Whitley Stokes

Irish Glosses

A mediaeval Tract on Latin Declension

Whitley Stokes

Irish Glosses
A mediaeval Tract on Latin Declension

ISBN/EAN: 9783337116422

Printed in Europe, USA, Canada, Australia, Japan

Cover: Foto ©Thomas Meinert / pixelio.de

More available books at **www.hansebooks.com**

IRISH GLOSSES.

A MEDIÆVAL TRACT
ON
LATIN DECLENSION,
WITH
EXAMPLES EXPLAINED IN IRISH.

TO WHICH ARE ADDED
THE LORICA OF GILDAS, WITH THE GLOSS THEREON,
AND A SELECTION OF GLOSSES FROM THE BOOK OF ARMAGH.

EDITED BY
WHITLEY STOKES, A. B.

DUBLIN:
Printed at the University Press,
FOR THE IRISH ARCHÆOLOGICAL AND CELTIC SOCIETY.
1860.

DUBLIN:
PRINTED AT THE UNIVERSITY PRESS,
BY M. H. GILL.

THE
IRISH ARCHÆOLOGICAL AND CELTIC SOCIETY.

MDCCCLX.

Patron:
HIS ROYAL HIGHNESS THE PRINCE CONSORT.

President:
HIS GRACE THE DUKE OF LEINSTER.

Vice-Presidents:
THE MOST NOBLE THE MARQUIS OF KILDARE, M. R. I. A.
THE RIGHT HON. THE EARL OF DUNRAVEN, M. R. I. A.
THE RIGHT HON. LORD TALBOT DE MALAHIDE, M. R. I. A.
VERY REV. CHARLES W. RUSSELL, D. D., President of Maynooth College.

Council:

EUGENE CURRY, ESQ., M.R.I.A.	PATRICK V. FITZPATRICK, ESQ.
REV. THOMAS FARRELLY.	JOHN C. O'CALLAGHAN, ESQ.
REV. CHARLES GRAVES, D.D., F.T.C.D., M.R.I.A.	JOHN O'DONOVAN, ESQ., LL.D., M.R.I.A.
	GEO. PETRIE, ESQ., LL.D., M.R.I.A.
REV. JAMES GRAVES; A.B.	REV. WILLIAM REEVES, D.D., M.R.I.A.
THOMAS A. LARCOM, Major-General R.E., M.R.I.A.	WM. R. WILDE, ESQ., F.R.C.S.I., M.R.I.A.

Secretaries:

REV. J. H. TODD, D.D., Pres. R.I.A. | J. T. GILBERT, ESQ., M.R.I.A.

A MEDIÆVAL TRACT
ON
LATIN DECLENSION,
WITH
EXAMPLES EXPLAINED IN IRISH.

HE following tract on Latin declension is taken from a volume of parchment MSS. marked H. 2. 13, and preserved in the Library of Trinity College, Dublin. The volume is unpaged, but the tract commences at the back of the 35th, and ends at the back of the 38th folio from the beginning.

Dr. O'Donovan thinks the tract in question was written about the year 1500. Mr. Curry considers it somewhat older. I do not venture to decide on its age. It is clear, however, that the scribe was a copyist, not a composer; and that his original was produced at a period considerably before the transcription.

The chief, indeed the only, value of the tract lies in the large number of Irish words (about 1100) which are placed as glosses to the Latin vocables exemplifying the different declensions. Many of these words are unregistered in our dictionaries; of others, the meaning

meaning has hitherto been guessed at rather than known. Still, some persons may ask, why should the Irish Archæological Society expend its funds in publishing a document which merely illustrates the Irish language? Let such persons try to understand that every contribution to a more accurate knowledge of this Irish language is ultimately a contribution to Irish history. For this can never be written until trustworthy versions are produced of all the surviving chronicles, laws, romances, and poetry of ancient Celtic Ireland. Moreover, immediate results of high historical importance may be obtained by comparison of the words and forms of the Irish with those of the other Indo-European languages. Chronicles may, and often do, lie; laws may have been the work of a despot, and fail to correspond with the ethical ideas of the people for whom they were made; romances may misrepresent the manners and morals of their readers and hearers; and poetry may not be the genuine outcome of the popular imaginative faculty. But the evidence given by words and forms is conclusive—evidence of the habitat, the intellectual attainments, the social condition of the Aryan family before the Celtic sisters journeyed to the West—evidence of the period at which this pilgrimage took place as compared with the dates of the respective migrations of their kindred—evidence of the connexions existing between the Celts and other Indo-Europeans after the separation of languages. I trust that the subjoined commentary will be found to have done somewhat towards the attainment of the objects here indicated; and have now only to acknowledge the helpful kindness of my friends, the Rev. Dr. Todd, Mr. Eugene Curry, Dr. O'Donovan, Dr. Siegfried, and the Rev. R. F. Littledale.

W. S.

Caraig Breacc. Howth,
August 16, 1858.

[It

A Mediæval Tract on Latin Declension.

[It was at first my intention to have printed the following tract exactly as it stands in the codex. But so corrupt did this appear on closer investigation, that it seemed preferable to correct the text wherever it was likely to embarrass the reader, always, however, giving in a foot-note the lection of the MS. This I have done. Proper names have been spelled with initial capitals. Marks of punctuation have been introduced. The letters Q. and R. have been inserted before the Questions and Answers respectively. The examples have been numbered. All other interpolations have been enclosed in brackets.]

Q. Prima declinacio quot literas terminales[1] habet? R. Tres. Q. Quas? R. a, s, m. Q. Quot terminaciones habet? R. Quatuor. Q. Quas? R. a, as, és, am. Q. Da exempla. R. a ut poeta, as ut Eneas, és ut Anchises[2], am ut Adam.

Q. Quot genera habet hec terminacio .á. in prima declinacione?

R. Quinque, que sunt masculinum, ut hic poeta, femininum ut hec regina, neutrum, ut hoc pascha[3], commune, ut hic et hec avena, epicenum ut hic et hec aquila.

Q. Quot genera habet hacc terminacio ás in prima declinacione?
R. Unum genus, ut hic Eneas.
Q. Quot genera habet terminacio es in prima declinacione?
R. Unum genus, ut hic Anchises[4].
Q. Quot genera habet hec terminacio am in prima declinacione?
R. Unum genus ut hic Adám. Unde regula[5]—

Rectius as, es, a, dat declinacio prima,
Atque per am proprie quedam ponuntur Ebrea, ut supra.

Q. Que est agnicio prime declinacionis nominum?
R. Hec est: cujus genitiuus[6] et datiuus singulares, nominatiuus et

---

[1] MS. tirminales. [2] ansises. [3] pasca. [4] ancisses. [5] r̄. [6] genetiuus.

A Mediæval Tract on Latin Declension.

et vocatiuus plurales in ǽ diphthongo[1] desinunt, accusatiuus singularis in am productum desinit[2], accusatiuus pluralis in ás productum desinit, exceptis nominibus prime declinacionis que non declinant[ur], sic :—

1. hic poeta .i. ḟiliḋ.
   hic propheta .i. ḟáiṫ[3].
   hic psalmista .i. ṗailmćétlaiḋ[4].
   hic scriba .i. ṙaí.
5. hic citharista[5] .i. cṗuitiṗe.
   hic timpanista .i. timpanać.
   hic organista .i. oṗganaiḋ.
   hic sophista .i. ṙophiṗtiḋe[6].
   hic partista .i. ṗannaiṗe[7].
10. hic lanista .i. lućtaiṗe.

   hic legista .i. leṗaiṗe.
   hic decretista .i. ḋecṗeḋeć.
   hic patriarcha .i. naṗalaċaiṗ.
   hic scurra .i. cṗoṗan.
15. hic questionista[8].[quaestionarius] .i. ceṗtunać.
   hic archimandrita[9] .i. apo-eaṗṗoc.
   hic auriga .i. ġilla cinn eić.
   hic birría .i. biṗṗać.
   hic geta .i. ġeiḋ.

Feminina haec sunt :—

20. haec regina .i. ṗíġan[10].
   haec duxista. banċóiṗeć[11].
   haec abatissa .i. banab.
   haec priorissa. banṗṗioiṗ.
   haec sacerdotista. banṗaġaṗt.
25. haec ancilla. innilt.
   haec galea. at cluic.
   haec alea. taiṗliṗ.
   haec mitra[12]. baiṗín.

   haec tunica[13]. inaṗ.
30. haec manica. muincille.
   haec allea [allium]. ġaiṗleoġ.
   haec lacerna. ṗleṗtan.
   haec cirra [cirrus]. ciaḃ.
   haec chirotheca. lámann[14].
35. haec spica. ḋiaṗ.
   haec lasciuia. bṗaiṗe[15].
   haec falinga. ṗallainġ.
   haec

[1] diptongo. [2] desinunt. [3] faidh. [4] sailmcetlaid. [5] sitarista. [6] sophistighi. [7] riġonista. [9] arcimantrica. [10] righan. [11] bantaisech. [12] mittra. [13] tonfca. [14] ciratheca. amann. [15] h. lassina braisi.

haec camisia[1]. léine.
haec gena. gruaid.
40 haec lingua[2]. tengad.
haec pera. tiac.
haec trulla. lorad.
haec decima. dechmad.
haec candela. coinnill.
45 haec gelima. punnann.
haec fistula. fedán.
haec barba. féróg[3].
haec nouerca. lermátair[4].
haec carruca. ferrac.
50 haec phoca. rón[5].
haec caphia .i. cennbarr[6].
haec claua lorg.
haec penna penn[7].
haec poena[8] pian.
55 haec iolla [jula?]. maroc.
haec olla. crocan.
haec vesica. riataire[9].
haec creta cailc.
haec caustoria [καυστήριον?]. adarc.
60 haec plumba [plumbum]. luaide[10].
haec norma. riagail.

haec tabella tabaill.
haec cantilena cantairect[11].
haec mitreta tuireog.
65 haec parra medar.
haec parricula gocan.
haec tabula cláp.
haec ancora ancoire.
haec lympha .i. uirce imill[12].
70 haec aptempna [ἐπίδεμνια?] rer no capp.
[haec] trabecula taebán tellaig no comlad[13].
haec caliga .i. arran.
haec ligula. laindep.
haec corrigia. traigle.
75 haec corona. coroin.
haec clerica. coroin.
haec coma[14]. folt.
haec glabella. deirged in fuilt[15].
haec palpebra. fabra.
80 haec pupilla mac imperan.
haec theologia[16]. diadact.
haec grammatica. grammatac[17].
                                    haec

camisa. [2] linga. [3] fesog. [4] lesmathair. [5] foca. ron. [6] cenbar. [7] pend. [8] pena. [9] fessica. siadaire. [10] luaidhi. [11] candaléna canntairecht. [12] h. limpausci .i. imill. [13] naucula taeman callaigh l. comla. [14] cómma. [15] fuilt. [16] tethologia. [17] gramatica. gramatach.

haec dialectica¹. ᵼiléctác.
haec ystoria. ρoaiρ.
85 haec mechanica. éolaρ oóiρ².
haec patena. oiʒen.
haec rhetorica³. oliʒi.
haec pantera naċaiρ⁴.
haec maxilla. leca ın ɔuinı⁵.
90 haec mala. leċail⁶.
haec bucca. ál.
haec gula. cράeρ.
haec mataxa. ulbu.
haec palma. baρρ.
95 haec alapa. baρoʒ.
haec plannta. bonɔ.
haec mentula ρeam .ı. ρpıu.
haec emenda .ı. cáın.
haec vena. cuρle.
100 haec mamma. cıch.
haec mammilla. cıchín⁷.
haec mammula⁸. uċh.
haec stella. ρeτla.
haec ethera [aether]. aóıρ.
105 haec aera. aıeρ.
haec cratera. ρcala.
haec cretella ʒneıɔell.

haec terra. τalam⁹.
haec tribula [tribulum].
ρuıρτ no ρʒıuρρe¹⁰.
110 haec villa. baıle.
haec villula .ı. aρτán¹¹.
haec via. ρlıʒe¹².
haec vita. beċu¹³.
haec herba. lub¹⁴.
115 haec silua. coıll.
haec virga¹⁵. ρlaτ.
haec virgula. ρlaıτín¹⁶.
haec grunna. moın.
haec gleba¹⁷. ρoɔ.
120 haec casa¹⁸. boτhan.
haec cassula. coċall.
[haec casula]. cρo¹⁹.
haec camera. campa no ρe-
ompa.
haec porta. ɔoρuρ.
125 haec valua. comla.
haec creta [crates] cliaτh.
haec digma²⁰. maρcaċ na
comlaɔ.
haec flamma²¹. laρaıρ.
haec cloaca. campaɔ.
haec

¹ dileta (with a hook over the *t*) ² h. mecanica. cal. doc. (undulating line over the last *c*). ³ rethorica. ⁴ nathari. ⁵ duine. ⁶ leth ail. ⁷ cichin. ⁸ mamula. ⁹ talum. ¹⁰ sust l. sgiursi. ¹¹ villola .ı. urtan. ¹² slighi. ¹³ beta. ¹⁴ luibh. ¹⁵ virgo. ¹⁶ virgola. slaitin. ¹⁷ glebo. ¹⁸ cassa. ¹⁹ h. cassula cochall no cro. ²⁰ or perh. drigma. ²¹ flama.

130 haec auia. ϝenmáṫaıϝ[1].
　　haec denia. ϝeċϝán[2].
　　haec scama [σκάμμα]. lanυ.
　　haec gemma. léʒ lóʒmaϝ[3].
　　haec fenistra. ϝuınneoʒ[4].
135 haec furca. ʒabal.
　　haec sportula. pellec.
　　haec trenga[5]. oϝϝaὐ.
　　haec urna. nılan.
　　haec guerra[6] coʒaυ.
140 haec alauda. ϝuıϝeoʒ.
　　haec garga[7] baıϝʒen.
　　haec quarta .ı. ceṫϝamaυ.
　　haec merenda. ϝϝuban.
　　haec buccella ϝϝubán maϝa[8]
　　　no ʒϝeım.
145 haec susurra [susurrus]. co-
　　　ʒaϝ.
　　haec tibia[9]. colϝa.
　　haec festucula[10]. ṫaıϝ.
　　haec homplata [ὠμοπλάτη?].
　　　monʒ ınṫ ϝlınυém[11].
　　haec junctura[12]. cenʒal.
150 haec gingiua. ϝeoıl na ϝıacal.
　　haec uvula[13] ϝıne ϝeaın.

　　haec biturría vel biturrea
　　　buṫun.
　　haec tectúra[14]. υıυean.
　　haec lorica. luıϝeċ.
155 haec antiquula. aıṫleme[15].
　　haec mica. míϝ[16].
　　haec vaghina. ϝaıʒın.
　　haec famula. cmle υabca.
　　haec vacca[17]. bó.
160 haec aqua. uıϝce[18].
　　haec idiogina. mb[uϝ].
　　haec binna. calϝṫaċ.
　　haec benna. ʒamaın aϝam.
　　haec juvenca[19]. calϝaċ.
165 haec muletrella[20]. cmnυeoʒ.
　　haec mulera. eυϝaċ.
　　haec opa[21]. coϝϝoʒ.
　　haec tunica sclerotica[22]. ʒe-
　　　alan na ϝúl[23].
　　haec taberna. ṫaıbeϝne.
170 haec rectoria. ϝeϝϝonaċṫ[24].
　　haec vicaria. bıcaıϝeċṫ.
　　haec capillanía. cabıllanaċṫ.
　　haec abbatia[25]. abυaıne.
　　haec vaccaria[26]. buaıle.
　　　　　　　　　　　　haec

---

[1] aua. senmathair. [2] sechran. [3] gema. legh loghmar. [4] fuindeog. [5] treoga. [6] gerra. [7] leg. quadra? [8] buccalla. [9] tipia. [10] pestucula. [11] ın ṫϝlınυém. [12] iuntura. [13] ugula. [14] deetura. [15] anticula aithleini. [16] mir. [17] vaca. [18] uisci. [19] iuṫéncca. [20] múcledla. [21] oba. [22] h. tonica scilarotica. [23] sul. [24] persunacht. [25] abacia. [26] uacaria.

175 hacc prouincia. ppóuınre.
   hacc metrop[o]litica ca-
      chaıp aıpoeapbuıʒ.
   hacc basilica. eaʒlaıp¹.
   hacc mellifolia [millefolium].
      aċaıpċalman².
   hacc testa. blaeɼc.
180 hacc sabribarra bɼoċpaċan.
   hacc uolua [valva?]. cen-
      baɼan.
   hacc artemisia³. buaċballan
      lıaċ.
   hacc ferina. luɼ na ɼıaŏ.
   hacc brecia [brassica?]. bıɼoɼ.
185 hacc genista. ɼecluʒ.
   hacc ca. ʒaɼıboʒ.
   hacc ganea. meɼoɼeċ.
   hacc concha⁴. ɼaeċoʒ.
   hacc gletealla [clitellae?].
      maɼıclaċ.
190 hacc solea⁵. bonn.
   hacc urla [orlus] .ı. bıle.
   hacc impedica. uaċċap.
   hacc medulla. ɼmıɼ.
   hacc coquilla⁶. ɼaeċoʒ beʒ.
195 hacc grangia. ʒɼaıɼɼeċ.

   hacc gallina. ceɼc.
   hacc aquila. ılun.
   hacc area⁷ apʒ.
   hacc cista cırċe⁸.
200 hacc merula. cıappeċ.
   hacc monedula⁹ caoʒ.
   hacc philomena¹⁰. ɼpıoeoʒ.
   hacc columba. colum.
   hacc lucifugia .ı. cɼebaɼ.
205 hacc capreola. ɼeɼıboʒ.
   hacc rostigola¹¹. coɼcaċ ma-
      ɼa¹².
   hacc aurigola. oɼeolan.
   haec urtica. nennċóʒ¹³.
   hacc arista .ı. connlaċ.
210 hacc stipula coınnlın.
   hacc fistula¹⁴. ɼeımın.
   hacc moneta monaŏan.
   hacc glaneta. ʒlacaɼıba.
   hacc pharetra¹⁵. ʒlacɼaıʒeŏ¹⁶.
215 hacc sagitta¹⁷. ɼaıʒeŏ¹⁶.
   hacc hasta. ʒa.
   hacc flabella. ɼeıŏeŏ ʒáıċe
      no bulʒa¹⁸.
   hacc fabrica. ceɼoċa¹⁹.
219 hacc massa. meɼʒan.
                           hacc

¹ bacilica eaglus. ² athair talman. ³ artimesia. ⁴ conca. ⁵ solia. ⁶ coqūima.
⁷ archa. ⁸ sista cisti. ⁹ monetola. ¹⁰ pilomena. ¹¹ leg. rusticula? ¹² mára. ¹³ neun-
tog. ¹⁴ festula. ¹⁵ faretra. ¹⁶ soiged. ¹⁷ sagita. ¹⁸ scideth gáibulga. ¹⁹ cerdea.

220 haec baudaca [balducta?]. bláṫaċ¹.
haec cernisia². líno.
haec urina. ꝼual.
haec fabula. ꞃgél³.
haec purpura. coꞃcaıꞃ.
225 haec cera. céıꞃ⁴.
haec serra⁵. ᵹlaꞃꞃ.
haec rota. ꞃoṫh.
haec fanilla.
haec cauicula [cavernula] .i. ꞃoċlaıb⁶.
230 haec litera. lıṫeꞃ.
haec syllaba. ꞃıllaıbı [?].
haec pagina⁷. leṫenaċ.
haec chiragra⁸. cꞃuꞃán na lám⁹.
haec luna. eꞃᵹa.
235 haec panca [pantex] meḋal.
haec aruina¹⁰. blonac.
haec monıꞃıcına [?]¹¹. monaḃ.
haec comprisura. ꞃaꞃcan.
haec troclia canṫaıꞃ.
240 haec cripica [rastrum]. cluaċ ꝼuıꞃꞃıb[e].

haec situla¹². ꞃıṫeal.
haec pista. ṫaeꞃ.
haec glassia [γαλαξία] mul-can.
haec prissura. ıᵹa.
245 haec pensa [pensum] cucan.
haec lapifulta. léce ınáꞃaın¹³.
haec prescna. bancoıᵹ.
haec rula. luċ ꝼꞃancaċ.
haec talpa. luċ ḋall.
250 haec lactura. laċhṫ.
haec amusca. amaıꞃc.
haec ascia¹⁴. ṫál.
haec scindula¹⁵. caꞃnoıbı.
haec scupa [scopae]. eꞃcaꞃṫ.
255 haec pustula. ᵹuıꞃín¹⁶.
haec onesta. nuꞃ.
haec grimaga baıneaċhlaċ.
haec picuta. meall.
haec mustella. eáꞃ.
260 haec muscipula. ꞃıòċaṫ¹⁷.
haec decipula .ı. concꞃo¹⁸.
haec sagena. ꞃꞃaṫaꞃ.
haec biga. caꞃꞃ.
haec antela [antilena]. uċṫaċ.
haec

¹ blathach. ² seruisia. ³ sgel. ⁴ ceir. ⁵ sera. ⁶ h. fanilla. fochluidh .i. cauicula.
⁷ pagena. ⁸ sirogra. ⁹ crupan na lam. ¹⁰ asugia. ¹¹ monifína (a hook rising out of the f). ¹² citola. ¹³ lec in arain. ¹⁴ assia. ¹⁵ sindola. ¹⁶ guirin. ¹⁷ musipula. fidh-cat. ¹⁸ decipola .i. con cro.

265 haec postella [postilena]. ᴛɪa-
    pać.
    haec crapula¹. laᴛhɪpᴛ.
    haec uva. cáep ꝑɪnemnać².
    haec lepra. lubpa.
    haec fragella. cnáɪmpɪać³ no
    ᴛoppan.
270 haec parma. coᴛun.
    haec pyromantia⁴. nellaᴅo-
    pachᴛ.
    haec chiromantia⁵. ᴅopnaᴅo-
    pać.
    haec ꝼᴛupna [?] clap ʒuaɪl.
    haec catapulta. pblínać⁶.

275 haec edibulta. cpoɪcɪnn maᴅ-
    pa allaɪᴅ.
    haec offa. coɪnmɪ́pı́⁷.
    haec cavea⁸. ᴅabać.
    haec calopeda. ꝼuɪpᴛe⁹.
    haec trica. ɪᴅ upćumaɪl¹⁰.
280 haec parvispendia. cepać.
    haec ophthalmia. ʒalap pú-
    la¹¹.
    haec pupina. cuɪlleać lɪʒeoc.
    haec coquina. cocᴛaɪp.
    haec babana. ᴛappach.
285 haec creatura coɪppeaʒaᴅ.

Ista sunt propria nomina uirginum:—

haec Maria.
haec Catarina.
haec Margareta.
haec Anna.
haec Lucia.
haec Brigada.

haec placenta. apan ʒeal.
his dominabus. baɪnᴛɪʒep-
na¹².

haec Elina.
haec Petronilla.
haec Alathia.
haec Osanna.
haec Melén.
haec Tegea.

his animabus. anɪm¹³.
his deabus. baɪnᴅea ɪn ᴛo-
paɪᴅ.
                                his

---

¹ capula. ² vua. caer linemach. ³ cnaimfiach. ⁴ piromanxia. ⁵ ciromancia. ⁶ cadibulta. ⁷ coinmir. ⁸ caba. ⁹ callidiba. suisti. ¹⁰ urcumail. ¹¹ obtolmia. galar sula.
¹² báinntigerna. ¹³ ainim.

A Mediæval Tract on Latin Declension.

290 his filiabus. ingen[1].
his natabus. ingen.
his libertabus. banṗóeṗ[2].
his amicabus. bancapa[3].
his equabus. láiṗ[4].
295 his mulabus. múl[5].
his asinabus. aṗṗal.

his lupabus. roġ allaiḋ.
Hoc pascha[6]. caiṗc.
hoc manna[7]. mainn.
300 hoc mammona. borluaiġeṽ[8].
hoc all. a [alacrimonia?]. ṗubaċúṗ.

Communia[9] sunt haec:—

hic et haec idiota. amaḋán[10].
hic et haec ádiiena. ḋeoṗaḋ.
hic et haec indigena. uṗṗaiḋ.
305 hic et haec Hibernigena. eiṗinnać[11].
hic et haec Scotigena[12]. albanać.
hic et haec Angeligina. ġallḋać[13].
hic et haec Normanigina. noṗmanać.
hic et haec Francigena. ḟṗanġcać.
310 hic et haec Romanigena. ṗomanać.
hic et haec romipeta[14]. oiliṫṗeć.

hic et haec Almanigina. almanach[15].
hic et haec cristigina. cṗiṗcin.
hic et haec alienigena[16]. comaiġceć.
315 hic et haec hermita [eremita]. ḋiṫṗebać.
hic et haec homicida. ḋunmaṗbtać.
hic et haec parricida. aṫhaṗmaṗbtać.
hic et haec matricida. máṫhaṗmaṗbtać[17].
hic et haec fratricida bṗáṫhaṗmaṗbtać[18].
320 hic et haec sororicida ṗiuṗmaṗbtać.

hic

---

[1] ingin. [2] banshaer. [3] bancara. [4] lair. [5] mul. [6] pasca. [7] mann. [8] h. mamona. bo sluaiged. [9] commonía. [10] amadau. [11] ibernigina. eirindach. [12] Scutigena. [13] galldacht. [14] romipida. [15] almancach. [16] alinigena. [17] mathar. m. [18] brathar. m.

hic et haec uxoricida. bean-
    mapbtac̀.
hic et haec genericida. cli-
    amuinmapbtac̀.
hic et haec uerbigina. cpip-
    taigc¹.
hee bracce² tpibup.
325 hee insidie³. cealg.
hee nuptie⁴. bainbe cíc.
hee nundine mópmapgau⁵.
hee rixe pepga⁶.
hee tabe inaoa.
330 hee atene [Athenae?]. at-
    píana.
hee tenebre. ɓopcaɓup.
hee latebre. ɓopcaɓup.
hee dinicie. nmupa.
hee diuine ɯaɓac̀t.
335 hee none. noínc⁷.
hee calende⁸. caillné.
hee nebule. néll⁹.
hee schole¹⁰. pcola.
hee mine. bagaip.
340 hic Andreas. anopiap.
hic Thomas. tomap.

hic Eneas. aengup.
hic Barnubas. apostoli.
hic Lucas.
345 hic Nemías. gilla na naom.
hic Malacias maolp̀ech-
    lainn¹¹.
hic Ysayas. çpac.
hic Tobias.
hic Elyas. elç.
350 hic Jermias. p̀aiṫ¹².
hic Ananias. p̀aiṫ¹².
hic Sacarias. p̀aiṫ¹².
hic Boreas¹³. an gaeṫ atú-
    aɩò.
hic Ancises. ppimaɓeċt.
355 hic Nestorides¹⁴. en.
hic Peliades. en.
hic Fetomsiades. en.
hic Latoniades. en.
hic Tebaydes. en.
360 hic Eneades. en.
hic Adam. e.
hic Joram. e.
hic Abraham. e.
hic Cayn. e.

Q. Secunda declinacio quot¹⁵ literas terminales habet? R. Tres.
Q. Quas?

---

¹ cristaighi. ² brace. ³ incidie. ⁴ nubtie. baindi. cich. ⁵ mormargad. ⁶ fergach.
⁷ nonne ndine. ⁸ callende. ⁹ nell. ¹⁰ scole. ¹¹ maolechl. ¹² faith. ¹³ borias.
¹⁴ Nastorrades. ¹⁵ quat.

Q. Quas? R. r, s, m.
Q. Quot terminaciones habet? R. ui.
Q. Quas? R. er, ir, ur, us, eus, um. Q. Da exempla. R. er, ut magister, ir, ut uir, ur ut satur, us ut dominus eus, [ut] Tatheus, um, ut templum. Q. Quot genera habet secunda declinacio? R. ui. Q. Quas? R. ut supra.

Q. Quot genera habet hec terminacio er in secunda declinacione? R. unum ut hic magister.

Q. Quot genera habet terminacio ir in secunda declinacione? Q. Unum ut hic uir.

Q. Quot genera habet hec terminacio us in secunda declinacione? R. quatuor.

Q. Que sunt? R. masculinum, ut hic dominus; femininum [ut] hec domina vel hec malus; neutrum, ut hoc vulgus; promisc[u]um siue epicoenum[1] ut hic [et haec] milgus.

Q. Quot genera habet terminacio eus in secunda declinacione? R. unum, ut hic Tatheus.

Q. Quot genera habet terminacio um in secunda declinacione? R. duo.

Q. Que sunt? R. femininum, ut hec dorcium, philorsium, glicerium; neutrum, ut hoc templum, simitherium.

Q. Que est agnicio nominum secunde declinacionis? R. hec est: cujus genitiuus singularis, nominatiuus et uocatiuus plurales in i productum desinunt, datiuus et ablatiuus[2] singulares in o productum desinit, [et genitiuus pluralis in orum] nisi sincupacio [i. e. syncope] fiat, ut duum pro duorum, datiuus et ablatiuus[2] plurales in is productum desinunt; accusatiuus pluralis in os productum desinit, exceptis alis nominibus secunde declinacionis que non sic faciuntur.

hic

[1] episcenum.   [2] oblatiuus.

365 hic magister. maξıρ ᴅeρ.
hic arbiter. bρeıṫeam.
hic presbyter[1]. ρaξaρᴄ.
hic minister ᴄımṫıρıξ.
hic faber. ξabann[2].
370 hic puer. macam.
hic liber. leabaρ.
hic caper. ξaḃaρ.
hic aper. ᴄoρc.
hic cancer. ρaρᴄán[3].
375 hic fiber. ᴅobρan.
hic linter. labaρ no ρlınncρı-
ᴀḋ.
hic gener. chamuın.
hic socer[4] compaṅaċ.
hic liber .a. um. neaċ ρaeρ.
380 hic pulcher[5].a. um. ρochρuıṅe.
hic niger .a. um. ᴅuḃ.
hic piger .a. um. leρc.
hic macer .a. um. ᴄṅuaξ.
hic acer .a. um. ξρuamᴅa.
385 hic acer .a. um. aξaρb.
hic dexter .a.um. ᴅeaρ.
hic sinister[6]. cle.
hic anser. ξeıᴅ.
hic onager[7]. aḋ allaıḋ.

390 hic ager. ρeρanᴅ.
hic suber. ρnámaċ[8].
hic in[s]cimagister maξıρ-
ᴅeρ aımρeρaċ.
hic eger a. um. eρlán.
hic tener .a. um. maeṫ.
395 hic uir. ρeρ.
hic semiuir. leṫρeρ[9].
hic leuir. ρeρ clí.
hic duum. uir ᴄıξeρne[10]
ᴅeıρe[11].
trium vir. ᴄıξeρne ᴄρíρ.
400 hic quadrum uir. ᴄaıρeċ ceṫ-
ρaıρ[12].
hic quinctum uir. ᴄaıρeċ
cúıξıρ.
hic satur. ρaṫaċ.
hic semisatur. leṫρaṫaċ[13].
hic dominus. ᴄıξeρne[14].
405 hic deus. ᴅıa.
hic animus. anum.
hic filius. mac.
hic natus. mac.
hic libertus. ρaeρ.
410 hic famulus[15]. baċlaċ.
hic molossus. mílċú[16].

hic

---

[1] prespiter. [2] gaban. [3] partan. [4] soces. [5] puplican (*sic!*). [6] senester. [7] on ag (*sic*). [8] snamach. [9] semuir. lethfer. [10] tigerna. [11] deisi. [12] cetrúir. [13] leth hsa-thach. [14] tigerna. [15] famulus. [16] malosus. milcú.

A Mediæval Tract on Latin Declension.

hic bufulus. bacl[ać] bṗe-
 all[án].
hic amicus. capa.
hic equus[1]. eać.
415 hic mulus. múl[2].
hic asinus[3]. aṗṗal.
hic lupus cu allaıð.
hic ursus. maṫḡamaın.
hic auus[4]. ṗenaṫaıṗ.
420 hic proauus[5] a aṫaıṗ ṗın.
hic atauus[6]. a aṫaıṗ ṗın.
hic clericus. cleıṗeać.
hic laicus[7] ṫuaṫa.
hic vitulus. lóeḡ[8].
425 hic oculus. ṗúıl[9].
hic monoculus. leṫ[h]caeć.
hic cecus. ðall.
hic cetus. mıl móṗ no ṗuaın-
 mech ðubaıṗ[10].
hic orbus. mac ðıleċṫa.
430 hic luscus. mınṫṗuıleć[11].
hic lippus maeṫṗuıleć[12].
hic aduocatus. aḃcoıðe[13].
hic juridicus[14]. ðlıḡṫıneć.
hic causidicus. ṗeṗ cúıṗı ðo
 ċonḡbaıl[15].

435 hic monachus[16]. manać.
hic homunculus[17] ðuıne beḡ.
hic canonicus. cananać.
hic discipulus ðıṗcıbul.
hic legitimus. ðlıṗṫınać.
440 hic cuipulus. ṗḡıan.
hic cutellus. ṗḡıan.
hic ungulus [ungula]. cṗuḃ[18]
 eić.
hic clauus [clavis]. ṫaıṗnḡe[19].
hic camus bṗaıḡðeć.
445 hic baietus. ṗaıṗṫı bṗóḡ[20].
hic tegulus. ṗcolḃ ṫıḡe[21].
hic archiepiscopus. aıṗðeaṗ-
 boḡ.
hic episcopus. eaṗboḡ.
hic archidiaconus. aıṗċın-
 neć[22].
450 hic legatus. ṫeaċṫaıṗe.
hic decanus. ðeḡanach.
hic prelatus. ṗṗelaıṫ.
hic prepositus. ṫıḡeṗne[23].
hic diaconus. ðećáın.
455 hic subdiaconus. ṗuḃðećáın.
hic acolytus. aclaıðe[24].
hic chorus[25]. ıncoṗaıð.
 hic

[1] equs. [2] mul. [3] assinus. [4] aus. [5] proaus. [6] ataus. [7] lacius. [8] laegh. [9] suil.
[10] ruaimnech dubain. [11] mintsuilech. [12] lipus mæthsuilech. [13] abhcoidi. [14] iuriti-
cus. [15] condmail. [16] monacus. [17] honumculus. [18] cru. [19] tairrngi. [20] brog. [21] tigi.
[22] airchindech. [23] tigerna. [24] acolitus. aclaidhi. [25] corus.

hic populus. ın pupul.
hic agnus. uan.
460 hic angelus. aınɜel¹.
hic gladius. cloıɷeam.
hic arcangelus. apcaınɜel.
hic pilus. puaınꝺe no ꝼoıl-
  cín².
hic capillus. ꝼoılcnín³.
465 hic digitus. méꝑláıme.
hic articulus. méꝑ coıꝑe⁴.
hic psalmus. ꝼalm.
hic uirsiculus. ꝼeꝑꝑán⁵.
hic sonus ꝼoɜuꝑ.
470 hic tonus. coın⁶.
hic semitonus⁷ [semitŏnium]
  lecċoın.
hic ditonu[s]. ꝺıcoın.
hic punnatus [prognatus?]
  macam ɜence⁸.
hic punctus. punc.
475 hic circulus. ceꝑcall.
hic murus. múꝑ⁹.
hic cibus. bıaꝺ.
hic discus. ın ɜaıllmıaꝑ¹⁰.
hic cupus. copán¹¹.

480 hic cepus [cippus?]. cep.
hic lectus. lebaıꝺ.
hic fimus. ocꝑać.
hic porcus. coꝑc.
hic uannus ꝛɜaıɜnen.
485 hic tignus [tignum] cleać.
hic collactaneus¹² comalca.
hic decius.
hic phaselus¹³. cuꝑać.
hic forulus. ꝛacc.
490 hic mantellus¹⁴. macal.
hic flosculus. blaċmaꝑ.
hic agnellus. uaınín¹⁵.
hic porcellus. oıꝑcnín¹⁶.
hic pullus. ꝛeꝑꝑać no ɜeꝛ-
  cać¹⁷.
495 hic palus. cuaılle¹⁸.
hic talus. ʋıꝑle.
hic callus.
hic catulus. cuılen.
hic murilegus¹⁹. cac.
500 hic dolus. cealɜ.
hic pediculus. míl éꝺaıɣ²⁰.
hic manipulus. ꝺoꝑnán²¹
  buana.

hic

---

¹ angilus. aingil. ² ruaindi l. fuiltin. ³ foiltnin. ⁴ merlaime-mer coisi. ⁵ fersa.
⁶ tóin. ⁷ semtonus. ⁸ gennti. ⁹ mur. ¹⁰ ingaill. mias. ¹¹ cipus copan. ¹² collucaníus. ¹³ facellus. ¹⁴ mancellus. ¹⁵ uainin. ¹⁶ oircnin. ¹⁷ serrac l. gerrcach. ¹⁸ cuailli.
¹⁹ morclius. ²⁰ peticulus. mil edaigh. ²¹ dornan.

A Mediæval Tract on Latin Declension.

    hic curellus. cnáimṗiaċ[1].
    hic columbus. colum.
505 hic curcolus [curlegius?].
        copcaċ mapa.
    hic gallus. coileaċ.
    hic milgus [milvus]. ṗpecán[2].
    hic figulus. cepo.
    hic cygnus[3]. ın ela.
510 hic corus. coileċ ꝼaiṫe[4].
    hic focus. ṫeallaċ.
    hic sotus. omnıo.
    hic minus ꝼeocaċ.
    hic loculus. ṗbopan.
515 hic pellicarius ṗꝼıꝼıvoıṗ.
    hic locus. ınaḋ.
    hic diuersarius. aıbıṗṗeoıṗ.
    hic iocus. cluıċe[5].
    hic Tartarus[6]. ıṗṗeaṗn.
520 hic infernus. ıṗṗeṗn.
    hic catholicus. caṫolıca[7].
    hic locanus. locan.
    hic xpianus. ꝼılla cṗıṗṫ.
    hic Persianus. Peṗṗen[8].
525 hic Donatus. Donncaḋ.
    hic Martinus. ꝼılla Maṗ-
        ṫaın.
    hic Malcus vıabul.

    hic Petrus. Peṫaṗ no Pé-
        ṫṗuṗ.
    hic Robertus. Roıbeṗṫ.
530 hic Valterus. Uaṫeṗ.
    hic Uilliahnus. Uıll[ıam].
    hic Gillialmus. ꝼıllıam.
    hic Uirgilius. Ḟeṗꝼal.
    hic Gillibertus. ꝼıllıbeṗṫ.
535 hic Ruaricus. Ruaıṗı.
    hic Ouidius. voctoṗ.
    hic Patricius. ꝼılla Páṫṗıcc.
    hic Laurencius. Lauṗınṫ.
    hic Clemencius. Clemenṫ.
540 hic Diarmicius. Dıaṗmaıv.
    hic Lodauicus. Loċlann.
    hic Mauricius. Muṗchav.
    hic Eugenius[9]. Eoꝼan.
    hic Grigorius. ꝼṗıꝼoıṗ.
545 hic Cornelius. Concubaṗ.
    hic Thitheus. macnahoıvċe[10].
    hic Orp[h]eus Uaıṫne.
    hic Thateus. Ṫavꝼ.
    hic Matheus. Maṫha.
550 Hec diphthongus[11]. veóıṗ.
    hec synodus[12]. ṗenav naoṁ.
    hec cristallus. [crystallum].
        cloċ cṗıṗvaıl.
                        hec

[1] cnaimfiach, and leg. corvellus?.   [2] prechan.   [3] cignus.   [4] coilec gaithi.   [5] cluithi.
[6] tarturus.   [7] cathholica.   [8] presen.   [9] augenius.   [10] mach na hoidhchi.   [11] diptungus.
[12] sinatos.

hec paradisus. paippup.
hec quercus. daip.
555 hec malús. aball.
hec corylus[1]. coll.
hec fraxinus. puinopeog.
hec alnus[2]. pepnog.
hec prunus[3]. opoigin.
560 hec buxus. beiċe[4].
hec taxus. ibap.
hec ficus. piċaball[5].
hec pinus[6]. cpano gíup.
hec laurus. cpano lauíp.
565 hec brucus. ppáeċ[7].
hec cornus. cpano mucop.
hec colus. cuigel.
hec fusus. pepipaio[8].
hec domus. ceach.
570 hec socrus. bean dobpaċap
[recte máchaip do mná].

hec nurus[9]. bean domeic.
hec penus. cugan.
hec jacinthus. lég[10] logmap.
hec carbassus. long luaċ.
575 hec abyssus[11]. in paipge[12].
hec aulus. bpu na hoige[13].
hec byssus. ppoll[14].
hec humus. in uip.
hec papyrus[15]. paipep.
580 hec porticus. dopup bip.
hec Egiptus. Eigipc.
hec acirus. peopup.
Hic bubulcus. buaċaill bó[16].
hic subulcus. buaċaill mucc[17].
585 hic rubus. múine.
hic remulus. cuipgeaċ.
hic dumus[18]. opip.

Hec sunt nomina adiectiua que non comparantur:—

hic primus .a. um céd neach.
hic secundus .a. um indapa neaċ.
590 hic tercius .a. um. an cper neaċ.
hic quartus .a. um. in cechpuma neaċ.

hic

[1] corrolus. [2] anlús. [3] brunus. [4] bruxus. beithi. [5] fichus. fidhabhall. [6] pinnus. [7] fraech. [8] fersad. [9] murus. [10] iacingtus. leg. [11] abisus. [12] infhairghi. [13] hoighi. [14] bissus. [15] papirus. [16] bo. [17] muc. [18] tomús.

A Mediæval Tract on Latin Declension.

hic quinctus .a. um. ın cuıgeḋ neaċ.
hic sextus ın ꝼeıꞃeḋ neaċ.
hic captus .ı. ᵹabáılꞇeċ.
595 hic cuculatus .a. um. cuꝑꝑacaċ.
hic capuciatus .a. tum. aꞇanach.
hic tunicatus¹ .a. tum. ınaꞃaċ.
hic manicatus. muıncıllec.
hic falingatus .a. tum. ꝼallaınᵹeċ.
600 hic bracatus² .a. tum. ꞇꞃıbuꞃaċ.
hic coronatus coꞃonꞇa.
hic inuidus³ .a. dum. ꝼoıꞃmꞇeċ.
hic blaesus⁴ .a. um. ᵹoḋ.
hic surdus . a. um. boḋaꞃ⁵.
605 hic claudus .a. um. baccaċ.
hic auratus .a. um. óꝛḋaıᵹe⁶.
hic argenteus⁷ .a. um. aıꞃᵹeꝺaċ.
hic ferreus .a. um. ıaꞃnaıᵹe⁸.
hic plumbeus⁹ luaıḋeaṁaıl¹⁰.

610 hic stanneus¹¹ .a. um. ꝼꞇanaṁaıl.
hic aereus¹² .a. um. umaṁaıl.
hic fundatus ꝼunꝺamınꞇeċ.
hic fessus .a. um. ꞅcıꞇeċ ón r̄lıᵹı¹³.
hic lassus .a. um. ꞅcıꞇeċ ó obaıꝛ¹⁴.
615 hic festinosus .a. um. [festinus] ꞇınnıꞅneċ no ꞇınnıꞅnaċ.
hic libidinosus .a. um. ꞅalaċ.
hic infestinosus neṁꞇınuıꞃneċ.
hic procus .a. um. ꞃuıꝛᵹeċ.
hic fornicarius .a. um. aḋallꞇꞃaċ.
620 hic famelicus .a. um. ᵹoꞃꞇaċ.
hic strabonus .a. um. ꝼıaꞃꞃuıleċh¹⁵.
hic orbatus .a. um. ꝺallꞅuıleċ¹⁶.
hic cecus .a. um. ḋall.
hic monoculosus .a. um. leꞇċaeċ¹⁷.
625 hic linguosus¹⁸ .a. um. ꞇenᵹꞇaċ.

hic

¹ tunicatus. ² braxatus. ³ inuidus. ⁴ blesus. ⁵ boghar. ⁶ ordhaighe.
⁷ argeteos. ⁸ iarn. i. ⁹ plumpeus. ¹⁰ luaigheam. ¹¹ staneus. ¹² aureus.
¹³ on shl. i. ¹⁴ o obair. ¹⁵ strubosus .a. um. siadshuilech. ¹⁶ dall shuilech.
¹⁷ lethcaech. ¹⁸ lingosus.

20 A Mediæval Tract on Latin Declension.

hic bilinguosus[1] .a. um. [bilinguis] ƿótengtać.
hic caritatosus .a. um. ꝺépcać[2].
hic uerbosus .a. um. bꞃiaćꞃać.
hic aglossus [ἄγλωσσος] .a. um. ꞃbeȝać.
630 hic radiculosus .a. um. ꞃonamaiƿeać.
hic egenus .a. um. ꞃaiȝeać.
hic crispus .a. um. caꞃta.

hic sanus .a. um. ꞃlán.
hic insanus .a. um. eꞃlán[3].
635 hic zelotypus .a. um. éƿmuꞃ[4].
hic densus .a. um. ƿluith.
hic acidus[5] .a. um. ȝoiꞃt.
hic urbiculatus .a. um. ballać.
hic lubricus .a. um. ꞃlemain.
640 hic amplus .a. um. ꞃaiꞃꞃinȝ.
hic neruosus[6] .a. um. luaćȝaiꞃeć.

Nunc de nominibus significantibus plenitudinem:—

hic formosus .a. um. ƿealbóa.
hic strumossus [ventosus] .a. um. uétaiƿ.
hic gulosus[7] .a. um. cꞃaeꞃꞃać.
645 hic barbosus .a. um. ꞃéꞃóȝać[8].
hic uentossus [ventosus] .a. um. ȝaećmaꞃ.
hic uentriosus .a. um. bꞃonnmaꞃ[9].

hic pédiculosus .a. um. mílećֿ[10].
hic lendosus[11] .a. um. ꞃnećać.
650 hic peditentosus[12] .a. um. coꞃꞃínećֿ.
hic phlegmosus .a. um. cꞃomꝺtilleć[13].
hic rugosus[14] .a. um. ȝeꞃbać.
hic maculosus .a. um. bocoiƿeć.
hic animosus .a. um. anmać.
hic

---

[1] bilingosus. [2] caritatinus .a. um. d. cach. [3] slan. eslan. [4] eelopidus .a. um. edmur. [5] accidus. [6] neurosus. [7] gulossus. [8] barbossus a. um. fesogach. [9] neutriossus .a. um. brondm. [10] milech. [11] lentossus. [12] pedidendus. [13] flegmosus .a. um. croindtilli. [14] rugossus.

A Mediæval Tract on Latin Declension.

655 hic famosus .a. um. clú-
  map¹.
hic difamosus .a. um. míclú-
  map².

hic spadosus .a. um. bṗeal-
  lac.
hic retrocosus .a. um. ppe-
  bac.

Nomina adjectiua que comparantur :—

hic albus .a. um. ɢeal.
660 hic doctus³ .a. um. τeɢaiṗɢe.
hic bonus .a. um. maiṫ.
hic malus .a. um. olc.
hic magnus .a. um. móṗ⁴.
hic paruuus .a. um. beɢ.
665 hic clarus .a. um. ṗoluṗ.
hic candidus .a. um. τaiṫne-
  maṫ.
hic auarus .a. um. ṗannτaṫ.
hic dignus⁵ .a. um. ḋinɢbala.
hic indignus .a. um. míḋinɢ-
  bala⁶.
670 hic multus .a. um. imḋa.
hic purus .a. um. ɢlan.
hic rarus⁷ .a. um. τeiṗc.
hic paucus .a. um. beɢ.
hic durus .a. um. ḋainɢen⁸
  no cṙuaiḋ.
675 hic madidus .a. um. ḟliuṫ.

hic ignauus .a. um. ḋoċené-
  laċ⁹.
hic longus .a. um. ḟaḋa.
hic curtus .a. um. cumaiṙ.
hic firmus .a. um. ḋainɢen⁸.
680 hic infirmus .a. um. éḋain-
  ɢen¹⁰.
hic iustus .a. um. ḟíṗénaċ.
hic iniustus .a. um. ainṗíṗé-
  naċ¹¹.
hic fetidus¹² .a. um. bṙén.
hic sordidus .a. um. ṡalaṫ.
685 hic gnarus .a. um.
hic ignarus .a. um.
hic gnauus .a. um.
Hoc templum. τempoll.
hoc tabernaculum. τaib-
  eṙne¹³.
690 hoc pennaculum.

  hoc

¹ clumar. ² míclemar. ³ doctus .a. um. tegaisgí. ⁴ mor. ⁵ dingnus.
⁶ midingbala. ⁷ rarrus. ⁸ daingin. ⁹ ignaus .a. um. docinclach. ¹⁰ edaingen.
¹¹ firenach, ainfirenach. ¹² fetitus. ¹³ tuiberni.

hoc simitherium [κοιμητή-
ριον]. peilic.
hoc feritrum [elicpum hod.
O'D.].
hoc sepulcrum. aölucaö.
hoc lucrum. coail.
695 hoc miraculum. mipbail.
hoc monaculum. baclog.
hoc cúnábulum. cliban.
hoc sinabulum.
hoc jentaculum¹. ɔinep.
700 hoc cribrum. cmacap.
hoc molendinum². muilino.
hoc atrium. gappga.
hoc torritorium³. cipaö.
hoc nestibulum⁴. oplap.
705 hoc stirpidivortium. pcoc-
ponna⁵.
hoc lumbarium. cpip cpi-
bimp.
hoc epiglotum. pgop-
nác[an].
hoc gernonum. cpombeol⁶.
hoc chartaceum⁷. pgeota.
710 hoc sacritegium. pgeota.
hoc pistrinum⁸. muilleano.

hoc cla[u]strum. cliacac.
hoc prostibulum. cech na
mepopeac.
hoc rediniculum in bpaic-
cin.
715 hoc silintrum.
hoc uentilogium. bile.
hoc stragulum⁹. in ceip.
hoc lolium ɔicen.
hoc plectrum cpanö. glepta.
720 hoc igniferrium. ceiní
[ceine] cpeapa.
hoc scrupulum. bubpuöan.
hoc teretorium. cuaipgin.
hoc herbagium. cluain ga-
bála¹⁰.
hoc caldarium. coipe¹¹.
725 hoc castrum. longpopc¹².
hoc monasterium. mainip-
cep.
hoc suffragium. popcacc¹³.
hoc refectorium. ppomocec.
hoc dormitorium. coöalcec.
730 hoc coopertorium. ppeilp.
hoc dolium¹⁴. cunna.
hoc corium. peice¹⁵.
hoc

¹ gentaculum.   ² mulindinum.   ³ tritorium.   ⁴ uescibulum.   ⁵ stipifortifartium, stoc ronna.   ⁶ gernooɔum. cromceol.   ⁷ cartesium.   ⁸ prostrinum.
⁹ straulium.   ¹⁰ .gabála.   ¹¹ colldarium. coiri.   ¹² longport.   ¹³ sufragium. furtacht.   ¹⁴ doleum.   ¹⁵ corcum. scichí.

A Mediæval Tract on Latin Declension.

hoc cotium.
hoc ingenium intlect¹.
735 hoc senium. renáir².
hoc ymagium.
hoc incendium. lorcað.
hoc martyrium³. mapτpa.
hoc salarium. τaile⁴.
740 hoc solarium. roilep.
hoc sellarium. reallað.
hoc equitium. ʒroiʒ⁵.
hoc palatium
hoc collum. mumél⁶.
745 hoc dorsum. ʊpuim.
hoc gyrgyrium⁷. ceilebpað
   eoin. no cpanð τoċap-
   τaiʒ⁸.
hoc cerebrum. inċinn⁹.
hoc scamnum¹⁰. pτol.
hoc firmamentum. ꝼipma-
   munτ.
750 hoc rubigorium. mip pluc.
hoc inuentorium. luaċ ꝼaip-
   néipi.
hoc exilium. innapbað.
hoc alimentum. oil[emain].
hoc armentum. aipʒe¹¹.

755 hoc crementum. τoipnaċ.
hoc incrementum [decre-
   mentum]. miτoipinaċ¹².
hoc indumentum. ċðaċ.
hoc iumentum. óʒùaṁ.
hoc monumentum. aðlacað.
760 hoc testamentum. τimna.
hoc instrumentum. inpτpu-
   minτ.
hoc tegmentum. ðioin.
hoc augmentum. méðuʒuð¹³.
hoc fragmentum. ppuipcċ.
765 hoc folium. ðuillen.
hoc psalterium. raltaip.
hoc pulmentum. liċé.
hoc dipodium¹⁴. uaiċne.
hoc pauementum. bioʒað¹⁵.
770 hoc lamentum. caí.
hoc sementum.
hoc centum. céð.
hoc ducendum [ducenti]. ðá-
   ċéð¹⁶.
hoc tricendum [tercentum].
   τpí céð¹⁷.
775 hoc quatricentum [quadrin-
   genti]. ceiτhpe¹⁸ .c.

hoc

---

¹ inntlecht. ² seonoir. ³ martirium. ⁴ tailf. ⁵ groidh. ⁶ múinel. ⁷ ʒʒium
⁸ .dochartaigh. ⁹ cerebrum. incind. ¹⁰ scanum. ¹¹ airgi. ¹² mitormach. ¹³ me-
dug. ¹⁴ ffodium. vaithne. ¹⁵ pavimentum. ¹⁶ da .c. ¹⁷ tri .c. ¹⁸ ceithri.

hoc quincentum [quingenti] cúıg .c.
hoc sexcentum [sescenti] ꞃé[1] .c.
hoc frumentum. cꞃuıṫneċc.
hoc hordeum[2]. eoꞁna.
780 hoc [a]mersiamentum. méıꞃ-ꞃı.
hoc stagnum. loċ.
hoc mulsum. lemnaċc.
hoc serum. meög.
hoc butyrum. ım [ımm].
785 hoc unguentum. unnımınṫ[3].
hoc aurum. óꞃ.
hoc argentum. aıꞃgeꝺ.
hoc plumbum. luaıöe[4].
hoc stannum. ꞃꝺan.
790 hoc ferrum. ıaꞃuꞃn[5].
hoc metallum[6]. mıṫall.
hoc praesumpticium[7] luaċ leꞃa.

hoc alministrum. bealaċ.
hoc nuchum. ꞃꞃeḃan[8].
795 hoc gladiolum. ꞃoıleꞃcaꞃ.
hoc propheticum[9]. ꞃgaꞃ-ṫaċ.
hoc falcastrum. ꞃıöba.
hoc bonum. maıṫ.
hoc malum. olc.
800 hoc candidus. (sic) caıṫnea-mnaċ.
hoc album. geal.
hoc nígrum. ꝺuḃ.
hoc flauum. buıöe[10].
hoc fuscum. ꞃaḃaċ.
805 hoc multum. ımöa.
hoc paruum. beg.
hoc modicum. meꞃuꞃöa.
hoc minimum. ꞃobeg.
hoc magnum. móꞃ.
810 hoc porrum. luꞃ.

Nunc dicendum de nominibus heteroclitis:[11]—

—— ínleman.
hoc coelum et plur. hí coeli[12] nem.
hoc castrum. lonǵꞃoꞃṫ[13].

hoc rastrum. ꞃaꞃcaıl.
815 hoc epulum ⁊ plur. hec epule. ꞃoıǵı.
hoc delícium héc. cic.

hoc

[1] sc. [2] ordium. [3] ᴚinnimint. [4] luaighi. [5] iarund. [6] mithallum. [7] proseumeticum. [8] srebhand. [9] profeticum. [10] buidhi. [11] ercocledus. [12] h. celum ⁊ plur híi celi. [13] longport.

A Mediæval Tract on Latin Declension.

hoc filum uel fila ꞅnáiṫe¹.
hoc claustrum .ri. ra. claurꞅꞃa.
hoc frenum .ni. na. ꞅꞃian.
820 hoc capistrum .ri. ra. aḋarṫaꞃ.
hoc scarletum.
hoc balneum .e. uel.a. ꞅoṫꞃaʒaḋ.
hoc nasturtium². bıꞃuꞃ.
hoc admidulum.

825 Hic Tartarus haec .ra. iꞅꞅeꞃn³.
hic sibilus est hominis⁴, sibela feminae prius ın ꞅéo ꞅoꞃē
hic infernus. na. ıꞅeaꞃnaoa
hic menalus .a.
hic dindimus .a.
830 hic avernus .a.
hic pelleus [pileus] aꞇ ꞅıll
hic intimus .a. ıbꞃać

Q. Tercia declinacio quot literas terminales habet? R. xi.
Q. Quae sunt? R. a, e, o, c, l, n, d, r, s, t, x.
Q. Da exempla. R. a, ut poema: e, ut sedile: o, ut uirgo: c, ut lac: l, ut mel: n, ut nomen: d, ut Dauid: r, ut pater: s, ut ciuitas: t, ut caput: x, ut felix.
Q. Quot genera habet hec terminacio a in tercia declinacione? R. unum genus, scilicet neutrum, ut hoc poema.
Q. Quot genera habet hec terminacio e in tercia declinacione? R. unum, scilicet neutrum, ut hoc sedile.
Q. Quot genera habet hec terminacio o in tercia declinacione? R. sex. Q. Quae? R. masculinum, ut hic ordo, femininum, ut hec dulcedo, commune, ut hic et hec homo, omne [i. e. omnigenum], ut centripondio⁵, promiscuum siue epicoenum⁶, ut uespertilio, dubium, ut hic vel⁷ hec margo.

Q. Quot

¹ snaithi. ² nastorsium. ³ ifern. ⁴ cebelus .c. hois. ⁵ oc. ut cento p̄sto. ⁶ episenum. ⁷ et.

Q. Quot genera habet hec terminacio e in tercia declinacione?
R. unum, scilicet neutrum, ut hoc lac.
Q. Quot genera habet hec terminacio l in tercia declinacione?
R. quatuor. Q. Quae? R. masculinum, ut hic sol: femininum, ut hec Micol: neutrum, ut hoc mel: commune, ut hic et hec nigil.
Q. Quot genera habet hec terminacio n in tercia declinacione?
R. tria. Q. Quae? R. masc. ut hic Titan: fem. ut hec siren[1]: neut. ut hoc nomen.
Q. Quot genera habet hec terminacio d in tercia declinacione?
R. Unum, scilicet masc. ut hic Dauid.
Q. Quot genera habet hec terminacio r in tercia declinacione?
R. Sex. Q. Quae? R. Masc. ut hic pater: fem. ut hec máter: neutr. ut hoc cadauer: commune, ut uber: omne, ut par: prom[i]scuum siue epicoenum[2], ut turtur.
Q. Quot genera habet hec terminacio s in tercia declinacione?
R. Septem. Q. Quae? R. masc. ut hic abbas: fem. ut hec caritas: neutr. ut hoc uas: commune, ut hic et hec sacerdos: omne genus, ut sapiens: prom[i]scuum siue epicoenum[2], ut phoenix[3], ut cortex[4].

Q. Que est agnicio tercie declinacionis nominum? R. hec: cuius genitiuus singularis in is correptum[5] desinit, datiuus in í productum desinit, accusatiuus sing. in em uel in im correptum desinit[6]: uocatiuus similis suo nominatiuo: ablatiuus desinit in é correptum [uel í] productum desinit excepto[7] fame et nocte: nom. et acc. et uoc. plur. in es productum desinunt[8], genitiuus pluralis in um uel in ium correptum[9] desinit: datiuus [et] ablatiuus plurales in bus correptum[9] desinunt[10].

Nunc

[1] sciren. [2] episcnum. [3] fenix. [4] corcortex. [5] coruptum. [6] coruptum desinit in í. [7] accpto. [8] desiniunt. [9] correbtum. [10] desinit.

A Mediæval Tract on Latin Declension.

Nunc de nominibus tercie declinacionis, ut sequitur:—

Hoc poema. pilidect.
hoc dindyma[1]. ɼeman.
835 hoc prolemma[2]. aðbapðact.
hoc cataplasma. céıpín[3].
hoc dogma. poıpceðal.
hoc doma. mullać cıɼe[4].
hoc énighma. popɼɼać no ınɼap.
840 hoc chrisma[5]. cpıpmal.
hoc nomisma[6]. monað.
hoc sophissma. poıpıpt.
hoc apostema[7]. nepcoıð.
hoc phlegma[8]. cpoınðtılle.
845 hoc anathema. coınðcalbćað.
hoc fantassma. taðbaıp.
hoc sperma. coımpepc.
hoc idíoma. aðbapðact.
hoc thema[9]. aðbap.
850 hoc sedile. pınðeocan.
hoc ouíle. cpo caepać[10].
hoc mónile vel munile. ppoıpćé.
hoc missale. lebap aıćppınð.

hoc gredale. ɼpeðáıl.
855 hoc trobiale. cpoıbel.
hoc lectóric. pcuıoıp.
hoc manuale. lámcuaɼ.
hoc cubile. leabaıð ın ðaım all[ta].
hoc corporale. coppopap.
860 hoc mare. muıp.
hoc praesepe[11]. maımðpép.
hoc cepe[12]. ınneamaın.
hoc rete. lín[13] ıııpcí.
hoc gausape. pcapaıð.
865 hoc cete. mil móp[14].
hoc tempe. maćaıpe.
Hec locucio. uplabpaıð.
hec lectio. aıceć̇t.
hec accio. acpa.
870 hec oracio. ɼıðð̇c[15].
hec constructio[16]. cumtać.
hec preposicio. pemteć̇tap[17].
hec coniunctio. compocul[18].
hec interjectio[19]. ınćepıacc.
875 hec comparatio. compapáıð[20].

hec

[1] dindíma. [2] prolema. [3] ceirín. [4] tighi. [5] crisma. [6] momíssma. [7] apastema. [8] fethma. [9] téma. [10] caeirach. [11] p. cepe. [12] sepe. [13] lin. [14] mil. mor. [15] guidhi. [16] construccio. [17] remtoṡc. [18] comfuccul. [19] interdeccio. [20] comparaíd.

hec intencio. ınnᴛınoeaċ.
hec opinio. baŋamaıl.
hec electio. ᴛoɣa.
hec racio. olıɤeò.
880 hec consecratio. coıρρeᵹnaò.
hec ornacio. cumòaċ.
hec famulacio. muᵹρaıne.
hec fornicacio. aòallᴛρaρ.
hec consolacio. comρólaρ¹ no comaıρle.
885 hec nominacio. aınmneaċaò.
hec dominacio. ᴛıɤeρnaρ.
hec generacio. ᵹeınemaın.
hec correctio. ceρᴛaċaò.
hec operacio. oıbρıuᵹuo.
890 hec planacio. ρcıòe².
hec castigacio. ceρᴛuᵹuò.
hec associacio³. compaŋᴛuρ.
hec supplicacio. ᵹuıòe⁴.
hec monstracio⁵. ᴛaıρbenaò.
895 hec annunciacio. ᖷoıll[ρıuᵹuò].
hec collacio. compaŋáıo.
hec communicacio⁶. comaıneachaò.
hec ministracio. ᴛımᴇıρeċᴛ.
hec procuracio. òenaṁ⁷.

900 hec fictio⁸ ooılbᴛıuᵹuo.
hec pericio [peritia]. eolaρ⁹.
hec adulacio. molaò.
hec coequatio. comᴛρomuᵹuo.
hec simulacio. coρmaıluρ.
905 hec disimulacio. eᵹcuρmaılıuρ.
hec sequestracio. uρlamaρ.
hec prolongacio. ᖷaıoıuᵹuo.
hec satisfaccio. lóρᵹním¹⁰.
hec remuneracio aᴛcumuleò.
910 hec deduccio¹¹. oıρluᵹuò.
hec compilacio. ceᵹal.
hec reuolucio. eıᴛellaò.
hec computacio. comaıρeṁ.
hec benediccio¹². bennachᴛ.
915 hec malediccio. mallaċᴛ.
hec remigacio [reptatio?]. lamaccan.
hec mitigacio. aılᵹıneċ[ᴛ].
hec talliacio. comma.
hec caro. colunò.
920 hec fortitudo. laıoıρe¹³.
hec multitudo. ımaò.
hec magnitudo. méıo.
hec

¹ comsholas. ² reidhi. ³ asociacio. ⁴ suplicacio guidhi. ⁵ mostracio. ⁶ comunicacio. ⁷ forcuracio denamh. ⁸ fixio. ⁹ colus. ¹⁰ lorgnim. ¹¹ dedicacio. ¹² benndiccacio. ¹³ laidiri.

hec paruitudo. loiġeḋ.
hec raritudo. ceipce.
925 hec latitudo. leitne.
hec celsitudo. aiṗḋe.
hec pulchritudo. maiṗṗe.
hec egritudo. eṗláne.
hec longitudo. ꝼaiḋe¹.
930 hec triplicacio. cṗipulca.
hec quadruplicacio. cecaṗḋuḃlaḋ.
hec limpitudo. uiṗꝣemlacc.
hec arundo. cuṗcuṗlac² no ꝣilcac.
hic hirundo³. ꝼainleoc.
935 hec hirudo⁴. náic. eṗcuinꝣ uṗcoiḃec⁵.

Propria nomina:—

hic. Odo Aoḋ.
hic Catto. caiḋ.
950 hic Plato. plaic.
hic Uato. [Pluto?] ploic.
hic Apollo. ꝣṗian.
hic et hec homo ḋuine.
hic et hec uirgo. óꝣh⁹.
955 hic et hec nemo. nemḋuine.

hec ymago. ḋealḃ.
hec indago. loṗꝣaṗecc.
hec norago. ṗaeḃcoiṗc⁶.
hec rubedo⁷. ḋeṗꝣe.
940 hec sangis suga [sanguisuga]. ꝣeṗṗꝣuin.
hec fuligo. ṗuiche.
hec calido [calor]. ceṗ.
Hic ordo. oṗḋ.
hic cardo. meṗlac na comla.
945 hic carbo. ꝼmeṗóiḃ⁸.
hic mango. ꝣilla naneac.
hic uel hec margo bṗuac.

hic et hec latro ṗlacaiḃe¹⁰.
hic et hec Brito bṗecnac.
hic et hec pseudo. ꝼaic bṗéꝣac¹¹.
hic et hec praesto. ꝼiaḋnaiṗe¹².
960 hic et hec par. comcṗom.

hic

---

¹ In the MS. teirei, leithní, airdí, maissí, eslaní, faidi. ² curcuslach. ³ crundo.
⁴frundo. ⁵ urcoideeh. ⁶ urago. saebhcoire. ⁷ rubido. dergi. ⁸ smeroid. ⁹ ogh.
¹⁰ slataidhi. ¹¹ ceudo [over which is the gloss " .i. longa fallsa"] faith bregach.
¹² psto. fiadhnaisi.

hic et hec impar. eɼcomtɼom.   hic et hec dispar. eɼcomtɼom.

Ista sunt nomina :—

hic Issac.
hic Melchisedech.
965 hic [hec] ambago¹.
hoc lac. bainne².
hoc allec. ſgaoan.
hic Daniel.
hic Michael.
970 hic Raphael.
hic Uriel.
hic Samuel. mascula sunt.
hic sol .i. ɼрian.

hoc mel. mıl.
975 hoc fel. ɔomblaſ áe.
hoc animal. ainmıoe³.
hoc sál et dicitur hic sal .i. ſalann.
hic tribunal.
hoc ceruical⁴. céſcaıll.
980 hic Aníbal. aınm ɔuını⁵.
hic et hec consul comaſleac.

Propria [communia?] sunt nomina :—

hic et hec praesul. eaſſoɼ.
hic et hec exul. ınnaſbtac.
hic et hec nigil. ſuſacaıſ.

985 hic et hec [im]provigil. neıſſuıſecáſı.
hic et hec pugil. ɼlecaıſe.

Nomina indeclinabilia :—

hoc nil neımthní.
hoc nul. neımthní.

hoc Pean. ɼрian.
990 hoc Titan. ɼрian.

Hoc

---

¹ ambaca.   ² bainde.   ³ ainm .i.   ⁴ seruical.   ⁵ ainmidhi duine.

A Mediæval Tract on Latin Declension.

     Hoc nomen. ainm.
     hoc praenomen[1]. remainm.
     hoc cognomen. comainm.
     hoc stramen. tuige[2].
995 hoc tegimen. didin.
     hoc pronomen. arron an-
       ma.
     hoc flamen. ridan. gaicte.
     hoc lumen. roillre[3].
     hoc flumen. sruth.
1000 hoc limen. tairrec[4].
     hoc polimen. rlirceog.
     hoc carmen filideċt.
     hoc agmen. sluag.
     hoc fragmen. sbrimleaċ.
1005 hoc trolliamen. marog.
     hoc odomen. [abdomen]
       blonacc.
     hoc culmen. mullaċ.
     hoc cacumen. rind.

     hoc semen. ríl[5].
1010 hoc geminen[6]. cmnad.
     Hic rén. ára.
     hic splen. realg no dreap-
       ran.
     hic lién. intinne iachta-
       raċ[7].
     hic pecten rlind.
1015 hic lyricen[8]. cruitire.
     hic tubicen[9]. rdocaire.
     hic fidicen. tédaire[10].
     hic cornicen. gilla adaire.
     hic lamen [flamen?]. rei-
       deaḋ[11].
1020 hic siren. muirouchu[12].
     hic Caton.
     hic Simon.
     hic Samson.
     hic Phaethon.
1025 hic Lycaon[13].

Propria nomina villarum :—

Hɛc Calidon.
hec Babilon .i. confusio.
hec Elicón.

     hic delphin[14]. mucc mara.
1030 hic Cayn colach.
     hic iubár. deallrad.
                   hic

---

[1] áinm h. pronomen.   [2] tuighi.   [3] soillsi.   [4] tairrsech.   [5] sil.   [6] genímen.
[7] .iasachtarach.   [8] liricen.   [9] tibicen.   [10] tedaire.   [11] séideagh.   [12] cirén. muruchu.
[13] feton hic licaon.   [14] delipin. muc.

hic hepar¹. áe.
hic sutolar. brócc.
hic lar. íctar na comlaḋ.
1035 hic Cesar. pí.
hic Lastar. pí.
hic Nár. rruċ.
hoc far. iċ in arba.
hic naris (pars corporis) srón (ir fluuii Náris).
1040 hic sequester [sequax] lenmunaċ² (extat hic sequestris).

hoc calcar. rbor an eiċ.
hoc pluuinar. rruċ.
hoc torcular. cláp³. carta.
hoc bostar. buaile ḋam.
1045 hoc nectar .c. ɼrinóí roilcí.
Hic pater. aċhair.
hic frater. bráthair⁴.
hic imber. braen aimrire.
hic cucumer. culaṗan.
1050 hic September⁵. mí.
hic October. mí.

Feminina⁶ hec sunt:—

hec mater. máthair⁷.
hec mulier bean.

hec linter. rlinn criaḋ.

Communia sunt:—

1055 Hic et hec puber caetar-[aċ].
hic et hec uber. uth.
hic et hec degener. ḋocinélach⁸.
hic et hec et hoc pauper. boċt.

hoc uber rine octa⁹.
1060 hic campester ⎫
hec campestris ⎬ maċaire.
hoc campestre ⎭
hic siluester ⎫
hec siluestris ⎬ cailltea-
hoc siluestre ⎭ mail.

hic

¹ epar. ² "hoc naris sron .is. flui. náris Hic sequester lenmunach. párs corporis extat. hic sequestris hoc calcar sbor an eich hoc sequestre." ³ torcular. clar. ⁴ brathair. ⁵ septimh. ⁶ feminea. ⁷ mathair. ⁸ docinelach. ⁹ apparently *senextus*.

A Mediæval Tract on Latin Declension.

hic pedester \
hec pedéstris } \
hoc pedestre /

hic celeber \
hec celebris } uacclan- \
hoc celebre / aide.

hic saluber \
hec salubris } uacclan. \
hoc salubre /

Video larem (.i. familiam) per larem (.i. per familiam) circa larem (.i. ignem) in lare (.i. in domo).

1065 Hic acer \
hec acris } ɡruamda. \
hoc acre /

hic volucer¹ \
hec volucris } etecail. \
hoc volucre /

hic paluster \
hec palustres } ɡóicamail². \
hoc palustre /

hic alacer \
hec alacris } eicioca- \
hoc alacre³ / mail.

Hoc polyandrium. uaid⁴. \
1070 hoc ner cappac. \
hoc cadauer. copp leɡap. \
hoc piper. pipup. \
hoc iter. pét pliɡed. \
hoc spinter. dealɡ. \
1075 hoc ruter. cac. ɡabap. \
hoc iuger. la oippzi. \
hoc uesper. nóm⁵. \
hic nutritor. aide⁶. \
hic honor. onoip⁷. \
1080 hic lector. leɡtoip⁸. \
hic amor. ɡrad. \
hic doctor. doccuip. \
hic decor. maipe. \
hic dedecor. mímaipe⁹. \
1085 hic labor. paethap. \
hic calor. tép. \
hic color¹⁰. dath. \
hic odor. boltanad¹¹. \
hic fetor. bpéntup¹². \
1090 hic factor. dénmupac¹³. \
hic fictor. doilbceoip. \
hic emptor. cennaide¹⁴. \
hic protector. dionɡte- oip.

hic

¹ hoc acris cithidemail Hic volucer. etechail hec uolacris, hoc volacre.   ² gaetham.
³ alice cathideam. h. alieris h. aliere.   ⁴ poliandrium.   ⁵ noin.   ⁶ oidi.   ⁷ onar. anoir.
⁸ leg. légtóir?   ⁹ maisi. dedicor. mímaisi.   ¹⁰ colar.   ¹¹ bolltanadh.   ¹² brentus.
¹³ denmusach.   ¹⁴ cend.i.

F

34   *A Mediæval Tract on Latin Declension.*

       hic tenor [tener]. boc.   hic auditor. ciṫcidóiṗ.
1095 hic textor. ḟiżidóiṗ¹.   Hoc cor. cṗoiḋeṡ⁵.
       hic nitor. ṫṗiallaṫóiṗ.   hoc equor. ḟaiṗże⁶.
       hic liquor². ḟluċiḋeċṫ.   hoc marmor. maṗmuṗ.
       hic conditor³. cumḋaiżṫóiṗ. 1105 hoc castor. ainmiḋe⁷.
       hic rector⁴. maiżiṗṫeṗ.   hoc ador aḋ⁸.
1100 hic senior. ṗenóiṗ.

                        Nomina communia⁹ :—

       hic et hec autor. użḋuṗ.   1110 hic et hec memor. cuim-
       hic et hec decór. maiṗi.   neaċ.
       hic et hec dédicor. mímai-   hic et hec immemor. micu-
         ṗi.   imneaċ.

      Nunc de nominibus comparatiuis tercie declinacionis :—

       hic et hec doctior¹⁰ et hoc   hic et hec peior et hoc .ius.
         .ius. níṗṫecoiṗċe.   níṗméṗa.
       hic et hec fortior et hoc   hic et hec durior et hoc .ius.
         .ius. níaṗlaidiṗ¹¹.   níṗ¹⁵cṗuaiḋi.
       hic et hec maior¹² et hoc   hic et hec mollior et hoc .ius.
         .ius. níṗmó¹³.   níṗ¹⁵ buiżi.
1115 hic et hec minor et hoc.us¹⁴. 1120 hic et hec auarior et hoc.ius.
         níaṗluża.   níṗṗannṫaiżi.
       hic et hec melior et hoc   hic et hec carior et hoc .ius.
         .ius. níṗḟeṗṗ.   ní¹⁶aṗuilé.

                                                                 hic

[1] figidoir. [2] licór. [3] cumdaightoir. [4] retor. [5] croidhi. [6] fairei. [7] ainmidhi. [8] adorad. [9] indecLe. [10] doctor. [11] nisalaid. [12] magior. [13] mo. [14] .ius. [15] nis. [16] ni.

A Mediæval Tract on Latin Declension.

hic et hec clarior et hoc .ius. nírroillri.
hic et hec debelior et hoc .ius. ní'armeaca.
hic et hec albior et hoc .ius. nurgile.
1125 hic et hec amabilior et hoc .ius. nírrocarcanaig[i].
hic et hec legibilior et hoc .ius. níarrolegca.
hic et hec laudabilior et hoc .ius. nírromolca.
hic et hec felicior[2] et hoc .ius níarconaichi.
hic et hec sapientior[3] et hoc .ius. níarglica.
1130 hic et hec benignior et hoc .ius nírcainruararigi[4].

hic et hec audacior[5] et hoc .ius. nírvana.
hic et hec amarior et hoc .ius. nírreipbe.
hic et hec loquacior[6] et hoc .ius. nírlabarcarge.
hic turibulus .i. raicec na cuire[7].
1135 hoc orologium .i. urralairci.
hoc collistrigium[8] .i. piloir.
hoc equicium .i. comrar no paing ancrair.
hoc equilibrium .i. comrar.
hoc manubrium .i. maive rgine.

[1] nisameata. [2] felitorum. [3] crudelior. [4] caenshuaraighi. [5] audatorum. [6] locatorum. [7] saithee na tuisi. [8] colosdrigium. [I have placed a mark of length over the *ai* in Nos. 1124, 1128, 1129.]

COMMENTARY.

[In the following Commentary I have made use of certain abbreviations, which, if not explained, might cause obscurity. Thus, "A. S." for Anglo-Saxon; "Beitr." for the *Beiträge zur vergleichenden sprachforschung auf dem gebiete der arischen, keltischen und slavischen sprachen*, herausgegeben von A. Kuhn und A. Schleicher, vol. i. Berlin, 1858; "Corm." for Cormac's Glossary; "gl." for "the gloss on;" "Glück." for C. W. Glück's *Keltische Namen* (München, 1857); "Lib. Hymn." for the Liber Hymnorum; "l. w." for "a living word;" "O. H. G." for Old High German; "O. Ir." for Old Irish; "O'R." for O'Reilly's Irish Dictionary (Dublin, 1817); "O. W." for Old Welsh; "r." for root; "Skr." for Sanskrit; "W." for Modern Welsh; "Z." for Zeuss, or Zeuss's *Grammatica Celtica* (Lipsiæ, 1853); "Zeits." for the *Zeitschrift für vergleichende sprachforschung* u. s. w. Berlin, now edited solely by Dr. Kuhn. Finally, I trust that Dr. O'Donovan and Mr. Curry will not be offended at finding their honoured names reduced to "O'D." and "C." respectively.]

1-5.—1. *Filidh* (gl. poeta), in O. Ir. fili gen. filed, a masc. d-stem, may perhaps be connected with the W. r. gwel, "to see;" cf. Velleda? Fili is declined in O. Ir. as follows:—

MASC. *d*-STEM.
Stem, filid.

	Sing.	Dual.	Plur.
N.	fili	dá fili	filid
G.	filed	dá filed	filed (n)
D.	filid	dib filedaib	filedaib
Ac.	filid (n)	dá fili	fileda
V.	a fili	a dá fili	a fileda

Hence *filidecht* (gl. poema, gl. carmen), Nos. 853 and 1002, *infra*. The .i. which so frequently occurs is for idón, "to wit," "namely." 2. *Fáith* (= vâtis) gen. fátha (= vâtayas?) cognate with Lat. vâtes, a masc. i-stem, declined in O. Ir. thus:—

MASC. *i*-STEM.
Stem, fáthi.

	Sing.	Dual.	Plur.
N.	fáith	dá fáith	fáithi
G.	fátha	dá fáithe	fáithe (n)
D.	fáith	dib fáithib	fáithib
Ac.	fáith (n)	dá fáith	fáithi
V.	a fáith	a dá fáith	a fáithi

3. *Sailmchétlaid*,

3. *Sailmchétlaid,* from salm = psalmus, is also an i-stem, as is cétlaid, which is not found in O'R., but must mean "singer," cf. crochairchétlaid gl. tibicen Z. 198 (crochuir, aerachair gl. crus Z. 744). 4. *Sái,* leg. súi? a masc. t-stem? of obscure origin,—unless we assume that a *p* has dropped out. It occurs, spelt *sui,* in Lib. Hymn. 3ᵃ (p. 72, ed. Todd), "roleg [read rolég] iarsein i Corcaig corbo *sui*" (he afterwards studied in Cork till he became a *sui,* a learned man, sage) acc. pl. seems to occur in the same MS. in the pref. to S. Cuchuimne's hymn, fo. 6ᵛ: rolég *suthe* codruimne¹. 5. *Cruitire* (leg. cruittire, gl. citharista, gl. lyricen, *infra*), a masc. ia-stem = crottárias, formed from crott = crottā, W. erwth, a fem. ā-stem. cf. chrotta Britanna, Venant. Fortun. 7, 8, cited by Z. 77, crottichther gl. citharizatur Z. 77. Note in cruitire the vowel-change (umlaut) of the *o* of the root into *ui,* effected by the *i* of the penultima; note also the non-aspiration of the *t,* though flanked by vowels, in consequence of its original duplication. Engl. crowd-er (fiddler) is from W. crwth, where *tt* has, according to rule, become *th.* cfr. O. H. G. hrotta, Ang. Sax. rót (fem.).

6-10.—6. *Timpanach.* 7. *Organaidh.* 8. *Sophistidhe.* All formed by adding Irish terminations to foreign roots. 9. *Rannaire* (gl. partista), a personal noun (masc. ia-stem) from rann (a part) a fem. ā-stem = W. rhan; cf. O. W. rannam (gl. partior) Z. 1078. In O. Ir. rannaire was thus declined:—

Masc. ia-Stem.
Stem, *rannária.*

	Sing.	Dual.	Plur.
N.	rannaire	dá rannaire	rannairi
G.	rannairi	dá rannaire	rannaire (n)
D.	rannairiu	dib rannairib	rannairib
Ac.	rannaire (n)	dá rannaire	rannairiu
V.	a rannairi	a dá rannaire	a rannairiu

And

¹ Suthe may here be a derived abstract subst. which occurs, spelt súithe, in the Amra Choluim Chille (*Leb. na huidre,* 10 a, a): Bái sab *súithe* cecdind (gl. no nas, no in .i. ba [sab] *snithe in each dindsenchas*) .i. roba sab daingen nosoad cech niummus. No robasniabb. No sabb cech denna .i. cecha airechta cosa-riceed Colum cille. No basoabb isuthemlacht cechberlai coclethi. No robonertmar isint[s]uithe coriacht coclethi. "He was a chief of science in every hill (gl. or above, or in, i. e. he was [a chief] of science in every hill-science), i. e. he was a firm chief who used to return every wealth [of knowledge]. Or he was a sage-abbot. Or a chief of every hill, i. e. of every assembly to which Columcille came. Or he was a good abbot in the knowledge of every tongue to perfection. Or he was mighty in the science to perfection" (coclethe. lit. according to C. "to the ridge or the top of anything"). In H 2. 16 (T. C. D.) col. 691, the passage and

And rann was thus declined:—

FEM. *á*-STEM.
Stem, ranná.

	Sing.	Dual.	Plur.
N.	rann	dí rainn	ranna
G.	rainne	dá rann	rann (ṅ)
D.	rainn	dib rannaib	rannaib
Ac.	rainn (ṅ)	dí rainn	ranna
V.	a rann	a dí rainn	a ranna

luchtaire (gl. lanista) not in O'R., who, however, has luchdaire, "whirlpool," as to which meaning, quære. Perhaps we may compare the name of Lucterius, chief of the Cadurci, also spelt LVXTIIPIOS.

11-15.—11. *Lexaire* (gl. legista), a hybrid from lex, as 12, *decredech* from Lat. decret-um, medializing the tenuis *t*. In O. Ir. we should probably have had crehoilidech. 13. *Uasalathair* (patriarch), a masc. stem, declined in O. Ir. like cathir (which, according to Ebel, is a stem in *r* taking the determinative suffix *e*—cf. Goth. brothrahans—but should, perhaps, like Ainmire, ruire, Fiachra, Fiacha, Lugaid, Echaid, cáera, nathir, &c., be rather considered a stem in *e*); cathir was thus declined:—

	Sing.	Dual.	Plur.
N.	cathir	dí chathir	cathraig
G.	cathrach	dá cathrach	cathrach (ṅ)
D.	cathraig	dib cathrachaib	cathrachaib
Ac.	cathraig (ṅ)	dí chathir	cathracha
V.	a chathir	a dí chathir	a chathracha

If uasalathair be a stem in r, it is compounded of uasal = ὀxala (ὀxalla?) high (cf. Uxellodunum) and athair = Skr. pitar, Gr. $\pi\alpha\tau\acute{\eta}\rho$, Lat. pater, Eng. father, with loss of the initial *p* as is common in Irish and Welsh: cf. lán (full) = W. llawn, Lat. plénus, Skr. root par; lear (many) with plérus, $\pi\lambda\acute{\eta}\rho\eta s$; iasc = W. pŷsg = piscis = fish; lia = $\pi\lambda\epsilon\acute{\iota}\omega\nu$; lethan (broad) with $\pi\lambda\alpha\tau\acute{\upsilon}s$, Skr. pṛthu; the O. Ir. intensive particle and verbal prefix ra-, ro- = Skr. pra, Lat. pro; the prefix il- = $\pi o\lambda\acute{\upsilon}$, Skr. puru, Goth. filu; ire (ulterior) = $\pi\epsilon\rho\alpha\hat{\iota}os$, ath (ford) = $\pi\acute{\alpha}\tau os$, and other instances brought forward by Ebel, Beitr. i. 307. Athir was thus declined in O. Ir.:—

gloss above quoted stand thus: Bai saph saithi cach dind .i. *robai corbasai ⁊ corbo hap saitheamlachta dindscanchas .i. iter ecna ⁊ filidecht ⁊ faistine* (wisdom as well as philosophy and prophecy).

Masc. r-Stem (Noun of Relationship).
Stem, athar.

	Sing.	Dual.	Plur.
N.	athir	dá athir	athir
G.	athar	dá athar	athre (ṅ)
D.	athir	dib nathraib	athraib
Ac.	athir (ṅ)	dá athir	athra
V.	athir	a dá athir	a athra

14. *Crosan* (gl. scurra), W. croesan (buffoon), primarily a cross-bearer in religious processions, "who also," says Dr. Todd (Irish Nennius, p. 182), "combined with that occupation the profession, if we may so call it, of singing satirical poems against those who had incurred Church censure, or were for any other cause obnoxious." The exercise of this profession was sometimes not unattended with risk—Muirchertach mac Erca having been expelled from Ireland ar na *crossana* do marbad (after having killed the Crossans, Ir. Nenn., *ubi supra*). In the Cornish vocabulary, printed by Z., *scurra* is glossed by barth, i.e. bard. 15. *Cestunach*, apparently formed from the base of the Lat. questio.

16–20.—16. *Ardeaspoc* (archbishop), O. Ir. ardepscop, where the first element ard (high) = Lat. arduus, Gr. ὀρθός for ὀρθϝός, Skr. úrdhva: epscop is of course from episcopus. 17. *Gilla cinn eich* (gl. auriga), "a servant (*gillie*) at a horse's head;" *gilla* = O. W. name Gildas, apparently a stem in *s* (Dauid in *gilla* dana, Colmán's hymn, "D. the bold youth"); *cinn* the locative of cenn (head), W. penn, a masc. a-stem, and thus declined in O. Ir.:—

Masc. a-Stem.
Stem, cinna.

	Sing.	Dual.	Plur.
N.	cenn	dá chenn	cinn
G.	cinn	dá cenn	cenn (ṅ)
D.	ciunn	dib cennaib	cennaib
Ac.	cenn (ṅ)	dá chenn	cinnu
V.	a chinn	a dá chenn	a chiunnu
Loc.	cinn		

eich = eci = akvai, gen. of ech, a masc. a-stem = ceas = akvas, cf. Skr. açvas, Gr. ἵππος, Lat. equus, O. H. G. chu, &c. v. *infra*. 18. *Birrach*, says C., is "a heifer between the ages of one and two years;" the Lat. birria is obscure to me. Festus (sub v. burrum, ed. Mueller) has "burra," a heifer with a red muzzle. O'R. has "biorrach," a boat, a cot, a currach (which word I have never met in a MS.). This reminds one of baris, a flat Egyptian rowboat, in Propertius, 3, 11, 44, βᾶρις in Herodotus. 19. *Geidh* (gl. geta), leg. *géidh*, is afterwards the gloss on anser (goose). 20. *Righan* (queen), a fem. â-stem. Cf. Skr. rájní, Lat. régina. Skr. root, ráj, reg-ere.

21–25. In *bantóisech* (duchess), *banab* (abbess), *banprioir* (prioress) (leg. banphrioir), *bansagart* (priestess), the first element is ban (woman, female), W. bun (Myvyr. Arch. i. 575) = gvaná, Gr. γυνή, Boeotian βάνα (see Ebel, Beitr., i. 160), tóisech (princeps Z. 61), a derivative from tús (initium), out of which a r has certainly fallen (cf. O. W. touyssogion principes Z. 6) as in dia (God) = Skr. dévas, núe (new) = navias; cf. the Gaulish base novio in Noviodunum and Noviomagus, Vedic navya, náí (a ship) = Lat. navis, Boind, the Boyne = Bovindâ (Βονουίνδα, Ptol.) &c.; *sagart* is of course from sacerd-os, with the provection of the medial frequent in derived words (cf. apgitir alphabet] = abecedarium). 25. *Innilt* (gl. ancilla), "a handmaid."—O'R.

26–30. *At cluic* (gl. galea), "hat of (the) skull," cf. clogad, "helmet," O'R. We should, I suspect, read atchluic; cf. *atanach*, gl. caputiatus, *infra*. 27. *Taiplis* (alea), perhaps nothing but the English "tables" (backgammon, or some such game with dice), with the provection of the medial above alluded to. 28. *Bairín* (gl. mitra) leg. bairrín? and cf. barr gl. cassis, gl. frons, frondis Z. 51. 29. *Inar* (gl. tunica) *inarach* (gl. tunicatus) *infra*, loc. sing.: Senoir broit buide (leg. buidi?) *inair* glais go glanmét (leg. glanméit), "an old man in a yellow cloak, in a blue tunic of full size." Harleian 1802, fol. 5ᵇ (tunica is glossed by fuan in Z., W. gwn, Eng. gown). 30. *Muincille* (gl. manica), afterwards *muincilleeh* (gl. manicatus), "a sleeve, cuff," O'R.

31–35. *Gairleog*, from Eng. garlick, A. S. garleac, garlee. 32. *Slestan* (gl. lacerna) not in O'R., is apparently a deriv. from sliassit (gl. poples Z. 22), of which the dat. pl. sliastaib is glossed by femoribus in the Leabhar Breacc copy of Gildas' Lorica : slestan, therefore, is probably a cloak, covering the thighs and hams. With the connected O. Ir. sliss, cf. W. ystlys (side, flank). 33. *Ciabh*, "a lock of hair," O'R., l. w. Cirrhus is glossed by mong in Z. 34. *Lámann* (a glove); cf. W. llawes, deriv. from lám (hand) = lámá, lábá? and this, perhaps, from the root LAB (Skr. labh), cf. λαμβάνω—the root-vowel being lengthened (vriddhied?). 35. *Dias* (gl. spica, "an ear of corn," O'R., probably W. twysen, although W. *t* = Ir. *d* is irregular), occurs in Z. 577 : nin (leg. nín) *dias* biis archiunn focheirt (non ή spica est antequam seminas). Oengus céle dé (Félire, Nov. 24) calls Cianan of Daimliac "caiu-*dias* diar tuirind" (a fine ear to our wheat).

36–40. *Braise*,

36-40. *Braise*, "hastiness, rapidity, intrepidity, boldness," O'R., which does not agree very well with lascivia (playfulness, licentiousness). The dat. sing. of the word occurs in the Leabhar Breacc copy of the Félire of Oengus (June 19):—

Luid afuil forocnu (.i. *foroenchaire*)
fiadsluagaib comnrassi: (.i. *coslatra no cosolam*)
donrig batar nissi (.i. *batar niss no umla no innraice no comadais*)
Gervassi Protassi (.i. *duos* [duo] *fratres erant, et in Eleidie sunt reliquia suo qui* [reliquiae suae quae] *per somnium Ambrossio ostensa* [ostensae] *sunt*).

Their blood flowed at the same time (i. e. at the one accusation)
Before hosts, with boldness (i. e. strongly or quickly);
Just unto the King [of heaven] were (i. e. they were obedient, or humble, or fit, or suitable).
Gervassi [and] Protassi.

Cf. W. brysiaw, "to hasten, hurry." 37. *Fallaing*, l. w. (mantle) a fem. i-stem, *fallaingech* (gl. falingatus), *infra*, occurs in Giraldus Cambrensis, Topogr. Hib., 3, 10, "gens ista, hibernica, vice palliorum *phalingis* laneis (al. falangis nigris) utitur," cited Z. 95; falluing is perhaps connected with pallium. Cf. the W. adage, *mal y Gwyddyl am y ffaling*, "like the Irishman for the cloak." 38. *Léine* (gl. camisia¹ = chemise), gen. leined, Corm. v. Lendan, a shirt, probably connected with lín (flax), W. llin, lin-seed, lin-um, λίν-ον. 39. *Gruaidh* (a cheek), occurs in Cormacan éces' Circuit of Ireland, ed. O'D., v. 23. (I have restored the ancient spelling):—

rob imde dér dar *gruaid* ngrinn
oc bantracht Ailig fuiltfind.

(There was many a tear over a comely cheek among the fair-haired women of Ailech), cf. O. Ir. gruad, gl. mala, Z. 28, Corn. grud. 40. *Tengad* (tongue), whence *infra tengtach, dotengtach*. In O. Ir. this was tenge gen. tengad, a d- (or t-?) stem, but identical in root with the Lat. lingua = dingua, O. H. G. zunga, Engl. tongue, Skr. jihvā. Very remarkable is the irregular representation of a Latin medial (*d*) by the Irish tenuis (*t*); cf., however, ithim = admi, edo. The W. form tafod (Corn. tavot, tongue) is to me altogether obscure; it seems to occur in the corrupt Gaulish plant-name ταρβηλοδάθιον, which Z. reads ταρβοταβάτιον (ox-tongue)."

41-44. *Tiach* (gl. pera), "a bag, pouch, wallet," O'R. The word seems to occur in an
obscure

---

[1] "Volo pro legentis facilitate abuti sermone vulgato: solent militantes habere *lineas* quas *camisias* vocant."—Jerome, cited by Diez, Etymolog. Wörterbuch, 82.

G

obscure passage in the St. Gall Priscian (Z. præf. xv.), "Tiach didiv mad ferr lat. i. d. o. o." 42. *Losad*, leg. losaid? Corm. losait, a "kneading-trough," gen. loisde, O'D. Gram. 90. If losad be the modern form of losait, it was a fem. i-stem, the declension of which is in the oldest Irish identical with that of the masc. i-stem. 43. *Dechmadh*, a tithe, tenth, identical with the ordinal (dechma-d = da(n)kama-tha, formed by adding the superl. suffix *tha* to the ordinal?). 44. *Coinnill*, Corn. cantuil = candela, and probably borrowed from the Lat., a fem. â-stem, gen. coinnle, O'D. 90, for cainnle, caindle; cf. caindlóir, gl. acoluthum, i. e. candelarium, Z. 1060.

45-50. *Punann*, punán in O'R., gelima is a "corn-sheaf;" and O'D. informs me that in his boyhood the word was used in this sense in the county of Kilkenny; the primary meaning, however, is "load," and the word seems borrowed from the Lat. pondus—like W. pwn, pyniaw. 46. *Fedán* (gl. fistula), perhaps derived from fid (arbor) = vidu (wood), gen. feda, W. and Corn. guiden, Breton, gwezen. Cf. O. Sax. widu, Ang. Sax. wudu, O. H. G. witu, the Gaulish Viducasses, and the name of the Irish river Οὐϊδουα (vidvâ) in Ptolemy (see Glück, 116). 47. *Fésóg* (a beard), fésóc, Corm. v. Croutsaile, apparently a diminutive. 48. *Lesmáthair* (stepmother), cf. W. llysfam, Bret. lesvamm; so Ir. lessmac (stepson) = Bret. lesvab: lessathair (stepfather), Corn. W. llysdad, Bret. lestad: lesainm (nickname), W. llysenw. I am not sure that Z. is right (p. 1104) in identifying this *les* with the Cornish *els*(privignus). 49. *Sesrach* (gl. carruca, a plough, Fr. charrue), fem. â-stem, absurdly derived by O'R. (who spells the word seisreach) from seiscar each. 50. *Rón* (gl. phoca) Corn. W. moel-ron (sea-calf, seal).

51-55. *Cennbarr* (gl. caphia), by which the scribe probably meant some kind of covering for the head. 52. *Lorg* (a club, cudgel), Corn. lorch, gl. baculus, Breton, lorchen (temo). 53. *Penn*, obviously from penna, as is—54. *Pian* (= péna) from poena. In— 55. *Maroc* (leg. maróc), gl. iolla, the Irish and Latin are equally obscure; maroc once seemed to me connected with W. myr(cmmets), Engl. pismire, Zend, baēvarĕ maoirinãm, decem millia formicarum (Spiegel), &c. (see Kuhn, Zeitschr., iii. 66; Försteman, *ib.* 80; Pictet, *ib.* v. 349). And if so, iolla might well be considered a blunder for iulus, ἴουλος (centipede). But Dr. Todd has pointed out in Du Cange the word jula, "piscis genus," which comes nearer to iolla; the gen. sing. maróci for maróce occurs in a passage from Mac Conglinni's Dream cited by Dr. Petrie (Round Towers), but the context affords no assistance in determining the meaning of the word. Is maróc identical with maróg (gl. trolliamen) *infra*?

56-60. *Crocan*, gl. olla (leg. croccan, W. crochan, boiler, pot), now crogan, "a pitcher" —O'R., seems a different word from crocann, gen. crocainn, which occurs in a gloss on fel. Z. 740; ainm in *chrocainn* im bí bilis, i. e. name of the membrane [the gall-bladder]

bladder] wherein is the bile, and of which crocenn gl. tergus (Z. 80) seems a by-form = W. croen (a skin, hide); crocann is certainly not olla, but tergus, in the poem of Cormacan éeces above quoted:—

> rob iat ar taigi cen rainn
> ar cochaill chorra (?) *crocainn.*

And on the whole we may safely say that Z. erred in comparing (p. 740) Ir. crocann with W. crochan.   57. *Siataire* (gl. vesica, if I am right in so reading "fessica, siadaire") seems connected with siataim, O'R., "I puff, swell up," cf. W. chwythu, "to blow, to breathe."   58. *Caile* (gl. creta), "chalk, lime," O'R., W. calch, perhaps a deriv. from calx, calcis.   59. *Adhare* (gen. adhairee, *infra*) is "a horn, trumpet," O'R., the adj. adarede, gl. corneta is in Z. 780. Here adhare probably means "a drinking-horn." With caustoria compare "Costarium, Costerium, ut Costrellus, Poculum vinarium," Du Cange. What is the *adhare leaga* (cornu medici) of Irish medical MSS.? A substitute for a cupping-glass?   60. *Luaidhe* = Engl. lead.

61–65. *Riaghail*, gl. norma, cf. rēgula, whence, of course, it is derived, but apparently with a change of declension, regula being a fem. â-stem, whereas the umlaut in riaghail points to a stem in *i* (in Z. 22, riagul, riagol, are exactly = rĕgula). A similar remark applies to—62. *Tabhaill.*   63. *Cantairecht*, apparently a hybrid from the Lat. cantor, but possibly a pure Irish word from the root can, Skr. çans; though the first *t* is hard to account for.   64. *Tuireog*, gl. mitreta: here both Irish and Latin are obscure to me.   65. *Medar* (gl. parra): parra is said to be a wheat-ear; I have not met medar elsewhere.

66–70. *Gocan* (gl. parricula): gogan is "cackling, prating," according to O'R., but I suspect gocan to be the name of some small bird, cf. *gocan* na cubhaig, "avicula quæ cuculum comitatur" (Highland Society's Dict., i. 500).   67. *Clár* (gl. tabula) in Z. claar (W. clawr, clawr, O.W. o clorion, tabellis, Z. 170), abl.: hi *claar* cridi (in tabulā cordis), Z. 1082.   68. *Ancoire* = ancora is from the Latin; ingor is the pure O. Ir. form, see Z. 1107, W. angor, Corn. ancar, Bret. cor.   69. *Uisce imill* (lympha), "water at the edge" (niseeán, gl. aquula, Z. 281; lán di *uisciu*, "full of water," Z. 595); uisce is perhaps an example of the rare derivative suffix -scia; cf. the man's name Muirsce = moriscias; but may possibly be connected through the Vedic form utsa, "a well," with the root und (vaud), to which belong ὕδωρ, ûdus, water, &c.; *imill*, nom. imell, in O'R. imeal, W. ymyl.   70. *Sess no carr* (seat or car). Sess from the root sad, Lat. sed-eo, ἕζομαι, &c.; cf. fiss and fid, &c.; sess ethar in Corn. is the thwart of a boat (ethar, gl. stlata, Z.); perhaps the abl. may be in that obscure passage in Patrick's hymn, Crist illius, Crist iss*ius*, Crist inerus; *carr*, which subsequently glosses

biga,

biga, is the well-known Gaulish carrus. The four-wheeler of Cæsar and Livy is now represented by the Irish carracutium. What *aptempna* can be, is to me exceedingly problematical.

71–76. *Taebhán*, which I have written for tæman (aspirated *m* for aspirated *b* is not uncommon in O. Ir.), C. explains to be the cross-beam between each pair of rafters; *teallaigh* is gen. sing. of teallach, which glosses focus, *infra*; taebhán teallaigh may therefore mean the little beam (trabecula) over a fire, from which pots are hung; taebhán *comladh* would mean the bar of a door (comla, gl. valva, *infra*). 72. *Assan* (caliga), in O'R., asán s. f. "a stocking or hose," W. hosan. 73. *Lainder* (a shoe-strap, shoe-string); O'D. suggests that this may be connected with the Engl. lanyard. It seems identical in meaning with—74. *Traighle*: neither word is in O'R. Can traighle be connected with O. Ir. traig (foot), acc. pl. traigid, a neuter t-stem = Corn. truit, O. W. troet (plur.), and cf. τρέχω, Goth. thragja, Skr. trksh, and the Scythian name Ταργι-ταος mentioned by Herodotus (Ebel, Zeits. vi. 400)? The Celtic root TRAG occurs (as Z. 6, has shown) with the intensive particle ver in the Gaulish vertragi: αἱ δὲ ποδώκεις κύνες αἱ κελτικαὶ καλοῦνται μὲν οὐέρτραγοι κύνες φωνῇ τῇ κελτικῇ, Arrian. de Venat. c. 3. 75, 76. *Coroin*, gl. corona, gl. clerica (leg. coróin?), from corona, apparently with change into the fem. i-declension; but probably an instance in the sing. of that usurpation by the acc. of the place of the nom. which is common in the plur. The acc. plur. occurs in the Book of Armagh, 180, *a*. 2—coirnea, gl. coronas—which shows that the word belonged to the â-declension. Corn. curun.

77–80. *Folt* (gl. coma), falt, Z. 251, abl. o folt, Z. 65, = W. gwallt, Corn. gols, gl. caesaries, Z. 1101, occurs in a quatrain concerning the Norsemen, quoted by Z. 928, from the St. Gall Priscian [Z.'s reading of the last line is dondlaechraidlainn oaloth lind]:—

Is acher in gáith innocht,	Bitter is the wind to-night:
Fufuasna fairgge find-*folt*:	The white-haired sea is enraged:
Ní ágor[1] reimm mora minn	The passage of a clear sea is not undertaken
Dond laechraid lainn oa Lochlind.	By the fierce heroes from Lochland.

The gen. sing. in—78. *Deirgech in fuilt*, stripping (?) of the hair, i. e. baldness (for deirgech I suspect we should read deirgecht); *in* O. Ir. ind. gen. sing. masc. of the article, which was thus declined:—

STEM.

---

[1] Ágor (for agthar = agitur? cf. *agat* clesamnaig "agant joculatores," Seirgl. Conc.) is probably the O. Ir. form of *aghar*, which is thus explained in O'Davoren's Glossary (Mus. Brit. Egerton, 88): "Aghar .i. gaibther no innsaighther, *ut est* Athgabáil *agar* a fai[th]che neme[d] is cóir dia ditiu." *Aghar*, i. e. is taken or is advanced, *ut est*, a distress that is taken from a privileged person's green ought to be protected. Ní agor might be rendered non timeo. Cf. agathar, Gr. ἄχεται, Z. 45.

STEM, SAN(D)A.

	Masc.	Fem.	Neut.
Sing. N.	int, in :	ind''	au, a (= sanad ?)
G.	ind', in'	inna :, na :	ind', in'
D.	(s) ind', (s) in'	(s) ind', (s) in'	(s) ind', (s) in'
Ac.	(s) in (ṅ),	(s) in (ṅ)	(s) au, (s) a (= sanad ?)
Plur. N.	ind', in'	inna :, na :	inna :, na :
G.	inna (ṅ), nan		
D.	(s) naib, (s) mab	in the three genders.	
Ac.	inna :, (s) na :		

In the dual *in* appears in every case, and for all genders.

79. *Fabra*, according to O'R., is not only "eyelids" and "eyelashes"—both which meanings may be attributed to palpebra—but also "eyebrows;" cf. O. H. G. prawa, ὀφρύς, Skr. bhrû. 80. *Mac imresan* (pupil of the eye), mac = O. W. map = maqvas (gen. maqi, in two of Dr. Graves' Ogham inscriptions), originally son, is here obviously in a transferred sense like pupilla, primarily an orphan girl. In Early Middle Irish mac imresan was mac *imlesen* (leg. immlesen), lit. "son of exceeding light"? Is hé tene na súla in mac *imlesen*, "the fire of the eye is the pupil;" Seirglige Conculainn, edited from Lebar na huidre, by Mr. Curry, Atlantis II. 383.[2]

81–85. *Diadhacht* (gl. theologia), a fem. â-stem, from dia (God), gl. deus, *infra*, a masc. a-stem = dêvas, which was thus declined in O. Ir. :—

Sing. N.	dia : = dêvas	Dual.	Plur. dé' = dêvi
		(Not yet observed.)	
G.	déi', dé' = dêvi		déa (ṅ) = dêvân
D.	dia' = dêvu (dêvâi ?)		déib : = dêvâbis
Ac.	dia (ṅ) = dêvan		déo : (for déu)=dêvûs (dêvâns)[3]
V.	a dé' = dêve		a déo :

Grammatack.

[1] The turned comma (') indicates that aspiration (of the initial letter of the word following) is caused by the forms to which it is added, and which therefore must have ended in a vowel. The mark (:), which has been suggested by the Skr. *visarga*, represents a lost final *s*. The forms to which *visarga* is added do not aspirate. N. B.—The *s* in brackets is found after the non-aspirating prepositions, and certainly belongs to the article. Dr. Siegfried was the first to make this important observation. This article in O. W. was *ir*, in Corn. and Bret. *an*.

[2] "In the Hebrew Bible," writes Dr. Todd, "the pupil, or 'apple of the eye,' is literally 'Daughter of the eye.'—Ps. xvii. 8."

[3] Compare Goth. vulfans, Gr. ἵππονς (Ahrens, Dial. ii. § 14, 1), O. Pruss. daivans and Skr. forms like kumârâṅç-cha (puerosque) Nalas, 8, where the dental s of âns (= -a + ans) has regularly become ç

Grammatach, dilechtach, sdair, are obviously *fremdwörter* (grammatica, dialectica, historia). 85. *Eolas dóir*—if I read aright—("an ignoble art"); éolas occurs in Z. 42, spelt heulas: the nom. pl. masc. of the related adjective éolach (gnarus) in Z. 252; ammi néulig (where the so-called prosthetic *n* is nothing but the old termination of the 1st pers. plur. of the verb subst. ammi (n) = ἐσμεν, W. ym, asmasmi); dóir is the opposite of sóir (free, noble), which words are produced by prefixing the inseparable particles of quality *do* (= Skr. dus, Gr. ἐυς?) and *so* (= Skr. su, Gr. ευ), to a root which remains obscure to me[1]. Perhaps we should read caladau doenna, "scientia humana."

86–90. *Oighen* (a pan) seems to stand alone; O'R. spells it oigheann. 87. *Dlighi* (gl. rhetorica): here there is either an omission (? labradha, i. e. of speaking) or a blunder: for dlighi must stand for O. Ir. dliged, lex, regula (cf. W. dleet, Z. 166, pl. dilehedion, Z. 293, O. Sloven. dlŭgŭ, debitum), passing into the consonantal declension, like the Mod. Ir. pearsa, gen. pearsan = O. Ir. persan, gen. persine (a person). 88. *Nathair,* gl. panthera, is surely a blunder, nathair (O. Ir. gen. nathrach), declined like cathir, *supra* = W. nadr, being "a snake, adder, viper, serpent"—O'R., perhaps originally a water-snake, &c. = Lat. natrix. 89. *Leca in duini* (maxilla), leaca in O'R. (gen. leacan), is, however, not jaw-bone (maxilla, the mobile os), but "cheek;" duini, gen. s. of duine (homo), n. plur. in O. Ir. dóini, a masc. ia-stem, originally, perhaps, as Dr. Siegfried conjectures, related to Zend daêna faith, and the root DHYAI (think, meditate), as Skr. manu (homo), Engl. man, is from the root man (think). 90. *Lethail* (gl. mala), apparently one of the class of compounds noticed by O'D. (Grammar, p. 338), who, after quoting in his text leathchuas (one ear), leathchos (one foot), leathlámh (one hand), leathsúil (one eye), gives the following note:—"When leath, which literally means half, is thus prefixed, it signifies 'one of two,' such as one ear, one eye, one leg, one hand, one foot, one shoe, one cheek. It is never applied except where nature or art has placed two together; but in this case it is considered more elegant than aon, one." We shall find lethchaech (gl. monoculus), *infra;* leth retains its original meaning in the following words: lethchil (half-biassed), Corm. v. Cil; lethfer (gl. semivir), *infra;* lethgute (a semivowel, Z. 968); lethmactbail (half a cheese), Corm. Prull; ledmarb (half-dead), Z. 825, lethóm (half raw, Adamnán's Vision, óm = Skr. âmá, Gr. ὠμός); lethsathach (gl. semisatur), *infra;* mala is glossed by gruad in Z. 28.

91–95. *Áil* before the palatal ch. The hypothetical dat. dêvâbis is to be compared with a Japetic instrumental daivâbhis, for which we should find in the Veda dialect dêvêbhis, and in classical Skr. dêvâis.

[1] My reason for hesitating to identify *do* with *dus* and *ἐυς* is, that *do* aspirates (cf. dochrud gl. indecor dochruidigther gl. turpatur, Z. 833); and should therefore have originally ended in a vowel. The *s* may, however, have dropt off at so early a period that its former presence was unrecognised when the practice of aspiration was introduced.

91-95. *Ail* (gl. bucca) is probably connected with the root al, nourish, Lat. ăl-o (cf. lám from r. lab, Skr. labh); ail gl. esca occurs in Z. 996, and cf. irail (nom. irál?) in the following gloss: hi precept sos[celi] ocus in *iráil* hirisse, "in preaching the Gospel, and in nurturing (?) faith", Z. 996. 92. *Craes*, gl. gula; *craessach*, gl. gulosus, *infra*, also means "gluttony," as in the following passage cited from the Leabhar Breacc by Dr. Todd (Ir. Nennius, pp. 170, 171): isé focuinn malarta dona tuathaib ⁊ dona cellaib icambit na ríg ⁊ na aircindig atta (?) dilsi do *craes* ⁊ do racbaidecht int sacgail; and in Z. 41, where the word is spelt crois; cf. W. croesaw, to welcome? 93. *Ulba* (gl. mataxa), I have never found elsewhere; mataxa (μάταξα) means in Martial "raw silk;" it also meant "a cord or line." W. ulw (cinders) is the only Celtic word I know resembling ulbu. 94. *Bass* (gl. palma), acc. pl. bassa, gl. palmas, Leabhar Breacc copy of Gildas' Lorica. 95. *Basog* (gl. alapa) is obviously a derivation from bass.

96-101. *Bond* (gl. planta), bonn gl. solea, *infra*, = W. bon (base, sole), found in most Indo-European tongues: Skr. budhna, Gr. πυθμήν, Lat. fundus for bundhus, O. H. G. bodam, Engl. bottom, O. Norse botn (Kuhn, Zeitschr., ii. 320), Huzvâresh and Parsi bunda, "ground, root" (Spiegel, Zeitschr., v. 320). 97. *Feam* (gl. mentula), "a tail," O'R., who also has feamach, "dirty," which adjective Pictet (Zeitschr., v. 348) compares with the Skr. root vam, vomere, ἐμέω, &c. As to *priv*, I doubt if I read the contraction (pu) rightly, and cannot explain it, unless perhaps as a derivative from the Lat. privus. 98. *Cáin* (gl. emenda, i. e. "damni reparatio," "satisfactio de jure laeso vel de illata injuria," DuCange) a fem. i-stem; "rent, tribute, a fine, amercement," O'R., cáin seems to occur in Z. 592 : Is tacáir dúun, acháin fochell asarchorp. 99. *Cusle* (gl. vena), with the *u* infected, cuisle, O'R. The voc. sing. is frequently heard in the conversation of the Irish peasantry: achushla (i. e. a chuisle) mochridi, "O vein [or pulse] of my heart!" Cuisle is a fem. stem in *n*, and perhaps derived (by the frequent change of *p* into *c*) from Lat. pulsus. The W. word for vein, gwyth, must on no account be compared with O. Ir. féith, gl. rien, gl. fibra, which, as Dr. Siegfried remarks, is the W. gwden, Eng. withe, Lat. vitis, vieo, ἰτέα, O. H. G. wida, Skr. vitikâ, a tie, fastening (Kuhn, Zeits., ii. 133). 100. *Cich* (gl. mamma), dat. pl. cichib (gl. mamillis), Leab. Breacc. Gild. Lor. 101. *Cichín* (gl. mammilla) should probably be written cich, cichín, as the present Irish is cioch, "a woman's breast," O'R.

102-105. *Uth* (gl. mammula), leg. úth? = (W. uwd pap, i. e. pulmentum?), if connected with Skr. ûdhas, Gr. οὖθαρ, uber, udder, M. H. G. euter, is an instance of an Ir. tenuis irregularly representing a Skr. aspirate medial. 103. *Retla* (gl. stella), gen. retlan (Vis. Adamn.), in O'R.; "readhlann, s. m. a star." 104. *Aoir* (aether) is W. awyr

awyr = Lat. aer = O. Ir. aér, Z. 114: dat. sing. *responsit mulier*, Ius atcondaire hisind *aeur* ⁊ ni accai hi talmain a leitheid ⁊ atbélsa no abéla ingein fil imbruind no abélam diblínaib mani thomliur inlussin. "The woman answered, 'the herb thou perceivest in the air, and on earth thou seest not its like, and I shall perish, or the child in my womb will perish, or we shall both perish, unless I eat that herb."—Trip. Life of Patrick, iii. 36. Cf. r. var, to surround. Whether in—105. *Aier* (gl. aera), the aera is for aer, or whether *aier* is era, is to me obscure.

106–110. *Scala* (gl. cratera), "a great bowl," O'R.; Corn. scala (gl. patera), Z. 1122, Goth. skalja, Eng. shell, O. H. G. scala (O. French jale, jalon, galon, Eng. gallon?). If Z. is right (G. C. 1122) in thinking scala a German word, when and how could it have come into Irish? 107. *Greidell*, "a gridiron," O. W. gratell (gl. graticula, Z. 1094), Ital. gradella, Fr. greille, Engl. grill, from craticula (Mart. 14, 21), Med. Lat. graticula, a dimin. of crates (see Diez, E. W. 180). 108. *Talam* (gl. terra), gen. talman (= talmanas), a fem. n-stem, perhaps identical with W. talm, the m of which, by the phonetic laws of Welsh, must stand for mn, mm, or mb. Talam has nothing to do with Skr. dhanvan, which Kuhn (Beitr., i. 368, 369) has identified with the Lat. tellus for telvûs; talam was thus declined in O. Ir. :—

Fem. *n*-Stem.
Stem, talaman.

Sing.	Dual.	Plur.
N. talam	dí thalam	talmain
G. talman	dá talman	talman (n)
D. talmain	dib talmanaib	talmanaib
Ac. talmain (n)	dí thalam	talmana
V. a thalam	a dí thalam	a thalmana

109. *Suiste no sgiurse* (tribulum), "a flail or a scourge," suist = fustis, W. ffust as srian = frênum, W. ffrwynn, seib = faba (Skr. r. bhaksh, Gr. φαγ), W. plur. ffa, srogell = flagellum, W. ffrowyll, &c. *Sgiurse* seems taken from the Engl. scourge. The etymology of—110. *Baile* (gl. villa), the Bally so common in Irish topography, is obscure to me. If, notwithstanding the singleness of its *l*, we connect it with the Med. Latin ballium, we are only led from one difficulty to another—for who shall explain ballium? The earliest instance I have met of the occurrence of baile is in the Trip. Life of Patrick, iii. 12: tanic victor do ingabail (leg. imgabáil?) patrice asin port corraboi immuiniu draigin boi i toeb in *baile*. "To avoid Patrick, Victor went from the house till he was in the brake of thorns at the side of the *baile*."

111–115. *Artán*,

111–115. *Artán*, as I venture to read the urtan of the MS. (gl. villula), I have not met elsewhere. It is a dimin. of art, "a house, tent, tabernacle," O'R. 112. *Slighe* (gl. via), a base in *t*, if sligthib, gl. naribus, in Gildas' Lorica be correctly spelt. Says Cormac: *Slige*, din, do seuchad charpat sech araile, dorónta fri himcomarc dá carpat .i. carpat ríg ocus carpat epscoip, con dechaid each ác díb sech araile. "*Slige*, then, for the passage of chariots by each other: made for the passage of two chariots, to wit, a king's chariot and a bishop's chariot, so that each of them may pass by the other." 113. *Bethu* (gl. vita), a masc. t-stem = O. W. bywyt, Bret. buez, O. Ir. gen. sing. bethad acc. bethid (n) = bivataten (or -tin ?). The root is biv (the adj. biu = bivas); cf. Skr. jiva for giva, Goth. qvius, Eng. quick, Gr. βίος, Lat. vivus. 114. *Lubh* (gl. herba). gen. lubac, lube, Z. 18, 777; abl. dind luib (gl. de rosa), Z. 232, = Eng. leaf, Goth. laufs: lub-gartóir (gl. olitor), Z. 45; lub-gort (a garden), in the so-called Annotations of Tirechan preserved in the Book of Armagh; cf. the Corn. luworch guit gl. virgultum, Z. 817. 115. *Coill* (silva), a fem. i-stem, W. cell, pl. celli, Corn. kelli, gen. coille in Cormac v. Ana :—Ba bind gair *choille* loinche Um ráith Fiachach maic Moinche, i. e. "Sweet is the voice of the wood of blackbirds [ad v. vox silvae merulosae] round the ráth of Fiacha son of M." Coill in Z. is always spelt caill, and only occurs in compounds: mirtchaill, gl. myrtetum, escalchaill, gl. esculetum, olachaill, gl. olivetum, gen. pl. innan olachaille, gl. olearum, Z. 821. May we identify this word with Lat. collis?

116–120. *Slat* (gl. virga), a fem. â-stem = slattâ, is, with its diminutive *slaitín*, to be compared with the W. llath, yslath. Compare—118. *Móin* (gl. grunna, a bog), apparently a fem. i-stem, with W. mawn (turves). In W. mign (masc.), migen, mignen (fem. a bog, quagmire), the *g* must have been a *c*, which could hardly have fallen out in Irish. 119. *Fód* (gl. gleba), leg. fód, "a clod of earth, sod, soil, land."—O'R. 120. *Bothan* (gl. casa); perhaps we should read bothán ("a little tent," according to O'R.), from both (house), W. bod, cf. Eng. booth; *both* seems to occur in composition in Cormac: tic iarum Find don fuar-*boith* deóg lai, con faca in colainn cen cenn: "colann sund cen cenn," ol Find; [afterwards Find came to the hut in the evening, and he saw the body without the head : "a body is here without a head !" said Find].

121–126. *Cocall* (gl. cassula). Cf. "The cuculla, sometimes called casula and capa, consisted of the body and the hood, the latter of which was sometimes specially termed the casula." In a note, Dr. Reeves, from whose noble edition of the Vita Columbae I have made this quotation, spells the word cassula. Cocall is one of those Celtic words

H which,

which, by the influence of the Church, has become universal. Diefenbach (Celtica, i. 122) quotes Martial:—

> Gallia Santonico vestet te bardo*cucullo;*
> Circopithecorum penula nuper erat.

And compares Bret. kougoul, Corn. cugol, Engl. cowl. 122. *Cro* (leg. cró?), before which I have ventured to put casula, the dimin. of casa, occurs *infra* (cro cáerach, gl. ovile), and is explained "a hut, hovel, pen, cottage, fortress" (?) by O'R. 123. *Camra no seomra* (gl. camera); the former is from the Latin, the latter from the Anglo-Norman. 124. *Dorus* (gl. porta), W. drws, Corn. darat [*sic* in Z., but daraz in Lhwyd] (ostium), Lithuanian durrys, Skr. dvâra, Gr. Οὔρα, Lat. fores, Goth. daur, Slav. dver, Engl. door, dat. plur. dinaib *doirsib* (gl. de portis), Z. 749. 125. *Comla* (gl. valva), gen. comladh, *infra*, occurs in the Leabhar Breacc, cited by Petrie, R. T., 400: *comla* gered friss ⁊ gerrcend maróei (leg. maróce?) furri (a gate of suet to it, and the short head of a *maróc* upon it). 126. *Cliath* (= crates, *hurdle*), Med. Lat. cleta, O. W. and Corn. cluit = cletâ, mod. W. clwyd, occurs in the Irish name of Dublin, Baile an atha cliath (the town of the ford of hurdles), also in Z. 21, 114. Fr. claie, Provençal cleda.

127–131. *Marcach na comladh* (gl. digma) is altogether obscure to me; marcach is literally horseman—W.; "marchauc (equestris) ortum e Gallico vetusto marca (μάρκα, τριμαρκισία, ap. Pausan.)," Z. 47. 128. *Lasair* (gl. flamma), gen. lassrach, marg. gloss on Patrick's hymn in Lib. Hymn. The 3rd pers. sing. pret. act. of the verb lasaim occurs in Fiac's hymn:—

> Dofaith fades co Victor, ba hé aridrálastar:
> *Lassais* in muine im bai, asin ten adgládastar.
>
> He went southwards to Victor, he it was that spoke to him:
> The bramble-bush wherein he [Victor] was flamed—from the fire he called.

The word is probably connected with loscad, Z. 143, W. llosg, Corn. leski. 129. *Camradh* (gl. cloaca). O'R. cites from Shaw, camrath, "a gutter, sewer, jakes;" I have not met the word elsewhere. 130. *Senmáthair*, "a grandmother" (O. W. henmam), from sen (old) = sinas, W. hen; cf. Zendhana (Spiegel), Gaulish senomagus, Lat. sen-ex, Sen-e-ca (compar. siniu, Z. 283, and sinithir [Lib. Hymn. gloss on the Altus Prositor]), O. W. superl. hinham, leg. hinam, Z. 305, and máthair = μήτηρ, mater, mother, Skr. mâtṛ (mátar), from the root mâ (to create?), was declined in O. Ir. like athir (v. *supra*), except in the gen. plur., which was máthar(n). 131. *Sechrán*(gl. devia, i.e. deviatio), O'R. seachrán, "an error, straying," has been taken into the Anglo-Irish dialect in the phrase, "going on the shaughraun."

132–136. *Land* (gl. scama), if we take scama to be for scamma, an arena = σκάμμα, "a place "a place dug out and sanded"[1], land is the W. llan, "area, yard, church." It occurs as the last element of a compound in Z. 168: isind ith-*laind*, gl. in area (i. e. in the threshing-floor). If, however, as is more likely, scama is for squama, we may quote O'R.: "lann, s. m. a scale of a fish." 133. *Lég lógmar* (a precious stone), lég (stone), O. Ir. liacc, W. llech; cf. the river-name Licca in Venant. Fortun. Z. 174, and the O. Sax. leia, i. e. leja for léa = léha lapis, Glück, 19. In O. Ir. liacc is a ce-stem, and either masc. or neut., I have not ascertained which. *Lógmar* is an adjective, formed by adding the common suffix -mar to lóg (merces, pretium): gen. sing. "*stipendium* ainm ind *lóge* doberr do míledaib ar míltc" (stipendium is the name of the price that is given to soldiers for military service), Z. 577; hill*uag* mo saethir ("in reward of my labour"), Book of Dimma macc Nathi; lóg. W. llog, is perhaps connected with Lat. lŏcare, loc-arium. May we also venture to adduce Goth. laun, Engl. loan? 134. *Fuindeog*, "fuinneog, s. f. a window," O'R., reminds one of the O. Norse vindauga (wind-eye), Engl. window; Ir. seinistir, W. ffenestyr, Corn. fenester, Bret. fenestr, are directly from the Latin. 135. *Gabhal*, gl. furca, (W. gafl, hardly gebel, a pickaxe), in Z. 731 is gabul (gl. furca, gl. patibulum), which spelling is strange, as the Med. Lat. is gabalus, gabala, gabalum, O. H. G. gabala, Engl. gavelock. 136. *Pellec* (gl. sportula, a small basket) is "a basket made of untanned hide," as O'D. considers. It occurs in Cormac's Glossary, and comes, of course, from pelliceus (made of skins), and this from pellis = Eng. fell, &c.

137-141. *Ossadh* (gl. treuga = truce). 138. *Milan* (gl. urna), not in O'R., is one of a long series of names of different-sized water-vessels, of which we shall hear more when C. publishes his invaluable glossaries. 139. *Cogad* (war), gen. cogaid, n. plur. cogtha, O'D. Gr. 87, like some other nouns of his first declension (a-stems) is, I strongly suspect, a neuter. How else can we account for the vowel-ending in the nom. plur. of aonach, ualach, mullach, cádach (O. Ir. étach, a neut. a-stem), bealach, órlach, sgéal (O. Ir. scél, a neut. a-stem), &c.? Neuter a-stems were thus declined in O. Ir.:—

A NEUTER a-STEM.
Stem, forcitala.

	Sing.	Dual.	Plur.
N	forcetal (ṅ)	dá forcetal	forcetla
G.	forcitil	dá forcetal	forcetal (ṅ)
D.	forcitul	dib forcitlib	forcitlib
Ac.	forcetal (ṅ)	dá forcetal	forcetla
V.	a forcitil	a dá forcetal	a forcetla

With

[1] See an interesting note by Dr. Todd, Lib. Hymn.. 75.

With cog-ad Glück compares the Gaulish name Cog-i-dumnus, *sed qu.* as the *g* is unaspirated in Mod. Irish. Cf. Marti *cocidio?* hardly the Lat. pugna. 140. *Fuiseog* (gl. alauda), "s. f. a lark"—O'R.; cf. W. guichell, "a bird," Pughe. The Welsh name for a lark is uchedydd, Corn. evidit, Bret. echouedez. 141. *Bairgen* (gl. garga) = W., Corn., and Bret. bara (panis), Z. 1122[1]; in O'R. *báirghean*, "a cake;" gen. sing. for dénma *bairgine*, gl. pistor, i. e. vir faciendi panis, Z. 462. The word often occurs in the conversation of Anglo-Irish children, barnbrack (O. Ir. bairgen brecc, speckled cake) being one of their favourite comestibles. Garga I have been unable to find in any Lat. dictionary.

142–146. *Cethramadh* (fourth, O. W. petguared, now pedwyryd, m. petguared, now pedwared fem.). The -ma- here seems inorganic, and introduced from the false analogy of sechtm-ad, ochtm-ad, nóim-ed, dechm-ad. A similar remark applies to óenmad = W. unvet, Z. 330. 143. *Sruban* (gl. merenda, a luncheon) I have not met with elsewhere. O'R. has srúbóg, "a mouthful of any liquid;" and srubhóg, "a cake baked before the fire." With the latter our sruban is probably connected. 145. *Srubán mara* (buccalla, i. e. buccinula?), is apparently a "cockle" (srubán, O'R.). *Greim* (gl. buccella, a morsel), stem in n; cf. O. Sax. gruomon (mica). 145. *Cogar*, "s. m. a whisper," O'R. 146. *Colpa* (gl. tibia, the shinbone) does not agree very well with O'R.'s "calpa, s. m. the calf of the leg." The word occurs in Corm. v. Ferend.

147–151. *Tarr* (gl. festucula, a little stalk or straw), now means "the lower part of the belly," and is still found in a phrase used in reference to a childless man, viz., nír' fás dadam assa tharr. 148. *Mong intslindein* (gl. honplata), "hair of the shoulder," i. e. mane, which meaning does not agree well with that of ὠμοπλάτη (shoulder-blade), for which word I am indebted to one of my friend Littledale's ingenious conjectures. Observe the form of the gen. sing. masc. of the article before aspirated *s*. In O. Ir. *d* before an *s*, or *sr*, or *sl*, which has been flanked by vowels, regularly becomes *t*. The proof of this proposition, which would occupy overmuch room here, may be found in Part IV., vol. I., of the "Beiträge" before referred to. It is enough here to say that int slindein may be proved to have been sandislindeni; and that the Mod. Ir. ant ech, "the horse" (phonetically written an t-ech) was of old san(d)as akvas. 149. *Cengal* (gl. junctura), W. cengl, both probably from Lat. cingulum. 150. *Feoil na fiacal*, "flesh of the teeth," i. e. gums; feoil, a fem. i-stem in Z. 23, ind *féuil*, "the flesh;" fiacal, gen. pl. of fiacail, a fem. i-stem[2], which occurs in one of the St. Gall incantations

---

[1] Bara and gouin (wine) compose the Fr. word baragouin (gibberish).

[2] In the gen. pl. Mod. Ir. has lost all declensional distinction between fem. stems in *d* and *i*; in the old language the gen. pl. of fiacail would have ended in *e*. Thus nime, dúle, caille, are respectively the genitives plur. of nem or nim (heaven), dúil (a thing), caill (a wood).

incantations, Z. 926: ind ala *fiacail* airthir a chinn (one of the two teeth in the front of his head), the adj. *fiaclaich* gl. dentatam, acc. sing. fem. of fiaclach, is in Z. 22. 151. *Sine seain*, the uvula, lit. John's teat; sinsean in O'R.

152-156. *Butun* (biturría); *butun*, according to O'D. and C., is now used for a blacksmith's paring-knife. The Lat. biturría is obscure; perhaps it may be for biturrius, bitorius, Fr. butor (bittern); if so, we should probably read the Irish word *butur*, which word, however, is not known. Batura (patena in Diefenbach's valuable collection of Med. Lat.-Germ. glosses) is the only other Med. Lat. word I know like biturría. 153. *Didean*, "protection, defence," O'R., which corresponds well enough with tectura, occurs *infra* in the form *didin* (gl. tegmentum, gl. tegimen). In O. Ir. the word is *ditiu* (gl. teges, gl. velare, Z. 79), gen. *diten*, dat. *ditin*. 154. *Luirech*, W. lluryg, from Lat. lórica (a corslet of thongs), which alone furnishes the etymon, viz., lorum. The earliest instance of the occurrence of this word is in Fiac's hymn, v. 26 :—

Ymmon doroega it' bíu bid *lúrech* diten do cách:
Immut il laithiu in messa régat ôr bérenn do bráth.

The hymn thou hast chosen in thy lifetime shall be a corslet of protection to every one:
Around thee on the Day of Doom the men of Ireland shall come for judgment.

(Here *luirech* is used in its secondary signification of a religious composition supposed to protect the soul in the same way that a corslet guards the body.) In the poem commencing "Cris Finnáin," Z. 933, we find the word with its primitive meaning: lurech dé dum' indegail ota [leg. ótá] m' ind gom' bond, "God's corslet to protect me from my crown to my sole." 155. *Aithléine* (gl. antiquula, if I read the Latin rightly) means, according to C., "a shirt cast-off" (on account of its age); cf. *aithle*, " an old cloak" —Corm. "*Aith*, or *ath*," says O'D. (Gram. 272), "has a negative power in a few words, as *aithrioghadh*, 'to dethrone;' *aththaoiseach*, 'a deposed chieftain;' *aithchléireach*, 'a superannuated or denounced clergyman;' athlaoch, 'a superannuated warrior, a veteran soldier past his labour.'" I have not met examples of this power of *aith-* in Z., where *aith-* (= Skr. ati, beyond) generally has the force of the Latin *re-*. 156. *Mir* (mica, offula) occurs in Z. 25 (with the neut. article), as the last element of a compound: *a conmir* (gl. medicatis frugibus offam), " the dog's-bit."

157-161. *Faighin*, W. gwain, Corn. guein, Bret. gouin = vagina; whence Ital. guaína, Fr. gaîne. 158. *Caile dabhca* (gl. famula), "girl of (the) tub;" *caile*, a fem. iâ-stem, occurs in Corm., and is compared by Bopp with Skr. kanyâ, Z. kainé (maiden), as aile (another) = anyâ. Hence the diminutive *cailín*, so often heard in the conversation of the Irish peasantry. *Caile* was thus declined in O. Ir. :—

A Fem.

A FEM. *iá*-STEM.

Stem, caliá.

	Sing.	Dual.	Plur.
N.	caile	dí chaili	caili
G.	caile	dá caile	caile (n)
D.	caili	dib cailib	cailib
Ac.	caili (n)	dí chaili	caili
V.	a chaile	a dí chaili	a chaili

Dabhca, gen. of *dabhach*, which subsequently glosses caba; cf. Eng. tub? 159. *Bó* (a cow), O. W. *bou* (in *boutig*, gl. stabulum, i. e. domus vaccarum, Z. 1079) = βοῦς, Lat. bos, bov-is, Skr. gâus, gen. sing. " monasterium quod Latine Campulus Bovis dicitur, Scotice vero *Ached-bou*," *Vita Columbœ*, ed. Reeves, p. 121, where two other readings of the Irish are given, viz., *acketbbou*, *achadh bó* : gen. dual. macc dá *bó*, Corm. sub v. *Deal.* 160. *Uisce*, "water" (whence "whiskey," i. e. *uisce beathadh*, aqua vitae), has been considered *supra*. 161. *Adhbar*, gl. idiogina (ideogina?), afterwards glosses thema, and is, according to O'R., "a cause or motive; a subject or matter to be converted into some other form." Tordelbac[h] a mac, *adbur* ardríg erend : "Tordelbach his son, *materies* of a monarch of Ireland" (i. e. crown-prince), Annals of Boyle, cited and translated by O'D., Gram. 445. Adbar occurs in Z. 337 : rothia *adbar* fáilte "erit tibi causa lætitiæ."

162-166. *Calptach* (gl. binna); Ir. and Lat. here equally obscure to me. O'D. thinks *calptach* an unfledged bird, sed qu.; binna is explained præsepe in the Med. Lat. Dictionaries. 163. *Gamain arain* (gl. benna) is also obscure to me; O'D. says that *gamain* is a yearling calf; but what is *arain*, and what is benna? 164. *Calpach*, gl. juvenca (spelt *colpach* by O'R.) is, according to C., a heifer from her second to her third year. 165. *Cuindcog*, O'R., *cunncog*, "s. f. a churn, a pail" = W. *cunnawg*, milk-pail. 166. *Edrath* gl. mulcra, or, perhaps, mulca), is, according to O'D., " milking-time; but we may also read the Ir. word *edradh*, and compare O. Ir. étrad (libido), the dat. and acc. sing. of which are found in Z. 433, 452.

167-172. *Corrog* (gl. oba, for which I have put opa, is obscure, opa, i. e. a hole) seems connected with O'R.'s *corr*, "a pit of water." 168. *Gealán na súl*, " the white of the eyes;" *gealán*, from *gel*, white; O. Ir. comp. gilither, O'D., Gr. 120. Christ is called by Oengus céle dé, " the white sun that illuminates heaven with much of holiness" (*gel*-grian forosna riched cu méit nóibe); *súl* gen. pl. of *súil*, of which more

infra.

infra. 169. *Taiberne,* from Lat. taberna, as—170. *Personacht* from persona, *Bicairecht,* from vicarius, and—171 and 172. *Cabillanacht,* from Med. Lat. capellanus.

173–176. *Abdaine,* better *abbdaine* (abbey), a fem. iā-stem; gen. sing. occurs in Leab. Breacc, cited by Dr. Petrie (Tara, 76), isin nomad (leg. noi maid?) bliadain déc *abbdaine* Cormaic (in the nineteenth year of the abbotship of Cormac), whence it appears that abbdaine is applicable to the office as well as the place. 174. *Buaile* (gl. vaccaria, a cow-house), spelt *buaili, buailidh,* in O'R., occurs *infra* in *buaile dam,* gl. bostar. It is from the Lat. bovile, with loss of the *v* between vowels, according to rule in Irish. 175. *Proibinse* (province) is proibhinnse in Keating, who calls the Pale *proibhinnse Gallda;* it is, of course, from the Lat. província. 176. *Cathair airdeasbuig* (oppidum archiepiscopi): *cathair* has been considered *supra,* No. 13. Note in airdeasbuig the transposition (p) s-b-g for p-s-e-p; and compare cengedais with πεντηκοστή, coisreachad (*infra*) with consceratio, eisdeacht = O. Ir. étsecht, and beurla = O. Ir. bélre.

177–181. *Eaglais,* O. Ir. *eclais,* gen. *ecaillse, ecolso,* a fem. i-stem, from ecclesia, with change of declension. 178. *Athairtalmhan,* yarrow, milfoil; literally *pater telluris:* wrongly spelt by O'R. *atairtalmhuin.* Athair and *talmhan*—gen. sing. of talam—have already been noticed. Observe the non-aspiration of the *t* in talman, in consequence of athair being a consonantal base. 179. *Blaese* (gl. testa) is *blaose,* a shell in O'R. 180. *Brothrachan* (gl. sabribarra). Brothrach, according to O'D., is a royal garment. 181. *Cenbaran* (gl. uolua); here again the Ir. and Lat. are equally obscure to me.

182–186. *Buathbhallan liath* (gl. artemisia, wormwood, mugwort) is, according to C., "the great thistle;" according to O'D., "the gray ragweed;" *liath* (gray) = O. Welsh *luit* (fuscus), now *llwyd.* 183. *Lus na fiadh* (herb of the deer); *lus,* W. *llysieuyn,* pl. *llysiau; fiadh* gen. pl. of *fiadh* (s. m. gen. *fiaidh*); W. *hydd?* though certainly Irish *f* can never be = W. *h.* 184. *Biror,* afterwards spelt *birur* (gl. nasturtium), W. *berwr,* Corn. beler, is now *biolar* (cresses), with change of *r* to *l.* Biror is fancifully derived by Cormac from *bir,* edge, and *or,* hair, the cresses being, as it were, the hair on the edges of wells and rivers. 185. *Feelug* (gl. genista, broom), not in O'R. 186. *Garbog* (gl. ca) is "the coarse brassica," according to C.

187–191. *Merdrech* = meretrix, from which it is derived. 188. *Facchog,* a shell, cockle? occurs *infra* (194). 189. *Marclach,* "a horse-load," according to C. (marclach cruithnechta occurs in the Trip. Life of P.), from *marc* (horse)—W. and Corn. march, which we have met above in *marcach.* 190. *Bonn* (gl. solea) = bond, v. *supra.* 191. *Bile,* masc. iā-stem, correctly explained "a border" by O'R.; W. byl, masc. "briu, edge." The word occurs in a beautiful old poem attributed to Columbcille, and quoted in full by Dr. Reeves. (Vita Columbæ, 285, 288.) Unfortunately the spelling has been modernized. I will try to restore the pure orthography, and adopt Mr. Curry's translation:—

Diambad lim Alba uile	Were all Alba mine,
O' thá brú co á *bile*,	From its centre to its border,
Rop ferr limsa ait taige	I would prefer to have the site of a house
Occam ar lár caem-Daire.	In the middle of fair Derry.
Is aire caraim Daire	The reason I love Derry is
Ar á reide, ar á glaine	For its quietness, for its purity,
'Sar imad á aingel fínd	And for the multitude of its white angels
On chiunu co roich araile.	From the one end to the other.

192-196. *Uachtar* (gl. impedica); uachtar is the upper part, O'R.'s *uachdar*; but impedica is altogether obscure to me. *Uachtar* also means "cream;" and uachtar go tóin, "cream to the bottom," is, according to C., "a plant supposed to possess the property of turning all the milk into cream when the milk-pail is scoured with it." 193. *Smir* (marrow); W. *mer*, cf. O. Norse smior (butter), Eng. smear, occurs in the exceedingly old tale of the "Fled duin nan géd," ed. O'Don. p. 70:—Ní roan sum din co tardad cnáim for méis dó . . . ocus toimlid á *smir*, ocus á feoil asáaithli; "he stopped not till a bone was brought on a dish to him, . . . and afterwards ate [eats] its marrow and flesh." 194. *Facchog beg*, a periwinkle, lit. "a little shell." 195. *Grainsech* (gl. grangia), *grainseach*; O'R. "a grange, a farm." 196. *Cerc*, O'R. *cearc*, a hen; cf. *crcedae*, gl. gallinaceus, Z. 765; the resemblance to the Gr. κίρκος seems accidental.

197-201. *Ilur* (eagle); W. *eryr*; Corn. gl. *er*; Bret. *erer, er*; Goth. ara, gen. arius; O.H.G. aro. 198. *Arg* (from arca), "a chest, coffer,"O'R.; so 199—*Ciste* is from cista. 200. *Ciarsech*, a hen blackbird, perhaps connected with ciar (fuscus), whence the name Ciarán, which occurs in an old obituary notice (Z. praef. xxxii.), bás Muirchatho maic Mailedúin hi Cluain maccunois á imda-*Chiarain* (death of Muirchad, son of Mailedúin, in Clonmacnois, from Ciarán's bed). With ciar = céra, we might, perhaps, compare κελαινός, Skr. kála, Lat. cal-igo. 201. *Caog* (gl. monedula, a jackdaw); cf. W. *coeg*-fran = coeg + bran. Engl. chough.

202-206. *Spideog* (gl. philomena), "a nightingale," O'R.; generally applied to the robin redbreast. 203. *Colum*, for columb = columba; cf. Lat. palumba; *ciadcholuim*, gl. palumbes, Z. 752; cf. Corn. *colom*; gl. columba, *cudon*; gl. palumba, Z. 1113; W. *colomen*; Bret. *koulm, klom*. The final *b* is still retained in *Colomb* cille (Book of Armagh, 15 *b*, 2), gen. sing. "eductio martirum, i. e. ossuum *Coluimb cille*" (ib. 16 *a*, 1), "*Columb* crag" (Vita Col., ed. Reeves, 19, 20); and in the tenth century inscription on the case of the Book of Durrow (see Vita Col. ed. Reeves, 327), which Rod. O'Flaherty has copied on a fly-leaf at the beginning of that MS.:— ✠ Oroit acrs acus bendacht *cholcimb* chille do flavnd macc mailsechnaill dorig herenn lasandernad acumeldachso ([the] prayer and blessing of Columb of [the] Church for Fland, son of Mailsechnall, for [the] King of Ireland, by whom this case was made). 204. *Crebhar* (gl. lucifugia); *creabhar* is a woodcock, according to O'R.: cf. W. *creyr*, a heron. 205. *Ferbog* (gl. capreola, a roebuck), in O'R. *fearboc, carb, earboc*; Gael. *carb, earbag*, Corn. yorch, gl. caprea, Z. 1115; W. iwrch, Bret. iourc'h. The unaspirated *b* in ferbog is a medialized *p*; cf. heirp (gl. dama, gl. capra), Z. 78. May we also compare Lat. hirpus, hircus, Sabine fircus, with which Weber (Zeits. vi. 320) connects Tacitus' alces, A. S. elch (Eng. elk)? 206. *Corcach mara* (gl. rostigola, *infra* gl. curiolus), some kind of sea-bird, perhaps the curlew. The nearest thing I know to rostigola is rusticula, but this is a heath-cock.

207–211. *Dreolan* (leg. dreólan?); W. drywyn, a wren, = Ir. drean, " the king of all birds;" the "avis regulus," for which aurigola seems to stand. 208. *Nenntóg* (gl. urtica, a nettle). spelt with two n's—O'D. Gr. 19; O'R. *neantóg, neanta;* nenaid (nettles) occurs in Cormac, but I omitted to note where. 209. *Connlach* (gl. arista), a collective, "stubble," "straw"—O'R.; applied in Clare, according to C., to *stalks* of rape; arista, however, is the beard of an ear of grain. 210. *Coinnlin* (gl. stipula, a corn-stalk), applied, according to C., to a *single* stalk of rape; cf. connall, gl. stipulam, colligendo, Z. 731; W. *cynnull* yd, "ingathering of corn." 211. *Seimin* (gl. fistula, reed), "a bulrush"—O'D.; "blackheaded bog-rush," O'R.; probably a deriv. from séim (gl. macer; gl. tenuis, Z. 23, 261).

212–216. *Monadan* (gl. moneta), bogberry, leg. mónadán, l. w., perhaps connected with móin, a bog. 213. *Glacarba* (a handful of corn); *glac* (hand, palm); *arba* (for arban?) O'R.'s "*arbha*, s. f. corn" (he is wrong as to the gender, for ith *in* arba, gl. far, occurs *infra*); cf. W. erfin. 214. *Glac saiged* (gl. pharetra); here *glac* must mean a quiver-like receptacle; soiged, better saiged, = sagittân; gen. pl. of *saiged*, anciently saiget; W. *saeth*, from Lat. sagitta: for if the word were Celtic, the initial *s* would have become *h* in Welsh. Thus, in Colmán's hymn (Lib. Hymn. fol. 5 *b*):—

> Cech martir, cech dithrubach, cech nóeb robai in genmnai,
> Rop sciath dunn diarn imdegail, rop *saiget* uan fri demnai.
>
> Let every martyr, every hermit, every saint who lived in purity,
> Be a shield to us, to defend us; be an arrow from us against demons!

216. *Ga* (gl. hasta) = gaisas; gaide (gl. pilatus, Z. 64) = gaisatias, the *s* being lost between vowels, as in siur (sister); iaran (isarn = iron); giall (a hostage) = O. H. G. kisal; iach = esox, esucius, W. cawg (salmon), Corn. chog, &c. Cf. with gaisatias, n. pl. masc. gaisatii, gaisati, the Gaulish tribe-name Γαισάτοι, Polyb., which, however, seems

seems a stem in *a*, not in *ia*. See Z. 64, note; W. gwaew, pl. gwewyr, Z. 119, Corn. gew, Z. 152, seem the O. Ir. faebur (edge), Corm. v. *Dimess*. 217–221. *Seidedh gáithe no bulga*, gl. flabella (a blast of wind—cf. flabra—or a bellows; cf. flabellum); *seideadh*, O'R.; W. chwythiad, Ir. siataim = Bret. c'houézaf Corn. huethaf; *gáithe*, gen. s. of *gáith*, a fem. i-stem, which we have already found in the quatrain quoted from the St. Gall Priscian; *bulga* (bellows?) must be connected with *bolg* (bag); O. Ir. bolc, gl. uter; bulgas Galli sacculos scorteos vocant, Festus, Z. 17; Goth. balgs, and Aeol. βολγος (= μολγός, hide). 218. *Cerdcha* (gl. fabrica), a smithy, forge, occurs twice in Cormac (sub vv. *Cu* and *Nescóit*). In Z. 70 it is spelt cerddchae, and glosses officina; *cerd* (formator, faber), gen. *cerda* (cerdcha, .i. teg cerda, Corm.); acc. *ceird* (Brogan's hymn, 79) is a masc. i-stem, from the root CAR, Skr. kr̥, to make, whence also *cerd* (art), a fem. i-stem; gen. dual; mic dá *cerda*, pseudo-Oengus, cited by Dr. Todd, Lib. Hymn, p. 85. *Cae, ca* (W. cae, caiou, gl. munimenta, Z. 291), has probably lost a *g*; cf. O. H. G. hag (stadt), N. H. G. gehege, Fr. haie, Eng. hedge. 219. *Mesgan* (gl. massa), leg. mesgán, now, I believe, applied to a lump of butter, shaped like a sod of turf. 220. *Bláthach* (gl. baudaca) is buttermilk; gen. *bláthaigh*. 221. *Lind*, leg. *linn?* (gl. cervisia), ale; O'R., *linn, lionn*, s. f. Gael. *leann*, W. llyn.

222–226. *Fual* (gl. urina), stem, vôla; cf. Skr. vâr, vâri (water); οὖρον, harn?; gen. *fuail*, occurs in one of the St. Gall incantations (Z. 926). "Ar galar *fudil*" (against disease of the urine, strangury?). "Domesuresa diangalar [mo] *fuáil*-se" (I save myself from great disease of my urine). "Focertar inso degrés i maigin hi tabair *thúal*" [thúal = do fúal]. (Let this be placed continually in [the] place wherein thou makest thy water). 223. *Sgél* (gl. fabula), O. Ir. scél (narratio, nuntius), nom. and acc. plural scéla; a neuter a-stem[1]; gen. plur. scél (n), which before *b* becomes scél (m),

---

[1] The mod. Irish nom. and acc. pl. is *sgéalta* (*sgéal-t-a*), as in *scol-t-a* (sails); *ceol-t-a* (melodies); *neal-t-a* (clouds), where the *t* is what Bopp would term an inorganic addition to the base, but what Curtius would call a determinant. Another inexplicable *t* is found in some dialectical verbal forms: thus, *biamuis-t* (let us be), in S. Leinster and E. Munster (O'D. Gram. 169); glanamuis-t (let us cleanse), in Kilkenny (ib. 180); *glanfamuis-t, glanfabhuis-t* (we would, you would, cleanse), Kilkenny (ib. 182). All through Ireland this *t* occurs (sometimes medialized) in the 1st and 2nd pers. plur. pres. act., and 1st pers. sing. fut. act., as *glanamai-d* (we cleanse); *glan-t-aidh* (ye cleanse); *glanfa-d* (I will cleanse). Cf. ar sein *bera-t-sa* einech do sgena [ib.], "on him I will take revenge (?) of daggers" (Rumann, Petrie, R. T.); compare also tánais-t-e (second), O'D., Gram., 123, for Z.'s tanise. The so-called determinant is not used in the O. Ir. declension, but a *t* occurs in two or three conjugational forms. Thus, *guidmi-t*, Z. 143 (we pray); *logmai-t* (we forgive); *proimfimi-t* (we shall prove); in perfects like *asrubar-t* (I said), *asrobar-t* (he said), and in the third pers. plur. of the secondary present, e. g., *domel-t-is* (they were

(m̐), as in a verse in a poem on the characteristic virtues of the saints of Ireland (Rev. Dr. Kelly's "Calendar of Irish Saints"):—

> Caras Scuithin na scél mbinn (bendacht ar chách doroinne!)
> Aindre áilne uchtgela, etarru dogní oige.
>
> Scuithin of the sweet legends loved (a blessing on every one who hath done so!)
> Maidens beautiful, white-bosomed, [and] among them preserved his chastity.

The long é seems to indicate the loss of a consonant. 224. *Corcair* (leg. *corcuir?* gl. purpura), from which it seems formed by changing the *p*'s into *c*'s (as in *case*, from *pascha*; *cengcedais* from *pentecoste*; cf. *necht* = *neptis* (W. nith, Skr. naptri, N. H. G. niftel); *secht* (ṅ) = *saptan*; *fescor* = *vespera* = a Skr. divas-para, Bopp), and altering the declension. Perhaps, however, *corcuir* is not a foreign word. Z. 744, has *dubchorcur*, gl. ferrugo, and compares the name of the Dalmatian island, Κύρκουρα, Corcyra. The Welsh is *porphor*. 225. *Céir* (wax); W. *cwyr* = cēra; but the Irish *céir* seems an i-stem. The Cornish and Bret. are *coir*, *koar*. 226. *Glass* (gl. serra), a lock, manacle, occurs in the poem of Cormacán éces (ed. O'D.), v. 57:—

> Ocus ní thardad air glas   And there was not put upon him a manacle,
> Na geimel alainn amnas.   Nor polished tight fetter.

The dimin. glasán (gl. serrula) occurs in Z. 281.

227–231. *Roth* = Lat. rŏta (a wheel); Z. 82, the *t* being aspirated between the *o*, and the *a* which originally ended the word. Under such circumstances in Welsh *t* always becomes *d*. We find, accordingly, that the Welsh for wheel is *rhod;* cf. Lith. ratas, O. H. G. rad. We may also compare Skr. ratha (waggon), Zend, rathaéstā. 229. *Fochlaidh*, "a cave" in Cormac, occurs in the Irish Nennius, p. 116: int ochtmad ingnad, *foclaid* fil i tír Gucut ocus gaeth tribith ass (the eighth wonder, a cave which is in the land of G., and wind for ever [blowing] out of it). Cf. O. W. claud (fossa), Z. 622, W. goglawdd, Ir. cláidim (I dig), W. cloddiaw. 230. *Liter* (a letter) = Lat. littera. Double *t* becomes *th* in Welsh; we find, accordingly, *llythyr-en*. 231. *Sillaidhi* (if I read the word rightly) seems a curious hybrid, consisting, as it does, of the first syllable of syllaba, *plus* an Irish termination. Cf. *siolla*, O'R.; W. *sill*. In Z. 968,

eating); *asber-t-is* (they were saying). The declensional *t* occurs frequently in the plurals of O. Welsh nouns, cf. *etin-it* [now edned], *bronnbreith-et* (volucres ventre variegatæ), *merch-et* (filiae, now merched). I do not find a *t* in the British conjugation, except in perfects act., like *a gant* (cecinit), *ae gwant* (feriit). In this *t* (= *dd?*), and in that of the corresponding Irish perfects, I am inclined to recognise the reduplicating root dhā.

968, the word is, as might be expected, sillab, fem.; sillaid occurs in Leab. Breace in the nom. pl. of sillad, Gael. *siolladh*.

232–236. *Lethenach* (gl. pagina, a page of a book); the gen. *lethinig* (leg. lethenig?) occurs in Harl. 1802, 13 *a*; line moite [O. Ir. m' aite] hí tus ind *lethinig* sea. Rob cennais dia for anmain maelissu, "a line of my tutor's [written by him] is at the beginning of this page. God be gentle to Maelissu's soul!" Is *lethenach* weakened from lethanach? **233.** *Crupán na lám* (gl. sirogra, i. e. chiragra, χειράγρα, gout in the hand); crupán I have not met elsewhere. O'R. has *crúpadh* (contraction, Gael. *crúpadh*); *crúpaim* (I contract); *crupog* (a wrinkle), to which it seems allied. **234.** *Esga* (gl. luna); in O. Ir. aescae, Z. 247; gen. ésci, Z. 1074, s. n. The adj. esca, which occurs in the Félire of Oengus, is glossed by cain no alaind no *lucida* in the Leabhar Breace copy of that (philologically) valuable composition. Note neph-éscide, unmoonlit (gl. σκοτομήνη), isin nep[h]-aescaidiu (gl. in σκοτομήνη), Z. 830. **235.** *Medhal* (gl. pauea = paunch?) though the unaspirated *d* in O'R.'s *maodal*, "a belly, a paunch," is certainly correct. Gael. *meadhail* is "mirth," "joy." **236.** *Blonac* (lard); cf. W. *blonry* (lard, grease). Corn. *bloneg*; gl. adeps.

237–241. *Monadh* (subsequently glossing momissma, i. e. νόμισμα, coin), seems here to mean a mint. In Gaelic *monadh* means a mountain; cf. W. mynydd, di-minid sursum, lit. ad montem, Z. 571, and also a heath. **238.** *Farcan* (gl. comprisura), (leg. *farcán?*), is "a knot in wood," according to C.; O'R. has "*farcán*, s. m., a corn or welt on hands or feet." **239.** *Cantair* (gl. troclia), "cantaoir, a press"—O'R.; "into which wood is put to be straightened," adds Mr. Curry. In Gaelic *farchan* is "a little mallet." **240.** *Cliath fuirsidh* (gl. eripica, a harrow); as to *cliath*, v. supra: *fuirsidh* seems the gen. sing. of *fuirse*, harrowing, O'R. **241.** *Sitheal* (gl. situla, bucket) is "a bowl, a cup," according to O'R.; W. hidl, a cullender?

242–246. *Taes* (= dough, Goth. daigs, N. H. G. teig?), W. toes. **243.** *Mulcan* (gl. glassia, i. e., γαλάξια? a kind of milk-trumety) is O'R.'s *mulachán*; s. m., "a kind of soft cheese; cheese curds pressed, but not in a vat." Cf. Goth. miluks, Eng. milk, O. H. G. miluh, mulgere, mulcere, ἀμέλγω. **244.** *Igha* (gl. prisura), perhaps O'R.'s *iodha*, "the cramp, rheumatism, any kind of pain;" "a stitch in the side," according to C. **245.** *Cocan* (gl. pensa, a day's ration) is *cucan* (gl. penus, store of food, provisions) in Z. 80. This is a different word from *cucann*, gl. pistrinum, gl. coquina, gl. culina, Z. 740, though they come from the same root, viz., cak, or pak. Cf. O. W. coc, gl. pistor; Cornish *cog*, gl. coquus; whence *keghin*, (gl. coquina), Z. 1095, 1122; cf. Skr. pacámi; Lat. coquo, coqu-in-o, and popina; Lithuanian kĕpu; Gr. ἀρτοπόπος, ἀρτοκόπο-ς (bread-baker), which last word Messrs. Liddell and Scott derive from ἄρτος and

and κόπτω. See Curtius, Zeitschr. iii. 403¹. 246. *Léce in árain* (calculus in the kidney); as to léce r. *supra*; *árain*, abl. of aru; gl. rien, Z. 20; Welsh *aren*, perhaps connected with Lat. rên; *sed qu.* Lapitulta is, perhaps, a blunder for lapillula.

247–251. *Bancoig*, gl. presena. Both words obscure, and probably corrupt. Shall we read *banchoigle* and proseda, a prostitute? *Banchoigle* occurs in O'R., with the meanings, "a female companion, a cup gossip." *Banchoigreach* in Gaelic is "mulier aliena." 248. *Luch francach* (lit. French mouse) is certainly a rat (cf. Welsh *llygod ffrengig*, rats), but what is rula? With *luch* (O'R. s. f. a mouse), cf. W. *logod*, Z. 82, *llyg* (a field-mouse). 249. *Luch dall* (gl. talpa, a mole), lit. blind mouse; *dall* (blind), which glosses cæcus, *infra*, and occurs in composition with *súilech*, in *dallsúilech* (gl. orbatus), *infra*, is the Welsh *dall*, pl. *deillion*, Z. 296. 250. *Lacht* (gl. lactura), in in O'R. *lacd*, "milk;" Corn. lait (leg. laith); W. *llaeth* = Lat. lact (lac, lactis) is, perhaps, as Bopp has suggested, an old passive participle formed by the Skr. suffix ta². On this word, and on the interesting identification of Ir. bliocht, W. blith, with γάλακτ (γλακτοφάγος, γλάγος), where the Celtic *b* and the *γα* are the last remnant of the word for cow (Skr. gav, Ir. bó), see Grimm, Gesch. d. d. Sprache, II., p. 1000. 251. *Amuise* (gl. amusca) I cannot explain.

252–256. *Tál* (gl. ascia, adze), cf. Lat. tálea (a cutting for planting); inter-taliare, and the crowd of words connected therewith; Ital. taglia; Span. tajo; Fr. taille, tailleur; Engl. tailor, and fee *tail* (feudum talliatum); and M. H. G. teller (a plate), Diez, E. W. 339. 253. *Casnoidhi* (gl. scindula, shingle), leg. casnaidhi? is "chips, or shavings of wood," according to O'D. and C. The nom. sing. *casnaidh* is in O'R. 254. *Escart* (gl. scupa, i. e. scopæ, a besom?), probably from *es* (= Lat. ex), and the root SCAR, whence etarscar-tha (separationis), Z. 254–5. But scupa is probably a blunder for stupa, and we may compare the Gaelic *eascard*, or *ascart*, s. m. "tow," "coarse lint." 255. *Guirin* (gl. pustula), Gael. *guirean*, W. goryn, from gur (pus); Corn. v. Nescoit; W. gor; cf. French gour-me, and perhaps O. Norse gor (dung), gor-m-r (slime). 256. *Nus* (gl. onesta, i. e. colostra?) is, says O'D., the beestings or new milk of a cow after calving: "*nus* quasi novus," says Cormac; and though it is
of

---

¹ Dr. Smith, in his Latin Dictionary (sub v. coquo), is wrong in including the English *bake* in this class of words. *Bake*, as Curtius points out, is the Greek φώγειν.

² This suffix (Lat. -tus, Gr. τός) is found (without addition) in Irish, not, as might be expected, in the part. perf. pass., but in the pret. pass. in -d, plur. -tha (Ebel. Beitr. i. 162). Ebel here speaks of *vocalic* verb-stems. The tenuis is preserved in the sing. of the pret. pass. of *consonantal* verb-stems: e. g. rocet (was sung) = pra-can-ta, tairchet (was prophesied), ad-ra-nac-t (was buried), &c. The termination of the part. perf. pass. O. Ir. -the, te, mod. Ir. -*tha*, -*ta*, really stands for ta + ya (see Ebel, Beitr. i. 162).

of course absurd to identify *nus* with novus, the word may really come from the root nov, which in Irish would lose the *v*. Gael. *nùs*, *nds*, gen. sing. *nùis*.

257–261. *Baineachlach* (gl. grimaga), a female servant, a she-post-boy! if O'R. be right in his explanation of *cachlach*. 258. *Meall* (gl. picuta, i. e. picota), a mound, hillock, a masc. a-stem, with which Glück, 138, has connected Mellodunum and Mellosectum. W. *moel* (a conical hill) is represented by the Mod. Ir. *maol*. 259. *Eás* (gl. mustella, weasel), a dimin. form in O'R., viz., *easóg*; another mod. word for this animal is *nas*, which is nes in Z. 60. 260. *Fidhchat* (gl. muscipula), literally wood-cat, a humorous word for a mouse-trap. 261. *Conero* (gl. decipula, a snare, a trap), "a wolf-trap," conjectures C., from *con*, base of *cu* (dog, a wolf is called *cu allaidh*), and *cro*, gl. casula (*supra*).

262–265. *Srathar* (gl. sagena, a fishing-net or seine), Gael. *srathair* (clitellæ). I suspect the scribe has blundered here, for srathar is certainly "a straddle," as O'R. explains the word; W. ystrodyr, f. from Med. Lat. stratura. It occurs (with its *s* aspirated by the nom. sing. of the fem. article) in the St. Gall Priscian, Z. 929:—

Gaih do chuil isin charcair :	Take thy corner in the dungeon :
Ní róis chluim na colcaid :	Thou gettest neither down nor flockbed :
Truag insin, amail bachal,	That wretched one ! like a slave,
Rot giuil ind *srathar* dodcaid.	The miserable *srathar* sticks to thee.

This, however, does not enlighten us much as to its meaning. 263. *Carr* (gl. biga, a two-horsed chariot) has been noticed *supra*. 264. *Uchtach* (gl. antela), a poitrel, or breast ornament for horses, from *ucht*, breast (also the brow of a hill, as in conrici *hucht* noinomne, "to nine-oaks' hill," Book of Armagh, 17 *a*, 1), mod. gen. ochta, a masc. u-stem. The following is a paradigm of these stems:—

MASC. *u*-STEM.
Stem, bithu.

	Sing.	Dual.	Plur.
N.	bith	dá bith	betha
G.	betha	dá betha	betha (ṅ)
D.	biuth	dib bethaib	bethaib (*for* bithuib)
Ac.	bith (ṅ)	dá bith	bithu
V.	a bith	a dá bith	a bithu

Iu—265. *Tiarach* (gl. postella, i. e. postilena = W. *pystylwyn*), a crupper, may, I suspect, be found the *tlar* conjectured by Z. 567, as a designation for the western regio mundi. In Ireland the west is the back; the east, the front (airthir a chinn, in the front

front (east) of his head); the south is the right hand (des) (cf. Dekkhan, from the Skr. dakshina) the north, the left (tuath). In Kerry I have heard an English-speaking peasant talk of a tooth in the *wesht* side of his jaw, meaning the back part.

266-270. *Laithirt* (gl. capula, i. e. crapula, drunkenness, debauch, also the headach resulting therefrom) is pleasantly derived by Cormac from *laith* (ale), and *ort* (killed) thus: *Laithoirt* .i. laith ron ort .i. ol cormac, "laithoirt, that is, *laith*, which killed us, i. e. a drink of ale (*corm* dat. s. *cormaim* = W. *cwrw*, κοῦρμι, Dioscor., see Dief. Celt., i. 123). 267. *Cáer finemnach* (gl. uva), literally bacca vitea: cáer, gl. bacca, Z. 37; W. cair: *finemnach*, an adj. formed from *finemain*, a vine, which is found in the Leabhar Breace Sermon on S. Brigit, cited by Dr. Todd (Lib. Hymn. 65): Is aire sin isé á samail etir dúlib, colum eter énaib, *finemain* eter fedaib, grian uas rennaib. ("Hence it is that her type among created things is the Dove among birds, the Vine among trees, the Sun above the stars.") 268. *Lubra* (gl. lepra, leprosy), cf. W. llyfrith, "eruptive, pimpled." 269. *Cnaimfiach no torpan* (gl. fragella, cornix *frugileya?*): *cnaimfiach* (which glosses curellus, *infra*, No. 503) means, according to C., "the great eagle," and is also applied to a raven (*sic* O'R.); to a rook in Scotland. It is hard to say what the first element of the compound can be: if we read *cnáimfiach*, we might compare *cnám*, bone, a masc. i-stem, o chnáim gl. ex osse, Z. 1002, n. pl. in chnamai, Z. 237, acc. pl. cnámi, Z. 609, cf. κνήμη, and *fiach*, gl. corvus, Z. 1030; cf. N. H. G. weihe, O. H. G. wiho, wigo (milvum), uuiio (milvus). *Torpan* is a crab (cancer), according to C., Gael. *tarpan*. 270. *Cotan* (gl. parma, a small round shield) I have not met elsewhere.

271-275. *Nelladoracht* (gl. piromanxia, pyromantia?) is, according to C., "astrology," Gael. *neuladaircachd*, from *neuladair* (astrologer). The first element of the word seems *néll*, a cloud. I know not if the Irish practised νεφελομαντία. 272. *Dornadoracht* (gl. ciromancia, leg. chiromachia, pugilism?), Gael. *dòrnadaireachd*, from *dornadáir* (a boxer): cf. *dorn*, W. *dwrn* (fist, hand): whence *dornán, infra*: nom. *durni* (gl. ut me colaphizet), Z. 336. 273. *Clas guail* (gl. sturna?), "the place on which charcoal was made," C.; *clas* here seems = the W. *clas* (a space, region). Its usual meaning is "furrow," "trench." *Guail*, gen. sing. of *gual* = Eng. coal, W. glo. 274. *Sblinach*, gl. catapulta (if I read this rightly), seems connected with *splin*, "a sharp dart of the eye;" *splincín*, "one who gives a sharp glance out of the corner of his eye;" and *splinc*, "a point of rock," "an overhanging cliff," O'D. 275. *Croicinn madra allaid* is "hide of a wolf," lit. "of a wild dog." What *edibulta* can be, or be put for, I cannot conjecture.

276-280. *Coinmir* (gl. offa), conmir in Z., v. supra, No. 156. 277. *Dabach* (gl. cuba, i. e. cavea), gen. *dabhcu, supra*, No. 158. 278. *Suiste* (flail), a lengthened form of of *suist* = fustis. *Calopeda* (if this be what the scribe's callidiba meant) seems a barbarous hybrid formed from καλον (wood), and pes (foot). 279. *Idh urchumail* (gl. trica, i. e. tricæ, hindrances) is a spancelling-chain: *idh*, a collar, chain; urchumail for érchumail, and this = *cumail* (holding), with the intensive particle *ér* = Gaulish ver, Lat. per, Gr. περι, prefixed. 280. *Cessacht* (gl. parvispendia, penuriousness). The adj. *cessachtach* occurs in S. Brogan's poem on Brigit:—

    Ni pu for seotu santach; ernais cen neim, cen mathim:
    Nir' bu chalad,[1] *cessachtach*: ni car in domuin cathim.

281–285. *Galar súla* (gl. obtolmia, i. e. ophthalmia), " disease of the eye;" *galar*, gen. galair in O. Ir., a neut. a-stem = W. *galar* (mourning, grief), *súla*, gen. sing. of *súil*, No. 425, *infra*. 282. *Cailleach ligeoch* (gl. pupina) is nearly unintelligible to me; *cailleach*, anciently *caillech*, has the meanings of " old woman" and " nun:" in Gaelic, *ligeoch* is " sly," *ligheach*, " flooded." 283. *Cochtair* (gl. coquina = cuisine), *vide supra*, No. 245. 284. *Tarrach* (gl. babana); of these two words I can make nothing as they stand. May we read torrach (pregnant), and babána, an Hiberno-Latin fem. subst. formed from babán (baby), and meaning a pregnant woman? In Gaelic *tarrach* is " the belly-thong of a pack-saddle, a girth." 285. *Coisreagad* (gl. creatura, i. e. the consecrated wafer?); for coisegrad = consecrata: the *n* being lost before *s* as in *mis* = mensis, *cis* = census, *mias* = mensa, &c.

286–298. *Aran* [leg. arán] *geal* (gl. placenta, a cake), " white bread." 287. *Baintigerna* (gl. dominabus). Here, and in the following twelve articles, the Latin words are in the dat. or abl. pl., the Irish being in the nom. sing. In baintigerna (lit. female-lord), note first the non-aspiration of the *t*, though originally between vowels, the Irish phonetic laws not admitting the combination *nth* (cf. banterismid, gl. obstetrix, Z. 820; o chaintaidliuch, gl. satisfactione, Z. 826, and verbs in the 3rd sing. pres. pass., such as frisduntar, gl. obstruitur, Z. 464); secondly, the change of the O. Ir. final *e* (= ia) to *a*; thirdly, the change of the *a* of *ban* to *ai*, which is owing to the influence of the vowel in the following syllable, viz., *i*, which has the power of changing a preceding *a* into *ai*; so *e* changes a preceding *a* to *i* (ai); but *o* causes no vowel-change. See Ebel, Beitr. 288. *Ainim*, in Z. anim (Corn. enef; Armor. éné) = anima, and declined like a fem. â-stem[2], but also declined as a stem in *n*[3] (= a Latin animo, -onis, if there were such a word), which curious fact Ebel (Zeits. vi. 213) was the first to notice. 289. *Baindea in toraid* (goddess of the fruit, Pomona? or growth, Ceres?); baindea, bandea

---

[1] = Goth. hardus, Eng. hard.
[2] Gen. anme, dat. anim; cf. *anam*-chairtea, gl. doctores, lit. soul-friends, Z. 10 (= anamacarant-i-ans).
[3] Dat. sing. anmin, acc. anmin(n), pl. anmin, anman(n), anmanaib.

bandea, Z. 279 (not bandia); where the ban seems superfluous, as dea = dḗvā = Lat. dea; *toraid*, gen. s. of *torad*; dat. torud (fructui), Z. 231; n. pl. *toirthe*, O'D. 88, for *tortha*, whence it would seem to be a neut. u-stem. Ebel (Beitr. 428) would connect this word with the root RAD; but consider the *t* in *toirthe* and in the adj. toirtheeh (fruitful), which occurs in Z. 778. 290, 291. *Ingen* (filia, nata), a daughter, girl; now *inghean*, Gael. *nighen*, which Bopp and Pictet, I venture to think, erroneously, have compared with the Skr. angaṇā, is literally, I suspect, "one who does not bring forth," from the neg. particle *in* (Z. 829), and the root GAN[1] (Skr. jan), to produce. Cf. the word *ingenas* in the following gloss (Z. 492), ma eterrosera fri a fer, ni teit co fer naile, act bed *ingenas*, which I render literally thus, "if she have separated from her husband, let her not go to another husband, but let there be not-bringing forth"—impartitudo, impartura, if I may coin a Latin word. Z. translates *bed ingenas* by sit innupta, obviously taking *ingenas* for an adj., or a concrete subst.; but the termination -*as* is only, so far as I know, used to form abstract substantives; see Z. 759 (curchas, gl. arundo, has yet to be explained). Ingen may, however, be for andegena (adgnata), cf. Cintu*gena*.

292–295. *Banchara*, a female friend; *cara* = W. *carant*, pl. *ceraint* (O. Ir. gen. carat = carantas, as Skr. bharatas = φέροντος[2]), is a stem in *ant*, like nāma (hater, enemy), gen. nāmat (= na + amantas); fiadu (God); dinu (ewe-lamb); brāge, throat (= Welsh *breuant*, windpipe); lóche (lightning); Nuada (a man's name); Brega (?) plur. Βρίγαντες (= in the Irish of Z.'s glosses, Bregait, Skr. brhantas), an Irish clan mentioned by Ptolemy. This class of nouns represents the Gr. participles in ων, οντος. Cara was thus declined in O. Ir.:—

MASC. *ant*-STEM.

Stem, carat from *carant.*

	Sing.	Dual.	Plur.
N.	cara	(Not yet observed)	carait
G.	carat		carat (ṅ)
D.	carait		cairtib
A.	carait (ṅ)		cairtea
V.	a chara		a chairtea

294. *Láir*

---

[1] The root GAN, when it means to be born, reduplicates in Irish (cf. no gignud, gl. nascebatur, Z. 417), as well as when it means to produce (nis gignetar tola, Oingus, Félire).

[2] The loss of the *n* before *t* in Irish is, however, purely the result of a phonetic law; the same loss in the Skr. gen. bharatas, and in the other weak cases, is the consequence of what may be called the *dynamis* of the language.

294. *Láir* (a mare); gen. lárach (declined like cathir, *supra*, No. 13). 295. *Múl* (afterwards glossing múlus, W. mul, N. H. G. maul); cognate with Lat. mûla, a she-mule. The adj. múldae, gl. mulionicus, is in Z. 30, where also are quoted the O. British name Epomulus = equomulus, and múlu, the O. Ir. acc. pl. of múl = mulus.

296–301. *Assal*, glossing, *infra*, asinus (W. asyn, he-ass; asen, a she-ass), I cannot believe to be a Celtic word. The vowel-flanked *s* would have been lost in Irish. Assal (O'R. asal) I believe to stand for asan, and to have been taken from the Lat. asinus: cf. Gaul. Ep-*asn*-actus, Gr. ὄνος for ὄσνος, Goth. asilus, O. H. G. esil, Lith. asilas. 297. *Sogh allaid*, she-wolf, lit. a wild bitch; as *cu allaid*, lit. wild dog, is lupus (v. *infra*); *sogh*, also *sagh. saidh, saith*, O'R., Gael. *saigh*. Hence *saighin*, "a little bitch," O'R.; saigir, "a bitch's heat," O'D. 298. *Caisc* = pascha, from which it is taken. Note, however, that it has become a fem. i-stem. In the O. Ir. the nom. is casc, which is declined like a c-stem; gen. casc = cascas; dat. caisc = casci; acc. caisc (n) = cascin (or -cn?). So—299. *Mainn* (manna) is mann in Z. 593; ni pu imdu do (leg. dó) in *mann* cid trén oc teemallad; "non fuit abundantius ei manna quamvis sollerti in collectione;" whence it appears that the word was either masc. or fem., which is curious, as the O. Ir. foreign-words generally follow the gender of the original vocables. 300. *Bosluaiged* (gl. mammona, riches), leg. hósluaiged, a deriv. from bósluag, "cow-host;" cf. Goth. faihuthraihns (μαμμωνᾶς), originally "cattle-throng," "*fee*-throng," v. *infra*, No. 1003. 301. *Subachus* (gl. all. a, leg. alacrimonia?), glossed by lætitia, Corm., and ilaritas (*sic*) in Egerton, 88, fo. 70: from subach (cheerful), opposed to dubach (*v. supra*, No. 85).

302–304. *Amadán* (gl. idiota, here a fool, idiot, *omadhaun*), which Pictet (Zeits. v. 325) rightly connects with Skr. a-mati, stupidity—mati is understanding—and Lat. amens. The root is MAN (think), whence Skr. manu, Eng. MAN, quasi thinker. 303. *Deorad* (gl. advena, a stranger, alien = the Scottish name Dewar, Gael. *deòradh*) also means a pilgrim, an exile, a stranger settling in an Irish chieftain's territory. See a valuable note by Dr. Reeves (Vita Col., 366), and one by O'D. (Battle of Magh Rath, p. 163), in which page the nom. pl. deoraid occurs. 304. *Urraidh* (gl. indigena), a native, also meant "a solvent yeoman," C.

305–310. *Eirinnach* (gl. Hibernigena), from the old name of this island, which is declined in the Book of Leinster and Lib. Hymn. nom. hériun (Maelmura Othna's poem) dat. dond erinn, gen. and acc. hérenn (see Fíacc's Hymn, vv. 7, 8, 10, and the *orthain* at the end, and the quatrain from Marianus Scotus, Z. 944). The origin of this name, notwithstanding the labours of Z. (G. C. 67) and Pictet (Beitr. 87), still remains obscure. One of Z.'s ideas is, that it is compounded of the intensive ér and rind (a star), (a star), which he thinks may also have signified an island, "quasi signum maris." Another conjecture of his is, that érrend is for iar-rend ("insula occidentis"). There are three objections to these theories: 1°, as Pictet observes, we never find the *r* doubled; 2°, the gen. of rind is renda, but the gen. of hérinn is hérenn; 3°, riud never means an island, though it certainly has the meanings of "star," "headland," and "point." Pictet, citing the Teutonic names for the Irish—Norse irar (Irishmen), Anglo-Sax. ira, ire (Irishman), asserts that Eirinn is derived "ohne zweifel aus dem ältesten volksnamen der Iren, der etwa Er oder Eir gelautet haben muss." The following theory has been suggested to me: Hérinn, which certainly is a stem in nn, iver-inn being the base in the nom. gen. and dat., iver-ann in the acc., represents a petrified AVARASMA (cf. Skr. avara, posterior, western, declined with the pronominal -sma, Ir. iar, after, aniar "in the west," Pictet, Beitr. i. 89). By weakening the vowels, dropping the final *a*, and changing *m* into *n* (cf. sui, "we," ex ASMI) we obtain ivarisn. From ivarisn hérinn may have arisen, by the assimilation of the *s* (cf. immunn = Skr. abhyasmân = N. H. G. um uns) the passage of *r* into a spiritus asper, the shifting of this breathing, and the drawing together of the i-a thus produced (cf. erthuaiscertach (gl. euroaquilo, Book of Armagh, 188, *b.* 2) = iarthnaiseerddach (gl. etesiarum, Z. 777); naueirchinninch = naui-airchinninch):—

  Nom. Sing. hérinn = hiarinn = iharinn = ivarinn,
   G. hérenn = hiarinn-as = ivarinn-as
   D. and Loc. hérinn = hiarinn-i = ivarinn-i
   A. hérenn = hiarann-en (-in?) = ivarannen (-in?)[2].

311–314. The only words here calling for remark are—311. *Oilithrech* (gl. romipeta, i. e. Rome-seeker), "a pilgrim" in O. Ir., alither, ailither, and—314. *Comaightech* (gl. alienigena, foreigner), now written *coimhtheach*, Gael. *coimheach*.

             315–325. *Dithrebach*.

[1] Cf. Ptolemy's Iver-n-ioi, Iver-n-is, Iver-n-ia ('Ιουερνία), and the W. Ewyrdonic (hibernicus, "westmanish"), Z. 814. But for these forms with *r*, Hérinn might be connected with Skr. apara.

[2] The most unfortunate circumstance in the investigations respecting the etymology of "Hérinn" is, that Prof. Pictet, to whom Celtic philology is much indebted, should have been deluded by our wretched O'Reilly, who actually has the following:—"Ibh, s. a country, a tribe of people."
Will it be believed that this ibh is nothing but the mutilated dat. plural of the Mod. Ir. *ó* or *ua* (grandson, descendant, in O. Ir. haue, Z. 1029, hoa, Fiacc, v. 2, nom. pl. háui, Z. 39, dat. pl. auib, *ibid.*)? See O'D. Gr. 108. Irish districts were often called after the tribe that possessed them: thus, la anu censelich, in the Book of Armagh (literally apud nepotes Censalaci), is correctly translated by O'D. (Gr. 436) "in Uy-Kinsellagh;" anu (leg. háun) is here the accus. pl. Dat. pl.: mac ind [f]irdana do *ib* Birnn, i. e.

315–325. *Dithrebach* (hermit), *supra*, dithrnbach ; cf. W. didryfwr from dithrab, "a desert," = di-trab : cf. A(d)trebates (possessores), from trab = W. treb (vicus), Lat. tribus, Goth. thaurp, Eng. thorp, N. H. G. dorf (Ebel, Zeits., vi. 422). *Marbtach* (slayer), in the following compounds, is from marb, "dead," = martva = Lat. mortuus? root MAR, Skr. mr̥. 320. *Siurmarbtach* (gl. sororicida), "sister-slayer :" siur = W. chwaer, chwïawr = svasâr, N. H. G. schwester, occurs in Z. in the dimin. siurnat, gl. sororcula, p. 282, acc. sing. : conuargaib focetoir in *siair*, "he straightway lifted up the sister" (Trip. Life of Patrick). A second form, sethair (?), occurs in sethar-oirenid (gl. sororicida), Z. 767 : a third form, pethair (?)—the Gaelic *piuthair*—in the Táin bó Cuailgne (Leb. na huidre); mac dechtere do *phethar*-su ; and a fourth form, fiar, fiur (Lib. Hymn. ed. Todd, p. 72), acc. sing. in the Trip. Life of Patrick : roboi bara do patricc fri *fiair* (lit. fuit ira Patricio contra sororem). 322. *Cliamhuin*, gen. *clémhna*, "son-in-law," in the plur. commonly signifies, in the Highlands, "any near relations by marriage." 324. *Tribus* (gl. braccæ), = W. trws, trows-ers.

326–330. *Cealg* (gl. insidiæ, *infra*, gl. dolus); cf. W. cele (trick). 326. Nubtic. *baindi. cich*, is very obscure ; bainne cich would be "breast-milk" (bainne, a drop): but this hardly agrees with nubtic, which can scarcely be for anything but nuptiæ. Dare we read *banais caich* nuptiæ cujusvis—*banais*, a deriv. from *ban*, as to which *vide supra*, and *caich*, the gen. sing. m. of each ? 327. *Mórmargad* (gl. nundinæ, market-day), great-market, margad, Corn. marhaz, is perhaps not derived from Engl. market (mercatus). 328. *Fergach*, leg. fergacht (gl. rixæ, quarrels), Gael. *feargachd*. Fergach is "angry," in Z., fereach for fergach, from ferg, anger, s. f., which Z. 71, compares with O. W. guerg. gl. efficax, and Gaulish Vergobretus, and Glück and Ebel (Beitr., i. 160) with Gr. Fέργον, Fοργή. Hence fairge, foirge, "the sea," Οὐεργίονιος (Vergivios) ὠκεανὸς, Ptol., and perhaps W. gweilgi (torrent, ocean). 329. *Inada* (gl. tabe), and—330. *Athfiana* (gl. atene), are obscure to me. Perhaps we should read Athenæ

("Son of the poet of Ily B." as Gilla mac Liacc is called in Harl. 1802, last page), literally "of the descendants of B." And yet the Professor compares with this fragment of the termination of a fragment (ib = bánib = âyavábo ? Cf. Vedic âyu proles, Dr. Siegfried), the non-existing Skr. root ibh, ibha (elephant) ἴφι, ἴφιος, and placing it before an imaginary "erna," soberly sets down "ibherna das land der Ernen oder Iren, oder vielleicht ibh-erin, mit hinzugesetzter griechisch-lateinischer endung," Beitr. i., 89). I cannot believe that the *h* which occurs in our MSS. so constantly at the beginning of Hérinn, háue (grandson), huile (all), huáir (hour), huasal (high, ὑψηλός), &c., is merely a freak of the scribe's. In Hérinn I am inclined, as above suggested, to attribute its presence to a shifting of the spiritus asper into which *v* has passed. Cf. in Greek ἵππος for ἱκϝος, Skr. açvas. A similar displacement has been remarked by Dr. Siegfried in biairn ("of iron"), *infra*, where the *h* has arisen from a vowel-flanked *s*. So, as Kuhn remarks, ἱερός = Ved. ishirá.

Athenæ for atene; if so, the glossarist absurdly meant to derive the city-name from áth fiana, "champion's ford."

331–364. *Dorchadus* (gl. tenebræ, gl. latebræ): dorchæ, obscurus (Z. præf. xv., 84); na dorche (tenebræ), Z. 237; cf. sorcha, "bright" (so-r'ch-a), Skr. r. ruch, and *r. supra*, No. 85. 333. *Inmasa* (gl. divitiæ), pl. of inmas, O'R.'s *ionmas, ionmus*, "treasure, riches." 337. *Néll* (for nebl = neblas?), "a cloud," hod. *néul*, W. nifwl, niwl, N. H. G. nebel, Lat. nebula, νεφέλη. 338. *Scola*, "schools," from schōla: gen. sing. in Colmán's Hymn, v. 40 (Lib. Hymn., 5 *b*):—

> Robet maccáin¹ flatha dé itimchuairt nascnlese!
> May the little children of God's kingdom be around this school!

339. *Bagair* (gl. minæ), n. sing. *bagar*, "threat," O'R.; dare we compare W. bwgwth, bygyliaeth (minatio), O. W. bicoled, recordia, Z. 802? 342. *Aengus* (Oingus, Book of Armagh, 13, *b*. 1, 19, *a*. 1, 19, *a*. 2), gen. Oingusso, *ib*. 18 *b*. 2, oingoś, leg. Oingosso, *ibid.*, a masc. u-stem, like Doilgus, gen. Doilgusso, Z. 18; Fergus, gen. Fergusso, Book of Armagh, 15, *a*. 2, fergosso, *ib*. 16 *b*. 2 (= W. Gwrwst?), Muirgus, Congus, Uarghus, and other nouns in -gus, = gustu? as Dr. Siegfried suggests to me². 345. *Gilla na naom*, "servant of the saints:" *naom* in O. Ir. is nóib, an adjectival a-stem. 353. *An gaeth atúaidh* (gl. Boreas), "the wind from the north," Gael. *gaoth á tuath*; *an gaeth*, O. Ir. in gáith (Z. 929), *a* (from) O. Ir. á; *túaidh*, cf. antúaid, "in the north;" aniartúaid, "in the north-west;" anairtúaid, "in the north-east;" fa dess no fa thuaith, "to the right or the left," Z. 566. 354. *Primaidhecht* (gl. anchises), inexplicable by me: prímaidecht would be "prime-tutorship," *vide oide*, oite, *supra*.

365–389. *Magisder*, W. meistyr, Corn. maister, all, of course, from the Lat. magister: O. Ir. acc. pl. magistru, Z. 615. 366. *Breitheam* (gl. arbiter), Z.'s brithem judex, a masc. u-stem, gen. brithemon, in a mutilated gloss preserved in the Book of Armagh, 187 *b*, 1, viz., suide bri[th]emon, gl. tribunal: dat. s. brithemain, Z. 269; cf. breth judicium, and the Gaulish Vergobretus (judicium exequens). A sister-form is found in

---

¹ MS. maccan.

² Dr. Reeves has favoured me with a list of names in -gus, which he has collected from the Annals, Calendars, and Pedigrees. From this I select the following, in hopes that some may be identified with Gaulish or Cymmric names: Alldghus, Artgus, Baothghus, Cuangus, Doedhghus, Donughus or Dongus, Eachtgus, Faelgus, Fiangus, Fianugus, Flathgus, Lergus, Miodhgus, Nialgus, Saergus, Snedgus. If Dr. Siegfried's conjecture be established, we have here the Celtic representative of the Skr. r. jush, γεύω, Lat. gustus, Eng. choose, Goth. kiusan. Cf. láimtech a des, diglach a *gus*, Seirgl. Conc. *Atlantis* ii. p. 382.

in O. Ir. bráth, O. W. braut, an u-stem, and is contained in the Gaulish *Bratu*spantium. Cf. A. S. braŚcan (sententiam dicere). 367. *Sagart* (gl. presbyter), from sacerd-os. 368. *Timthirigh* (gl. minister), leg. *timthiridh?* and cf. timthir-thid, servus, Z. 256; timthir-echt servitium, Z. 237; gl. ministratio, *infra.* 369. *Gabann* (gl. faber); cf. the Gaulish man's-name Gobannitius, Bret. Corn., and W. gof, all perhaps etymologically connected with fab-er; O. Ir. nom. goba, gen. gobann. Patrick invokes divers virtues fri brichta ban ocus *gobann* [MS. goband] ocus druad (against the incantations of women, and smiths, and druids). 370. *Macam* (gl. puer), a deriv. from mac, as to which *vide supra.* 371. *Leabar* (gl. liber, "a book"), W. llyfyr, Corn. liuer, is here apparently spelt according to "leathan re leathan," but the vowel-change in the penult is either owing to *umlaut* or assimilation; in O. Ir. either lobar or libur, a masc. u-stem. A Mid. Ir. gen. sing. occurs in a gloss on *a folaire* (leg. a phólaire), H. 3, 18, p. 523, viz., aium do teig *liubair,* "a name for a book-satchel," where, by the way, note *téig,* dat. sing. of *tiach* (gl. pera, *supra,* No. 41), a fem. â-stem, obviously from thēca, θήκη. A dimin. of lebar occurs in a quatrain which the scribe of the St. Gall Priscian seems to have extemporized while producing his invaluable MS. (see Z. 929):—

Dom'farcai fidbaide! fál,	The grove makes a festival for me,
Fom'chain lóid luin lúath, uad cél—	A blackbird's swift lay sings to me—I will not hide it—
Uas mo *lebrán* indlínech	Over my many-lined booklet
Fom'chain trírech inna nén.	A trilling (?) of the birds sings to me.

372. *Gabhar,* gabor, gl. caper, Z. 744, W. gafr (pl. geifr), a masc. a-stem, irregularly Lat. caper. (I say irregularly, because the Lat. and Gr. tenues (c, t, κ, τ) are, as a rule, represented by the same letters in Irish: so the Lat. and Greek medials (d, g, b, δ, γ, β) by Irish medials, which last (as in Gothic, Slavonic, and Lithuanian) regularly represent the aspirates: b = φ, Lat. *f,* d = θ, g = χ, Lat. *h.*) But by Benary's important law, the Lat. cap-er might be regarded as arising from a r. GABH, and thereby the Celtic form with two medials would become intelligible; cf. Gaulish Gabromagus (goat-field), O. Brit. Gabrosentum (goat's-path), Glück, 43. 373. *Torc* (gl. aper), acc. sing. torce, Book of Armagh, 18 *b,* 1, hence torcde, gl. aprinus, Z. 85. *Torc* = W. twrch, Bret. tourc'h, "a hog," Corn. torch, gl. magalis. 374. *Partan* (gl. cancer, "a crab"), etymologically inexplicable by me. The W. is cranc = cancer? 375. *Dobhran* (gl. fiber), masc. a-stem, is now an "otter" (ἐνυδρις), not a "beaver,"

---

[1] Cf. Leab. Breace, 121 *aa,* cited O'D., Gr. 370: is lirlu feoir no folt *fidbuide* illratha in marbnuda noibsea; literally, 'Tis more numerous than grass or a grove's hair, the many-blessings of this holy elegy (marbnud = W. marwnad).

A Mediæval Tract on Latin Declension. 71

ver," from dobur (water), which Pictet compares with dabhra, said to be Skr. for "ocean." The W. for "otter" is dufrgi, i. e. dufr + ci, "water-dog;" cf. W. rivername, Camdubr, and the Gaulish Verno-dubrum, Dubra, Dubris. 376. *Labar no slinneriadh* (gl. linter), "an ewer (?) or a clay-tile." 378. *Companach* (gl. soces, i. e. socer, socius?), formed from Lat. compagauus, the *g* being lost between vowels, as *always* in W., and sometimes in O. Ir. (*vide infra*, 550). 380. *Soeruidhe* (pulcher), i. e. εὔμορφος: ernidhe from cruth (forma), an u-stem: gunated gen. sing. in O. Ir. crotha = crutavas, non-gunated, crutto = crutvas. 381. *Dubh* (gl. niger) dub in Z., is in W. and Bret. du, Corn. gl. duv; cf. the river-name Dubis; and perhaps Lat. fuscus (blackish), for fubiscus? Engl. dusk? Dub also meant ink: is tana an *dub*, "thin is the ink" (Z. praef. xv.): cf. Danish blæk. 382. *Lesc* (gl. piger), n. pl. m. neb-*leisce*, gl. non pigri, Z. 830; *vide* leisg, O'R., W. llesg, Lat. laxus? 383. *Truagh* (gl. macer), = tróg, "miser," Z. 28; trogán (gl. misellus), better spelt in the Book of Armagh, 38, *a*. 1, trógán, a marg. gloss on "Judas scariothis," W. truan. 384. *Gruamda* (gl. acer) cf. W. grwm?, "surly, sour," O'R. 385. *Agarb* = acerbus, as *sagart*, O. Ir. sacart = sacerdos, which shows that the Lat. *c* before *e* was pronounced like *k* by the Irish. 386. *Deas* (gl. dexter), O. Ir. des, = W. deheu, Corn. dyghow, dex-ter, ἐεξιός, Skr. dakshina; cf. the Gaul. goddess-name, Dexsiva, Dexivia. 387. *Cle* (gl. sinister), leg. *clé*, is obviously a mutilation of a *cledh*, W. cledd, Bret. kleiz, which Diefenbach and J. Grimm have compared with Goth. hlei-duma (-duma = -timu, in Lat. dextimus). A sister-form cli occurs in the dat. sing. for laim *chli* (gl. a sinistris), Z. 67; duchli (gl. ad sinistram), Book of Armagh, 184, *b*. This comes close to Goth. hlei, and also to Skr. çri, which Bopp equates with hlei ("Vergl. Gramm." ii. 30, 2te aufl.). "Wenn ich recht habe," says the Master, "den goth. primitivstamm *hlei* auf das Skr. çri = kri, glück zurückzuführen, mit der äusserst gewöhnlichen vertauschung des *r* mit *l*, so sehen wir in der gothischen benennung des linken einen euphemismus, gleich dem worauf die griechischen ausdrücke ἀριστερός und εὐώνυμος sich stützen." 389. *Adh allaidh* (gl. onager), leg. *agh* allaidh: *agh*, "a beast of the cow-kind," O'R., gen. *aighe*, masc. and fem.: in Gael. "a hind," "a heifer," "often applied to cattle two years old, without regard to gender." If *gh* here stands for *ch*, we may compare *agh* with Skr. paçu, pecus, Goth. faihu.

390-394. *Ferand* (gl. ager), glosses iathmaige in the *orthain* after Fiacc's Hymn; ferann, which Dr. Reeves (Vit. Col., 449) explains as "jurisdiction of a monastic order," is perhaps the same word: induxit nivem supra totum agrum pertinguentem *ferenn*, Book of Armagh, 5 *a*. 2; cf. W. grwn, pl. gryniau, "a ridge, a lay, or land in a field." 391. *Snámach* (gl. suber, "the cork-tree"), something, apparently, that swims

swims or floats; cf. Skr. snâ, W. nawf. Odran is called abb sáer *snámach*, "a noble, swimming abbot," by Oingus, Fél., Oct. 27.   392. *Magisder aimfesach*, "an ignorant master;" aimfesach from the neg. prefix am (Skr. sâmi, ἡμι, semi?), and the root fis, the connexion of which with fid, Skr. vid, Fιĉ, wit, seems to rest on a desiderative formation.   Only a gunated base vivaits would explain O. Ir. forms like fésur, fiasur (scio), fiastar(scit), fésid (scitis), fiasmais(sciebamus), fiastais(sciebant); and perhaps we should read aimfésach.   393. *Eslán* (leg. esslán), from es = Gaul. ex, W. eh and slán, with which W. llawen may be identified, if we assume the existence of an original slavana.   394. *Maeth* (gl. tener, i. e. tener), irregularly = W. mwyth; compar. moithiu, gl. molliorem, Z. 283.

395–409. *Fer* (= vira-s, a masc. a-stem) = Lat. vir, Goth. vair, Lith. wyras, Skr. vara.   397. *Fer eli* seems to mean not levir (husband's brother), but a left-handed man (*supra*, No. 387), as if levir (for devir = ἐαϜήρ, Skr. devara) were a compound of lævus and vir.   398–401. *Deise, trir, cethrair, cúigir*, respectively the genitives sing. of dias (fem.), triur, cethrar (dunaib chethrairib, gl. quaternionibus, Book of Armagh, 178 *b*. 2), cuigur, O. Ir. cóicur (which respectively mean a combination of 2, of 3, of 4, of 5 persons); four of those numeral substantives which form so remarkable a feature in Irish.   O'D. and Z. suggest that the numeral substantives in -r are compounded with fer.   If so, the original *a* is preserved unweakened in nonbar (a combination of 9 persons), Corn. v. Nós = Skr. navanvara-m, hod. *nonbhar*, and in deichenbar, a combination of 10 persons, (gen. sing. deichenboir occurs in one of the inscriptions copied by my revered friend Dr. Petrie) now *deichneabhar*. Others, I may observe, compare fer, &c., with Skr. vira (hero), *sed qu.* on account of the long *i*.   402. *Sathach* (gl. satur).   403. *Lethsathach* (gl. semisatur); cf. Lat. sat-is.   404. *Tigerne, dia* (O. W. duw, Corn. duy), *anum* (anam) *mac* (O. W. map, Corn. mab), *saer* (sóir), have been already considered.   *Libertus* is glossed by sóirmug, i. e. free servant, in Z. 825.

410–418. *Bachlach* (gl. famulus, a slave) is "a herdsman, a rustic," according to O'R.   411. *Milchú* (gl. malosus, i. e. molossus, i. e. κύων Μολοττικός, a wolf-dog, quitter in the Cornish Vocab.) is explained "greyhound" by O'R., who spells the word *miolchu*; plur. mílchoin occurs in Lebar na Cert, 252, W. milgi, pl. milgwn.   412. *Bachlach breallán* (gl. bufulus) is obviously a term of great reproach; but what breallán is exactly, I know not; "a lubberly fellow with a hanging under-lip," says C.; perhaps it is connected in meaning with spado; cf. *breallach*, gl. spadosus, *infra*, *breall*, "foreskin," l. w.   418. *Mathghamain* (a bear), of uncertain derivation.

419–423. *Senathair* (gl. avus, grandfather), literally "old-father," *v. suprá*, No. 13.   420. *A athair sin* (gl. proavus, great-grandfather), "*his* father," i. e. the father of the

avus;

avus; so the same words at No. 421 mean the father of the *proavus*. *A*, O. Ir. *á* (the gen. sing. of the masc., and neut. pronoun of the 3rd pers. sing.) aspirates, must, therefore, have ended in a vowel, and has long since been identified by Bopp with Skr. asya. As to *sin* (for O. Ir. som, sem, Mid. Ir. sium, now *sean, san*), it is here placed as an emphasizing particle. The O. Ir. som has been compared by Bopp and Pictet with Skr. svayam; and their view is confirmed by the fact that the *s* in som is unaspirable (cf. dossom, ci, Z. 334), and must, therefore, represent a combination of consonants. *Tuata* (gl. laicus); cf. τουτιους in what, up to the recent appearance of M. de Belloguet's work, was presumed to be the oldest monument of the Celtic language, the Gaulish inscription, found at Vaison (Département Drôme):—CEΓOMAPOC OYIΛΛONEOC TOOYTIOYC NAMAYCATIC EIωPOY BHAHCAMI COCIN NEMHTON, which Dr. Siegfried has thus translated:—"Segomarus Villoneus, a citizen of Nemausus (Nimes), dedicated (?) this temple to Belesama"[1]. Cf. also Toutio-rix (a Gaulish name for Apollo) from tuath (people), O. Brit. tût, Z. 39, now tud, a widely scattered word. Oscan tovto, Umbrian tuta, tota (urbs), Goth. thiuda, O. H. G. diota, Lith. Tauta (Germany), all from the root tu (to grow, to be strong), as Aufrecht and Kirchhoff, Grimm and Kuhn have shown. 424. *Lóegh* (gl. vitulus, calf) = W. llo, pl. lloi, Corn. loch, Bret. lue; cf. uenierunt ad fontem *loigles* in scotica nobiscum vitulus ciuitatum, Book of Armagh, 10 *b*, 1, and perhaps the man's-name, Loiguire, *ib*., 7 *a*, 1 (but see Z. 126). The nom. and gen. sing. occur in Brogan's poem on Brigit, l. 52:—

In *locq* lia clam i carput, in bó indiaid ind *lóig*.
The calf with her leper in the chariot, the cow behind the calf.

425–428. *Súil* (gl. oculus), "eye," frequent in Z. It is also found in the Book of Armagh, 219, *b*, 1, where a grotesque profile occurs, opposite to which is written: [f]éccid in[s]róin *súil* bél, "behold ye the nose, eye, mouth." Súil is a fem. i-stem: its etymology is obscure to me. 426. *Lethcaech* (leg. lethchaech, gl. monoculus, "blind of an eye"); here, if caech be not a foreign-word (Corn. euic, gl. luscus), we have a trace in Irish of aksha, oculus, auge, eye, &c., for caech is = Lat. caecu-s = cā-icu-s, Skr. kā-aksha (Pott, E. F. i. 126, Benfey, Zeits. ii. 222). But I suspect caech is taken from the Lat., as Skr. ksh would have become *s* in Ir., as in Gr. cf. akshi with ὄσσε, ὄσσομαι. 427. *Dall* (gl. caecus), *v. supra*, No. 249, and cf. the adj. dallbrónach (blind, sad),

[1] Is not *Villoncos* the gen. sing. of Villoneus, governed by a *mapos* (filius), understood? Compare Correus, Abarcus. Eιωρου in the other Gaulish inscriptions seems always ιευρυ (ieuru). See De Belloguet, Ethnogénie gauloise, p. 197, ss.

sad), of which the gen. sing. m. occurs in the Book of Armagh, 11 *a*. 1, as a man's name: super fossam *dall*bronig. 428. *Mīl* (leg. míl) *mór, Ruainmech dubair*, gl. cetus (if I read the two last Irish words aright) are names for a whale, míl mór, "great beast," ruainmech dubair, i. e. r. of the water; ru-ainmech, great-animal? ru being an intensive prefix (= Skr. pra), and ainmech being probably, like ainmidhi, gl. animal, *infra*: anim, Lat. animal, &c., a deriv. from the root AN, to breathe. I have only once found ainmech, viz., in a poem attributed to Rumann (Bibl. Bodl. Laud, 610, fo. 10):—

| Rola curu[1] in gaeth ganmech | The sandful wind sent circles |
| Im iuber na da *ainmech*. | Round the estuary of the two *ainmechs*. |

Perhaps, indeed, the reading of the MS., *ruaimnech dubain*, "the hair-line of a fish-hook," may be correct. *Ruaim* is "the long hair of a horse's or cow's tail," O'D.; "cetus," would, accordingly, stand for seta.

429-439. *Mac dilechta* (gl. orbus, orphan, properly "bereaved"), "son of milklessness," according to C., *sed qu*. Gael. *dilleachdan*. 430. *Mintsuilech* (gl. luscus, here "purblind"), leg. mintsuilech, is O'R.'s mionsuilech, "weak-eyed" (the *t* in min-t has yet to be explained). *Min* = W. mwyn, main, Bret. moan, Gr. μᾱνός, Glück, K. N. 99. 431. *Maethsuilech* (gl. lippus, blear-eyed, which is fliuchdere in Z.), maeth, gl. tener, *infra*, W. mwyd. 432. *Abheoide*, taken from advocatus. Note the bh = dv, as in aibhersóir, *v. infra*, = adversarius, and cf. the Lat. bellum, bis = dvellum, dvis. 433. *Dlightinech* (gl. juridicus), the guttural assibilated in the sister form *dlistinech* (gl. legitimus), *infra*, from the root DLIG (dligim, debeo, Z. 431, Goth. dulg, *v. supra*, No. 87). 434. *Fer cúisi do chongbail* (gl. causidicus), "a man to maintain causes;" cúisi acc. pl. of cúis, from causa, with change of decl., acc. sing. cois, Z. 443. With congbail = con-gab-áil, cf. O'R.'s cungbhailim, O. Ir. congaibther, Z. 842; congbhalas, "stay, help, support," O'R. 435. *Manach* (Corn. manach)—437. *Cananach*, and—438. *Discibul* (W. dysgybl, Corn. discibel), respectively from monachus, canonicus, discipulus. 439. *Duine beg* (gl. homunculus, ad v. homo parvus), *beg*, in Z. becc, bec; gl. paulum, Z. 281, be[c]ca, gl. modicas, Book of Armagh, 183, *a*, 2, is the W. bach, cc always becoming ch in Welsh.

440-444. *Sgian* (gl. cnipulus, gl. cutellus), a knife, dagger, gen. sgine, *infra*; O. Ir. scian, gen. scine; W. ysgïen fem. ("a slicer, cymetar"), a fem. a-stem; cf. W. ysgíaw, Bret. skéja, to cut. Note, that ia here does not stand for an original *é* (if it
did,

[1] Curu (gl. gyros, Z. 1072) = Lat. curvûs.

did, the Welsh would have been ysgwyn, and the Irish gen. sing. scéine). Perhaps the original base was skidyanâ, from which first *d* and then *y* may have fallen. If so, we might compare scindo, scidi, σχίζω, Skr. chhid, &c. 442. *Crubh eich* (gl. ungulus), "a horse's hoof;" eich, gen. of ech. 443. *Tairnge*, "a nail, pin, peg," O'R. 444. *Braigdech* (gl. camus, horse-collar, *hame*); O. Ir. bráigtech, from bráge, gen. brágat, neck, throat, = W. breuant, an ant-stem, *supra*, No. 292.

445–456. *Paisti bróg* (gl. baietus), a patch on a shoe; paisti (leg. paiste?) is, perhaps, taken from Eng. patch; bróg, fem. according to O'R., O. Ir. bróce; cf. the Gaulish bracca. 446. *Scolb tige* (gl. tegulus); scolb is a wattle ("scollop"), pointed at both ends, used to bind down straw-thatch. *Tige*, gen. of teg (house), a neut. i-stem = tagi; cf. tegere, *et v. infra*, No. 446. 449. *Airchinnech* (gl. archidiaconus), princeps in Z., has been before noticed: dat. sing. nauairchinniuch (gl. nauiclero), Book of Armagh, 188, *b*. 2. 450. *Teachtaire* (gl. legatus), messenger, envoy, O. Ir. techtaire, tectaire, a personal noun, from techt, tect (venire), cf. Zend. tac (ire), Lith. tekù (curro), W. taith (journey), the Gaulish tribe-name, Tectosages, O. Ir. man's name, Techtmar. Techtaire is wrongly explained dispensator, gubernator in Z. 743, 888, though one would have thought the gloss in Z. 888 was decisive as to the word's not meaning gubernator: is hé in tecttaire maith condaig indocbáil dia thigerni, "he is the good *tectaire* (ambassador), who obtains glory for his lord." At p. 78 Z. probably mis-read tecttaire, gl. dispensator, for rectaire, which word is better spelt rectaire (ond rectairiu, gl. a villico, Z. 743), and rectire (gl. praepositus, Z. 245), 451. *Deganach*—452. *Prelait*—454. *Decháin*—455. *Subdecháin*—456. *Aclaidhe*—458. *Pupul*—460. *Aingel*—462. *Areaingel*, all from the Latin. Note, however, in pupul (Corn. pepel) the assimilation of the *o* of populus to the succeeding *u*, and note also that the stem of aingel, a masc. a-stem (Corn. ail) seems in O. Ir. to be extended in the acc. pl., which is always aingl-i-u, not angelu, anglu. Cf. Lagn-i-u (Leinstermen), Z. 944: coirn-e-a (coronas), a fem. â-stem: Boind-e-o, gen. sing. of Boiud (Bovinda, Boyne), Book of Armagh, 16 *a*, 2, 16 *b*, 1: ins-e-o, gen. sing. of inis (island), *ibid*. 18 *a*, 1: ailichth-i-u, gl. alternationes, Z. 256, an u-stem: cairt-e-a, friends, and náimt-e-a, haters, enemies, both ant-stems in the acc. pl.

457–464. *Coraidh*, a choir, is, like W. cor, from chor-us, or χορ-ός, but with an Ir. termination. 459. *Uan* (lamb), W. oen, Corn. oin, Bret. oan, a masc. a-stem, whence nainín, *infra*, has certainly lost a *g*, *v. supra*. 461. *Cloideam* (sword), W. cleddyf, in O. Ir. claideb, Z. 442. 469. *Ruainde* (leg. ruainne?), a single hair; *foiltín*, a dimin., and—464. *Foiltnín*, a double dimin. of folt, hair, as to which *v. supra*, No. 77.

465–479. *Mérldime*,

465–479. *Mérláime*, a finger (lit. digitus manus, as toe is—466. *Mér choise*, digitus pedis), mér (digitus), acc. dual; imber in dá mér (infer duos digitos), Z. 926; abl. pl. in e meraib (in digitis ejus), Z. 347. Mér seems to have lost a letter (*t?*) before *r*: cf. W. motrwy, a finger-ring; *eoise*, gen. sing. of cos, a fem. â-stem = Lat. coxa. 467. *Salm*—468. *Fersán*—470. *Toin*—471. *Lethtoin*—472. *Ditoin*—474. *Punc*—475. *Cercall*, all taken from the corresponding Lat. words: *fersán*, with the addition of the Ir. dimin. suffix án. 469. *Foghar*, gen. foguir (sonus, pronuntiatio), frequently in Z., see pp. 964, 965; root GAR, whence gair (vox), gairim (voco), &c., Skr. gir (vox). 473. *Macam gente*, a child begotten; gente, part. perf. pass. of geinim, root GAN, as to which *v. supra*, No. 291. 476. *Múr*, W. mur = mūrus, is probably taken from the Lat. "Mur," says C. (Cath Maighe Léna, 78, note °), "means simply a circular¹ wall, bank, or mound of earth; but it does not imply a dwelling, except for the dead." It sometimes meant a mound only, as in the passage to which the note is appended. 477. *Biadh* (gl. cibus); biad = bivata, βέϝοτο-ς, in O. Ir. is neuter, like the Skr. jivita (Lat. vita = vivita is fem.); cf. arbiathim, gl. lacto, gl. nutrio, Z. 431, gen. sing, in O. Ir. biith (Z. 250) = bivati, in Mod. Ir. *bidh* = W. bwyt, Corn. buit. 478. *Guillmias* (gl. discus), i. e. *gall* + *mias* : gall, foreigner (v. Galldach, *supra*), mias = mensa, O. W. muis, Z. 137. 479. *Copán* (gl. cupus), a deriv. from Eng. cup?

480–493. *Cep* (gl. cepus) I can hardly explain, unless as = Lat. cippus: *ceap* occurs in O'R., with many meanings, of none of which, save two, do I feel certain (ccap is a shoemaker's last, and isna ccapaibh is certainly "in the stocks"). Cf. icip, gl. in ligno (Book of Armagh, 181, b. 2; Acts, xvi. 24). 481. *Lebaid* (gl. lectus, a bed), O. Ir. lepaid: the abl. sing. occurs in the Leabhar Breacc (pref. to Secundinus' Hymn, Lib. Hymn, ed. Todd, p. 28): batar in oen *lepaid*, "they were in the same bed," and the gen. sing. at the beginning of the *Táin bó euailgne:* Feet nóen do ailell ɔ do meidb iarn dergud a *rígleptha* dóib i cruachan ráith chonrach arrecaim comrad chindchércaille cturru, "once upon a time, after Ailill and Medv had spread their royal couch in C. R. C., a pillow-conversation took place between them." 482. *Otrach* (gl. fimus, dung), O'R., also a dunghill, Gael. *ōtrach*. 483. *Tore* (gl. porcus). *v. supra*. 484. *Sgaignen* (gl. vannus, a winnowing-van), also a cullender, according to O'D.; in O'R. *sgaighneam*. 485. *Cleath* (tignum, a log, beam) is explained "a rib, rod, stake," by O'R. 486. *Comalta* (gl. collactaneus—ὁμο-γάλακτ-ος—a foster-brother), com-al-ta, involves the root AL, nourish (Lat. al-o), -ta, perhaps for -tava. Comalta occurs in the Scirglige Conculainn: fobith ba haite dó Fergus ocns ba *comalta* Conall Cernach, "because

---

¹ Cf. Skr. r. mur, circumdare, vestire ; Bopp.

"because F. was his foster-father, and C. C. was his foster-brother," Atlantis, ii. 372. 488. *Curach* (gl. phaselus, "a kidney-bean-shaped vessel, made (sometimes) of wickerwork," which answers tolerably well to the Irish curragh, W. cwrwg-l, whence Eng. corac-le. 489. *Sacc* (gl. forulus), W. sach = Lat. saccus, Gr. σάκκος, Goth. sakkus, Eng. sack (sacc is incorrectly spelt sac in O'R.). 490. *Matal* = Lat. mantélum? whence it is probably derived, the *n* being lost before *t*, as in sét, a road, W. hint, Goth. sinths, Eng. send, etar (between), Lat. inter, Skr. antar, and in the termination of the third pers. plur. pres. and fut. active of verbs (-at [= Lat. ant], -et, -it : -tet, -fit = Lat. -bunt). W. mantell (pl. mentyll, Z. 787) = Lat. mantellum. 491. *Bláthmar* is "flowery" (W. blodeuog), not "floweret" (flosculus), from bláth, flower = W. blawd, Corn. blez, Lat. flos, N. H. G. blüte. 492. *Uainín* (gl. agnellus), dimin. of uan = agnus. 493. *Oirenín* (gl. porcellus), double dimin. of orc = porcus, W. porch, with loss of initial *p*.

494-514. *Serrach no gercach* (gl. pullus, "a foal or a chicken"); gercach, "an unfledged bird," "a squalling child," C. 495. *Cuaille* (gl. palus, W. pawl), a pole, stake. 496. *Disle* (gl. talus), a die, W. dis. 498. *Cuilen* (gl. catulus, whelp), leg. cuilenn? (cuilennboce, gl. cynyps, Z. 740), W. colwyn, Corn. gl. coloin, Bret. kolen, compare Eng. *whelp*. 499. *Cat* (murilegus, cat, lit. mouse-catcher), for catt, W. cath, Corn. kat, Bret. kaz, a masc. a-stem; cf. Med. Lat. cattus, catta. 500. *Cealg*, v. supra, No. 326. 501. *Míl édaigh* (gl. pediculus, louse), lit. beast of the clothes; édaigh = O. Ir. étaig (étig, Z. 857), gen. of étach, a neut. a-stem. 502. *Dornán buana* (gl. manipulus, small handful of hay), dorn, W. dwrn, a fist: buain, gen. buana, "s. f. cutting, reaping, shearing," O'R. 506. *Coileach* (gl. gallus) = W. ceiliawg, Corn. chelioc. 508. *Preehán* (gl. milgus, i. e. milvus), a kite; cf. Gr. κίρκος? note in the Lat. *g* for *c*, as in ugula (*supra*) for uvula. 508. *Cerd* (gl. figulus), v. supra. (In the MS. the letters *eg* are just visible before cerd, but the scribe has evidently tried to efface them.) 509. *Ela* (swan), O'R. eala: W. alarch, pl. eleirch, Lat. olor. But who can account for ela? Can it have lost a *g* before the liquid? cf. Ἀγλυ, ὁ κύκνος ὑπὸ Σκυθῶν, Hesych. 510. *Coileck gaithe* (W. ceiliog gwynt), i. e. gallus venti, weathercock? 511. *Teallach* (gl. focus, fire-place, hearth), perhaps for tenlach, tened-lach. 512. *Oinmid* (gl. sotus), an oaf, W. ynfyd. The -*mid* = O. Ir. mit = manti, and probably involves the root man. 513. *Geocach* (gl. mimus), apparently from jocu-s (*sed* cf. N. H. G. geck), now "a strolling player." 514. *Sboran*, "a purse," O'R. sporán, W. ysbur.

515-533. *Sgingidoir* (leg. sgingidóir? gl. pellicarius, "a furrier"), is, according to C., a "packsaddle maker;" cf. W. ysgin (fur) = Eng. skin, seing, O'R., "part of the trappings of a horse." 516. *Inadh*, a place, O. Ir. inad, frequent in Lib. Hymn. 517. *Oibhirscour*

517. *Oibhirseoir* = adversarius.   518. *Cluithe* (gl. jocus), also cluiche, game, sport, an ia-stem.   The dat. sing. occurs in the Trip. Life of Patrick: Fecht aili do patrice ic *cluithiu* iter a comaistiu (.i. *a comaltud*), "at another time P. was playing amongst his coevals" (i. e. *his foster-brothers-and-sisters*).   With cluiche cf. cluichech (gl. ludibundus), Z. 778.   519, 520. *Iffearn*, iffern = infernum, W. uffern, Corn. iffarn, gen. sing. of iffern, viz. iffirnn in Z. 51.   522. Locanus (Lucanus), here identified with the Irish man's-name, Lochan; see O'D., Four Masters, A. D. 606.   533. *Fergal* is connected with ferg (anger), fairge (sea), Οὐεργίονιος (ὠκεανός) Ptol. "The proper meaning of the word [ferg] is," says Glück (K. N. 131), "motio, agitatio (compare Gr. ἔργον for Ϝέργον, ὀργή for Ϝοργή, from the root varg, Germ. werk)." Cf. Zend verez (agere). If Fergal be the W. Gwral-deg and = a Gaulish Virogalos, the elements are fer "man" (Skr. vara), and the root GAL, as to which see Z., 993 *n*.

534-548. Of the rest of the proper names note *doctor*, glossing Ovidius.   Hence there would seem to have been some Irish word resembling this name, and corresponding with W. ofydd, with which, however, Z. 3, would connect the Irish *ogham*.   540. *Diarmaid* seems = Derbomautis.   541. *Lochlann* is curiously like the old name for Scandinavia, Lochland, of which the dat. sing. occurs in one of the S. Gall quatrains above quoted.   542. *Murchad*, leg. muirchad, gen. muirchatho, Z. xxxii. = moricatus, a masc. u-stem.   543. *Eogan* is from εὐγενής.   545. *Concubar*, leg. Conchubar, the Anglo-Irish Connor; cf. Conchuburnensium (Book of Armagh, 9 *a*, 2), Conchobor, Z. 1133. Glück, 66, where note the aspiration of *c*. Does Con- stand for Cono- (cf. Cono-maglus, Cunobelinus), or is *c* aspirated in the combination *nc*, as in sancht (Brogan's Hymn, l. 23) = sancta; conchoimnucnir (efficit), Z. 853; concheehrat (amabunt), Z. 495; and perhaps tenchor (gl. forceps), Z. 84?   546. *Mac na hoidhche* means "son of the night;" *oidche*, O. Ir. aidche, a fem. ia-stem, Z. 257; áidchide, "nocturnal," Leab. Breacc, cited Lib. Hymn. ed. Todd, 27. In the *h* prefixed to *oidche* here, and to *oighe*, *infra*, No. 576, Bopp would see a relic of the *s* which terminated the fem. article in the gen. sing.   547. *Uaithne* is placed opposite orpens, i. e. Orpheus, because Uaithne is said to have been the inventor of music, under the singular circumstances described in a legend, which C. tells me is preserved in the Book of Leinster.   548. *Tadhg* (the "Teague" of English writers) is said to mean "poet."

550-554. *Deóir* (gl. diphthongus), in Z. deoger = defoger (guir, sonus), the *g* being dropt between vowels, as is the rule in Welsh, and as sometimes occurs in Irish. 551. *Senadh naom* ("holy synod"), cf. W. senedd, Corn. sened, from synodus.   552. *Cloch crisdail*, "stone of crystal."   553. *Parrtus*, leg. partus from paradisus, W. paradwys, the medial *d* being provected, as sometimes happens in foreign words: cf. aipgitir

gitir = abecedarium. Perhaps, however, the *t* may be owing to the practice pursuant to which *b*, *d*, *g* are written respectively *p*, *t*, *c*, when preceded by either *l* or *r*: see Z. 70, 71. 554. *Dair* (gl. quercus, oak-tree), gen. darach = daracas, a *c*-stem; cf. daur, gl. quercus, Z. 8; dairde, daurde, gl. quernus, Z. 764; daurauch, gl. quercetum, Z. 779, deruce, gl. glans: W. derw-en. Cf. δρῦς, δόρυ, Goth. triu, A. S. treóv, trŷv, Eng. tree, Skr. dâru (timber), Δαρούερνον (Britanniæ oppidum), Z. 8.

555–566. *Aball*, O. W. aball-en, Corn. auall-en = apple, apfel, Aballum, &c. Ubull *quasi* abull; aball, imorro, o burgg Etale dianid ainm Abellum .i. is ass tucad síl nan aball *prius* (Cormac's Glossary, Book of Leinster), "*Aball*, now, from a town of Italy called Abellum, i. e. it is thence that the seed of the apples was brought formerly." 556. *Coll* (W. coll-en, Corn. col-viden, Bret. kel-vézen) = coslas = hasel, corylus, whence κόρυλος. Z. 1118 compares the name Coslum, hod. Kusel, and the Slav. shcol, virga, baculus, "*primitus colurnus?*" whence, he says, the names of places Sebeska and Scheslitz. The adj. collde, gl. colurnus, in Z. 81. 557. *Fuindseog* (gl. fraxinus, ash-tree), leg. fuinnseog? and cf. O. Ir. huinnius (gl. fraxinus, Z. 751), uinsenn (Irish Nennius, 116); and, perhaps, Lat. ornus for osnus: Corn. onnen, Bret. ounn-en. 558. *Fernog* (gl. alnus, alder), W. and Bret. gwernen, E. Corn. guernen, "gall. vet. vern [vernâ] in nomine fluvii Vernodubrum;" cf. Vernosole (Glück, 35, 125). 559. *Droighin* (gl. prunus, blackthorn, sloe-tree), leg. *draighen*; draigen is used to gloss pirus in Z. 738; cf. W. draen, pl. drain, sed *vide* Z. 139 *n*. 560. *Beithe* (gl. buxus, box-tree), bethe, gl. buxus, Z. 728, apparently = W. bedw, birch, Lat. betula. The word occurs in a note on Christ's cross (Lib. Hymn. 7 *b*. in marg.): cedir a cos ⁊ cupris a tenga ⁊ gius in geind doratad trethe ⁊ *bethe* in clar in roscribad in titul, i. e. "Cedar its shaft, and cypress its tongue [the upper segment], and deal the piece (?) that was put across it, and box the board whereon was written the title." 561. *Ibhar* (yew), ibar in Corn. Another Irish word for yew, *eo*, is the W. yw, Corn. biuin, Bret. ivinen, O. H. G. iwa, N. H. G. eiben-baum, Fr. if, Sp. and Port. iva. 562. *Fichabhall* (as I read for the senseless fidhabhall, wood-apple), a fig-tree, from ficus and aball (malus), No. 555; cf. Corn. ficbren, gl. ficus, Z. 1118. 563. *Crand gius* (pine-tree). 564. *Crand lauir*, laurel-tree (leg. crandgiús, crandlauir), with giús, perhaps cf. bí, gl. pix, Z. 25, 764. 565. *Fraech* (gl. brucus, heather), O'R.'s *fraoch*, nom. pl. neut. inna dœrœ *fróich*, gl. vaccinia, i. e. rubræ cricæ, Z. 890, which Z. calls a solitary example of the occurrence of flexion in an adjective *preceding* a substantive. Cf. however, doadbadar sunt atá *nili* dána in spirto *et* as *nóindœ* in spirut (Z. 360), "here is shown that there are many gifts of the Spirit, and that the Spirit is single." With fraech cf. W. grûg. 566. *Crand mucor* (gl. cornus, cornel-cherry, dogwood-tree), "dogbriar," C.

567–568. *Cuigel*

567-568. *Cuigel* (gl. colus, distaff) = W. cogail, Corn. kigel, Bret. kigel, kegel = O. H. G. cuncla, N. H. G. kunkel, all, like Fr. quenouille, It. conocchia, from Med. Lat. conucula, for colucnla, from colus. 568. *Fersaid* (gl. fusus, spindle) cf. W. gwerthyd, Corn. gurhthit, Bret. gwerzid, and Lat. vert-o, verticillus, versatilis, Med. Lat. vertebrum, verteolus, "Et colus et fusi digitis ccciderc!"

569-575. *Tech*, tech in Z. 73. house (cf. coitchen communis = con-tech-en? Z. 73; tee-nate, gl. domesticus, Z. 769; cum-tach, ædificatio, Z. 843; daltech (gl. forum). Book of Armagh, 189 *b*. 2), apparently a sister form of teg, Z. 73 (gen. ind idul*taige*, gl. fani, Z. 822; dat. i *taig* rig, gl. in prætorio, Z. 280), which last is W. ty, pl. tai, Corn. and Bret. ti, τέγος, *thatch* (Skr. r. sthag?). 570. *Bean do brathar*, "thy brother's wife;" *bean do meic*, gl. nurus, "thy son's wife;" as to *bean v. infra*, No. 1053. *Brathar*, leg. bráthar, gen. of bráthair, a stem in tar, declined like athair, *supra*, No. 13; and = Skr. bhrátṛ, Goth. bróthar, Lat. fráter, Gr. φρητήρ, ἀδελφός, Hesych.; *do*—O. Ir. du, do—the possess. pron. of 2 pers. sing.; W. dy, Bret. da, = Skr. tava, the original *t* having been worn down to a medial in this frequently used word. The *d* of this pronoun, however, becomes *t* when the vowel is elided. Cf. tesérge, "thy resurrection," Book of Armagh, 18 *b*, 1; conicim tanacul, "I am able to save thee," *ibid.*, 186 *a*. Note that no word corresponding to Skr. snushá, Gr. νυός, Lat. nurus, Goth. snur, has yet been found in Celtic. Skr. çvaçrú, Gr. ἑκυρά, Lat. socrus, Goth. svaihro (mother-in-law), are represented by the W. chwegr, but no such Irish word can be quoted. It would, however, be rash to draw conclusions from circumstances like this, till we make more progress in collecting our ancient words and names, of which, perhaps, scarce one-third is accessible to the philologer. 572. *Cugan*, gl. penus, Z. 80, cucan, gl. penus. 573. *Lég loghmar* (read lóghmar), a precious stone – O. Ir. liacc lógmar, liacc = W. llech, a *flag*, a flat stone. Liacc is a fem. â-stem: is[ed] béss didu *ind liacc*: berir ilbeim friss *et* intí dothuit fair conboing a chnámi; intí for a tuit som, imorro, atbail side: "It is this, now, that the stone is: many a blow is given to it, and he that falls on it breaks his bones; but he on whom it falls *he* perishes," Z. 609: gen. in acclesia magná aird*liecc*, Book of Armagh, 9 *b*, 2: dat. for *leicc* luim, Fiacc, 16, "on a bare stone." 574. *Long luath* (gl. carbassus), "a swift ship;" long, gen. luinge (W. llong, fem., whence llynghes, a fleet), a fem. â-stem: is *long* from the Lat. navis *longa*, or may we refer it to the Skr. root langh (*salire*, ire)? The acc. sing. loing glosses vas in the Book of Armagh, 177 *b*, 1; carbasus, "cyn schiff das keyn bodem hat."—Dief. Med. Lat. Dict. 575. *Fairge* (sea), *v. supra*, No. 328, a fem. iâ-stem, O. Ir. fairgge, Z. 928; fairggæ, foirggæ, Z. 1125.

576-579. *Bru na hoighe* (gl. aulus), "the virgin's womb," leg. brú na hóighe (gl. alvus).

alrus). 577. *Sroll* (gl. byssus, βύσσος) is spelt sról, and explained "silk, satin, gauze, crape," by O'R., but byssus is a yellowish linen. With—578. *Uir* (gl. humus, the ground), Pictet compares εὐρύς, Skr. uru (large), fem. urvi (earth); gen. úire, Corm. v. Gaire; Corm. v. Mur, glosses ur by talam: so also sub v. *Ur*. Ur. tréide fordingair, úr chetamus .i. talam, ⁊ úr cech nuæ amail asmberar imb úr; úr dana cech nóle, inde dicitur isna br. n. [brethib nemed] lán dosiathach each núr .i. cech nóle. "Ur: three things it means; úr, in the first place, i. e. the earth; and úr, everything new, as is said, *imb úr* [fresh butter]: úr, then, is everything bad. Hence is said in the *Bretha nemed*, "fully *dosiathach* (?) is everything *úr*, i. e. everything bad.' " Adj. húrde, "ad humum pertinens," Z. 764. 579. *Paiper*, of course from papyrus, πάπυρος.

580–587. *Dorus lis*, "door of a *less*," now spelt lios, an a-stem, cf. Lissus: "a Dun, pronounced Doon [dún, cf. Eng. town] is an elevated, circular, enclosing wall or bank, within which a dwelling-house was erected. A Dun required to be surrounded by a wet fosse or trench [a moat] to distinguish it from the Rath which had not a trench ... Lios was another name for the Dun, but that it often contained within it more than one dwelling-house." (C. *Cath Maighe Léna*, 78, 79.) Cf. W. llys, a court, hall. The dat. sing. of less occurs in the Book of Armagh, 17 *b*, 1: Dirrógel ... ochter nachid con a scilb it[ar] fid ⁊ mag ⁊ lenu con all*ius* ⁊ allubgort; also in Patrick's Hymn: Crist il *lius*, Crist is sius, Crist in erus, "Christ in the court, Christ in the chariot-seat, Christ in the poop," i. e. Christ be with us while at home, or travelling by land or sea; the gen. pl. occurs in loig-*less*, before cited : in Gaelic, lios, gen. *lise*, is fem., and means "a garden." 582. *Feorus* (gl. acirus), *feoras* is explained "the spindle-tree, prick-wood," by O'R. (on whom, of course, no reliance can be placed), which reminds one of W. grwysen, gooseberry. Should we read acinus for acirus, or is it for acerus, galingale, sweet flag? 583. *Buachaill bó*, ad v. bubulcus bovum; buachaill (gen. muine *buachaille*, Book of Armagh, 17 *b*, 1) is bóchaill in Z. 28, 67; cf. W. bugail, Corn. bugel, gl. pastor. 584. *Buachaill muce* (swineherd) is lit. bubulcus porcorum; buachaill, like bubulcus and βουκόλος, merging its special meaning of cowherd in that of herdsman; cf. ἱπποβουκόλος, horscherd, and see Max Müller, *Oxford Essays*, 1856, p. 17. 585. *Múine* (gl. rubus, bramble-bush) occurs, as we have seen, in Fiacc, 24, and in the Book of Armagh. 586. *Airgeach* (gl. remulus, a small oar), but airgeach is a plunderer, O'R., also an owner of herds (nirbu airgech air slébe, Brog. 11; cf. *airge*, gl. armentum, *infra*, No. 754), and there is probably some mistake here. 587. *Dris* (gl. tomús, i. e. dumus, bush, bramble); cf. dris-tenach, gl. dumetum, Z. 777, driss, gl. vepres, Z. 139, Corn. dreis, gl. vepres, Z. 1118, W. dryssien (frutex), Z. 301.

588-593. As to these ordinals, *céd* (céd neach, "first anyone") is only found in Z.'s glosses in fochetoir, leg. fochétóir, statim, illico, lit. sub prima hora. The lengthened form cét-ne is used instead. But we find the adverbs cétu, ciatu, céta (primum), and Corn. has cétamus (imprimis), cét-aidche (first night), Fíacc, 32; cétbliadain, first year, Z. xxviii. The *t* is unaspirated, owing to *n* having been lost before it; this *n* is found in W. kentaf, kyntaf, Z. 230; Gaulish *Cintu*-genus, "first-born," = O. Ir. Cetgen, Book of Armagh, 11 *b*, 2. *Indara neach* seems simply the old indala noch (the second anyone), the liquid *l* becoming *r*, as in imlesen, *supra*, &c.; ala = W. eil, alter, secundus; ala occurs in Z. 313, with the meaning of "second," in connexion with the numeral deac, 10 : cethar brottae, 7 *ala* rann deac brotto (4 moments, and the 12th (2 + 10) part of a moment): with the meaning of "one of two:" indala fiacail, Z. 926. With ala we may, perhaps, connect the prep. al, gl. ultra, Z. 602, which occurs with a suffixed pronoun in Colmán's Hymn, 50 : Benedacht for Columcille con nóebaib Alban *alla*, "blessing on Columcille, with the saints of Scotland besides him." *Tres*, third, O. Ir. triuss, tris, gen. tres, Z. 316, is not easily explained: can it have been a distributive = Zend thrishva? or an old superlative in -istha? But how is gen. tres to be accounted for? A passing over to the *s*-declension is possible, but unlikely. *Cethruma*, O. Ir. cethramad, *v. supra*, No. 142. The dat. sing. neut. occurs in the Book of Armagh, 177 *b*, 2 : iár *cethramad* laithiu (gl. a nudus [nudius] quartana die). *Cuigedh*, O. Ir. cóiced = O. W. pimphet, Lat. quinctu-s : *Seis-ed* = O. W. chueeh-et = svocs-a-ta, Lat. sextu-s.

594-604. *Gabáilleeh* (gl. captus), from gabáil, W. cafael, cavail, Z. 160, capere. 595. *Curracach* (gl. cuculatus, i. e. cuckolded?), lit. crested. Horne Tooke was not so original as he supposed when he wrote, " In English we do not call them cuculi, but cuculati (if I may coin a word on this occasion)." 596. *Atanach* (gl. capuciatus), cf. Corn. hot, gl. caputium, W. hotan, hotyn (a cap). 597. *Inarach*—598. *Muincilleeh*— 599. *Fullaingech*—600. *Tribhusach*, adjectives, and—601. *Corunta*, a participle, from bases considered *supra*. 602. *Foirmtech* (gl. invidus). The subst. format, O'R.'s *formad* (envy, ox MAN, like μῆνις): acc. s. appears in the pref. to Patrick's hymn, Lib. Hymn., cited in Petrie's Tara, 32 : bid ditin do ar cech neim 7 *format*, "it will be a protection to him against every poison and envy;" cf. W. gorfynt. 603. *God* (gl. blaesus, lisping, speaking indistinctly), "stammering," according to C., who tells me that the Danes were called by the Irish na Gaill *guit*; cf. W. gyth (a murmur). 604. *Bodhar*, deaf, W. byddar, Corn. bothar, Bret. bouzar, Skr. badhira. (Hence Eng. bother?)

605-614. *Baccach* (gl. claudus, limping, halting, lame, W. bachawg, "crooked")
occurs

occurs in the acc. pl. masc., spelt bacachu, as a gloss on the word luscu, in the second line of the 17th couplet of Fíacc's hymn :—

Iccaid luscu la trusen, mairb dosfiuscad do bethu.

He used to heal the halt, with the lepers; the dead he used to raise them to life.

606. *Ordaighe* (gl. auratus), *ór*, gl. aurum, *infra*, gen. óir, from the Lat. aurum for ausum (Skr. root usb, urere). If the word were Celtic, the *s* would have been lost between the vowels. 607. *Airgedach* (gl. argenteus), from *airged*, gl. argentum, *infra*. in O. Ir. argat (gen. arggait, argit, Book of Armagh, 17 *b*, 1) = W. ariant, Bret. arc'hant, Corn. arhanz, Old Keltic Argento-ratum, Argento-magus, &c., Zend erezata, Lat. argentum, Osc. arageto, Skr. rajata. 608. *Iarnaighe* (leg. iarnaidhe?), gl. ferreus, from iarn, for isarn (iron), W. haearn, Corn. hoern, Z. 120; cf. the Gaul. Isarnodurum (iron door?), *iarunn*, gl. ferrum, *infra*; the gen. sing. seems to occur in Z. 926, ar fuilib *hiairn* for fhairn = isarni, the aspirate being displaced as in the W. and Corn. forms); cf. Skr. ayas, Eng. ore, Goth. eisarn (ferreus), from which the Celtic stem isarno can hardly be taken, the deriv. suffix -arn being common in Celtic, but rare in Gothic. 609. *Luaidheamhail* (gl. plumbeus), from luaidhe, gl. plumbum, *infra* (cf. Eng. lead, load?), and samhail = samalis = W. hafal, Lat. similis, Gr. ὁμαλός, &c. 610. *Stanamhail* (gl. stanneus), from stan (sdan, gl. stannum, *infra*). 611. *Umamhail* (gl. aereus), from ume (*humae* fogrigedar, "aes quod dat vocem, sonat, Z. 445), O. W. emed, Mod. W. efydd. 612. *Fundaminteeh* (gl. fundatus), from fundamentum. 613. *Scitheeh ón sligi* (gl. fessus, "wearied from the way," i. e. journey). 614. *Scitheeh ó obair* (gl. lassus, "wearied from work"), leg. scitheeh, and compare scíth, Z. 26, sciith, Z. 669 : ni confil bas *sciith* lim act rop ar Christ, "death is not a burden to me if only it be for Christ."

615-621. *Tinnisneeh* (O'R. tinneasnach), "speedy, hasty." 617. *Nemhtindisneeh*, "unspeedy, unhasty." 616. *Salach* (salacious, lustful), perhaps borrowed from salax, root sal (sal-io, ἅλλομαι, for σάλjομαι). Salach subsequently glosses sordidus, dirty = W. halawg, cf. halou, gl. stercora, Z. 1095 (the man's name Cennsalach, gen. sing. Ceinn*selich*, Book of Armagh, 18 *a*, 1, comes from cennsal, imperium), and hence would seem connected with O. H. G. salo, not clear, troubled, Fr. sale. 618. *Suirgech*. gl. procus, wooer (in O'R. suireach), perhaps connected with στοργή, στέργω; cf. seree, amor, W. screb, with the *s* preserved (*st* at the beginning of a word in Welsh, as a rule, loses the *t*, not the *s*). 620. *Gortach* (gl. famelicus, famished, starved), O. Ir. gorte (famine), a fem. iā-stem, Z. 1006 = gardh-ti-ā, Skr. r. grdh (avidum esse). 621. *Fiarshileeh* (if I read the word aright), gl. strabonus, squint-eyed; fiar, crooked = W. gwyr.

gŵyr. Bopp may be right in comparing fiar with Lat. rârus, Skr. vakra curvus, flexuosus. So Gaulish mâros seems Gr. μακρός.

625–629. *Tengtach* (gl. linguosus), dótengtach (leg. dothengtach?), gl. bilinguosus, hypocritical, double-tongued, from tenge (tongue), gen. tengad, *v. supra*, which, from these adjectives, would seem to have been a t-stem. 626. *Déreach* (leg. déireach?), charitable, from déire, alms, deserce (amor), Z. 78. 628. *Briathrach* (gl. verbosus), from briathar (word), a fem. â-stem. 629. *Sbegach* (ἄγλωσσος, clinguis, not glib of tongue), not in O'R.

630–634. *Fonamaideach* (gl. ridiculosus, facetious, droll), O'R. has fanambad, ridicule, and fonamadach, which he translates by "contemptuous;" "making game," is, O'D. tells me, the meaning now attributed to the word; cf. Eng. *fun?* 631. *Failgeach* (gl. egenus, needy, indigent). 632. *Casta* (gl. crispus, curled, crisped), from *casaim*. 633, 634. *Slán* (gl. sanus) *eslán* (gl. insanus), have been connected, *supra*, with W. llawen.

635–639. *Edmur* (gl. zelotypus), O. Ir. étmar [= Gaulish Iantumarus, Glück, 78], from ét zelus, Z. 22, aect, Z. 343 (forn *ét* fri saibapstalu darmchensa, "restra aemulatio pro me contra pseudoapostolos," Z. 607, Skr. r. yam(niti)? 636. *Dluith* (gl. densus), an adjectival i-stem; glosses denso in Gild. Lorica. Z. seems to have mistaken for the adj. dlúith the subst. dlúthe, wrongly rendered "apertus" in Z. 30, notwithstanding his glosses contain tri beulu *dlutai*, gl. fixis labris, Z. 1015, *dluthe* in tiuf[id] douaib conso[naib], Z. 1021; literally, connexion (coherence) of the aspiration to [i. e. with] the consonants (in χ, θ, φ). Dlúithe also means a chink: huand *dlúithi* seim, gl. tenui rima, Z. 261; and cf. dlúth, gl. stamen (the warp in a loom), Z. 30; tre chomdluthad, gl. per synaeresin, Z. 985, rundlúth, gl. densaverat, Z. 435. 637. *Goirt* (gl. acidus), perhaps connected with the verb in "ma *gorith* loch cith in e chuis nu in e laim," which Z. renders (p. 1006) "si dolet locus vel in ejus pede vel in ejus manu." 638. *Ballach* (gl. urbiculatus) is now not "rounded, circular," but "freckled," from ball (spot). Cf. W. *ball*, "eruption, plague." In Z. ball, a masc. a-stem, always means membrum, and agrees in form, declension, and gender with φαλλός. 639. *Slemain* (gl. lubricus, slippery, smooth), an adj. i-stem: a sisterform, of the a-declension, is slemon, which occurs in a marginal gloss on the Lib. Hymn. copy of the Altus Prositor; nom. pl. neut.: is airi asbertar étrumma ┐ *slemna* huare nád techtat tinfed, Z. 1022 (i. e. therefore are they called light and smooth, because they have not aspiration); slemna, gl. levia, Z. 737, slemon = W. *llyfn*, fem. *llefn*. Cf. N. H. G. schleifen, Eng. slip.

640–649. *Fairsing* (gl. amplus, spacious, roomy), farsinge, the subst. from this, occurs in Lib. Hymn., 5 *b*, Colman's Hymn, line 43, as a gloss on lethu:—

Robbem

Robbem cen es illethu la aingliu imbithhethu.

May we be without age, in space¹, with angels in eternal life!

641. *Luathgairech* (gl. nervosus), generally means "rejoicing," "exulting," from luath (swift), and gáire (joy), W. gware (play). Here it seems equivalent to energetic, vigorous in expression (quis Aristotele *nervosior?* Cic.). 642. *Dealbhdha* (gl. formosus), O. Ir. delbde, from delb (forma, figura, imago, paradigma), fem. W. delw, Z. 99, and cf. doilbthid figulus, Z. 987, indoilbthid, gl. figurate, Z. 984, dolbud (figmentum), Z. 768, leads one to think the root DAL which is, perhaps, etymologically connected with Lat. forma, Skr. r. dhṛ. 643. *Uchtard* (gl. strumosus, wenny) rather seems "high-breasted," from ucht and ard. 644. *Craessach*—645. *Fesógach*—646. *Gaethmar*—648. *Milech*, all from nouns noticed, *supra.* 647. *Bronnmar*, from brú, gen. s. hronn, W. bru (womb): a dimin. from brú occurs in the dat. sing.: his *bronnait* (gl. infra ventriculum), Z. 593. 649. *Snethach*, leg. snedhach (nitty), W. neddog, is interesting, furnishing, as it does, a hint as to what must have been running in the heads of the European Aryans at an early period, for sned, Z. 1126 (W. nedd-en, Bret. niz) is Slav. gnida, Gr. κόνις, κόνιδ-ος, N. H. G. nisse, Lith. gli(n)da, Lat. le(n)s, le(n)dis.

650–653. *Coisinech* (if I read the word rightly) means, I presume, taking short steps, going pedetentim, step by step, slowly. 651. *Croindtilli* is probably a blunder for crointsilech, an adj. formed from crontsaile, phlegm, spittle, derived by Corm. from grant (grey), and saile = saliva. 652. *Gerbach* (gl. rugosus, wrinkled, shrivelled) is now "scabby." 653. *Bocoidech* (gl. maculosus, spotted), leg. bocóidech? from bocóid, a spot, O'R.

654–659. *Anmach*, from anim, *v. supra.* 655. *Clúmar*—656. *Michlúmar*, from clú (gl. rumor, Z. 68, also fama), W. clyw; cf. Slav. slovo (verbum, sermo), slava (gloria), Gr. κλέFος, Skr. çravas, rumor. The W. for famosus is clodfawr = clotomáros (the O. H. G. Hlodomâr, Glück, 81); cf. with elod, Ir. cloth (fame, praise) = cluta-s, Gr. κλυτός, Lat. in-clytus, Eng. 'loud; Ir. cluas (ear) = W. clust (cf. Eng. 'list). The root reduplicates in Celtic. Thus in Irish: rot-che-chlad-ar (hears thee), Z. 496; cechluista .i. nocluinfithea (auditum erit, Brehon Law gloss). And in Welsh: ciglif (audivi), Z. 420 = Skr. çuçrâva. 657. *Breallach* (gl. spadosus) I cannot explain with any certainty; spadosus is, perhaps, a med. Lat. adj., from spado (σπάδων), an impotent person. 658. *Prebach*, kicking (preabaim, I kick, O'R.). Is retrocosus for calcitrosus?

¹ Perhaps we should rather translate "in greatness," "in grandeur;" lethe and fairsinge, like amplitudo, may well have attained to this secondary signification.

citrosus? or a barbarous hybrid from retro and the Irish cos (= coxa), leg from knee down, foot? 659. *Geal* (white), O. Ir. gel, *v. supra*.

660-669. *Tegaisge* (gl. doctus), *tecoisce*, gl. doctior, *infrá*: cf. sochoise, gl. docibilem, Z. 832; cosc (institutio) Z. 53; cossec, *ib.* 61; coscc, *ib.* 78: *coscitir* ind fir et doairbertar foréir dǽ, "the men are taught and brought under the will of God," Z. 618. I know not if O. Ir. écosc (habitus, forma), Z. 832, 235, or W. *dangaws*, demonstration; *arddangos*, to demonstrate, be connected with this word. 661. *Maith*, good, O. Ir. nom. pl. maithi, Z. 883 (an i-stem), W. mad; cf. the Gaulish name Teutomatus. 662. *Olc* (bad), n. pl. masc. uile, uilce, Z. 252; acc. pl. masc. ulcu, Z. 457. In the nom. and acc. pl. neut., when followed by *sa*, this adjective drops its proper termination: inna *olc*-sa, Z. 354, 676. 663. *Mór*, O. Ir. már, mór (W. mawr), great = μακρός? (the guttural was lost even in Gaulish; cf. Virdomarus, Brogi marus [W. bro, country], Segomaros [Skr. sahas, strength], Iantumarus [Ir. étmar], Nertomarus [Ir. nertmar¹]); cf. μέγας, mag-nus, Skr. mah-at, for maghânt, Goth. mik-ils, μεγάλου. 664. *Beg* (small), O. Ir. becc, W. bach, cf. Gaul. "*Becco* Mocconis fil.," Z. 77. 665. *Solus*, *v. supra*. 666. *Taithnemhach* (gl. candidus), from do + aith + nemh; cf. W. ednyf, ednyw (purity, vigour), with which we may, perhaps, connect Adnamatius, Namatius (Glück, 39), *namhain*, and Namnetes (Glück, 140). 667. *Sanntach* (greedy, avaricious, covetous) occurs in Z. 78, from sant, with which Z. wrongly compares the Gaulish tribe-name Santones, for W. and Bret. chwant (invidia, desiderium) points to an Old Celtic svauataka. Cf. Suanetes, Consuanetes (Glück, 28, 64). 668. *Dingbala* —669. *Midingbala* (worthy, unworthy), I can in nowise explain, unless, indeed, dingbala be from do-ind-gabál (acceptabilis).

670-674. *Imdha* (gl multus), in Z. 75, imde (multus, abundans) = ambitias, imda, gl. opulentus, *ib.* = ambitvas? cf. Ambitui, a Gaulish tribe-name; imbed (gl. ops copia, Z. 75), all from the prep. imm, W. amm, Gaulish ambi (circa) = Lat. amb, Gr. ἀμφί, Skr. abhi, Eng. um (in umstroke = circumference, Fuller), which has often an intensive meaning. 671. *Glan* (purus, mundus, clarus), mod. W. glân, with inorganic lengthening of the vowel (Glück, 187, justly compares the Keltic river-name Glana), act ranglana, gl. siquis emundaverit se, Z. 454, glantar as (eliditur, Z. 985), bói ní roglante and, Z. 1060; cf. Eng. clean, N. H. G. klein? 672. *Teirc* (gl. rarus), whence

---

¹ Curiously enough, we find many O. German names formed with this adj. and identical with Celtic appellations, e. g., Hadumar (= a Gaulish Catumáros), W. catmor, Hlodomar (= a Gaulish Clotomáros), W. clodfawr, &c., Glück, 78, 81. So Hincmar = Ex-cincomarus, Sigumar, Segimerus, hod. Siegmar = Segomaros.

whence teirce, *infra* (gl. raritudo), thin, scanty. 673. *Beg*, v. *supra*. 674. *Daingen no cruaidh* (gl. durus), daingen glosses firmus, *infra*, *édaingen* (infirmus), O'R.'s daingean, "strong, secure, close;" isin dun *daingen*, Z. 30, " in the strong fort ;" daingnigim (gl. mocuio), Z. *ib.* Apparently donjon, Eng. dungeon, are Celtic words, perhaps cognate with O. H. G. dwingan, Eng. twinge, tongs, tack (Zwecke): *cruaidh*, " hard, callous, severe," O'R.

675-694. *Fliuch*, moist, wet = W. gwlyp (= vlievas?); cf. *fliuchidhrcht* (gl. liquor), *infra*, fliuchaide (humidus, Z. 272; fliuchaidatu humiditas, Z. 66; fliuchaigim, gl. lippio, Z. 65; fliuchdere, gl. lippus, Z. 65; cf. Corn. glibor (moisture) = W. gwlybwr [= Lat. liquor], and O. W. rogulipias, gl. olivavit, Z. 420. If fliuch, gwlyp, be, as conjectured, from vlievas, we may be correct in comparing the word with Lat. lippus for vlippus (where *pp* may have sprung from *kv*, as in ἵππος, from *akra*, Skr. açva), O. Slov. vlŭgŭkŭ, humidus. 676. *Dochenélach*, low-born, ignoble; cenél genus, gen. ceneiuil = O. W. cenitol, Z. 172. The dat. sing. of cenél occurs in the following passage in the Book of Armagh, 17 *a*, 2, now for the first time correctly printed : Conggab patrice iarnaid puirt indruimm daro .i. druim lias, Fácab patrice adaltæ .n. and benignus aainm ⁊ fuitinse xuii. annís. Gabais caille lapatricc lassar ingen anfolmithe *dicheniul* caicháiu. Baiade and taresi .m. benigni trifichtea bliadne, " Patrick afterwards abode at a place [or house—observe the locative of *port*] in Druimm Daro, i. e. Druimm Lias. Patrick left his pupil there. Benignus was his name, and he was therein for 17 years. Lassar, a daughter of Anfolmid (?), of the race of Caichán, took the veil from Patrick [lit. cepit velum apud Patricium]. Three scores of years was she there after Benignus." 677. *Fada* (long), O. Ir. fota, Z. 942; fote, Z. 966, n. pl. bithfotai, semper longi, Z. 824. The subst. is fot, Z. 230, gen. fuit, Z. 66. 678. *Cumair* (short, brief), O. Ir. cumbair, whence cumbre (brevitas) ar *chumbri*, Z. 1074; cf. W. byr, Lat. brevis. 681. *Fírénach*—682. *Ainfrénach* (just, unjust): cf. fíriáu (verax, justus), Z. 115, &c.; gen. pl. hignimaib fer *fírean* (Patrick's hymn), firianugud (justice, justification), Z. 53, 346; firianigedar (justifies), Z. 445. Cf. W. gwirion, from gwir-iawn: *iawn* is " equity," " just," " meet;" cf. O. Ir. án (" wealth," nom. pl. and gen. pl. aue, dat. pl. ánib, acc. pl. anu, Z. 934, a masc. u-stem), with which Dr. Siegfried is inclined to connect the Zend yâna (see Haug, *Die Gáthá's*, p. 42). 683. *Brén* (gl. fetidus), brénaim (puteo), bréntu (foetor), Z. 1085; cf. W. braen (rotten), braenu (to moulder); perhaps connected with braigim pedo, Z. 431, the *g* being lost before *n*, as in the instances quoted *supra*. 684. *Salach* (gl. sordidus), v. No. 616. 688. *Tempoll*, from templum, as—689. *Tairberne*, from taberna, and—691. *Reilic* (gl. simitherium, a cemetery), from reliquiæ (observe the hard

$c = qv$,

c = *qu*, as in mac), gen. sing. timchell na *relgi*, "round the cemetery" (Leab. Breacc. cited Lib. Hymn. ed. Todd, 31). 693. *Adhlucadh* (gl. sepulchrum), *Adhlacad* (gl. monumentum), *infra*, No. 759, are etymologically obscure to me. Can they be a corruption of aduacul (sepulcrum), Z. 731 (i slebti *adranact* cremthann, "C. was buried in Sletty," Book of Armagh, 17 *b*)? with which, perhaps, νέκυς, Zend. naçu, Skr. r. naç, "to die," Lat. nex, nox, Ir. nocht, may be connected. 694. *Edail* (gl. lucrum), O'R. eadail, leg. éadail, W. *ennill* (masc.) = antalli? (gain, profit, acquired wealth). Gael. *cudail*, "treasure," cattle, feudail, "cattle," "herds," (with inorganic prefixing of *f*?).

695–699. *Mirbail* (gl. miraculum, wonder), an i-stem, acc. pl. dogni in noemog-sa na *mirbuli* mora (this holy virgin performed the great miracles), Leabhar Breacc, cited by Dr. Todd, Lib. Hymn. 65. This word is taken from mirabile. 696. *Bachlog* (gl. monaculum, i. e. monaculus?); should we read bachlóg, and is this a playful dimin. from bachal = baculus, crozier? Or is this word connected in meaning with bachlach (tarunlus), *supra*? and is monaculum a contemptuous word for servant, slave, a meaning often attributed to manach (monachus) in Irish, as will be seen from a note on S. Hilary's hymn in Dr. Todd's ed. of Lib. Hymn. 699. *Diner* (gl. jentaculum), from the English *dinner*.

700–708. *Criathar* (gl. cribrum, sieve) = crétara, Corn. croider, Bret. krouezer; glosses cerebrum in Z. 22 (the scribe having obviously mistaken cerebrum for cribrum): Skr. root kṛi, to pour out. Cf. κρησέρα, Benfey, G. W. ii. 171. 701. *Muilind* (gl. molendinum), *Muileand* (gl. pistrinum), *infra*, No. 711, mulenn (gl. pistrinum), Z. 740, is probably, like W. Corn. and Bret. melin, from the Latin mŏlendinum (mŏlo); cf. muilneoir, a miller, O'D., Gr. xxxiv. Though the word for mill may be a foreign word, the root is certainly in Celtic: cf. Ir. meilim (I grind), W. malu (to grind); and cf. μύλη, O. H. G. muli, Lith. malunas, Eng. mill. 702. *Garrga* (gl. atrium, hall), said to be "court-yard," "enclosure" (but read garga, and cf. Skr. gṛha, house?). 703. *Tiradh* (gl. territorium, if this be what our careless copyist had before him), leg. tíradh (kiln-drying), for tírsadh? tirme (ariditas), tirim (aridus), both in Z. 1070, gl. 15, ho tirmai .i. co na bí tírim (from dryness, i. e. that it be not dry), tír (terra), all from Skr. r. tṛsh (tars), to thirst, "ursprünglich offenbar trocknen, vgl. gr. τέρσομαι. Das goth. thaursja ich trockne, euphonisch für thursja (und dieses für tharsja) stützt sich wie das lat. torreo (aus torsco) auf die skr. causalform tarsháyâmi" (Bopp, vergl. gramm. zte ausg. i. 105). One would have expected the *r* doubled as in *carr* (*supra*), Skr. karsha, "dragging." 704. *Orlar*, leg. orlár? (gl. vestibulum, a forecourt), lár, W. llawr is solum. Can the *or* be = παρά? cf. Ar-morica, παραλία, or is *or* for

for *aur*, and this for *air*, Gaul. *are*, as in do*aur*chanim (gl. sagio), Z. 10.   705. *Stocronna* (stirpidivortium, separation of a stock), from stoc (stirps)—cf. Corn. stoc, gl. stirps—and ranna (leg. rannadh?), a division, parting. Note the assimilation of the first *a* in ranna to the *o* of stoc, and cf. ocond, ocon, oco, Z. 594.   706. *Cris tribhuis* (gl. lumbarium), "belt of the trowsers" (triblius, *v. supra*).   707. *Sgornachan* (gl. epiglotum, the epiglottis) : sgornachán, says C., is now "a long-necked fellow," cf. Gael. *sgòrnach*, "throat, neck."   708. *Crombéol*, gl. gernonum (if I read the words rightly), a moustache (cf. with gernonum O. Fr. grignon, grenon, guernon, "bart sowohl der oberlippe wie des kinnes," Diez, E. W. 182, and O. H. G. grani (plur.), M. H. D. gran, O. N. grön, there cited. I know not if there ever was such a word as granni, "long hair," O'R., but it is possible there was, as grannaidh (hair) occurs in Gaelic. I have never met crombéol, except in the Anglicised form crommeal :—

<blockquote>"They tell me the stranger has given command
That *crommeal* and cooluu shall cease in this land."</blockquote>

S. Ferguson.

709–719. *Ngeota* (gl. cartesium), spelt—710. *Sgéotha* (gl. sacritegium) seems to be a bag or wallet for carrying ecclesiastical books or utensils. C. quotes: *Sceóta* nau aidbheadh ar muin chléirig riachois, Book of Fermoy, 88 b, b.   711. *Muilleand*, leg. muileann (gl. pistrinum, a pounding-mill), *v. supra*, No. 701.   712. *Cliathach* (gl. clastrum) seems to be an enclosure made of hurdles, from cliath, as to which *v. supra*. In Gaelic this word means "the frame of the ribs," "the chest."   713. *Tech na merdreach* (gl. prostibulum), "the harlots' house."   714. *Braiccin* (gl. redimiculum, a band, girdle), is, perhaps, a garter (from bracc-a?).   716. *Bile* (gl. ventilogium, a weathercock, Dief.) seems a blunder ; *bile*, so far as I know, has in Ireland only the two meanings : "border," and "old tree" (such, e. g., as grows by a holy well or in a fort). In Scotland it also means "leaflet," "blossom."   717. *Ceis* (gl. stragulum, covering, rug, horse-cloth) is the Corn. peis, gl. tunica, pows (tunica), Z. 123, *peus* gruce, gl. torul, Z. 124, W. pais, pl. peisiau, Z. 1121. Cf. cass-ock?   718. *Dithen* (gl. lolium, darnel), O'R.'s dithein, W. llys *dyn*.   719. *Crand glesta*, leg. *glésta* (gl. plectrum, the stick for striking the chords of a harp or other stringed instrument); *crand* (W. pren), O. Ir. crann, has occurred frequently, *supra* : *glésta*, gen. sing. of glésadh ; cf. Gael. gleusadh, "a tuning," "act of tuning," &c.   O'R. has gleusaim, "I prepare, tune, arrange ;" gléus, "key or gamut in music."   Cf. W. glwys, "pure, pleasant."

720–724. *Teine creasa* (gl. igniferrium), fire of [the] girdle, i. e. flint-steel-and-tinder ; as to *teine* (MS. teini), *v. supra*, and compare Zend tafnu (hot) ex ᴛᴀᴘɴᴜ, as Ir. suan (sleep), W. hun is from sᴠᴀᴘɴᴀ ; *creasa*, gen. of cris, which occurs *supra* in *eris* tribhuis, gl. lumbarium. 721. *Dubhradan* (gl. scrupulum), leg. dubhradán? I have never met elsewhere; perhaps it is a dimin. of dubhradh, "shade, eclipse," O'R., and may mean "trouble," "anxiety," figurative meanings of scrupulus, properly a pointed pebble. 722. *Tuairgin* (gl. teretorium, i. e. tritura). The O. Ir. verb and subst. occur in Z. 853: dofuairee (triturat): ar is bés leosom in daim do *thúarcnin* ("for it is a custom with them for the oxen to thresh"); and pistor is glossed by fer dénma bairgine *tuarcain*, dofuaircitis inna gráu la arsidi, "a man who makes bread [lit. a man of making of bread] by pounding: among the ancients they used to pound the grains;" and tuarcun glosses tribulatio, comthúarcon, contritio, Z. 738. 723. *Cluain gabála* (gl. herbagium): *cluain*, of which the dat. occurs in Z. xxxii. hi *cluain* maccunois, is a meadow, a lawn, iu Scotch Gaelic also "a bower," = clôni, W. clyn, "brake," "thicket:" cf. Cluniâcum, hod. Cluguy; *gabála*, gen. of gabáil (capere, captio), and cluain gabála is, according to C., an Irish legal term for "an appropriated field, a field not held in common." 724. *Caire* (gl. caldarium, "a vessel containing warm water for bathing"), W. pair (caldrou), Corn. pêr. Fr. pair-ol, generally means caldrou (as in *Coire* Breccáin, Corm., now Corryvreckan). It also means "a hollow or cul de sac in the mountains," Reeves, Vit. Col. 88, where Coire Salchaiu occurs, and in this sense has been adopted into the English language as "corry;" coire = κακκια or πακκια, Γ. κακ, ρακ (No. 240, *suprá*), as dér = ἄκρυ, Goth. tagr; fiar, W. gŵyr = vakra, várus; sár = Skr. çakra, Lat. sacer; már = μακρός.

725-729. *Longport* (gl. castrum), leg. longphort = W. llongborth (ship-harbour); longport glosses *sosad* in II. 3, 18, p. 523. It is not easy to see how its elements— *long* ship (*v. supra*) and *port* (a house, place, harbour)—can when combined express the idea of castrum. *Port*, gen. and loc. sing. puirt, dat. sing. purt (Lib. Hymn. ed. Todd, 13) is, perhaps, connected with Zend peretu, Eng. ford. Dief. G. W. ii. 365. 726. *Mainister*, gen. manestreeh, Z. xxviii., from monasterium, but with a remarkable change to the e-declension. 727. *Fortacht* (gl. suffragium), here "a favourable decision;" cf. fortachtid, gl. fautor, Z. 766, 845; acc. s. fortachtain, Z. 270, a fem. n-stem, generally "assistance." The verb occurs in Leab. Breace (cited by Todd, L. H. 65), is hí *fortaigess* da [leg. dona, dna?] cech oen bis cumea ocus in guasacht (she it is, then, that helps every one who is in anguish and in danger); fortacht, Z. 195: co fordumthésidse, "that ye may help me," Z. 335: fortiag (gl. conniveo), Z. 438. 728. *Proindtech* (gl. refectorium), and—729. *Codaltech* (gl. dormitorium), are, respectively, compounds of *tech*, house, with *proind*, W. *prain*, from Lat. prandium, and *codal*, whence *codlaim*, I sleep, O'R. The O. Ir. contul (?) dormio (ma *conatil* si dormis, Z. 1053, *contuil* each úadib forsét, Fíacc, 31) appears connected with this.

Proindtech

Proindtech (spelt praintech) occurs in the Book of Armagh, 18 b, 1 : airm ifuirsitis in torce arimbad and furruimtis a*praintech*.

730-739. *Speilp* (gl. coopertorium, i. e. cooperinentum? cooperculum?) is explained "a belt, armour," by O'R., but by C. "a girdle or swathe of linen." 731. *Tunna* (gl. dolium, a large jar), exactly O. Norse *tunna*, is "a cask" in O'R.; hardly a Celtic word; cf. W. tynell, Corn. tonnel, Bret. tonel, French tonneau, M. H. G. tonne, Eng. tun, &c. 732. *Seiche* (gl. corium), "a hide, or skin," O'R., Gael. *seiche*, *seich*, *scie*. 734. *Intlecht* (gl. ingenium), in O. Ir. intliucht, intsliucht (= andesllictus?), intellectus, sensus, Z. 42, 849, 230, gen. intliuchta, Z. 63 : sliucht, Z. 970, a masc. u-stem, compounded with the prep. ind (= Gaulish ande) which aspirates, and the *d* of which becomes *t* before aspirated *s*. 735. *Senáis*, old age, from sen (old) = sena-s (Gaulish Seno-magus, Zend. hana), and áis (age), a masc. i-stem, which Ebel would connect with Skr. âyus, but this would be a solitary instance of the preservation of an original final *s*. Áis, perhaps, stands for âissi-s ex âivs-i-s: cf. O. W. *in ois oisoudh*, the mod. W. yn oes oesoedd, Z. 298 : Corn. huis. 737. *Loscud* (gl. incendium, burning); dat. sing. do *loscud*, Z. 768, loiscdib (gl. essis), *ib*. forloiscthe (gl. igne exanimatus), Z. 845 ; cf. Corn. lose (arsura, ustulatio), W. llosg, Bret. losk. 738. *Martra* (gl. martyrium), like martir, a martyr, Colm. 19, W. *merthyr*) is a foreign word. O. Ir. martre: filus trechencke *martre* dancu adrimiter ar cruich du duiniu[1] mad esgre baan martre ocus glas martre ocus dere martre, "now there are three kinds of martyrdom which are considered as man's cross, that is to say [lit. if thou sayest], white martyrdom, and green martyrdom, and red martyrdom," Z. 1007 ; dul *martre* tartarcennsi, Z. 618, "to suffer martyrdom for your sake;" hence martre appears to be a fem. iâ-stem. 739. *Tuile* (gl. salarium, wages), cf. W. *tal*, pl. *talion* (payment), τέλος, τελέω.

740-744. *Soiler* (gl. solarium, sun-dial? house-top? Germ. söller), Corn. soler (Z. iii.); solarium is glossed by solam in Z. 733, which looks a genuine Irish word, and gives a favourable idea of the material civilization of the Irish ecclesiastics in the eighth and ninth centuries, especially when we consider their native words for napkin (lambrat bís tar glúne, gl. mappa, gl. mantile, i. e. a napkin that is over the knees, Z. 613 ; lámbrat (gl. gausape), Z. 820), for canal, or, perhaps, water-pipe (lóthur, gl. canalis, lothor, gl. alveal, Z. 744, for bath: fothareud, Z. 893, *infra* fothragad); but, above all, for usury (fogbaidetu for fogaibthetu, Z. 844). 741. *Scallad* (MS. scall.), (gl. sellarium) a pantry, *séalladh*, "a cell, O'R. 742. *Groigh* (gl. equitium), a stud of horses, Gael. *greigh*, s. f., an i-stem = gragi-s, cf. Lat. greg (grex), W. *gre* (herd, stud).

[1] Lit. are counted for a cross to a human being : glas = glasta : cf. glastum, woad.

stud). 744. *Muinél* (gl. collum, neck), Gael. *muineal*, gen. *-eil* = W. mwnwgl; cf. muinde, gl. collarium, muinntorc, gl. torques, Z. 764, where is also muinæ, which I suspect is a misreading or misprint for muince (necklace); cf. mong, W. mwng, mane.

745-749. *Druim* (back, ridge): gen. sing. drommo, dat. druimm, occur in the Book of Armagh, 17 a, 1 : Issí inso coibse fétho fio ⁊ aedocht dibliadin rembas daú dumanchuib *drommo* liás ⁊ dumaithib callrigi it[er] crochaingel ⁊ altóir *drommo* liás nadconfil finechas for*druimm* leas act cenél fétho fio ma beith nech besmaith diib bescráibdech beschuibsech dinchlaind manipé dúcastar dús inétar dimuintir *drommo* liás l. diamanchib Maniétar dubber décrud dimuintir pátricc inte . . . ["This is the communication of Féth Fio and his bequest, two years before his death, to the monks of Druim Liás and to the nobles of Callrige, as well the chancel as the altar (i. e. as well the laymen as the clerics) of Druim Liás: Let there not be *finechas* (inheritance of kindred, *fine*?) on Druim Liás (i. e. let it not devolve according to the law of *finechas*) but the race of Féth Fio, if any one of them be good—if any one of the clan be pious and decent. If there be not, let it be seen if there be one of the family of Druim Liás, or of its monks. Unless one be found, place a member of Patrick's family into it."] Druim occurs in Z. in composition with the numeral nóin (9): mochoe noin-*drommo*, "Mochoe of Nendrum" (Nine-ridge), now Mahee Island, in Strangford Lough (Todd, L. II., 100). 746. *Ceilebradh coin* is "a bird's warbling," *ceilebradh*, from celebratio : the verb ceilebraim means "I bid farewell;" lasc *celebirsimme* (gl. cum malefecissemus), Book of Armagh, 18↓ *b*.; *ceileabhar*, "chirping like birds," O'R.; coin gen. sing. of én (Z. 82: gen. iud*eúin*, Z. 24) = atina, W. edyn. Cf. O. W. *etn-coilhaam* (gl. auspicio), Z. 130; ætinet (volucres), Z. 169; Corn. idne (auceps), Z. 784. Has an initial *p* been lost by these words, and dare we compare (with Dr. Siegfried) πέτομαι, πετεημαί, Lat. penna (for petna—W. *adan*), Eng. feather (O. W. eterinn, avis, singularis, Z. 300: atar, aves: collect. *ib*.). *Crand tochartaigh* is "a reel;" cf. tocharaim, "I wind up, I reel," O'R., Gael. *tachras*, "winding, act of winding yarn;" gyrgyrium (if I read the word rightly—in Med. Lat. generally girgillus) seems formed by reduplication from gyrare. (See Pott as to this word, Zeits. i. 309.) 747. *Inchinn* (gl. cerebrum), the brain, Gael. *eanchainn*, W. emennyd, Corn. impinion, Bret. empenn : gen. inchinne : La sodain dolléci dia feraib fidchilli don techtaire com boi for lár a *inchinne* (Táin bó Cuailgne in the Lebar na Uidre), thus rendered by O'D., Lebar na Cert. lxiv.: "With that he cast [one] of his chessmen at the messenger, so that it pierced to the centre of his brain :" inchinu is an i-stem, from *in* (= unde?), and *cenn*, head. The word is formed like ἐγκέφαλος. 748. *Stol*, leg. *stól* (gl. scanum, i. e. scamnum),

scamnum), W. ystawl, fem.: both, no doubt, from Eng. stool, A. S. stól.   749. *Firmamint*, like Corn. firmament, W. *ffurfafen*, of course from firmamentum.

750–758. *Mir plue*, gl. rubigorium, is altogether obscure to me. Possibly it may mean "the (top) red part of the cheeks." Cf. Gael. *mir*, "the top or summit:" *plue, pluie, ploe*, "cheek," O'R.   751. *Luach faisnéise* (if I read the last word aright) is "reward of information,"; inventorium from invenio, in the sense of discover ("seis, Pamphilam meam *inventam* civem?"). 752. *Innarbad* (gl. exilium), for indarbad: cf. indarpe (ejectio), Z. 591, gen. -pi, dat. -pu, Z. 246; indarbad expulsus est, O'D. (Ir. 291; isan *indarbe*, gl. in repulsam, Z. 247; aren *indarbe* analchi ood (that he banish vices from him), Z. 1003; tre *indarpae* .de. asin mascul (per ablationem syllabæ *de* a masculino), Z. 848; nachimr'indarpai-se quod non me repulit, Z. 848; nachitr'indarpither (ne sis exheredatus); *innarbar* hires dam trí drochgnimu, "Faith also is banished by evil deeds" (note the assimilation of the *d*); the *ind* (Gaulish ande, Skr. adhi) here signifying motion from something (Z. 848), which something is, in the present instances, arbe, orpe, heritage (gen. orpi), Z. 234. a neut. ia-stem, which = N. H. G. erbe, Aug. S. yrfe neut., as in Beowulf, 6093, ed. Thorpe. Cf. also na berat an *erpther* doib, "let them (slaves) not take away what is committed to them," Z. 458: nom*érpimem* (me trado, contido), Z. 431: nobirpaid (confiditis) ro *airpth*a (commissum est), Z. 7.   753. *Oilemain*, gl. alimentum, root al, as to which *v. supra*. 754. *Airge*, "a herd," O'R., *v. suprà*.   755. *Tormach* (increase).   756. *Mithormach* (decrease), *tormach*. leg. tórmach = do-for-mac-a, Z. 1051, gl. 26; tormachtaid (auctor), Z. 766; tormachtai (aucta), Z. 983; doformgat (augent), Z. 854; doformagar, tórmagar (augetur), doformmagddar (augentur), Z. 854.   Here again we find the Skr. root mah.   757. *Edach* (clothing), O. Ir. étach, Z. 442, éitach, Z. 1050, gen. ætig, Z. 857, étich, Z. 1051, a neut. a-stem, as in Z. 235, gaibid immib an*étach* macc cóimsa, "put around ye the raiment of sons of mercy." 758. *Ogdhamh* (gl. jumentum, a beast of burthen), lit. young ox; cf. ogbho, leg. ogbhó, O'R.; óg = O. Ir. óe (óelachdi, gl. juvenilia, oemil (= yavanca-milit), gl. tyro, Z. 60; oemiledu, gl. athletas, Gildas). Óe = O. W. ionenc, W. *ieuanc* = Eng. young = juvencus, which shows that our Irish word has not only lost *v* and *n* in the middle of the word, but *j* (*y*) at the beginning. The original is YAVANKA, the *a* in the first syllable being found in the Skr. comparative and the superl. yavishtha, and in Ἰάονες, which Lassen has equated with juvenes. The stem has been recognised by Dr. Siegfried in the O. Ir. comparative óa, "less" (= W. iau = Skr. yaviyâns), and superlative oam (gl. minimus, Z. 286) = W. ieuaf.   Z., p. 60.

---

[1] In the MS., faini, with an oval mark over ai, and a mark like a long z between n and i.

60, points out another word in O. Ir. which has lost initial *j*, viz., aig (gl. cristallus, Z. 60), the corresponding W. word iâ (= yag), ice, and the Breton adj. yen (= yagin), icy, still retaining the semi-vowel. Cf. also uisse with Lat. justus, from which, however, I do not think it taken. Consider A. Weber's remark (Ind. Stud. iv. 398), "yôs for yâvas, from √yu, to join: cf. Lat. jus, Zend yaos, in the verb yaozhda." In other words, such as ísu (Jesus), ice (salus), W. iechyt, íth (gl. puls, Z. 60), W. iot, the *j* has blent with the following vowel, and produced í. *Damh* will be considered *infra*, No. 858.

760–769. *Timna* (gl. testamentum), O. Ir. timne: "is taschide *timne* déc do chomalnad," Z. 897 ("it is necessary to fulfil God's commandment"). This timne is a neut. ia-stem. 761. *Instrumint*, like—766. *Saltair* (gl. psalterium) is a foreign word. 762. *Dídiu* (gl. tegmentum), O. Ir. dítiu, gen. díten, *v. supra*. 763. *Médugud* (gl. augmentum), from *méid*, gl. magnitudo, *infra*. 764. *Sprirech* (gl. fragmentum), from the same root, probably, as W. ysbwrial, sweepings, ysborion, refuse, *Spruilleach*, gl. fragmen, *infra*. 765. *Duillen* (gl. folium), W. dalen, deilen, Corn. delen, Bret. delien, pl. deliou, Ganlish dula in πεμπέδουλα quinquefolium: πεντάφυλλον Ῥωμαῖοι κιγκεφόλιουμ, Γάλλοι πεμπέδουλα [alia lectio πομπαιδουλά] Δάκοι προπεδουλά. Dioscorides, 4, 42, cited Z. 324. Z. thinks that dula = folium, b-l-at. Celtic *d* may certainly sometimes be = Lat. *f*, because we know that at the beginning of a word the latter often represents DH. The double *l* in duillen seems due to an original semi-vowel. Cf. φύλλον = φυλjον, fol-i-um. But what is the -en? A trace in Irish of the singulative forms of her Celtic sisters? 767. *Lité* (gl. pulmentum), Gael. *lit*, *lite*, is porridge. Cf. W. llith, "meal soaked in water." 768. *Uaithne* (gl. dipodium, if I rightly read this strangely contracted word, *ff = di f*, i. e. two f's) is a kind of rhyme in Irish verse, discussed in O'D. Gr. 418. Our scribe does not seem to have been very deep in Greek, ἀποδία being "two feet combined into one metre." 769. *Bidhgadh* (gl. pavementum). O'R.'s *biodgadh*, "stirring, rousing, startling;" Gael. *biodhgadh*, "a stirring up, sudden emotion."

770–777. *Cai* (gl. lamentum, "wailing, weeping") occurs in Corm., but I omitted to note where, also (spelt *coi*) in Lib. Hymn. (fol. 3, *a*, and p. 72, ed. Todd, where the mark of length is omitted). 772. *Cíd* (gl. centum), O. Ir. cét, Skr. çata-m, Zend çatĕ-m, ἑ-κατό-ν, Lat. centu-m, Goth. and O. H. G. themes, hunda, hunta. Here the Welsh and Bret., as usual, surpass the Irish and Cornish in retaining intact the combination nt; W. and Bret. cant, Corn. cans. In composition cét aspirates. Thus Conn cétchathach "100-battled Conn." 773. *Dá* (2), in O. Ir. inflected with dual-endings, nom. masc. and n. dáu for dvâv (originally dvâm?), gen. dá not

not aspirating = Skr. dvayòs? dat. dib(n)¹ (= Skr. dvâbhyâm?), acc. dá for dvâv. The fem. was nom. dí = dvai, Skr. dve, Lat. duae, gen. dá, dat. dib(n), acc. dí. In composition this numeral was dé, which is curious, as the Skr. is dvi, and Gr. δί, Zend and Lat. bi-, A. S. tvi. In O. W. dou masc. dui fem. 774. *Trí*, masc. and neut. (3) does not aspirate, having ended in the nom. originally in *s*; the O. Ir. forms for the fem. of this numeral are teoir, teora, gen. teora (n), dat. teoraib, acc. teora. Of these, teoir is obscure to me; teora, teora (n), seem to be formed from an extended theme. In O. Welsh, tri masc. teir fem, which last is the mod. *tair*. 775. *Ceithre* (4), I have never met in O. Ir., though cethri occurs in the Lib. Hymn. (a MS., I should say, of the eleventh century). The O. Ir. forms are cethir, masc. and neut. (= W. petuar, Skr. nom. masc. chatváras, neut. chatvári, Goth. fidvór), and ce-theora fem. Corn. (We may expect to find a cethoir = W. peteir, Skr. chatasra².) 776. *Cúig* (5), O. Ir. cóic = Lat. quinque, Skr. pánchan, Zend. panchan, πέντε, Æol. πέμπε, Goth. fimf, Eng. five. The non-occurrence of what may be called a trans-ported *n*³ after cóic before vowels and medials (except of course in the gen.) might be regarded as confirming Bopp's assumption that the final nasal in the Indo-Zend pancha-n is a later addition, were it not that the Welsh *pump* nasalises an initial medial, and should therefore, according to Aufrecht, Beitr. i. 105, have ended in *n*. However, this phenomenon seems quite modern (cf. pump gwraged, 5 women, not pump ngwraged, Z. 325, quoting the Mabinogion, iii. 101), and is probably owing to the influence of the *m*. 777. *Sé* (6), W. chwech = svees, originally KSVAKS, Zend. khsvas, the final *s* (= Lat. *x*, Gr. ξ, Skr. sh, Goth. hs) is retained in the ordinal ses-e-d,

W.

¹ As in the following examples: for *deib* indillib (according to two declensions), Z. 277; in *dib* inarib deac, Z. 312 (in 12 [2 + 10] hours); in an *dib* nairechtaib dermaraib (in their two vast assemblies), Adamnán's Vision, and with the *n* changed to *m* before *b*: Doluid Oengus con *dib* mbuidnib arachend dia marbud (O. went with two troops before him to slay him), Trip. Life of Patrick.

² A curious Celtic (Pictish?) form of this numeral is found in composition in the name *Cothir*-thiacus, given to S. Patrick, "because he served four houses (households?) of druids." It occurs in the following passage (Book of Armagh, 9, a, 2):—"Tirechán episcopus hec scripsit ex ore uel libro ultani episcopi cuius ipse alumpnus uel discipulus fuit. Inueni .iiii. nomina in libro scripta patricio apud ultanum episcopum conchuburnensium sanctus magonus qui est clarus [cf. "Apollini Granno *Mogorno*"] succetus qui est [deus belli—see the gloss on the Lib. Hymn. copy of Fiacc's Hymn, v. 2, where this name is spelt *succat*] patricius cothirthiacus quod seruiuit .iiii. domibus magorum et empsit illum unus ex eis cui nomen erat miliuc maccuboin magus." (See Lib. Hymn. ed. Todd, p. 27.)

³ Z. calls this a prosthetic *n*, which conveys an erroneous idea. Irish grammarians call it an eclipsing *n*. I have, I believe, proved that this *n* has almost always originally belonged to the termination of the word immediately preceding that to which it seems prefixed.

W. chweched. A remarkable form of this numeral is involved in mór-fes-er, seven persons, literally great-six-persons. I incline to the opinion that here, as in the forms fiur, fiar (= Skr. svasr), above quoted, the *f* was unaspirable, and stands for sv (cf. Ϝεξήκοντα, Ϝεξακάτιοι, Ϝέκτος, on the Tabulæ Heracl.)—that for this *f* we sometimes find *ph* written (cf. mo *phethar*-su for mo *fehar*-su, urphaisiu, gl. cancer, for urfaisiu); but that there is no good ground for regarding a form like the Gaelic *piuthair* as ancient.

778–788. *Cruithnecht*, gl. frumentum; gen. sing. cruithnechta, Z. 193; cruithnechtide, gl. ceritus, Z. 765. 779. *Eòrna* (gl. hordeum), barley: here, as in óe (= young), perhaps both *y* and *v* have been lost; and, if we assume the addition of the Celtic derivative syllable -arn-, we may compare Skr. and Zend yava, Gr. ζέα. 780. *Méirse* (gl. merciamentum), cf. Fr. merci, Lat. merces. 781. *Loch*, gl. stagnum = lacu-s, gen. sing.: ótha erích drommo .nit. englais tamlachtæ dub*locho*, Book of Armagh, 17 *a*, 2, a stem in *u*, gen. dual: dún dá *lacha* (Fled dúin nan géd, 80) = lac(u)ás? Loch = Lat. lacus, Bret. and Corn. lagen. 782. *Lemnacht*, gl. mulsum, i. e. wine mixed with honey (lemnach, gl. mulsum, Z. 777), is O'R.'s leamnachd, "sweet milk," *et sic hodie*. 783. *Medhg* (gl. serum, whey), W. maidd, O. Fr. mègue, Germ. matten. 784. *Im*, leg. *imm* (gl. butyrum), in Corm. imb (O. W. emmeni, Z. 130, W. ymenin, Bret. amann). Imm occurs in the nom. sing. with the masc. article in a MS. of T. C. D. (H. 3, 18, p. 433), cited in Petrie's Tara, 190: ni ba leghtha int*im*, "the butter was not dissolved;" gruth ┐ *imm*, pref. to Secundinus' hymn (Todd, Lib. Hymn. p. 32), "cheese and butter" (gruth = Eng. curd). Gen. sing.: Fecht naile luid rechtaire ríg bretan do chuinchid chisa grotha ┐ *imme* comuime pátricc, "at another time the steward of the King of the Britons came to Patrick's nurse to demand tribute of cheese and butter."—Trip. Life of Patrick. Dr. Siegfried has acutely suggested that the *b* of imb may be for *g* (cf. bó = Skr. gàus, broon [gl. molac, Book of Armagh, 10, *a*, 2] = Goth. qvairnus, bíu = Skr. jiva), and that the word may, accordingly, be connected with the Skr. anji, ointment, *ungere*, &c. Cf. Germ. *anke*, butter, and see Grimm, Gesch. d. d. Spr. ii. p. 1003. 785. *Unnimint* (gl. unguentum), seems derived from a Med. Lat. ungimentum, or perhaps from Eng. ointment. *Ór, Airged, Luaidhe, Sdan, Iaran*, have been noticed *supra* (606–610). 791. *Mitall*, from metallum. 792. *Luach lesa* is, says C., "the reward paid by a pupil to his tutor;" fer lesa, he says, is "a guardian." Cf. *leasughadh*, "education," O'R.; Gael. *leasachadh*, improving: *luach* seems a sister-form of ló-g, lua-g, gen. lóge, Z. 432, dat. luag, *supra*. The root seems LAV, found in Lat. Lav-crna, lû-cru-m, Skr. lô-ta (booty, *loot*), λη-ΐ-s, λάτρι-s (hired servant), Goth. lau-n, anda-launi, Curtius, G. E. i. 329. 793. *Bealach* (gl. alministrum)

alministrum) I cannot explain : alministrum is like almunicium (amice ?), Dief. Lat.-Germ. Gloss. : bealach generally means "a road," or "a mountain-pass," "defile." *Beoladh* is " anointing." 794. *Srebhan* (gl. nuchum, a membrane) : *srebhan na hinchinne*, "membrane inclosing the brain," C.; cf. sreibnaide, gl. membranaceus, Z. 765.

795-808. *Soilestar* (gl. gladiolum), sedge, flaggers, fleur de lis, O'R.'s *feleastar*, *feleastrom, seilistrom, sileastar, seilisdeir*, and *soileastar*! The last form comes nearest to the Lat. salicastrum, " bitter-sweet," and if this be the etymon, we should write *sailestar*: W. and Corn. elestren. 796. *Sgartach* (gl. propheticum) is "roaring out," according to O'D., Gael. *sgairteach* (clamosus), from *sgairt* (exclamatio). 797. *Fidhba* (gl. falcastrum) is the W. gwyddif, "a hedging-bill," O. W. gudif, gudhyf scalprum, from fid = wood, and the root BEN, BE, Z. 44. With gudif I should be inclined to compare a word *undimm*, which Z. gives as a gloss on lignismus (a woodman's axe, lignicisimus, Ducange). But in the facsimile, published by Vicomte H. de la Villemarqué, of the part of the MS. (Bibl. Bodl. 572, fo. 42) from which Z. purports to take this form, it stands distinctly *undimin*[1]. *Maith, Ole, Taithneamach, Geal, Dubh, Imdha, Beg, Mór*, have been noticed *supra* (from 659 to 673). 803. *Buidhe* (yellow), buide, gl. flavus, Z. 727, an adjectival ia-stem. Such stems were thus declined :—

	Masc.	Fem.	Neut.		Masc.	Fem.	Neut.
Sing. N.	núe	núe	núe (n)	Plur.	núi	núi	núe
G.	núi	núe	núi		núe (n)	núe (n)	núe (n)
D.	núu	núi	núu		núib	núib	núib
Ac.	núe (n)	núi (n)	núe (n)		núu	núi	núi (núe)
V.	núi	núe	núi		núu	núi	núi (núe)

And adjectival a-stems were thus declined :—

	Masc.	Fem.	Neut.		Masc.	Fem.	Neut.
Sing. N.	mall	mall	mall (n)	Plur.	maill	malla	malla
G.	maill	maille	maill		mall (n)	mall (n)	mall (n)
D.	maull	maill	maull		mallaib	mallaib	mallaib
A.	mall (n)	maill (n)	mall (n)		maullu	malla	malla
V.	maill	mall	maill		maullu	malla	malla

Adjectives agreeing with nouns in the dual are always put in the plural. 804. *Riabhach*

---

[1] In the "Archives des Missions Scientifiques et Littéraires," v° vol., facsimile No. IV., Paris, 1856.

ach (gl. fuscum, swarthy): etymologically obscure to me. 807. *Mesurdha* (gl. modicum), from mensura, with the usual loss of *n* before *s*. Cf. mesraigthe (gl. modestus), Z. 743. O. W. doguomisur (gl. geo, i. e. mensuro), Z. 1076. 808. *Robeg* (gl. minimum), from heg, by prefixing the intensive particle *ró*, ro = Lat. pro, Skr. pra.

810–816. *Lus* (gl. porrum) = leek, Corn. les, W. llysiau, "herbs." What (811) *inlemau* can be, I know not. 812. *Nem* (heaven) also once *nim*, in Z. ní artu ni *nim* ní domun ní muir ar noihbriathraib rolabrastar Crist assa chroich, "neither height nor heaven, nor depth nor sea surpasses[1] the holy words that Christ spoke from his cross," Z.; W. and Corn. nef, Bret. énv: cf. Slav. nebo, "heaven." *Nem* (gen. sing. nime, gen. pl. a choimdiu secht *nime!* "O Lord of seven heavens," Oingus)—is a fem. i-stem = nami, perhaps for nahi, originally a stem in *s*, like Skr. nabhas, Gr. νέφος—(*m* from *bh*, as in lám, from r. labh). Original stems in *s* have, with the exception of mí, mouth, gen. mfs, invariably ceased to be inflected according to the consonantal declension. Thus, clú, "glory" = Skr. çravas, κλέϝος. The following have gone over to the vocalic declension: geine, Lat. genus, γένος: lige, "bed" = λέχος: suide, "seat," Skr. sadas, ἕδος: corp, Lat. corpus: ucht, Lat. pectus. With the suffix *arn*—hiarn, iarann (Gaulish isarno-), Skr. ayas, Lat. aes. What the *s* in áis, óis ("age," which Ebel compares with Skr. âyus) can be, is not easy to say, *v. infra*, No. 1071. 814. *Rastail* (gl. rastrum), rastal in Corn., O'R.'s rásdal (a rake), perhaps from the Lat. rastrum; cf. W. rhasgl, O. W. rhascl, gl. sartum, Z. 1093. 815. *Foighi* (gl. epulum), leg. foighdhe? and cf. Z. 1059: leisee na pronn .i. fri fognam gréssich *foigde*, ad v. "pigri τῶν prandiorum, scil. in servitio continuo epuli," acc. sing. inn áis déed caras *foigdi* cáich, Z. 457; dat. sing. nírbommar utmuill oc *foigdi*, Z. 481. In the last two quotations foigde seems to have the meaning of the Gaelic *faighe, faighdhe*, "begging, a public begging from house to house;" "an asking of aid, in corn, clothing, or other stuff, usual with young persons newly married, or about to stock a farm."

817–825. *Snáithe* (a thread), snáthe, gl. filum, Z. 20; dat. sing. snáthiu, Z. 232; Corn. suod-en, W. ysnoden (vitta), *snood*, W. and Corn. noden, filum, Bret. neud, neuden. Cf. also O. W. notuid, "needle," Bret. nadoz. O. Ir. verbal forms, apparently connected with these words, are: co atomsnassar (gl. uti ego inserar), Z. 472; insnastis (gl. consuerunt exserere), Z. 452; nach nastad [leg. *nascad*: cf. ronaisc, Ir. Nennius, lxxii., Mod. Ir. nasgaim] in cretmech ⁊ na coméitged dó, "Let him not bind the believer, and let none accompany him," Z. 599.—1 Corinth. vii. 15. The connexion of these words with Skr. r. nah, Lat. nectere; νέ-ω, Lat. ne-o; νήθω, ΝΑΠΗ-, no

---

[1] Lit. [is] over.

no doubt exists, but is not easily made out. 819. *Srian*, a bridle = frēnum, W. ffrwyn, all perhaps connected with the Skr. root dhṛ tenere (see Pott, Zeits. i. 120). But whether srian, ffrwyn, are taken from the Lat., we shall not be able to decide till the nature of initial Welsh *ff* is more thoroughly understood. 820. *Adhastar* (halter), O'R.'s adhastair, cf. W. eddestr, eddestl, eddestlawr, a steed. 822. *Fothragadh* (gl. balneum), gen. sing. a conelæ *fothairethe*sin, Z. 893, "this kind of bath," dat. pl. fothairethib, Z. 238, an u-stem. 823. *Birur* (cress), Mod. Ir. *biolar*, W. berwr, berw, berwy, Corn. and Bret. beler. 825. *Iffern* (gl. Tartarus), *v. supra*.

826–832. *Infēd fosē* I cannot explain, unless we read *in fēd fosclaidh*, "the whistling (sibilus) of a chink;" *fēd* = W. chwyth, blast, chwythell, whistling: cf. *sétfethchaib*, flatibus, Z. 856. 827. *Ifearnadha* seems a neut. adj. plur., formed from iffern = infernum. 831. *At pill* (gl. pelleus, pileus, πῖλος, hat of felt? But indeed *pill* may be an hibernisation of the Latin pellis. *At* is of course from the English *hat* = Lat. stem *cas*-sid, from *cad*-tid (Lottner, Zeits. vii. 180), *v. supra*, *at* cluic. 832. *Ibrach*— if I read the word rightly—(gl. intimus) is obscure to me; the only word I know resembling it is *iubrach*, which C. and O'D. say is a wooden drinking-vessel, broad at bottom and narrow at top.

833–841. *Filidhrecht*, *v. supra*, No. 1. 834. *Geman* (or perhaps gemen, gemin), gl. didyma, δίδυμα, apparently from Lat. gĕminus, as W. gefell from gemellus. 835. *Adhbardacht*, πρόλημμα (afterwards glossing idioma), πρόλημμα, literally "what is taken beforehand," here apparently equivalent to "advantage" (πρόλημμα ποιεῖν τινι, "to give one an advantage"), a formation from the prep. *od* and the r. BAR, Skr. r. bhṛ (bhar), φέρ-ω, fer-o. 836. *Céirin*, κατάπλασμα, a plaster, probably from céir, wax; cf. W. cwyren, a cake of wax. 837. *Foircedal*, gl. dogma, O. Ir. forcetal, forcital (doctrina), gen. -til, a neut. a-stem[1]. The verb forchun, forchanim, præcipio, frequent in O. Ir., occurs in Z. 195, 440, fut. part. pass. forcanti (leg. forcanti), Z. 84; forcitlid, preceptor, Z. 85; forcitlaidecht (magisterium), Z. 771. The root can (Skr. çans, Lat. can-ere, cens-ere, Goth. han-a, καν-άζω), also occurs in doarchet, doairchet, tairchet, "it was predicted," Z. 468; doaurchanim (gl. sagio), Z. 440; foacanim (gl. succino), Z. 440; dorencanas, perspexit, Z. 856; isdo fordoncain, Z. 1060, leg. ised do fordoncain, "this is what it teaches us." The root in question reduplicates: furdubecchna (-ec-ch'n-a), gl. qui vos commonefaciat), Z. 496: tairchechuin, gl. predixit, tairchechnatar predixerunt.
ibid.;

---

[1] *For* (the Gaulish ver-, as *foirge* is to be compared with *Vergivios*) has been compared with Skr. upari (Ebel, Beitr. i. 309). *Sed quære*, for Celtic *v* never (so far as I know) is = Skr. *p*. And as Gaulish exhibits no tendency to eject *p*, the theory that *ver* arose from *vari* [u(p)ari] is untenable.

ibid.; rochachain, cecinit, Leb. na Cert, 136; doairreechnatar .i. rotairnngestar, Brehon Laws, O'D.[1] 838. *Mullach tighe* (gl. doma), mullach (gl. culmen, *infra,* gl. vertici, Gildas' Lorica), generally means top, summit, head. Here "roof," a meaning which doma has in Eccl. Latin. 839. *Forsgath no ingar* (gl. enigma). I can throw no light on these Ir. words (which I have never met elsewhere), unless we read the first forsgáth, and connect it with sgáth = shade, shadow, αἴνιγμα being a dark saying. Cf. furastar (= furasctar?), gl. fuscetur, Z. 472. The Gael. iongarach is "purulent." 840. *Crismal* (gl. chrisma, anointing, unction), a hybrid from Eccl. Lat. chrisma, or perhaps Gr. χρῖσμα. 841. *Monadh* (νόμισμα, a coin), from Lat. moneta, generally means "money," whence W. mwnai.

842–850. *Soiphist* (sophisma) is certainly a foreign word, and perhaps involves a blunder. 847. *Nescoid* (gl. ἀπόστημα = imposthume, abscess) is nescoit in Corm. Its etymology is obscure to me. 844. *Croindtille,* v. *supra,* No. 651. 845. *Coindealbthadh* (gl. anathema), cursing with bell, book, and *candle.* 846. *Tadhbais* (gl. phantasma) is O'R.'s tadhbhas, "a spectre." Taidbsiu, a stem in tián (= dn-ati-*bhás*-tiän?) occurs in Z. 581, 196, 233, 456, 1016, with the meanings of manifestation, proof.

[1] Other reduplicating roots in O. Ir. are BA (die), bebais, Félire, 23rd April: rombebe, Z. 496 (where several instances are collected): beba Fiacc, 12. BAR (bear, Skr. bhṛ) dubbert, "he gave," Book of Armagh, 18 *b,* 1 : atróport [*p* for *bb*] flaith 7 aithech inso huile itosuch iar tabuirt baithis dúaib, "prince and peasant granted all this immediately after the administration of baptism to them," *ibid.,* 17 *a,* 2. BU (BHAV), "be :" is airi doroign dia geinti hore nár'*babe* la Iudeiu creitem, "for this cause it is that God chose the Gentiles, because the Jews had not faith" (ad v. "quia non fuit apud Judæos fides," Z. 602): robbu (fuit), Z. 481, is, according to Lottner, an imperfect, and is for ro-bv-u, not (as one would think at first) for a Skr. prababhúva. CANG, "go :" cechaing (.i. roching) Félire: dacheachaing, "he advanced," Fled d. n. góed 66. CAR, "love," conchechrat "they will love," Z. 495 (for conchecharfat). CLU, "hear," rotchechladar, "hears thee," Z. 496. CLUS, "hear :" cechluista .i. rochluinfithea, O'D. DÁ, "give," adcho-*dad*-ossa, Z. 852; adcotedae [ad-cont-*did*-ae], "he granted," Book of Armagh, 18 *a,* 1: cf. laprai .... ἀλλανοιτακος ϛεδε ματριβο ναμανσικαβο βρατουεϛ, in the Nismes inscription (*Rev. Archéol.* 1858, p. 44), translated by Professor Siegfried, "Iartai .... Ilanoitacus [Illanoitacis *filius*"?] dedit Matribus Nemausicis ex imperio [ipsarum]." GÁ, "go :" hit hé magistir don*gegat* inhi (leg. indi) asindisset a tola feisne doib, Z. 1057, "these are the masters to whom they will go, those who preach their own wishes to them." GAN, v. *supra,* No. 290, note 1. GES, "beseech :" gigestesi dia linn ara fulsam ar fochidi, Z. 496, "Ye used to beseech God that we might endure our tribulations." GRANN, "follow :" adroigegrannatar, "they were persecuted," Z. 496 (cf. ingrented, persecutor, Z. 265 ; ingrimmim ingraimmaim [in-grann-man-bi] persecutioni, Z. 268 ; ingramman, ingremmen, persecutiones, Z. 266, 463). STÁ, "stand :" sesaimm = ἴστημι for σίστημι, Skr. tisluthâmi (Zend hiçtâmi). r. sthâ, Lat. si-st o. Bopp, Gloss. 387. Whence is sinsair .i. rosaidestar, Brog. 1 ?

proof. The related verb is also of frequent occurrence: doadbat, tadbat, demonstrat, Z. 852, 360, for tadbad-d; doadbadar, taidbadar, demonstratur, *ibid.*; *taidbdid* form doscire friss, Z. 458, "show your love to him;" *doaidbdetar* fisi doib, "visions are revealed to them," Z. 521; an donaidbdem, "when we shall demonstrate," Z. 670; from these forms it would seem that the root was B-D. The D, however, may represent a later formation (cf. φα-ί-Οω, and φά-ος); perhaps the root DNA agglutinated. 847. *Coimpert* (σπέρμα, seed, semen genitale, offspring), obviously a compound of co-imb-bert (r. bar, Skr. bhṛ), the *bb* becoming *p*, as in idpart, oblatio, &c. The genitive singular of coimpert, in the sense of "conception," occurs in the following passage from the Wanderings of the Curach of Maelduin, cited and translated in Dr. Petrie's Round Towers, 378: gabais Ailell a laimh lais 7 dodatrascair, 7 dogni coibligi fria 7 asbert an caillech fris: "ni segda," ol si, "ar comrue, ar is aimsir *comperta* dam." 848. *Adhbardacht*, and—849. *Adhbar* have been already noticed. 850. *Suidheocan*, leg. suidhechan (a seat, bench), an extended form of suide (seat), Z. 60, 140.

851–855. *Cro caerach* (gl. ovile, sheepfold), as to *cro*, v. *supra*; caerach, leg. cáerach, gen. pl. of cáera, a e-stem = cáirax, v. *supra*, No. 13: cf. cáirchuide, ovinus, Z. 37, 235, and the Gaulish tribe-name, Caeracates, Caerosi. This curious word may, perhaps, be connected with κριός. 852. *Proisté* (gl. monile, vel munile, a necklace) is said by C. to mean "a goad, a spike," which agrees well with the Cornish gloss on monile: scil. dele, leg. delch = Ir. delg spina. Proiste is probably taken from the Fr. *broche*, and this, according to Diez (E. W. 71), from Lat. brocchus, broccus, a projecting tooth. 853. *Lebhar aithffrind*, a missal, lit. liber offerendæ: aithtfrind, leg. aiffrind, gen. of aiffrend, now aifrin, from the Lat. offerenda, with change of declension and gender, as scribent, scribend, from scribenda, and legend, gen. -ind, from legenda, Z. 462. 854. *Gredháil*, gl. gredale, i. e. gradale, Eng. grail, "that book which containeth all that was to be sung by the quire at high mass; the tracts, sequences, hallelujahs; the creed, offertory, trisagium; as also the office for sprinkling the holy water," Burn, Eccl. Law, ii. 303. 855. *Troibel*, gl. trobiale, i. e. troperium? "the book which containeth the sequences, which were devotions used in the church after reading the epistle," *ibid.* iii. 799.

856–860. *Stuidis* (gl. lectório, leg. lectoriale), a deriv. from the base of Lat. studium, studeo, here, perhaps, having the meaning of the Eng. "lectureship." 857. *Lámtuagh* (gl. manuale), lit. hand-axe or hand-bow, *tuagh* (axe), O'R., tuag nime "arcus coeli," Z. 28. 858. *Leabaid in duim allta* (gl. cubile), lit. bed of the wild ox, *daim*, gen. sing. of dam, ox; dat. sing. daum, Z. 250; n. pl. ar is bés leosom in *daim* do thúarcuin, "for with

with them there is a custom for the oxen to thresh," Z. 853. *Dam* would also appear to mean a deer: cf. the adj. damde, gl. cervinus, Z. 764; but perhaps this is from the Lat. dāma (fallow-deer), and we should read dámde. I know not if W. dafad, pl. defeid, sheep, dafates, a flock of sheep, can be connected with *dam*. 859. *Corporas*, gl. corporale. I cannot explain. 860. *Muir* = Gaulish mŏri, W. and Corn. mor, Lat. māre, which I cannot think Bopp is right in comparing with Skr. vāri, water (Ir. fual?). Rather hold with Curtius (Zeits. i. 33) in referring it to the Skr. root mr̥ (mar), "welche in der bedeutung sterben am geläutigsten, in μαραίνω und dem mit e weiter gebildeten marceo die allgemeinere bedeutung des welkens hat (vgl. Skr. mr̥iṇ). In Skr. maru, die wueste, so wie in marut, wind, tritt noch bestimmter der begriff des verwuestens hervor; mare bezeichnete demnach das meer als das unfruchtbare, als den tod der vegetation, wie nach der gangbaren erklaerungsweise ἀτρύγετος." Curtius also compares Ἀμφί-μαρο-ς, Lith. mar-ios, Goth. mar-ei. Muir in Z. is a fem. (or neut.?) i-stem (gen. s. mora, Z. 1000), as appears from the termination of the adj. agreeing with its nom. pl. in Mora són nítat lora [leg. lóra] sidi leu, which Z. (1000) correctly translates maria hic, non sunt sufficientia ipsa eis. But note here, if *muir* be fem., the anomaly of an i-stem passing over to the â-declension in the nom. pl.

861-865. *Maindsér* (gl. praesepe) is of course from the Eng. manger. 862. *Uinneamain* (gl. cepe, onion), Gael. *uinnean*, W. *wynwyn-in*. These forms remind one of the Lat. únio, whence Fr. oignon, &c., are said to be taken. Perhaps the name of the vegetable is originally Gaulish (oinnio?), which the Romans may have assimilated to their únio, "a single large pearl." The word foltchep is, I may observe, glossed by barr *uindiuin* (leg. uinniuin) in H. 3, 18 (MS., T. C. D.), p. 526. 863. *Lin uisci* (gl. rete), fishing-net, water-net, lit. "net of [the] water:" lin, gl. retis, Z. 25 : ished insin al*linn* ingaib diabul peccatores (gl. laqueum diaboli), Z. 1052, "this is the net in which the devil takes sinners." 864. *Sgaraid* (gl. gausape), O'R.'s sġoráid, scároid, table-cloth. 865. *Mil mór*, v. *supra*, No. 428.

866-870. *Machaire* (gl. tempe, i. e. feld, anger, awe [aue], Dief.), a field, plain :—

 Adaig dúnn uili mallei
 Immachaire (leg. machairiu ?) háue Carpri.—Corm. Ecces, vv. 119, 120.

gen. sing. fo diamraib in *macairi* moir minscothaigsin; *Cogad Gaedil re Gallaib* (ed. Todd, 76), a masc. ia-stem: Gael. *machair*, gen. macharach, s. f. machaire bán, is still a living expression for a grass-field : W. magwyr, " wall, enclosure, field," Bret. móger, "wall" = Lat. măcēria, " wall, enclosure." 867. *Urlabradh* (gl. locutio), Corn. lauar, W. llafar. Another form of this word is erlabra, which occurs in Lib. Hymn. (pref. to

the

the Magnificat;): ocus is inti doratad *erlabra* do Zachar[1] ("and it was there that speech was given to Zacharias"), and, apparently with a transitive meaning. is an infin. in Patrick's noble hymn: cluas Dé dom' éstecht, briathar Dé dom' *erlabrai* lám Dé domm' imndegail "God's ear to hear me, God's word to plead for me (*erlabraidhe* advocate, O'R.), God's hand to protect me." 868. *Aicecht* (gl. lectio), I have never met elsewhere. It seems to occur in the "*Uraicecht* nan Eiges," O'D. Gram. p. lv., but this is, perhaps, a corruption of the Lat. praeceptum. 869. *Acra* (gl. actio), is a lawsuit, pleading, perhaps from the prep. ad, aith, and GAR; cf. adgaur, gl. consentio, i. e. addico, Z. 987, adobragart, "he addressed you," Z. 838. 870. *Guidhe* (gl. oratio), in Z. guide is sometimes a fem. ia-stem; tri *guidi* acc. sing. Z. 258: and sometimes masc. or neut.; oc du *guidiu*-siu a dæ, "in supplicating thee, O God," Z. 346. The verb guidim occurs at pp. 55, 993, *guidimse* Dia nerutsa[2] (I pray God for thee), guidimm vel adjuro (gl. testor), Z. 1050, gl. 21; nosnguid som "he asks them," Z. 441. Can this be connected with gáid in the gloss con dartin do ar *rogáid* dom, Z. 450, "that I should give him what he asked of me," rogad (rogavi): 1st pers. plur. pret. act. rogadammar, Z. 442, 443; 3rd plur. in Fiacc's Hymn, 9:—

> *Gadatar* co tissad in noeb, aran imthised lethu
> Aru tiutarrad o chlóen tuatha herenn do bethu.
>
> They besought that the saint should come, that he should journey far and wide,
> That he should turn the tribes of Ireland from evil unto life;

for the latter forms seem referable to the Skr. r. gad, to speak, of which, however, Böhtlingk and Roth give no Vedic examples. The W. gweddi seems connected with the Skr. r. vad.

871–875. *Cumtach* (gl. constructio) is generally used in the spiritual sense of edificatio in Z. (*cumtach ñecolso*, Z. 229), sometimes in that of structure, and glosses fabrateria, Z. 777[3]. I agree with Z. in regarding the word as a compound, cum-tach; the *cum* being a frequent form of the prep. con, and tach (= taca), being radically connected

---

[1] In the Leabhar Breacc this passage runs: ocus is indte thucad *hirrlabra* do Zach.

[2] Observe the so-called prosthetic *n* here: it is nothing but the *n* of the old accusative termination, dévan.

[3] In the Book of Armagh: duhbert Pátricc *cumtach* du Fiacc idon clocc ⁊ menstir ⁊ bachall ⁊ poolire, i. e. Patrick gave a *cumtach* to Fiacc [containing] to wit, a bell and a *menstir* and a crozier and a booksatchel. This cumtach, a neut. a-stem, seems a deriv. from the root of cum-main, box, or basket, Lib. Hymn. 3 a, cuimin, "a little chest or box," O'R. O'D. Gram. 437, derives it "from the verb comhad or coimead [O. Ir. *coimet* arfuacht, "a defence against cold," Corm. cited O'D. 294] to keep or preserve."

nected with tech (house): cf. Foirtchernn (Book of Armagh, 16 a, 2) = Ver-*tig*-erna-s, Vortigern, cuimtgim (gl. architector, gl. construo), Z. 439, comrótgatar, Z. 843. Is this root TAK, in the Vedic *tak*-ma-s, "child," with which Curtius connects τέκ-ος, τόκ-ος, τέχ-νη, τεῖχ-ος, τοῖχ-ος, τύκ-ος, and of which Skr. r. taksh, to fabricate (whence takshan = τέκτων¹), seems an intensive. But indeed there are three roots, T-G, T-GH, T-K, the relations of which I am unable to settle. 872. *Remthechtas* (gl. prepositio), see Z. 750; rem, a form of ren (before), and *techtas*, an abstract from techt, venire (cf. W. taith, Gaul. Tecto-sagi, "march-sustaining:" and Skr. and Zend r. tanch, ire). Remthechtas also meant anteposition: alaaili diib hí *remthechtas*; alaili dam it coitchena eter *remthechtas* et tiarmoracht, "some of them are in anteposition; others also are common between anteposition and postposition," Z. 985. As an infinitive, the word occurs in Patrick's Hymn: Intech dé dom remthechtas, "God's way to come before me." Cf. tairm-*thechtas* (transgressio), Z. 750. 873. *Comfocul* (gl. conjunctio), com + focul: focul dictio, Z. 968, taken from the Lat. vocabulum (focbhul, foevul), which would account for the non-aspiration of the c. Focul occurs in the nom. of the sing., dual, and plural in the following passage, from a fragment of Cormac's Glossary, preserved in the Book of Leinster: Trefocla .i. trifoccuil bite ind .i. dáfoccul dimolud dobrith forculu indimderggtha dofarci antress (leg. in tress) foccul .i. foccul indimdergtha ┐ aire; "*Trefocla*, i. e. three words that are in it, i. e. two words of praise it gives behind the reproach, which makes the third word, i. e. a word of reproach and satire." From which curious definition it would seem that *trefocla* was a composition apparently satirical, but really laudatory. 874. *Interiacht*, and— 875. *Comparáid*, from the Latin. (The O. Ir. words for preposition, conjunction, interjection, and comparison, were remsuidigud, comaccomal, interiecht, and condelgg, Z. 982.)

876–880. *Inntindeach*, like—880. *Coissegradh*, a hybrid from the Latin. 877. *Baramail* (gl. opinio), baramhuil, O'R., Gael. *barail*, an opinion, conjecture, supposition, apparently a compound of samail, but what *bar* stands for I cannot conjecture. 878. *Togha* (gl. electio), O. Ir. togu, a stem in *d* (or *t*?) = du-vagн-ad (or -at?): is dichéin immunr'ordad condan maicc togu, lit. it is long ago we were ordained that we should be sons of election, Z. 475: Gael. *tughadh*. 879. *Dlighedh* (gl. ratio), v. *supra*. 880. *Coissegradh* (gl. consecratio), like W. cysegriad, a hybrid from the Latin consecro (the *n* being lost before *s*, as usual), O. Ir. coisecrad: Asbert fiacc frisinaingel nandrigad

¹ Cf. the Gaulish con-*tex*-to-s (in the inscription of Autun), and perhaps O. Ir. Tassach (St. Patrick's artificer) = Tax-aca-s.

drigad contísed patrice dothoorund a luie leis ⁊ dia *choisecrad* ⁊ combed húad nuggabad [gg, ⁊⁊ = ng, Z. 282] aloce Dulluid iarsuidiu patrice cufíace ⁊ durind aloce les ⁊ cutsecar [leg. cu-t-secar], "Fiace said to the angel that he would not go till Patrick came to measure his place with him, and to consecrate it, and so that it might be from him he should receive his place. Patrick afterwards went to Fiace, and measured his place with him, and consecrated it," Book of Armagh, 18 *b.* 1.

881–885. *Cumdach* (gl. ornatio)—so O'R. *cúmhdach,* "an ouch, an ornament;" in Z. 1046, *cumtach* bas uisse fri hiriss (gl. cum verecundia et sobrietate *ornantes* se), "an adornment that is fitting to faith." 882. *Mughsaine* (gl. famulatio, service, servitude), from *mugh,* O. Ir. mug, gen. moga, a masc. u-stem (= Goth. magus), and *saine,* which termination, forming abstract substantives from other substantives, occurs twice in Z. 739, viz., in coccilsine (gl. societas, céle, socius), and in faithsini (gl. prophetiæ, fáith, propheta). The termination is probably = -ss-an-ia, st-an-ia. 883. *Adhalltras* (gl. fornicacio), adhaltras, Z. 750, a hybrid from adulter. 884. *Comsólás no comairle* (gl. consolatio), "consolation or counsel:" comsólás, sólás, from Lat. sólátium, which the Irish of old probably pronounced sólátsium[1]. (N.B.—I doubt if this be a different word from solás, happiness, the opposite of dolás, grief, which latter may either be derived from dolere, or have been produced on the erroneous hypothesis that the first syllable of sólas was the well-known particle of quality): *comairle,* in putting down which the glossarist evidently took consolatio for consultatio, occurs in Z. acc. sing. tre dag*comairli,* Z. 826, nom. pl. ni rubtar gáitha tor *comairli,* Z. 481, "your counsels were not wise," whence the word appears to be a fem. iá-stem. The acc. sing. of the airle in com-airle occurs in the following gloss (Z. 1060): arna érbarthar ochretsit nintá *airli* armban, ad v. "ne dicatur ex quo crediderunt non-est-nobis animus nostrarum mulierum," and the nom. sing. (compounded with dag, "good") in "ban buidich, is sí ar dag*airle,*" Z. 1051, where I suspect Z. should have read arndagairle. Comairlle (with two l's), occurs in Z. 51, and he explains it by voluntas. I have never found the word with this meaning: but if Z. be correct, we might, perhaps, regard it as = com-are-valiá, and recognise therein (with Dr. Siegfried) the Skr. r. vr (ex vak), to choose, *wale, will,* velle, cf. W. ewyll (du-valya), to will, Bret. ioul, Ir. tol (du-valá). Cf. airlam (paratus, promtus), Z. 733 : irlithe (obediens), Z. 766 : irladigur (obedio), Z. 839. 885. *Ainmneachadh* (gl. nominatio), a deriv. from ainm, a name, declined *infra,* No. 991.

886–890.

---

[1] *C* before *i,* in Latin words, was probably also pronounced *ts :* cf. comirsire, Z. 233 = commerc-i-ari, kommerziren.

886–890. *Tighernas* (gl. dominatio), W. teyrnas, "kingdom," from tigerne, as to which *v. supra*. 887. *Geinemain* (gl. generatio), from r. GAN, "to produce," as to which *v. supra*, Gael. *gineamhuinn*; cf. Vedic janiman, janman, "birth." 888. *Certachadh* (gl. correctio), Gael. *ceartachadh* (W. ceryddu, corrigere, seems for cerythu, and connected with correctus); cf. Lat. certus. The element cert enters into the composition of many words in O. Ir. Thus, cocert (mendatio), cocart, corrige, cocarti, emendandum, Z. xiv.; conaicertus (emendavi), foceirt deponit, &c. 889. *Oibriugudh* (gl. operatio), from *obair* (in Corm. opair, gen. *oibre*, a fem. i-stem = from Lat. opera (not opus, Skr. apas); cf. oipred, Z. 80, 476, gen. oipretho, Z. 766: dat. (sensu obsceno) oc ind oipred, Z. 593, acc. amal rongab comadnacul dúun ata comeisséirge act rocretem *oipred da̅*, Z. 1040, gl. 15, "as we have co-burial there is co-resurrection, if we believe in the working of God." 890. *Reidhe* (gl. planatio), leg. *réidhe*, levelling, smoothening, from *réidh*, "plain, level, smooth," which occurs in Z. 1067 (with the meaning of "easy"), is reid foglaim in besgnai, "easy is the learning of morality;" and in Colman's Hymn, v. 33:—

    Amal foedes in aingel tarslace Petrum a slabreid
    Doroiter[1] dun diar fortacht, rop *reid* remunn cech namreid.

    As He sent the angel that delivered Peter from his chain,
    Let him be sent to us to help us, let everything unsmooth be smooth before us.

Cf. Bret. *reiz*, "aisé, facile."

891–896. *Cestugadh* (gl. castigatio), W. cystwyad, is, I suspect, a foreign word, as certainly is—892. *Compantus* (gl. associatio), from compagau-u-s; cf. however, O'R.'s *céasnugadh*, which suggests a connexion with césad (W. cystudd?), rocéss, pertulit, passus est, Z. 434. 893. *Guidhe* (gl. supplicatio), *r. supra*. 894. *Taisbenadh* (gl. monstratio), Gael. *taisbeanadh*, "act of revealing, showing, or disclosing," O. Ir. taispenad: ó ruscaith tra do Sechnall in moludsa do dénam, luid dia *taispenad* do patraic, i. e. "now when Sechnall had finished making this hymn [lit. this praise] he went to show it to Patrick" (Pref. to Secundinus' Hymn, cited from Leabar Breace, by Dr. Todd, Lib. Hymn. 31); gen. sing. ó dochotar imorro iccun *taispenta* ind immnin do griguir, "when, however, they had done showing [lit. come into the end of showing] the hymn to Gregory" (Lib. Hymn. pref. to Altus Prositor). Taispenad for taipsenad (taid-bs-ten-ad) *v. supra*, No. 846. 895. *Foillsiugudh* (gl. annunciatio), rather manifestatio: this word occurs, spelt foilsigud, in Z. 16, the gen. sing. foilsichtho,

---

[1] Read dorfoiter, i. e. do-ro-foid-ther.

sichtho, Z. 85, foilsigthe, 255, and is derived from follus, Z. 664, folus, Z. 748, 751, "plain," "manifest." *Soillsiughadh* is, perhaps, a sister-form (soillse, light, Z. 51, 257).

896-900. *Comparaid* (gl. collatio, cf. comparit, Z. 973, W. cymharu, to compare), and—897. *Comaineachadh* (gl. communicatio), both appear foreign words; compare, however, with the latter comnactar: aní nad *comnactar* dóini trian cene, "that which human beings do not comprehend (or conceive of) by their understanding," Z. 447, 702: comain occurs in Cormac, and also in Z. 1050, gl. 18, with the sense of "obligation," "debt." Comman occurs in Fiacc's Hymn, v. 27, with the meaning of "communion," "the Lord's Supper:"—

> Anais tassach di[a]áis, intan dobert *comman* dó :
> Asbert moniefed[1] pátricc : bríathar tassaig nirbu gó[2].
>
> Tassach remained after him, when he had administered the communion to him :
> He said that Patrick would come : Tassach's word was not false.

The cognate W. words are cymyn, "bequest, testament," cymanfa, "congregation" (m = mm). Cf. Lat. communis from commoinis, Goth. gamains, O., M. and N. H. G. gemein. 898. *Timthirecht* (gl. ministratio), cf. *timthirigh*, *supra*, occurs in Z. 260: *timtherecht* cacha dúlo "servitus omnis creaturæ," and also spelt timthirect, timthrecht, at pp. 771, 237, timdirecht (acc. sing.), p. 777 (do-imu-tir-echt). The root seems TAR, Skr. tṛ, to go; compare ἀμφίπολος and Skr. parichara, "servant," lit. "one who goes about." 899. *Dénamh* (gl. procuratio), O. Ir. dénom, dénum, gen. sing. dénmo, Z. 733, means "a doing," "to do" (cf. dénmusach, gl. factor, *infra*), a stem in *u*. Cf. denim (facio), Z. 430; dene (fac), Z. 457; dened (facite), Z. 458 (leg. dénim, déne, dénid); dénti (faciendum), Z. 473; denmid, gen. denmada (gl. factoris), Z. 766. 890. *Doilbtiugud* (gl. fictio), from delb, as to which *v. supra*.

901-906. *Eolas* (peritia), leg. *eólas?* et *v. supra*. 902. *Moladh* (gl. adulatio) laus, cf. molor (I praise), Z. 444; Bret. meulet laudatus, Z. 107, W. *mawl*. The etymon may be MAGALA, cf. μεγάλον, and the Gaul. Magalus, Magalius, Glück, 50, as móidim, another verb for I praise, is to be compared with Gaulish Mogit-marus. Molad occurs in Z. 989: Is bées donaib dagforcitlidib *molad* in gni innanétside ara carat an rochluinetar, "it is a custom of [lit. "to"] the good teachers to praise the intelligence of the hearers,

[1] Gloss: .i. cosabull iterum, "that is to Sabull [Saul, in the county of Down, lit. "barn"] again." Note the interesting form mo-n-iefed wherein mo, also spelt mu, is a verbal prefix, only occurring four times in Z. See Z. 419. Tassach was Patrick's artificer, and Bishop of Rúith-Choloptha, now Raholp.

[2] Gloss: quia uenit patricius iterum co sabull.

hearers, in order that they may like what they hear:" is huisse a *molath* (gl. laudandus), dat. sing. molud, *supra*, No. 873, Z. 459. 903. *Comtromugud* (gl. coæquatio), leg. comtrummugud, equalization, balancing, lit. "making-equally-heavy," from trumm, tromm, W. trwm (nipsa *tróm*—leg. trom̄—for nech, gl. nulli onerosus fui, Z. 585); *tromm* occurs subsequently in composition: tromchride (gl. jecur), Z. 825, i. e. heavy-heart; cf. étrumma, "non gravia," Z. 252; etrumme "dissimilis," Z. 843; cutrummus, similitudo, Z. 751; hi cutrumus, ad instar, Z. 451; cutrummi, similes, Z. 843; fortrumme, opportunitas, Z. 843. 904. *Cosmhailius* (gl. simulatio), cosmilius in Z. (cf. ecsamlus, diversitas, Z. 751, 851), from the adj. cosmail (W. cyfal, cyhafal), i. e. co-samail con-samali-s, the *simplex* of which Bopp has justly compared with Lat. similis (an i-stem, as in Irish), to which we may add W. hafal, Gr. ὁμαλός (an o-stem); cf. also Skr. sama, Goth. sama, Eng. same, Slav. samŭ. Observe in—905. *Egcosmailius* (gl. dissimulatio) an example of the mod. Ir. practice of writing the so-called eclipsing letter before the original tenuis. It need hardly be said that all the phenomena of eclipsis (amongst which I by no means count the apparent change of *s* into *t*) are explicable by reference to the medializing influence of *n* on *c*, *p*, *t*, and *f*, and to the tendency of *b*, *d*, and *g*, respectively, to become assimilated to a preceding *m*, *n*, and *ng*. *Egcosmailius*, however, seems merely an example of the ordinary sinking of the O. Ir. tenuis to the corresponding medial.

906-910. *Urlamas* (gl. sequestratio, properly "a depositing of money, &c., in dispute") is wildly guessed at by O'R. "possession, supreme power and authority; captivity," but is correctly explained by C. (who spells the word *urlámas*) "the placing anything in the custody of a person; as in the laws *urlámas coitcenn* means the placing of contested property in the hands of an indifferent custodian, until its true owner is defined by law." Cf. irlam (paratus), Z. 252; erlam, Z. 7; compar. erlamu, Z. 284. 907. *Faidiugud* (gl. prolongatio), from fot, length, *v. supra*. 908. *Lórgním* is exactly satis-factio. With lór, lour, laur, Z. 123, 309, 607, 889, 1000 (enough), cf. W. llawer multus, multitudo, Z. 123. Hence O. Ir. loure, sufficientia, and Z. 30, compares Lauro, Lauriacum, Laurentius. *Gním*, gen. gnímo, is of frequent occurrence in Z., and is connected with the root of do-gním, facio (= du-genáiu?). 909. *Atheumiledh* (gl. remuneratio) seems from aith = ati (Gaulish *ate*), which stands for the Lat. re-, and *cumal* (a fem. â-stem), said to mean the value of 3 cows, which occurs twice in the following passage: digéni cummen cétaig ríthæ friéladach m[acc]maile odræ tigerne cremthinnæ arech[1] .n. donn ríthæ intechsin fricolmán. nam bretan archumil .n. arggit[2] Luid in
*chumals*in

---

[1] Observe the transported *n* of the acc. sing. of ech, viz. ech (ṅ).

[2] Observe the transported *n* of the acc. sing. of cumal, viz. cumil (ṅ). The passage above quoted is

chumalsin dufurlóg ochtir achid: "Cummen made a mantle, *which* was given to Éladach, son of Máel Odra, lord of Cremthinne, for a brown horse. This horse was given to Colmán of the Britons for a *cumal* of silver. This *cumal* went in addition to the price of Ochter Achid" (Book of Armagh, 17 *b*). 910. *Dísliugudh* (gl. deductio), if I read the word aright, seems literally "a leading away from the road, or path," di-slig-ud, *v.* slige, *supra*, and cf. *dísligeach*, "deviating," O'R., Gael. *dísleach*, "straggling."

911–916. *Cengal* (gl. compilatio), *v. supra*, No. 147. 912. *Eitelladh* (gl. revolutio, leg. evolatio?) I have never met elsewhere. O'R. has *cataladh*, a flight, *citeallach*, "flying, bouncing," Gaelic, *itealaich*. 913. *Comairemh* (gl. computatio), Gael. comáireamh, apparently a weakened form of comáram, W. cyfrif numeratio, from áram, numerus, W. cirif, rhif, A. Sax. rím, gerím (cf. rhyme?), see Z. 912. 914. *Bennacht* (gl. benedictio), O. Ir. benedact, bendacht, W. bendithio, "to bless." 915. *Mallacht* (gl. maledictio), O. Ir. maldacht, maldact, gen. maldachtan, acc. maldactin, Z. 584, from maledictio, Z. 270, W. melldith (*ct* always becoming *th* in Welsh, *cht* in Irish). 916 *Lamacean*, leg. *lámagán*, which, according to O'R., means "groping," Gaelic. *lámhagan*, "handling."

917–921. *Ailginecht* (gl. mitigatio), connected with O'R.'s *ailghean*, soft, smooth, kindly; álgenaigim, algenigim (gl. lento, gl. tardo), Z. 431. 918. *Comma* (gl. talliatio); there is probably some blunder here (leg. *comain*, remuneratio?). I have never met "comma" elsewhere. 919. *Colund* (gl. caro), in Z. 740, colinn, gen. colno, colna, perhaps connected with kravya, κρέας, caro, O. H. G. hréo, gen. hréwes, cadaver. Cf. the W. calaned, "carcasses;" perhaps, also, calon, "heart." 920. *Laidire* (gl. fortitudo), deriv. from *láidir* (fortis), of which the compar. occurs *infra*. 921. *Imad* (gl. multitudo), O'R.'s *iomad*, for immad, imbad, imbed, gl. ops, copia, Z. 75 (cf. Ambitui), a deriv. from imb = Gaulish ambi = Skr. abhi, Gr. ἀμφί, Lat. amb-, N. H. G. um, Eng. um-, in Fuller's umstroke, circumference.

922–926. *Méid* (gl. magnitudo), in Z. méit = W. *maint*, Corn. myns, a fem. i-stem = maganti? 923. *Loighedh* (gl parvitudo), *laget*, Leab. Breacc, cited Lib. Hymn. ed. Todd, 30, W. lleiad (diminution); cf. laigiu minor, Z. 283. W. llai (= ἐλάσσων for ἐλαχίων, and levior, Skr. laghíyâns), superl. lugimem, Z. 1128, W. lleiaf. 924. *Teirce* (gl. raritudo), from teirc, gl. rarus, *supra* = duseirg; cf. scirg-lige, "bed of consumption,"

difficult. *Rithæ* seems the 3rd sing. imperf. pass. of an irregular verb, the 3rd plur. imperat. act. of which occurs in Z. 238: ni *riat* na dánu diadi aran indeb domunde (gl. non turpe lucrum sectantes, sint diaconi), "let them not give the divine gifts for worldly advantage," 3rd pl. pret. pass. ro-*ratha*, Fiacc, 25. Cf. the Cornish *ry*, *rey*, "to give" (Norris' *Cornish Drama*, ii. 282), W. rhoi.

tion," ar ni aill *seirge* oc cúrsagad, "for no loss (?) is weakness in reproaching," Z. 1056. 925. *Leithne* (gl. latitudo), W. llydanedd, from the adjectives lethan, llydan (Z.'s lethit. p. 770, acc. sing. is from *leth*). 926. *Airde* (gl. altitudo), derivatives from *lethan*, broad, and *ard*, high, as to which *v. supra*.

927-931. *Maisse* (gl. pulchritudo), O'R.'s *maise*, *maisi* (gl. decor), Mímaisi (gl. indecor), *infra*, 1083, 1084. 1108, 1109. Maisse occurs in Z. with the intensive er- prefixed: is fuasnad dut' menmainsiu tuisled ho *ermaissiu* firinne trimrechtrad na tintathach, Z. 1064. gl. 4, "It is a disturbance to thy mind to fall from the love- liness of truth, owing to the variance (trimrechtrad = tri in-brechtrad?) of the inter- preters." Hence maisse in O. Ir. must have been either a masc. or a neut. in-stem; cf. W. maws, "pleasant." 928. *Eslaine* (gl. aegritudo). 929. *Faide* (gl. longitudo), from *slán* and *fot*, as to which *v. supra*. 930. *Tripulta* (gl. triplicacio), W. triphlygiad, a deriv. from tripul, triplex, threefold, not met elsewhere. *Diabul*, of which the dat. sing. occurs in Z. 968; a buith ar consain *diabuil* (gl. pro duplici consonante digamma positum, i. e. "its being for a double consonant"), has, perhaps, lost the guttural (but cf. ἁπλόος, διπλόος), which is preserved in the W. plygu, to double, root ᴘʟᴀᴋ, Skr. prch, πλέκ-ω, plic-o, plec-t-o, O. H. G. flch-t-an. 931. *Cethardubhladh* (gl. quadruplicatio), W. pedwardyblyg (cf. Ir. dublaighim, I double), the Ir. and W. -dubladh, dyblyg, losing their primitive meaning of "two-folding" in the general idea of "folding." Cf. cóicdiabail, "five-folded," *infra*, note on No. 1053.

932-936. *Uisgemlacht* (gl. limpitudo), a deriv. from uisgenuail (uisce-samail). 933. *Curchuslach no gilcach* (gl. arundo): for curchuslach perhaps leg. curchaslach, the middle syllable being represented by a contraction which may be read either *as* or *us* (curchas, gl. arundo, Z. 84). The syllable -lach, perhaps originally a subst., occurs frequently in Z.: teglach, "family;" góithlach, "swamp;" mátharlach, "ma- trix;" mimaselach, "hinge;" óclach, "a body of youths;" aslach, "persuasion;" ellach, "union," &c. Here, perhaps, the scribe mistook arundo for arundinetum. Z.'s curchas seems derived from a stem identical with that of the Lat. cárex. 933. *Gilcach* (O'R.'s *giolcach*, "reed," "broom," also a place where reeds grow: Gael. *cuilcearnach*), occurs in Corm., and also in a passage from the Brehou Laws, cited by Dr. Petrie, R. T. 62. losa feada, raith, aiteand, dris, fraech, eideaud, *gilcach*, spin, which he thus translates: "The Losafeada [shrubs] are tern, furze, briar, heath, ivy, broom, thorn." 934. *Fainleoc* (gl. hirundo), leg. fainleóc, a dimin. of fannall (= W. gwennol, Corn. guennol, Bret. guénnéli), which glosses hirundo in Z. 731, Gael. *ainleag*. Cf. *vanellus* cristatus, the lapwing. Does the diminutival suffix cóc stand for yavanka? 935. *Náit. escuing urcoidech* (gl. hirudo, horseleech): *náit* (cf.
"naid,

"naid, sf. a lamprey." O'R.), seems = nànti. *Escuing erchoidech* is lit., according to O'D., "noxious eel." *Escuing* (= O'R.'s *escu*, *easga esgan*, Gael. *easgann*, I have not seen elsewhere; *urchoidech* is Z.'s erchoitech, gl. nocens, Z. 199. 936. *Dealbh* (gl. imago), W. *delw*, a fem. â-stem = a Gaulish delva.

937-941. *Lorgarecht* (gl. indago, investigation, tracing from), lorg, m. track, W. llyr, which occurs in Corn., and also in Z., spelt lorc, gl. trames, whence also lorgairim, I track, investigate; lorgaire, tracker, investigator; lorgair, a dog (cf. Eng. lurcher); lorgad = W. llyriad. Compare also fin*lorg*, which word I have only met in Bishop Sanctáin's hymn, l. 2: dia dam *finlorg* [.i. darmesi] dia tuathum [.i. frim atnaith] dia dom thuus [.i. remun] dia dessam [.i. frim asoer], "God to follow me, God at my left hand, God to precede me, God at my right hand." In Corn. and Bret. we have *lergh, lerc'h:* see Norris, C. D. ii. 428, where the old Cornish trulerch (gl. semita) is ingeniously explained as = truit-*lerch*, "foot-trace." 938. *Sáebchoire* (gl. urago, i. e. vorago, whirlpool) is spelt in Z. 37, sáebchore, in Z. 827, sáibchore, and glosses syrtium. The first element of the word is obviously sáeb, sóib, falsus; the last, coire, core, Z. supposes to mean "places" (cf. coór, gl. locus, Z. 29), but perhaps it is the *coire*, gl. caldarium, *supra:* cf. Corryvrecan, i. e. Coire Bhreccáin. 939. *Derge* (gl. rubedo), rust, lit. "redness," from *derg*, O. Ir. derc (cf. derc martre, *supra*), whence the diminutive adj. dercaide (gl. rubvenus), Z. 1008[1]. 940. *Gerrguin* (gl. sanguisuga, leech, "bloodsucker") is O'R.'s gearrghuiu, "a horseleech." The deriv. is obscure, but cf. Gael. geàrr, "cut," "bite," Irish gearradh, "cutting:" *guin* seems an i-stem from r. gonaim, vulnero, gonas, who wounds, Corm. náram*gonat* fir, "let not men wound me," Z. 933; *gerrguin* may therefore be lit. "that which wounds by biting. *Geal tholl*, a Gaelic word for leech, seems connected with W. gel, gelen, gelue, Corn. ghel, Bret. gwelaouen, gweleouuen: Pictet compares Skr. jalukâ. 941. *Suithe* (gl. fuligo, soot) = W. swta, where the sibilant and tenuis are preserved, because swta is from the Eng. soot.

942-946. *Tes* (gl. calido, *infra*, gl. calor), "heat;" so in O. Ir.: gen. in *tesa*, gl. caloris, Z. 231, Corn. tes, gl. fervor, Z. 1112, W. tes, Bret. tez. Can tes be = tepsu? Skr. r. tap, Lat. tep-ere, the ultimate connexion of which with Skr. dah, Vedic dabh, ταφ, is not yet clearly understood. 943. *Ord* (gl. ordo), W. urdd, is órd, ordd in Z.: ní pu libsi intórd-so act ba la amiresselnn (this order was not with you, but with the unbelievers), Z. 666, gen. uird, Z. 70. Hence it appears that the word is a masc.
a-stem

---

[1] Other adjectives formed by this suffix are rotaide, "reddish," Vit. Adamn., and fliuchaide, "moist," "damp," from fliuch, "wet."

a-stem = árda, and cognate with, but not, like N. H. G. ordn-ung, taken from Lat. ordo, a stem in n. Orddan, a deriv. from this word, occurs in Fiacc's Hymn, v. 25 :—

> Asbert [t]*orddan* do mache : do crist atlaigthe¹ buide :
> Dochum nime mosrega : roratha duit du guide.
>
> He said, "Thy dignity *shall be* at Armagh : to Christ offer thanks :
> To heaven thou shalt come : thy prayers have been granted to thee."

The dat. sing orddain occurs in Ultan's Hymn to Brigit. Cf. also with órd the Gaulish Ordo-vices. 944. *Merlach na comla* (gl. cardo, hinge), "the *merlach* of the door." I have never met *merlach* elsewhere; shall we read mérlach, and connect it with mér, "finger"? 945. *Smeróid* (gl. carbo), O'R.'s "*smearóid*, s. f. a burning coal, an ember;" cf. perhaps, W. marwydos and Germ. schmoren. 946. *Gilla naneach* (gl. mango), "servant of the horses:" in the MS. the article is written along with its subst. (*naneach*), and in Mod. Ir. nan each would be written phonetically ua n-each, but this transportation of the termination of the gen. plur. of the article must be of very recent origin, as in Scottish Gaelic it is preserved at the present day with the na. In O. Ir. there can be no question that the final n of the longer form "innan" was transported to the following substantive beginning with a vowel or medial; but I never find any indication that this was the case with the short form "nan."

947-951. *Bruach* (gl. margo), *sic* in Z. 28 ; a word still used by Lowland Scotch curlers; cf. the Gaulish Ande-brocirix, Brocomagus, Eng. brink? 948. *Aodh*, in the Book of Armagh, Áed, a man's name, O. Ir. gen. Áedo, Áeda, Áido (connected with the Gaulish tribe-name Aedui, for áidvi). Aed, Z. xxxii. means "fire" (aed .i. tene, Corm. W. *aidd*), and is related to Gr. οἴθω, αἴθος, αἰθίοψ, ἰθαίνεσθαι, Hesych., Lat. ædes, æstus, æstas (Curtius, Griech. Etymol. 215), Ved. édha, m. édhas, n. "fuel;" vriddhi-form áidh, f. or áidha, m. O. H. G. eit, "fire," Ang.-Sax. ád, &c. The name Áed is either an i- or an u-stem, I cannot say which: it is formed by vriddhation from a root IDH = Skr. indh, to kindle. The name in question occurs in the following passage from the Book of Armagh, 18 *b*, 1: Epscop *aed* bói isléibti luid duarddmachæ

---

¹ Observe this interesting form of the 2nd pers. sing. imper. It also occurs in Z. 840, atlig-the buide, and in the Book of Armagh, 178 *b*, 2 : nutasigthe (nu-t-asigthe) du gallasn (gl. calcia te gallicas tuas), which gloss should have been cited *supra*, No. 72. Compare the Mid. Ir. forms notgebtha darabési ol pátraice, "put thyself in his place, said Patrick." – Pref. to Fiacc's Hymn. Gaibthi cloich isin tailm, a Loig! "Put a stone into the sling, O Loeg!" Seirgl. Conc. Dr. Lottner regards these forms as taken from the 2nd pers. sing. of the secondary present, which in the indic. ended in -*the* (noscomalnithe, Z. 1054, gl. 29).

duarddmachæ birt edoct cusegéne duarddmachae dubbert segene oitherroch aidacht dud*aid* ⁊ adopart *áed* aidacht ⁊ achenél ⁊ a celis dupátrice cubbráth Fáccab *áed* aidacht la conchad luid conchad du art machæ contubart fland feblæ acheill dóo ⁊ gabsi cadessin abbaith. "Bishop Áed was in Sléibte (Sletty): he went to Armagh: he gave a bequest to Segéne of Armagh. Segéne gave another bequest to Áed, and Áed gave a bequest and his race and his church to Patrick for ever [lit. "to the Judgment"]. Áed left a bequest with Conchad. Conchad went to Armagh. Fland Feblæ granted his church to him, and he himself (cadessin = fadessin) took the abbey." Coilboth mac oingusso maic cogin, brecán mac *aido*, *ibid.* 18 *b*, 2. 951. *Ploit* (gl. uato) seems for *Plait* (gl. Plato).

952-956. *Grian* (gl. Apollo, *infra*, gl. sol, gl. Pean, gl. Titan), sun = gréna, gen. sing. gréne, gréine, a fem. â-stem, and possibly connected with the name of the Gaulish Apollo, Grannos, which Dr. Siegfried compares with the Vedic ghraṇs, or ghraṇsá, m. "sun-glow, sunshine, light." This is referred by Böhtlingk and Roth to the root ghar, whereto also belong Skr. gharmá, "heat," ghṛṇi, "sun;" θερμόν, fervere, Ir. garaim, and Eng. warm. The Gaulish Grannos appears in many Latin inscriptions along with Sirona (= Σελήνη? or perhaps, with Glück, goddess of long life, Ir. sír, W. hir); cf. also Apollini Granno Mogouno, with which Dr. Siegfried has compared Skr. maghavan, gen. maghónas, an epithet of Indra, &c. As to—953. *Duine* (gl. homo), W. dyn, Corn. den, and—954. *Nemduine* (gl. nemo), *v. suprà*. 955. *Ogh* (gl. virgo) = ógá, is apparently connected with óg integer, óge integritas, virginitas, Z. 28, and occurs in Ultán's Hymn in praise of Brigit, line 7:—

> Dorodba iunnun ar colla[1] cisu
> In chroeb com bláthaib, in máthair isu:
> Iud fir-*óg* iumain, con orddain adbail (leg. aidbil?)
> Biam sóer cech inbaid lam' nóeb do laignib.

> She has abolished within us our flesh's taxes,
> The branch with blossoms, the mother of Jesus:
> The beloved true-virgin, with vast glory—
> I should be safe at every time with my saint of Leinster.

The abl. plur. in Colmán's Hymn, line 48:

> Bendacht for érlam Brigit con *ógaib* hérenn impe,
> A blessing on Patron Brigit with Ireland's virgins around her!

Sometimes

[1] Note here an instance of the governed preceding the governing substantive.

Sometimes in the nom. sing. the ó is resolved, and we find *uag*, gen. uaige: feil már Muire *uaige* (the great festival of Mary the Virgin), *Félire Oingusso*, May 3. 956. *Slataidhe* (gl. latro), apparently from *slat* (gl. virga), v. supra. Gael. *sladaidh*.

957-966. *Bretnach*, from Bretan (Colman nam *bretan*, supra, No. 909), for Brettan = Britt-ana. Zeuss thinks that O. W. brith (gl. pictus) is connected with this name, W. *th* arising from *tt*. But W. *th* may also represent an original *ct*. Cf. O. W. œtinct bronn-*breithet*, "volucris pectore variegata," Z. 1087, and O. Ir. mrecht, varius, mrechtrad, varietas, ílmrechtrad, multa varietas, Z. 822. The following forms connected with a word so famous as *Briton* will probably interest: D. M. Phileti *Brittae* (Mommsen Röm. inschriften der Schweiz, 124). Com-bretonium (Glück, 66). Marti *Britonio* (Orelli, No. 1358). Matribus *Brittis* (from *Britte*burgum, in Bavaria, Orelli, 2094). The Greeks write Βρεττανία, Βρεττανοί = W. Brython. 958. *Fáith brégach*, lit. "lying prophet," O. Ir. brécach, from brée, a lie, acc. s. bréic dolum, Z. 79, breic, gl. mendacium, Z. 23; im brecairecht (gl. in astutia), Z. 580. 959. *Fíadhnaise*, in Z. fiadnisse, a neut. ia-stem, "witness, testimony," root vɪᴅ, gunated; cf. nuiadnisse (novum testamentum), Z. 823, 824, for nufiadnisse. Fiadh = W. gwydd. As to—960. *Comtrom* (gl. par), and—961, 962. *Egcomtrom* (gl. impar, gl. dispar), v. supra, No. 903. 966. *Bainne* (gl. lac), milk, occurs in Cormac v. Arg, and is probably connected with banna "drop" (ni conteshad *banna* ass, Brogan, l. 88), and the Corn. banne, gl. gutta vel stilla, Bret. bannec'h, Z. 1119, from bann, a jet?

967-976. *Sgadan* (gl. allec), in Corm. scatan, is a herring, W. ysgadan, cf. Eng. shad, N. H. G. schade; probably a foreign word. 968. *Mil* (gl. mel), honey, cf. Lat. mel, mellis, for melt-is, Gr. μέλι, μέλιτ-ος, Goth. milith : Mod. Ir. gen. *meala*, a fem. i-stem, W. Corn. and Bret. mel. Neither in Irish nor in Greek does the *l* stand for *d*; cf. *meadh* = W. medd = μέθυ, Skr. madhu, O. H. G. metu, Lit. med-u-s, "honey" (in the Mid. Ir. mesce, "drunkenness" (= med-scia), *d* has been lost). 995. *Domblas áe* (gl. fel), lit. "bitterness of the liver;" *do-mblas*, opposite of so-mblas, gen. somblais, "sweetness, sweet," which occurs in the Ir. Nennius, 196, tipra uisce *somblais* i taeb in corainn, "a well of sweet water in the side of the Corann;" blas = W. blas, "taste :" the -m- perhaps for -imm. As to *áe*, v. infra, No. 1032. 976. *Ainmide* (gl. animal), beast, brute; hence *ainmidheach*, brutal, brutish, O'R. 977. *Salann* (gl. sal), salt, *sic* in Z. 740, acc. sing. dinebloich dorigne *salard* (leg. salann), "of the stone she made salt," Brogan's poem on Brigit, 40: sailti, "salted," Lib. Hymn. ed. Todd, 20; cf. ἅλς (masc.), sal, sāle, Goth. and Engl. sal-t, Lett. sahls, Slav. solŭ. "In Greek," says Lottner (Zeits. vii. 24), "ἅλς, as is well known, also means 'sea' [it is then feminine], and is radically connected with ἅλλομαι [from σάλjομαι], Lat. salio, which we find again

in

in Sanskrit in the forms sal, sar (sṛ), 'to go.' Thence salila, 'water,' sarit, 'river,' saras, 'lake' = ἕλος. Hence it clearly results that water is denoted by all these words as the 'bounding, leaping, billowing,' just as this meaning also lies in the Greek σάλος, Lat. salum, ' the (leaping) sea-flood.' The passage from this fundamental idea (*grundanschauung*) to that of the 'salty,' could only take place on becoming acquainted with a great salt sea. And so there can be no doubt that the European peoples were still unsevered when they reached the sea, whilst the primeval abodes (*ursitze*) of the stem lay remote therefrom;" W. halen, Corn. haloin, halein, Bret. hal, halen, holen; Z. compares the Gaulish name Salusa.

979-981. *Cércaill* (gl. cervical), and no doubt taken from the Latin, which, of course, is from cervix, neck or nape. Note the lengthening of the *e*, produced by way of compensation for the loss of the *r*, and cf. futures like taiccéra, dogéna, ashéra, dobérat (Z. 1126), for taiccerfa, dogenfa, asherfa, doberfat. 980. *Aníbal* (Annibal), *Ainm duini*, "nomen hominis." 981. *Comairleach* (gl. consul), from comairle consilium, *v. supra*.

982-986. *Easpog* = O. Ir. epscop, from episcopus; cf. O. W. pl. escip, Z. 684, Corn. ispak. 983. *Innarbtach* (gl. exul) = indarbtach, *v. supra*. 984. *Furachair* (gl. vigil). 985. *Nemfuireachair*, "unwary." O'R. has *furachar*, "watching, watchful, wary;" Gael. *furachail*, careful, *furachras*, vigilance. Cf. W. gwarchad, "a guarding," gwarchadw, "to watch," gwarched, "to ward, to watch," &c. 986. *Gleoaire* (gl. pugil), cf. O'R.'s gleic, "wrestling, jostling, combat, conflict, contest;" Gael. *gleachdair*: pugil is glossed by cuanene in Z. 27.

987-996. *Neimthni* (gl. nil, gl. nul), leg. *neimhni; nem, nemh*, is a mod. form of the O. Ir. neb, neph (pronounced nev?), and ní is a thing: cf. do nephní, gl. ad nihil, Z. 830. The acc. sing. *ní* occurs in Z. 584, 586; and the nom. (or perhaps the acc.) pl. in Z. 442; na ní ararogartsom (res quas mandavit). This is one of the stems in *i* (like Hí, "Iona," lit. "humilis") noticed in the Beitr. 462. 991. *Ainm* (gl. nomen), name, W. enw, has been noticed *supra*. It may here be further observed that ainm seems = ágnâmant = Gr. ὄ-νοματ, the -gnâmant, -νοματ being the Lat. gnomen in cognômen, agnomen (for ad-gnômen)[1]. If, however, ainm was originally an *ant*-stem, it is, so far as I know, the only one in which the *t* has been medialized, and then
                                                                                                                assimilated

---

[1] It is well known that the Gr. stems in *μαρ* represent Skr. bases in *man*, Latin, in *men*. To identify these we must assume a common prototype *mant*. Curious, if a trace of this prototype be preserved in the second *n* of anmann.

116   *A Mediæval Tract on Latin Declension.*

assimilated to the preceding *n* (cf. clann, cland = W. plant). At all events, in the oldest Irish, ainm is a neuter *ann*-stem, and thus declined:—

	Sing.	Dual.	Plur.
N.	ainm (ṅ)	dá ṅainm	anmann
G.	anma, anmae	dá anma?	anmann (ṅ)
D.	anmaimm	dib ṅanmannaib	anmannaib
Acc.	ainm (ṅ)	dá ṅainm	anmann
Voc.	ainm (ṅ)	a dá ṅainm	a anmann

992. *Remainm* (gl. prænomen), W. rhagenw, and—993. *Comainm* (gl. cognomen), W. cyfenw, are compounds with *rem*, *com*. 994. *Tuighe* (gl. stramen, i. e. stratum), "straw-thatch," O'R.; cf. W. to, pl. toau, "layer, roof," toad, "roofing," Z. 163, 874; comtoou, gl. stemicamina, Z. 291; cf. the Gaulish names Togirix, Togidia, Togiacus, Τογιοσουμνος (leg. Τογιοσουμνος?), Togius, Togitius, &c., and O. Ir. Toiguire, Book of Armagh, 2 *a*. 995. *Didin* (gl. tegimen), O. Ir. dítiu, g. díten, *v. supra*. 996. *Arson anma* (gl. pronomen), a pronoun, lit. "in lieu of a noun."

997–1001. *Sidhan gaeithe* (gl. flamen), "a blast of wind," leg. *sidan g.*, and cf. Gael. *séideag*. 998. *Soillse* (gl. lumen), *v. supra*. 999. *Sruth* (gl. flumen, gl. pluuinar, No. 1042), a river, gen. srotha, srotho, W. ffrwd, in O. Ir. a masc. u-stem. Pictet compares Skr. srotas, river, from sru, fluere (from sbhrav?). Cf. the Gaulish river-name Φρουτις (Frutis), as Glück, 35, reads Ptolemy's Φρουεις. Cf. also the Gr. r. ρυ in ρέω ρεύ-σω, ἐ-ρρύη-ν, ρεῦ-μα, ρυ-τός, &c. Lat. ru-o, riv-us, ru-mis (mamma), Lith. srov-e, srav-a. Curtius, G. E. i. 318, 319. The O. H. G. strou-m, Eng. *stream*, have a *t* which I do not understand. 1000. *Tairsech* (gl. limen), threshold; so in Cormac: *táirsech*, O'R., perhaps a deriv. from the prep. tars, Skr. root tar, to stride over or across, an old participle of which Bopp finds in the Lat. trans: cf. W. trothwy, and traws, tros; Bret. treuzou, from treuz. 1001. *Sliseog* (gl. polimen), Gael. *sliseag*, "a chip, shaving;" cf. the Eng. "slice." The glosser seems altogether to have mistaken the meaning of polimen.

1002–1006. *Filidecht* (gl. carmen), *v. supra*, No. 1. 1003. *Sluagh* (gl. agmen) = slóga, W. llu, Corn. luu: so in Z. 27, who justly compares the Gaulish (Belgic) Catuslōgi, "battle-hosts." He also compares λόχος, a troop, which seems a different word from λόχος, an ambush, childbed. Dare we compare O. H. G. slahan, Eng. slay, slaughter? 1004. *Shruileach* (gl. fragmen), in O'R. *spruilleach*, "a small scrap, crumbs, fragments, offal," cf. W. ysbwriaL. 1005. *Maróg* (gl. trolliamen). I now feel convinced that *maróg* (Gael. *marag*, "gut of an animal," "sausage," "pudding") is the modern

form

form of maróc, gl. iolla, i. e. hilla, *supra*, No. 55. Trolliamen is obscure to me.
1006. *Blonacc* (gl. odomen, i. e. abdomen), the same as *Blonac*, which glosses arvina,
No. 236. So in A. S., we have the same word for lard and paunch. Blonacc : W.
bloneg : : seboce : hebawg. Perhaps the *cc* (W. *g*) stands for anc&. Cf. the Gaulish
derivatives in anco, enco, inco, unco, Z. 773, 774.

1007–1011. *Mullach* (gl. culmen), *v. supra*, No. 838. 1008. *Rind* (gl. cacumen), frequent in Z., nom. s. ar *rind*-siu, 254, generally a neut. i-stem, gen. s. renda, rendo, acc. frisa *rind*, Z. 236, nom. pl. n. rind, Z. 257 : na rind astoidet (gl. signa radiantia), but renda (masc.) in Adamnán's Vision (early middle Irish) : Isat lána *renda* nime ocus redlanda ocus firnamint ocus ind uli dúl don uallguba dermair dogníat anmanna na peedach fo lámaib ocus glacaib inna nánnut nemmarbdasin, " Full are the constellations of heaven, and the stars, and the firmament, and the whole world of the mighty lamentation which the sinners' souls make under the arms and hands of those immortal enemies."
The following is a paradigm of the O. Ir. declension of neuter i-stems :—

NEUT. *i*-STEM.
Stem, fissi.

	Sing.	Dual.	Plur.
Nom. and Acc.	fiss	dá fiss	fess
G.	fessa, fesso	dá fisse ?	fisse (ṅ) ?
D.	fiss	dib fissib	fissib
V.	a fiss	a dá fiss	a fess

Rind is always rendered signum coeleste, constellatio, by Z., and unquestionably this must be its meaning in "ainm *renda*, gl. pisces," Z. 255; but its primary meaning seems "point," "mark" (cote in *rinnd*, gl. ubi . . . aculeus ? Z. 361, where note the *masc*. article, in dá *errend*, gl. stigmata, Z. 254, and in this sense it is connected with the verbs tornther, Z. 595 (leg. tornder); dofoirnde, Z. 974; tóirndet (do-fo-rindet), dofóirndet, Z. 433, significant, tororansom, gl. signavit (do-fo-ro-rand-som), Z. 854 ; trimirothorndiussa (gl. transfiguravi), Z. 850 (where the *d* of the root is dropt or assimilated : in dofoirde, dofoirdet, Z. 56, the *n* of the root is lost). Hence it came to mean "the point of a weapon," "a headland" (W. rhyn), "the top of anything," " a star." 1009. *Sil* (gl. semen), W. hil. (There is another Welsh form, sil, where the *s* is unexplained.) Z. compares the names Silo, Silus, Silius Italicus. 1010. *Emnad* (gl. geminen, a doubling), O'R.'s *eamhnadh* ; cf. emou, "a couple, twins," Corm. Mac na trí findem*na*, "son of the 3 fair twins," Scirglige Conc., Atlantis, ii. 386 ; mat

anmann

anmanu adiechta *emnatar*, and is écen comacomol hi suidib ("if nouns adjective are doubled, there a conjunction is necessary between them," lit, *in* them), Z. 671. Cf. Skr. yama, "twins," unless we regard (e. g.) emnatar as an early corruption of geminantur. 1011. *Ara* (gl. ren), O. Ir. áru, gl. rien, Z. 20, gen. áran, W. aren, pl. ciryn, Corn. acran (Lat. rien, rénes?).

1012-1016. *Sealg no dreassan* (gl. splen, the spleen) would be in O. Ir. selg no dressan, but I have never met either gloss elsewhere, except in O'R. (who has sealg, but not dreassan), and in O'D. Gram. 397, "mór cosmhailius risint seilg," "great resemblance to the spleen." Selg (Bret. fielc'h) seems to stand for s(p)legâ; cf. $\sigma\pi\lambda\acute{a}(\eta)\chi$-$\nu o-\nu$, $\sigma\pi\lambda\acute{\eta}\nu$, Skr. plihan, Lat. lien. 1014. *Int-inne iachtarach* (gl. lien), the milt or spleen, certainly a blunder, for the Irish words mean "the lower gut"—inne, "a bowel, entrail," O'R., iachtarach, an adj. from iachtar (O'R.'s iachdar), the lower part of anything, O. Ir. ichtar, Z. 147 n., 592, which seems connected with the prep. *is*, "infra." The suffix -tar (as in echtar = W. eithyr, uachtar = W. uthr, &c., Z. 823) seems identical with the Skr. comparative suffix, -tara. 1014. *Slind* (gl. pecten) a weaver's reed or sley), so Z. 723. 1015. *Cruitire* (gl. lyricen), *v. supra*, No. 5. 1016. *Sdocaire* (gl. tubicen, a trumpeter), from *sdoc*, a trumpet, O'R., Gael. *stoc*, "trumpet," "sounding-horn."

1017-1030. *Tédaire* (gl. fidicen, lute-player), from *téd*, Gael. *teud*, string of a musical instrument, in O. Ir. tét, gl. fidis, Z. 79 = W. tant, pl. tannau, Skr. tantu, pl. tantavas, Skr. r. tan, Lat. ten-d-o, $\tau\acute{a}\nu\nu\mu\alpha\iota$, $\tau\epsilon\acute{\iota}\nu\omega$. The *n* of this root seems preserved in scim-*tana*, gl. exilem, Z. 23, cf. Eng. thin, $\tau\alpha\nu\nu$, tenuis, &c. 1018. *Gilla adhairce* (gl. cornicen, horn-blower), lit. "lad of [the] horn;" adhairce, gen. sing. of adharc, "horn, trumpet," O'R., whence the dimin. adercéne, Z. 282, and the adj. adaredae, gl. corneta, Z. 780; cf. also adircliu (gl. cornix), Z. 727. 1019. *Séideadh* (cf. seidedh gáithe, *supra*), "blowing, blast," O'R. 1020. *Muirduchu* (gl. siren), lit. sea-music? The nom. pl. occurs in a passage from Keating, cited in O'D. Gr. 177: trialluid for muir agus teagmhaidh *murdhuchainn* dóibh, "they put to sea, and sirens met them;" cf. duchann, "i. e. ceol, music," O'R., with which our -duchu seems connected: cf. also W. dyganu, "to chant." Siren is glossed by muirmóru in Z. 28 = W. morforwyn, "sea-girl" (morynyon puellæ), Z. 202. 1029. *Mucc mara* (gl. delphin), lit. "pig of [the] sea" (cf. W. morhwch, Corn. morhoch, Bret. morhouc'h, lit. sus maris), mucc mora, gl. dolphinus, Z. 1114; cf. muccfoil, gl. hara, Z. 198 : mucc = W. moch, and cf. meichat, meichiat, "swineherd," Z. 106, 806, and the Gallo-Latin inscriptions, DEO. MERCVR. *MOCCO* (Muratori, i. 51, Orelli, 1407) MAR. ET *STI*, MER. ET *SVI* (de Betouw, *De aris et lapidibus ad Neomagum et Santenum effossis*, &c.

&c., Noomagi, 1783). 1030. *Colach* (gl. cayu) is explained "incestuous, impious, wicked." It occurs in the gen. sing. masc. in a citation from Leab. Breacc. (Petrie, R. T. 369) : ba mór tra diumus ┐ adclos, ┐ bocasach in ríg *cholaig* (leg. colaig?) sin, and its root occurs in Patrick's Hymn, where Patrick speaks of cech fiss a *rachuiliu anmain duini*, "every knowledge that hath depraved man's soul." Cf. cuil (gl. piaculi), Muratori, *Antiq. Ital.* iii. 891, cuilech (gl. prostibulum, Z. 431, gl. profanus, Z. 834), cuiligim (gl. prosto), Z. 431; œrchuilecha (gl. tam nefarii ausus), Z. 838; W. cwliawg. 1030. *Deallrad* (gl. jubar, radiance, splendour, brightness), Gael. *dealradh*, masc.

1032–1036. *Ae* (gl. hepar, liver), leg. *áe*, gen. sing. *supra*, No. 975, gen. pl. in Gael. *áinean*, O. Ir. óa (gl. jecur), Z. 28 = W. afu, Corn. aui, Bret. avu, may all, notwithstanding their great dissimilarity, be connected with ἧπαρ, jecur, and Skr. yakṛt. 1033. *Bróce* (gl. sutolar), a shoe, "brogue," in Hiberno-English, is the W. brycan, where I do not understand the *c*; Gaulish bracca seems Bret. bragez. 1034. *Ichtar na comladh* (gl. lar), "the lower part of the door." 1036. *Rí* (gl. Cæsar), a king = O. Ir. ríg, a masc. g-stem, and thus declined :—

	Sing.	Dual.	Plur.
N.	ríg	dá ríg[1]	ríg
G.	ríg	dá ríg	ríg (n)
D.	ríg, rúi	dib rígaib	rígaib
Acc.	ríg (n)	dá ríg	ríga
Voc.	a ríg	a dá ríg	a ríga

The word occurs frequently in Gaulish proper names: nom. sing. reix, rix (= ríg-s, n. pl. ríges, cf. Lat. rēg (rēx), Goth. reik-s, Skr. ráj, in samráj, svaráj (Kuhn, Ind. Stud. i. 332)).

1037–1041. *Sruth*, a river, *v. supra*, No. 999. 1038. *Ith in arba* (gl. far, spelt, meal, grits). Ith, gen. etho, etha, Z. 15, differs from ith (gl. puls), Z. 26 = O. W. iot (gl. puls), Z. 60, now uwd, Z. 1122, Corn. iot. *Ith* (O. W. *it*-laur, gl. area, now *yd*, Corn. hit, Z. 1109) has been compared by Kuhn (I. S. 358) with O. N. acti. *Arba*, O'R.'s *arbha*, corn, perhaps connected with W. erw, "acre," Lat. arvum. 1039. *Srón* (gl. naris), a fem. â-stem, acc. s. sróin, *supra*, srónbennach, gl. rhinoceros, Z. 28. Srón glosses nasus, Z. 28, and, like W. ffroen, seems to have lost a guttural before

---

[1] Cf. O. W. dou *rig* Habren, "duo reges Sabrinæ," Z. 157.

before *n*: cf. Corn. fruc, Z. 89, where Norris would read *friic*, Gr. ῥύγχος. The *s* in the Irish form is put for *f*, as in srian, W. ffrwyn, Lat. fraenum, &c., and the resemblance of *srón* to srenim (gl. sterto, Z. 14 = sternuo, πτάρνυμαι) is therefore accidental. 1040. *Lenmunach* (gl. sequester), from lenamain, O'R.'s *leanamhain*, "following, pursuing." The root len in Z. 1022, gl. 14: *lenaid* din gutai thoisig, gl. ex superiore pendens vocali, Z. 1051, gl. 25, ar mad peethad inti for a taibre grad, *lenit* a peethe dindí dobeir au grád, "for if he be a sinner on whom thou conferrest a holy-order [lit. a degree], his sins depend from him who confers the order" (1020). 1041. *Sbor an eich* (gl. calcar), lit. spur of the horse; *sbor*, perhaps not from the Eng. spur. Cf. W. yspar, yspardun (éperon), Bret. spern, "thorn." *Eich*, gen. sing. of ech.

1042-1046. *Sruth* (gl. pluvinar), *v. supra*. 1043. *Clár casta* (gl. torcular, a winepress or oil-press), lit. a board of twisting (a mangle?), *clár, v. supra; casta*, gen. of *casad*, O'R.'s *casadh*, "a bending, twisting," &c. 1044. *Buaile dam* (gl. bostar, a cow-house), *buaile*, gl. vaccaria, *supra; dam*, "ox," *v. supra*. 1045. *C. grindi foilcí* (gl. nectar), I cannot explain, unless the Irish be put for c[eannach] grinde no foilce, "reward of baptism, or washing." I am indebted to C. for the following curious glosses: *Biathad grinde no crinde* .i. biadh cretme .i. bathais .i. log in baistithi (H. 2, 15, MS. in the Library of T. C. D., p. 61, *b*), "food of belief, i. e. baptism, i. e. the reward of the baptized one." *Crinne* .i. ainm do baisti, ut est biathad crinne .i. logh na baisti intan imlinn ⁊ imbiadh doberar .i. ó ní is credintibus bautisium [.i.] in baithis creidmedhe (O'Davoren's Glossary), "a name for baptism, *ut est* 'biathad crinne,'" i. e. reward of the baptism when much ale and food are given, i. e. since there is *credentibus baptisma*, i. e. the baptism of believers." With *foilce* cf. folcaim, gl. humecto, gl. lavo, Z. 78, Gaulish Volcatius, Volcae, Z. 66, W. golchi, lavare, Z. 151. 1046. *Athair* (gl. pater), O. Ir. athir, is declined *supra*, No. 3, and has, as before observed, lost the initial *p* (the root is pâ, "to protect, to support, to nourish"): hence aitherrechtaigthe (gl. patronymicum), Z. 972. Welsh has lost the word corresponding with *athair* (W. tad = Skr. tâta, carissimo). The Breton compizrien (compatres) is, perhaps, a loan-word, but cf. W. athrach, "relationship," cyfathrach, "affinity" (ach, "pedigree").

1047-1051. *Bráthair* (gl. frater) = brother, O. W. brawt, pl. brodyr, Corn. braud, broder, declined like athir, and found in all the Indo-European languages; Skr. bhrâtr (acc. bhrâtar-am), Zend. brâtar, *et v. supra*, No. 570. The root, according to Bopp (Gloss. 253), is uncertain. Prof. Max Müller, however, says that "the original meaning of bhrâtar seems to have been he who carries or assists" (*Oxford Essays*, 1856, p. 16). In accordance with this view we may suppose bráthair to stand for an

original

original bhrâtar, root bhrâ, from bhar (bhṛ, Ir. ʙᴀʀ, robar-t, tulit, Z.). In Old Irish this noun in the nom. sing. and gen. and dat. pl. (bráithre, bráithrib) seems to have gone over to the *i*-declension. Cf. the decl. of the Lith. stems dug-ter, mo-ter, gen-ter, seser, Schleicher, *Handbuch der Lit. Sprache*, i. 193. 1048. *Braen aimsire* (gl. imber, rain-shower). *Braen* (leg. bráen) seems bróen, " pluvia," in Z. 41; so in Colmán's Hymn, l. 53 :—

    In spirut nóeb ron*braena*, crist ron*sóera*, ron*séna*.

    The Holy Spirit rain upon us! Christ deliver us (and) bless us!

Braen is explained "a drop" by O'R.; so, Gael. *braon*, and this certainly seems its meaning in Ir. Nennius, ed. Todd, 206: fofrith fer móruleach ind ⁊ *braena* fola derge tairis, "a great-bearded man was found therein, with drops of red blood over him." It is perhaps radically connected with W. bwrw, to cast, to throw: bwrw gwlaw, to rain. *Aimsire*, gen. of aimser, "time," "season," W. amser. 1049. *Cularan* (gl. cucumer, cucumber) is cularain in O'R.; cf. W. cylor, "earth-nuts," Bret. kéler. 1050, 1051. *Mí* (gl. September, gl. October), W. mis, a month. The gen. sing is mís, = má(n)s-as, one of the few stems in *s* remaining in Irish, if, indeed, there be another. Cf. mís-tae, gl. mensurnus, gl. menstruus, Z. 256; and Skr. más, " moon," " month," Zend. maonh-, μήν, μείς, Lat. me(n)s-is (from ᴍᴀɴs, as can-is from ᴋᴠᴀɴ).

1052–1056. *Máthair* and *Bean* have been noticed *supra*, but with respect to *máthair* = mátar-i. I may here quote Prof. Max Müller (*Oxford Essays*, 1856, p. 15): "Among the early Arians mátar had the meaning of maker, from ᴍᴀ̂, to fashion; and in this sense, and with the same accent as the Greek μήτηρ, mátar, not yet determined by a feminine affix, is used in the Veda as a masculine. Thus we read, for instance, *Rv.* viii. 41, 4 :—Sáh mátá pûrvyám padám. He, Varuṇa (Uranos), is the maker of the old place." 1053. *Bean* (gl. mulier). O. Ir. ben, must have had some curious irregularities in its declension. I have not yet found all the O. Ir. forms, but the following list will probably prove correct so far as it goes :—

	Sing.	Dual.	Plur.
N.	ben		mnáa
G.	mnáa		ban (n)
D.	mnái		mnáib
Acc.	mnái (n)	(dí mnái?)[1]	mnáa
V.	a ben		a mná

Here

[1] Dotháet cúchulainn iarsin co tard a druim frisinlííc ⁊ bahole amenma leis ⁊ dofuit cotlud fair conaccai

Here there seem to be three bases: 1°, bani (ben) = gvani, Skr. jani; 2°, bana (ban) = gvanâ = γυνή, Bœot. βάνα, Vedic gnâ, for ganâ; and 3°, a lengthened form mnâvâ, for bnâvâ, for banâvâ (W. benyw, Corn. mennyw) = gvanâvâ. What is the form *bándû*, "goddesses," Z. 280? Perhaps a double plural (nom. sing. bandea, *ibid.*, gen. sing. bandeae, Z. 1029). 1054. *Slinn criadh* (gl. liuter, i. e. later), "a brick, tile;" cf. W. pridd-faen, pridd-lech, lit. "clay-stone," where pridd = *criadh*. 1055. *Catharach* (gl. puber) = W. cedorawg, cf. W. caitoir, gl. pubes, Z. 48, hod. cedor, "hair of pubescence," Bret. kezour, pubertas. 1056. *Uth* (gl. uber), leg. úth, gen. útha, see *supra*, No. 102. I think now that úth may have lost an initial *p*; cf. W. piw, "dug," "udder."

1057-1061. *Docinelach* (gl. degener), leg. *dochinélach*, from do, the particle of quality before mentioned, and cinélach, an adj. formed from cenél, as to which *v. supra.* 1058. *Bocht* (gl. pauper), gen. sing. masc. ind aissa *boicht*, Z. 250; dat. pl. donaib *bochtaib*, Z. 823: cf. boctán, gl. pauperculus, Z. 111, and perhaps W. bychodawg (= boxâtâco?), Corn. bochodoe, gl. inops, Z. 295. Cf. Skr. bhiksh, "to beg," bhikshu, "beggar." 1059. *Sine ochta* (gl. uber), if this be what the scribe meant, *sine*, nipple, has occurred *supra*, No. 151, No. 1039: *ochta*, gen. sing. of ucht, breast: *v. supra*, No. 812. 1060. *Machaire* (leg. machairech?), gl. campester, *v. supra*, No. 866. 1061. *Caillteamhail* (gl. silvester), from caill and amail (= samail, samali), apparently with the insertion of *t* before aspirated *s* (caill-t-seamail), as in min-t-súilech, No. 430: however, *coill* makes its nom. pl. *coillte* in modern Irish.

1062-1065. *Uachtlanaidhe* (gl. celeber), *Uachlan* (gl. saluber), have each the peculiar mark which the scribe seems to have placed where he was not sure of the correctness of his Irish gloss. Certainly he was right in putting this mark here. Celeber is glossed by *erdairc* in Z.; saluber in O. Ir. would be slán, sleinech, or sláintech. 1065. *Gruamda* (gl. acer), from *gruaim*, surliness, Corn. v. Groma. Cf. W. grwm, Eng. *grum.*

1066-1074. *Etechail* (gl. volucer), in O'R. *eitcaccail*, "volatile;" cf. *cite*, quill, feather (= pettia?). 1067. *Góithamhail* (gl. paluster), cf. góithlachde (gl. paluster), Z. 41; isin *goithluch* (gl. in palude), Z. 822. 1068. *Eithidemail* (gl. acris, leg. alacris?), *eithideamail* (gl. alacris), apparently formed from a personal subst. eithid, "goer,"

---

indamnái [O. Ir. indimnái?] cucai indalanai brat úaine impe alaili brat corcra cóicdiabail imsude ("then Cuchulainn went and put his back against the rock, and his heart was low, and sleep came upon him. He saw the two women [coming] towards him—one of them [with] a green cloak around her, the other [with] a red, five-folded cloak round her").—*Seirglige Concalainn.*

"goer," which I have not met, though *cathaim*, " I go," *cathadh*, "going," occur in O'R. With *eathaim* Bopp compares the Skr. r. at, ire. 1069. *Uaidh* (gl. polyandrium), πολυάνδριον, a common burial-place) should probably be read *uaigh*, "graves." 1070. *Earrach* (gl. ver), O. Ir. errach, gen. erraig (it luathider gáith *herraig*, "they are swifter than the wind of spring;" Scirg. Conc. *Atlantis*, No. iii. p. 110). This interesting word (stem (v)erraka, for vesraka? root vas, to clothe) seems to have lost the initial r, like *úrde*, viridis, W. guyrdd, Z. 66, uisce = vad-scia? water. *Errach* is derived by Cormac from the Lat. vēr, but vēr, though it may come from the same root, is formed differently. Vēr is = verer = ves-era, the vowel-flanked *s* becoming *r* as usual, and the thematic *a* being lost, as in *čap* = Fϵσαp, and as is usual when *r* precedes it. See Benfey, G. W. i. 309. 1071. *Corp leghas* (gl. cadaver), "a corpse that dissolves" (decomposes, decays); *corp*, gen. cuirp, now a masc. a-stem, like W. corff, pl. cyrff: both corp and corff, no doubt, were originally *s*-stems, but have gone over to the vocalic declension: r. *supra*, No. 812, and seem taken from the Lat. corpus. *Leghas*, 3rd sing. pres. relative of *leghaim*, the verbal subst. of which occurs in Z. 580, 614, illobad et *legad* (in corruption and dissolution); cf. also lechdacha, liquids (in grammar), Z. 968. *Leghaim* (cf. W. lliaw, lliad) is etymologically obscure to me, unless indeed Bopp be right in comparing it with a Skr. layámi, r. li (liquefacere, solvere). As to the forms legh-as (pl. legh-ate), fut. leghfas, pl. leghfate, Schleicher, Beitr. i. 503. would regard them as the participles present and future active, only preserved in the nom. form of the sing. and plur. The form in *s*, he thinks, expresses the Lat. *ns* (the loss of *n* before *s* being common in Irish), while that in *te*, in the nom. pl. m. and f., would correspond with the Lat. *ntēs*. It must, however, be observed that both these forms aspirate: thus, ar cech duine *midus th*rastar dam ("against every one that meditates evil to me," Patrick's Hymn): cid druailnide *mbes chechtar* in da rann, Z. 472, "quamvis sit corrupta utraque duarum partium:" *bes chuibsech*, Book of Armagh, 17 a, 1. Plur. *failsigdde phersin* "quae significant personam," Z. 198; *beta thuicsi* "qui sunt electi," Z. 197. Hence, when the practice of aspiration was introduced, these forms must have ended in a vowel, not in *s*; and I follow Professor Siegfried in regarding them as having arisen from the agglutination of pronouns, the relative construction being originally an inverted one. 1072. *Pipur* (gl. piper), from the Lat. 1073. *Sét slighedh* (gl. iter): int-*seuit* bite hí each crich (paths that are into every country, lit. boundary), Z. 237. Hence, sét appears to have been a masc. a-stem = senta. Glück has compared the O. Brit. name Gabro-sentum, which in Mod. Ir. would be *Gabharséd*, "goat-path;" Cf. also W. hynt, f. Bret. hennt, m. Corn. cun*hinsic*, just, Z. 145; O. W. duguohintiliat (incedens), Z. 149; tidoihinto (?) per avia,

Z. 866. The Irish séitche (= sintáciá), "wife," originally an abstract noun, like aipche, has been referred by Dr. Siegfried to sét. So much for Celtic cognates. In Gothic we have "*sinths* m. (Schulze) Mal, z. B. in *ainamma sintha, traim sintham* einmal, zweimal, vrm. eigentlich Gang, Reise (= Mal in mehreren deutschen Sprachen) *gasintha, gasinthja* m. Gefährte, συνέκδημος; pl. genossenschaft, συνοδία." Dief. Goth. Wörterbuch, ii. 210, 211, where *hynt* and *scud* (= O. Ir. sét) are also compared, as well as O. H. G. sind (iter, trames), M. H. G. gesende (comes), A. S. gesið, sendan, Eng. send, &c. *Sligedh*, gen. sing. of sligi, gl. via, *supra*. 1074. *Dealg* (gl. spinter), O. Ir. delg, gen. deilg, thorn, pin, A. S. dale, has been compared *supra* with Corn. dele(h). It occurs in the St. Gall incantations, Z. 926, imm an *delg* (around the thorn), manibé an *delg* and (unless the thorn be there). Hence, it appears to have been a neut. a-stem.

1075-1079. *Cac gabhar* (gl. ruter), "goats' dung" (excrement), leg. *cacc g.* = W. cach; cf. Lat. caco, Gr. κακκάω, κάκκη, Skr. çakṛt, in the weak cases çakan, Lith. szeku: the German kacken infringes Grimm's law. *Gabhar*, W. gafar. As to *gabhar*, *v. supra*, No. 372. 1076. *La virrthi* (gl. juger, an acre) I cannot explain, unless the Irish be for lá-airthe, "a day's ploughing" (airthe, from aratio?), i. e. as much land as can be ploughed in a day; cf. W. aradu, to plough. There is probably some blunder in the gloss. 1077. *Nóin* (gl. vesper, evening), from the Lat. nóna (the third hour before sunset), with change of declension; W. nawn, A. S. nón, Eng. noon, Dan. noen. 1078. *Oide* (gl. nutritor), O. Ir. aite, which occurs in a gloss in Z. 1066, airdanimmart greim á *aite*, "his rearer's influence constrained him." (Note the genitive's identity with the nom., aite, not aiti. Perhaps, however, aite is the gen. plur.) The word also occurs in the Leabhar Breace Sermon on Brigit, cited by Dr. Todd, Lib. Hymn. 65 : Isé a hathair na noemoigise intathair nemda, isé a mac Isu Crist, isé a *haite* in Spirit nóeb, "this holy virgin's father is the heavenly Father: her son is Jesus Christ, her nurturer is the Holy Ghost." The non-aspiration of the *t* in aite can hardly be explained, except by assuming its original duplication (as in cruitire = crottaria); aite would then represent a primitive attia, which may be compared with Skr. attâ, mother; Lat. atta, Fest. Gr. ἄττα, Goth. atta, father; aithei, mother; O. Bohem. ot. 1079. *Onoir* = honor, whence it is taken, but with change to the i-declension, as in preceptóir, &c.

1080-1084. *Leghtóir* is from the Latin lector [lĕgo], which would regularly become lechtóir: the Irish root LÉG, read; in ro*lég* fanacc, did he read or not? Z. 1434, exhibits a strange lengthening of the vowel: cf. W. mag*ieyr* = macĕria. Lég enters into composition: act arroilgither (ar-ro-lég-fither) ind epistilse dúibsi berthir uaib Laudocensibus et doberthar ind æpistil scríbther do suidib con arlægthar (= ar-lég-atar) duibsi,

duibsi, "when this epistle shall have been read to you, let it be brought from you to the Laodiceans; and let the epistle that is written to them be brought so that it may be read to you." Z. 1044, con arlégidsi, gl. vos legatis, Z. 1044. In legai-s, the 3rd sing. pret., the verb in question seems to have passed over to the ai (é) conjugation:

> Inn insib mara torrian ainis, innib adrimi,
> *Legais* canoin la german, ised adñadat lini.- *Fiacc*. 6.
>
> In the isles of the Tyrrhene sea he remained, in them he meditated:
> He read the canon with Germanus; this histories make known.

Soleghta, soleghta, gl. legibilior, *infra*. The root senin has also been borrowed, and we find it in what is supposed to be the oldest MS. containing specimens of the Irish language, viz., the Book of Dimma (Library of T. C. D.). Thus, at the end of St. Matthew's Gospel: oróit¹ dodimmu rod*scrib* ["pray ye for Dimma who wrote it"] pro deo ⁊ benedictione; at the end of S. Luke's: oroit dodianchridiu diaro*scribad* ["pray ye for Dianchride, for whom was written"] hic liber et dodimmu ["for Dimma"] scribenti, amen . . . (Dimma is supposed to have written this A. D. 620). 1081. *Gradh* (gl. amor). Bopp (Gloss. 107) refers this to the Skr. r. grdh desiderare appetere, with which gorte (famine, Goth. gredus, hunger) has been connected *supra*: cf. also O. N. grád, Eng. greed. 1082. *Doctuir*, from the Lat. Anamchara, lit. "soul-friend," is the beautiful O. Ir. word for doctor, teacher. 1083. *Maisi* (gl. decor)—1084. *Mímaisi* (gl. dedecor), leg. maise, mímaise, et *v. supra*.

1085-1089. *Saethar* (gl. labor), in Z. sáithar (n.?), gen. sáithir: is uisse lóg a *sáithir* do chách (just is the reward of his labour to every one), Z. 1051; astorad *sáithir* do (Book of Armagh, 184 *b*, top margin), acc. sing. cen sáithar, Z. 251. 1086. *Tés* (gl. calor), gen. tesa, Z. 12 = W. tes, "sun-heat;" perhaps = tepsu, Skr. r. tap. 1087. *Dath* (gl. color), dat. pl. secht múir gloinidi con *dathaib* examlaib in a timchell, "seven chrystal walls, with various colours around it," Vis. Ad. 1088. *Boltanadh* (gl. odor), cf. ni *boltigetar* side *bolad*, "non odorem faciunt hi," Z. 447. 1089. *Bréntus* (gl. fetor), *v. supra*.

1090-1094. *Dénmusach* (gl. factor) from dénmus, O'R. *denmas*, an effect, and this from dénum, "to do." 1091. *Doilbtheoir* (gl. fictor) has been noticed *supra*. 1092. *Cennaidhe*

---

[1] The Lat. *oráte*, hibernicised. *Oratio* was also imported: I have not met the nom. sing., which must have been orathe, oirthe (cf. coibse, from confessio), but the acc. sing. *orthain* occurs in the Lib. Hymn., p. 32: Ninine écas dorine inn*orthainse* no fiac sleibte, "N. the sage made this prayer, or Fiac of Sletty."

Cennaidhe (gl. emptor), O'R.'s ceannaidhe, "a merchant, any dealer;" cethrar imorro roscennaigsim pátraic, "now four persons purchased Patrick" (Pref. to Secundinus' Hymn). 1093. *Didnightcoir* (gl. protector), O'R.'s didcanoir, "protector, guardian," from dítu, gen. díten, as to which v. supra. 1094. *Boc* (gl. tener), hod. bog, "soft, tender, penetrable," O'R., cf. *buigi* (gl. mollior), infra, Bret. bouk, "soft;" hence the Engl. "hog."

1095-1099. *Figidóir* (gl. textor), figheadóir, O'R., "a weaver," from the causal verb figim, I weave, Corm. (W. gwau, gwëu, Bret. gwéa, to weave). Bopp (Gloss. 335) refers to the Skr. r. vê, texere, suere, and compares Lat. vieo, Gr. ἤ-τριον, Lith. udis, textura; see also Diefenbach, G. W. i. 148, 431; Benfey, Gr. W. i. 287. To the Engl. "weave," web, O. H. G. web-an, &c. (see Curtius, G. E. i. 261), we cannot yet quote the corresponding forms in Old Irish and Welsh. 1096. *Triallatóir* (gl. nitor, attempter). The stem from which this noun is formed occurs in the Lib. Hymn. (pref. to Fiacc's Hymn): "dentar *trial* [mo] berthasa, ol Dubthach, con accadar Fiac, "Let an attempt be made to tonsure me," said Dubthach, "so that Fiac may perceive it." 1097. *Fliuchidect* (gl. liquor), from fliuchaide humidus, Z. 272, v. supra. 1098. *Cumdaightóir* (gl. conditor), cf. cumtach, ædificatio, Z. 229, 777, 1046. 1099. *Maigister* (gl. retor, leg. rector), from Lat. magister.

1100-1104. *Senóir*, from the Lat. senior (which would, I think, more regularly have become sinóir); W. henwr = hen-gwr, a Gaulish senoviro-s. 1101. *Eistidóir* (gl. auditor), cf. O'R.'s *cistim*, "I hear;" by metathesis for O. Ir. étsimm, cf. héitsidi (auditores), éitset (audiunt), Z. 23, 87; foćitsider (subintelligitur), Z. 34; foétsecht, subintellectio, Z. 771: the preservation of the *t* suggests the loss of an *n*. 1102. *Croidhe* = cradia, cridio, in O. Ir. au ia-stem, neuter like Skr. hrdaya, Zend zeredha-ya, Goth. hairtô, and Slav. srŭdĭce, while Gr. καρδία, and Lith. szirdis, are fem. The gen. and dat. of cride occur in the following gloss from Cormac: *Torc*, .i. nomen do *chridiu* ut etan dixit. Ni fó¹ in dam dom mo thuirce .i. mo *chridi* im chliab cotĺ forerith. " *Torc*, i. e. a name for the heart; as Etan said, 'not good is the throbbing of my *torec*, i. e. of my heart in my bosom which is trembling.'" Cf. also luath*chride*, gl. cardiacus in the Leyden codex of Priscian; Dian*chride*, supra, No. 1080. What is the *crid* in fom*chrid*ichfidersa (gl. accingar), Z. 475; fo*chrid*igedar (gl. accingit), Z. 476? Perhaps we may connect with this *cris*, gen. *cresa*, a girdle: Bret. dar-*greiz*, "the girdle or the middle of the body." *Croidhe* is always spelt cride in Z. (the *o* in *croidhe* being introduced to mark the broad pronunciation of the *r*). I know not if W.

craidd

---

¹ Fó (*s* being lost between vowels, and *au* becoming *ó*) = Skr. vasu, Zend vôhu.

craidd were ever a stem in ia. 1103. *Fairge* (gl. equor), v. supra. 1104. *Marmur*, marble, from Lat. marmor.

1105–1109. *Ainmidhe* (gl. castor), an animal. 1106. *Ad*, hoc ador *ad* should, perhaps, be read (as O'D.) suggests) hoc ador *torad*: torad is "fruit" in O. Ir., dat. sing. torud, Z. 231. 1107. *Ughdur* (gl. autor), from auctor: cf. O. Ir. augtortás = auctoritas, W. awdur. 1108, 1109. *Maisi*, *Mimaisi*, v. supra.

1110–1112. *Cuimneach* (gl. memor), co-m'n-ech. 1111. *Micuimneach* (gl. immemor), root MAN, as to which v. supra: cf. ní *cuman* lim, gl. nescio; cuimnigedar (gl. reminiscentis), Z. 843. 1112. *Tecoisce* (gl. doctior), cf. *tegaisge*, supra, would have been in O. Ir. tecaisciu. The -*iu*, -*u* in the O. Ir. comparatives from iûs, and this from iâs = Skr. íyáns (strong theme), O. Lat. -iōs, Goth. iza, Gr. ἴων. The *nis* (spelt *nías*, *niis*, *niis*, *infra*) preceding the adj., is = ní is, ní as, "a thing which is," *is*, *as*, being, as I conjecture, respectively the third sing. indic. of the roots AS, ÂS, the principal fragments of which remaining in O. Ir. are as follows:—

	Sing.	Plur.
Pres. indic. 1.	am, amm[1]	ammi (ṅ)[2]
2.	at	adib[3], ada
3.	is, it[4]	hit, it
	as, at	(at)
Pres. subj. 3.	asu, aso	atu.

Impersonal Flexion.

| 1. | ismé, asmmé[5] | issnisni |
| 2. | istú | ississi, itsib. |

I cannot explain these forms solely by the root AS and the active voice. The átmaneforms of AS given by the grammarians are fictions. One is therefore thrown upon the root ÂS and the middle voice, of which last there are, I think, clear traces in the Celtic dialects.

---

[1] Arnamtomuad *namm* (= na + amm) in duine, Z. 702.

[2] Ammi néulig, Z. 252.

[3] Adib óis muintire, Z. 478; adib atrab do dia, *ibid*. Adib iressich, Z. 252. Before *m* the *b* is assimilated: *adimmaice*, Z. 251. What is the form *abi* in Z. 1043, gl. 18 : quasi dixisset *abi* mogasi dam atá far cóimdiu in nim, "as if he had said that ye are servants: your lord also is in heaven ?" A misreading for adi, i. e. adim ?

[4] Itsib ata chomarpi, Z. 894: ithé ciatu ruchreitset, Z. 570: rofess *it fás* infenechus icondelg ferb ndé, "it is known that the Feuechus is void in comparison with the words of God," Corm. v. *Ferb*.

[5] Z. 434, -mmé, from mé + mé ? Cf. Lat. meme.

dialects. In the first person sing. *am, amm* is the Skr. asmi, Gr. ἐμμί, εἰμί, Lat. sum, Lith. es-mi, Goth. im, Eng. am. Here Irish has retained the old form better than her Celtic sisters, the W. being wyf, Corn. of, Bret. off. The plur. ammi (ṅ) is startlingly like the Gr. ἐσμέν, both, perhaps, standing for an original as-masmi. That the *n* is part and parcel of the Celtic form seems proved by the uninfected *m* (= m + n) in the corresponding W. *ym*, Corn. *on*, Bret. *om-p*, as well as by the fact that *ammi* does not aspirate, and must, therefore, have ended in a consonant. In the 2nd person sing. *a-t*[1], like the W. *wy-t*, Corn. *o-s*, is formed by suffixing the pronoun of this person. But the *a* in *a-t* points to the Skr. âsê, Gr. ἦσαι, the 2nd pers. of the root *is*, to sit, to be, "from which," says Bopp, Gloss. 35, "the root of the verb subst. AS is, perhaps, shortened." Whereas the *wy* in *wy-t* rests on ê, ai, Skr. asi, Gr. εἶ. For the agglutination of the pronoun cf. O. N. er-t, Eng. ar-t, Goth. vas-t = Eng. was-t, O. N. var-t. The plural *ada*[2] seems from *adib*, which may = *adai* + *sib* the pers. pron. of the 2nd pers. pl.: cf. the Skr. âdhvê for âs-dhvai, Gr. ἦσθε. In the 3rd person *is* of course is = Skr. asti, Gr. ἐσ-τί(ν), Lith. es-ti, Eng. *is*. But, like the Lat. es-t, Goth. ist, it must have lost its terminal vowel at an early period, for it never aspirates. Indeed, in one instance (is nuisse, Z. 370) it seems to take a transported *n*, which would point to an old Celtic form ASTIN. But here, perhaps, Z. misread *n* for *h*. The forms *it, at*[3], in the sing. are obscure to me. Can they have passed over from the plur.? There *hit* (note the *metathesis aspirationis*, h-i-t = i-h-i(n)t), or *it is* = Skr. santi (for asanti), Zend. hěnti, Gr. (σ)εντί, εἰσί, Lat. s-unt, Goth. sind: other Celtic forms are W. and Bret. ynt, Corn. yns, *ens*. *As* aspirates, and must therefore have ended with a vowel at a comparatively recent period. It is generally used in dependent or relative sentences; and was, I believe, originally identical with the Skr. âstê: *at* seems to point to ἦνται, Skr. âsatê, for âsantai, the nasal of plurality being omitted, as in dadatê = δίδο-νται. The subjunctive forms *asu*[1] (*aso*), and *atu*, only occur in connexion with the conjunctions *ma*,

---

[1] Z. 1129.   [2] Ada baill, Z. 251.

[3] Is and *at* gniu tengad isind huiliu labramarni, "est officium linguae in omni quod loquimur," Z. 446. This is an example of the use of *at* as a *singular* form. But there can be no doubt that it will be found in the plural. I can, however, as yet only quote Middle-Irish examples, such as "*at* luide do láma *at* breeca do beoil *at* liatha do śúile," Leab. Breacc, cited O'Don. Gr. 350. *As* is often found in an absolute position. Thus *As* du Christ as immaircide in salm-so, "*it is* to Christ this psalm is inscribed," Z. 473: Sancti et justi it hé as chorp dosom. Christus *as* chenn ind noib *as* chorp, "Sancti et justi, it is they who are his body. *Christus* is head, the saints are body," Z. 197, where note the use of *os* in the plur.

[4] M-*assu* thol, Z. 671.

ma, "if," and *cia*, *cé*. "although," Z. 671, 673. *Asu* (*asa*), the *s* of which is sometimes doubled, appears to me identical with the Skr. imperative âstâm; and *atu* (the *t* of which is unaspirable, and must, therefore, have lost a preceding *n*) seems the Indo-European âsantâm. 1113. *Laidiri* (gl. fortior), positive laidir: *laidiri*, gl. fortitudo, *supra*. 1114. *Mó* (gl. major). This form occurs in Z. 285, as well as móo, móa, má, máo, máa, W. is mwy, Corn. moy, Bret. muy (where note the preservation of the primitive *i*). One thing is tolerably clear about these forms, that they have lost a vowel-flanked *g*: cf. Skr. mahíyâns, Zend. maçyóhim zãm = μείζονα γῆν, Bopp; Osc. mais, Lat. major, for mag-ios, Goth. maiza, μείζων, from μεγjων. So in the superl. O. Ir. maam.

1115–1119. *Lugha* (gl. minor), in Z. 283, 284, lugu, laigiu, W. llei = ἐ-λάσσων (ἐ-λαχjων), Lat. levior, Skr. laghíyâns, Eng. less. 1116. *Ferr* (gl. melior) = W. Corn. and Bret. guell, Z. 286: cf. Skr. varíyâns, ἀρείων. The second *r* in ferr, *l* in guell, represent the assimilated *y*: W. superl. goreu stands for varama. 1117. *Mésa* (gl. pejor), messa, Z. 285. The positive is the prefix mí- (Ebel) = Goth. missa (Dief. G. W. ii. 76) = Eng. mis: cf. Skr. mithyâ, "falsely." There are two other O. Ir. comparatives in -*sa*, viz., nesa, nessa, or nesso, "nearer," and tresa, or tressa, "firmer," "stronger." Nessa, W. nes, if connected with the Zend nazdista (proximus) = Skr. nêdishtha, may stand for nasdiâs: cf. Skr. nêdîyas. (With the superl. Ir. nessam, W. nesaf, Ebel has compared Umbr. Osc. nesimo.) Tressa, W. trech, Bret. tréc'h, seems to point to a Gaul. trexiâs, but this leaves its connexion with the positive trén unexplained, unless, indeed, this be = trexna.

1120–1124. *Sanntaigi* (gl. avarior), *sanntach*, *supra*, No. 667, 1121. *Dilé* (gl. carior), posit. *dil*; is *dil* lace maid [leg. maith] do dénum dúibsi, "she likes (lit. est gratum ei) to do good to you," Z. 283; nimdil, Z. 942; compar. diliu, Z. 283; superl. dilem: is hed as *dilem* lium rath precepte, "It is this that is dearest to me, the grace of teaching," Z. 604. 1122. *Noillsi* (gl. clarior), pos. sollus, solus. 1123. *Meata* (gl. debilior) = O. Ir. mettu, from O'R.'s meata, "cowardly, fearful, timid," reminds one of the Goth. ga*maids*, Eng. mad, but perhaps the resemblance is accidental. Cf. W. meth, "a miss," methiant, failure, decay, Corn. meth, pudor, Z. 223, méza, "timide," "honteux." 1124. *Gile* (gl. albior), pos. gel (= gila), *geal* (gl. albus), *supra*, No. 659. Cf. Lat. gilvus = O. H. G. gelo, Eng. yellow. "The stem," says Lottner (7 Zeits. 184), "is widely spread, but with other suffixes: Gr. χλωρός, Skr. hari, Sl. žlŭtŭ, Lith. geltas."

1125–1129. *Socarthanaighi* (gl. amabilior). 1126. *Soleghta* (gl. legibilior). 1127. *Somolta* (gl. laudabilior), all formed by prefixing the particle so (= εὖ) to adjectives formed respectively from the roots car, leg, and mol, as to which r. *supra*, and compare with *socarthanaighi* cairddine, for cairtine, "of friendship," Z. 740, cairddinigther (amari),

(amari), Z. 1129, which, however, are formations from the participial stem, carant. 1128. *Conaichi* (gl. felicior), cf. O'R.'s conách, "prosperity, affluence." 1129. *Glica* (gl. sapientior), O. Ir. gliccu : ar ni ɓa *gliccu* felsub olambieidsi si in Christo estis, Z. 1040, "for no philosopher is wiser than ye will be," &c.: the abstract derived from it occurs in a gloss on "sapientes in astutia," Z. 257, viz., isin tuaichli isin *glicci*, i foili, 1130 : cf. Goth. glaggvus, O. N. glöggr, A. S. gleav, N. H. G. klug, Dieffenbach, G. W. ii. 411.

1130–1133. *Cainsuaraighi* (gl. benignior), read *cáinfuarraighi?* compar. of *cáin-fuarach*, voc. sing., cain[f]uarraig, occurs in Gildas' Lorica. 1131. *Dana* (gl. audacior), leg. dána : the positive of this is dána, cited *supra* from Colman's Hymn, 12, and glossing davus in Z. 20. With *dána*, Glück, 92, connects the river-name Dánuvius (N. H. G. Donau, Eng. Danube), often wrongly written Danubius. Cf. also dánatu (audacia), Z. 769. The dat. sing of dána occurs in the Félire, Jan. 23 :—

Césad cebriani	The suffering of Cebrianus
clementi consádu :	And of Clement I celebrate :
ronsnadat dondríga	May they convey us to the Kingdom,
conandúnad *dánu*.	With their daring host.

1132. *Scirbe* (gl. amarior), pos. serb, O'R.'s scarbh = W. chwerw, O. H. G. sueran (dolere) cf. the Eng. *service* tree ; cf. the adverb int*serbu* (gl. amarius), Z. 563. Z. has also the subst. serbe, a fem. iâ-stem : gen. sing. o cech cenélu *serbe*, Z. 257, "ab omni genere amaritudinis," acc. sing. cen *serbi* peetho (gl. azyrni), "without the bitterness of sin." 1133. *Labartaighe* (gl. loquacior), pos. labartach, an adj. formed from the base labar, frequent in Celtic : cf. Corn. guir-leueriat, veridicus, gou-leueriat, falsidicus, Z. 98, W. llafaru, llefaru, to speak ; allafar, dumb (= Ir. amlabar, Z. 743), and in Irish, labrad loqui, sermo : conibad an dede sin im' labrad-sa, Z. 460, rolabrastar, *supra*, "he spoke," which comes from a deponent labra-r, Z. 444. Bopp, in his Glossary, p. 297, has referred the Mod. Ir. labhraim, I speak, labhradh, speech, to the Skr. r. lap loqui, sed qu.; cf. the Gaulish name Labarus. A form, apparently taken from the Lat. labrum, occurs in O. Ir., but unfortunately I am as yet only able to quote its acc. pl. :—

Sén, a christ, mo *labra*	Bless, O Christ, my lips (?)
a choimde secht nime!	O Lord of seven heavens ![1]

Before

---

[1] Verses prefixed to the Leabhar Breacc copy of the Félire of Oingus céle Dé ("God's companion"). In a MS. preserved in the Bodleian, however (Rawlinson, F, 95, fo. 59), this passage runs : Sén a christ mo *labrad*, a choimdiu secht nime,—and this I believe to be the true reading.

Before leaving the subject of the Celtic comparatives, I take the opportunity of referring to a paper on the subject by Dr. Ebel in the Beitr., vol. ii., pp. 78-80, and of printing a note with which I have been favoured by Prof. Siegfried: "I was long doubtful whether the Old Irish comparative in *iu*, *u*, was from -iân (like Greek) or -iâs (like Latin). I am now convinced it is from -iâs, whence by weakening, ius, iu. We have the analogy of the acc. pl. of masc. a-stems, which ended in -ús, not -ûn (ex -âns); this we know, because that case never appears with the transported *n*, as in the sing. fer (n). The Welsh termination of the comparative -*ach*, the Breton -*ock*, one would wish to explain likewise from -iâs. But I believe that this syllable (the Indo-European *iâns*) is totally lost in Welsh, as it is almost in Irish. No one will find this unnatural who knows that the original accent of the comparative was on the radical syllable. The termination -*ach* must then be some agglutinated word or particle, though such seems at first not offered by the Welsh lexicons. I would point to a possible connexion with ἐξ, ἔξω, ἔξοχα, W. *ch*-, Ir. *as*-, and especially with the unexplained *assa*, which occurs with the Old Ir. comparative in Z. 286. Cf. also the Welsh '*ech-doe*, day before yesterday, *ech*-nos, night before last.'"

1134-1139. *Naithech na tuise* (gl. turibulus, thurible, censer), "vessel of the incense:" *saithech*, occurs, spelt *soitheach* in the *Lebar na Cert*, p. 236. Dare we compare the W. *saig*? *Tuise*, gen. of *tus* (which occurs in composition in *tuslestar*, gl. turibulum, Z. 1120); *tus* is from the Lat. tus, and from the inflection of the adjective *dimór* in the following lines, it appears to have been feminine (Lib. Hymn. 7 *a*):—

Melchar tidnachtaid indóir	Melchar, giver of the gold:
Caspar tuce in*tus* dimóir	Caspar brought the excellent frankincense:
Patifarsat tuce inmirmaith	Patifarsat brought the good myrrh;
Conastarat[1] dondrig[f]laith.	He gave them to the kingly Lord.

The acc. is more correctly spelt *túis* in Harl. 1802, 5 *b* (*tuis* dodia dodégtidnaic). 1135. *Urralaisti* (gl. horologium, ὡρολόγιον) I have never met elsewhere. It is identical with the W. *orlais*, horloge. Cf. *próiste*, *cóiste*, from broche, coche. 1136. *Piloir* (gl. colostrigium, i. e. collistrigium, collum, stringo), French pilori, "Engl. pillory, aus dem deutschen pfilare?" (J. Grimm, Rechtsalterthümer, 725). 1137. *Compas no rainy antsair*, "a compass, or the carpenter's (or mason's) divider," O'D.; *sair*, gen. sing. of *sáer* = W. saer, a masc. a-stem. Cf. *sáir*dénmidecht, gl. artificium, Z. 771; *sáer* oc suidigud sillab, Z. 1018, "an artist in placing syllables;" n. pl. nitat *sóir* huili oc saigid for sunu, Z. 460, "all are not artists in disputing respecting sounds,"

[1] Cf. contarat, Z. 360 (4).

sounds," Corn. sair artifex, faber, Z. 142. How is it that the initial *s* is retained in Welsh? Ciaran macc int*sáir* ("Céranus filius *artificis*," Book of Armagh) is a well-known person in Irish hagiology, as is also the Gobhan *Sáer* in Irish tradition. The Highland name Macintyre = mac iutsáir. 1139. *Maide sgine* (gl. manubrium), handle of a knife; *maide*, lit. "wood," "stick," occurs in Corm., and Bopp compares it with Skr. manthâna (rudis); *sgine*, gen. of *sgian*, as to which *v. supra*, No. 440.

In conclusion, I have to repeat the expression of my great obligations to my friend and teacher, Professor Siegfried. To his genius or guidance are due all the novel truths brought forward in this Commentary, and he is in nowise responsible for the mistakes which it contains. I have also to request that my readers will, before forming an opinion on the contents of any of the preceding paragraphs, see whether the statements made therein have been corrected, completed, or modified in the Corrigenda and Addenda at the end of the volume.

APPENDIX.

APPENDIX.

It has been thought that the following Hymn, with the glosses thereon, would form an appropriate supplement to the foregoing Tract and Commentary. The poem in question is taken from the copy preserved in the so-called "Leabhar Breace," or "Speckled Book" of the Mac Egans (fol. 111, *a, b*), a manuscript in the Library of the Royal Irish Academy. In the opinion of Dr. Todd, this manuscript was produced in the latter part of the fourteenth century. It is a large and well-written codex, and contains many Irish tracts and poems, of which some (such as the "Vision of Mac Conglinni," and the "Calendar of Oingus") are of considerable antiquity.

I know nothing certain about the Gillas (or Gillus—the MS. allows of either reading) to whom the scribe attributes our poem. As, however, Laideenn, son of Baeth the Victorious (who would seem from the preface to have brought Gillas' production to Ireland), died in the year 661[1], we may perhaps presume that our Gillas was the celebrated Welshman, S. Gildas Badonicus, whose death is recorded in the Annals of Ulster, at the year 569.

[1] "This ecclesiastic was a pupil of S. Lactan, at Clonfert-Molua, now Clonfert-Mulloe, or Kyle, in the Queen's County, and died on the 12th of January (at which day he is commemorated in the Irish calendars), in the year 661."—Reeves, *Proceedings R. I. A.*, Nov. 8, 1858, where also may be found the obituary notices of Laideenn, contained in Tigernach and the Annals of Ulster. In the latter he is called Laidggenn *sapiens*. In the Bodleian Annals of Innisfallen we find at the year 651, Quies Laideenn mc. Baith hannaig. For this quotation, as well as for the following extracts from the calendars, I am indebted to Dr. Reeves:—

> Crist asrfanaid rindaig Christ's acute mystery-explainer is
> Laideend macc Baith bandaig. Laideend son of Baeth the Victorious.
>
> *Félire Oingusso*, Jan. 12.

(*rindaig* is glossed by *glic* in the *Leabhar Breace*, and the first line by "is rinnaith irrúnib crist, i. e. he is sharp-pointed in the mysteries of Christ." *Bandaig*, gen. sing. m. of *bandach*, is translated "victorious" on the authority of Colgan). Laidhgenn macc Baoith o Cluain ferta molua *et* as ann ata a adhnacul, Aois Cr. 660, "L son of B. of C. F. M. and there is his tomb, A. D. 660."—*Calendar of Donegal*, Jan. 12. So the scholiast on Marian Gorman at Jan. 12: Laideenn ó cluain ferta molua ⁊ is ann rohadnacht som .i. Laideenn mac bóith, "from C. F. M. and it is there he was buried, i. e. L. son of B." Denis mentions a Ladkenus Hiberniensis who made an abstract from the "Moralia" of Gregory the Great. But I am doubtful if this were the same as L., son of Baeth.

569. This Gildas was the son of Caw, a disciple of Iltut, and, in the opinion of his countrymen, an "egregius scolasticus et scriptor optimus" (Rees' *Cambro-British Saints*; Llandovery, 1853. pp. 120, 343 n). The Welsh origin of the hymn is indicated by its Latinity. Thus gibra (homo), cona (oculus), sena (dens), gigra (leg. gugra? caput), are, so far as I know, only found in the Folium Luxemburgense (see Zeuss, G. C. 1096, 1097, where the forms gibras, conis, sennarum, gugras, are quoted from Mone's edition in his *Die gallische Sprache*; Karlsruhe, 1851). If Gildas Badonicus were the author, and if, as is possible, the *mortalitas hujus anni* mentioned in the fifth and sixth lines were the Yellow Plague, we might attribute the composition of our hymn to the year 547, when that visitation was first inflicted on Britain, and when Gildas was 31 years of age. Dr. Reeves, indeed, has thought (*Proceedings of the Royal Irish Academy*, November 8, 1858) that the composer of our hymn was a later writer. But I understand that this eminent scholar has recently found reason to alter this opinion, which rested, no doubt, on the statement that Gildas was a contemporary of Laidcenn, involved in the assertion that the latter "venit ab eo [scil. Gilla] in insulam Hiberniam." However this may be, I do not think it desirable to go further into the question, agreeing, as I do, with Denis (Catal. Codd. Theol. Vindob., i. 3, p. 2932), who prints from a Viennese MS. of the fifteenth century some verses of the hymn in question, and observes thereon:—"Hymnus sat mendose scriptus, rudis et superstitiosus, quo quis omnes vel minimas partes corporis sui partes Deo protegendas prorsus ἀνατομικῶς adnumerat, ubi ad membrorum censum delabitur, Plautinum te cocum aut Merlinum Coccajum audire credas."

Herr Mone, the learned Director of Archives at Carlsruhe, has published the text of the following hymn from a Darmstadt MS. of the end of the eighth century, which attributes the composition to "Lathacan Scotigena." Mone's edition ("Hymni Latini Medii Aevi," Friburg, 1853, vol. i. p. 367), is followed by a commentary in German, from which I translate the following passages:—"As an example of Irish hymn-poetry of the seventh century, the above song is not without interest, for one perceives in it a national style of treatment which differs greatly from that of the other peoples. In minuteness of detail it agrees with the drawing of the ancient Irish figures (Bildwerk), particularly with that of the illuminations in the MSS., and this particularity (Specialisiren) is accordingly a national trait. See the 'Contributions of the Antiquarian Society in Zürich,' vol. vii., p. 73-75, 92"[1].

"The song rests on Rom. xiii. 12, 2 Cor. x. 4, especially Ephes. vi. 11, 1 Thessal.

v. 8.

---

[1] Hence it will be seen that Mone considers the author to have been an Irishman. And certainly the authority of a MS. of the eighth century is not to be despised. But I repeat that the peculiar Latinity of

v. 8. Hence also χιτών τῆς πίστεως in the Menæa, July 29. Quibus pro lorica Christus est, vim non metuunt. Ennod. pro syn. præf. Since the Fall, inasmuch as man's body became mortal, it has been capable of injury, and will remain so until he shall again receive an immortal body through the resurrection. And inasmuch as he has lost the garment of the original innocence, the *stola prima*, he needs against the perils of the earthly life, a defensive garment, as it were, an armour. The song moves in these ideas, to which allusion is made in other places. For example: νεκρώσεως τοὺς χιτῶνας ἐξάμενος προπετείᾳ τῆς ἀκρασίας, ἀλλὰ σύ με ἔνδυσον υἱὲ τοῦ Θεοῦ, στολὴν φωτεινὴν τῆς ἀναγεννήσεως. Triodion, E. 1. Gregor. Naz. Orat. xlii. p. 681, says:—'Ἀδὰμ τοὺς δερματίνους ἀμφιέννυται χιτῶνας, ἴσως τὴν παχυτέραν σάρκα καὶ θνητὴν καὶ ἀντίτυπον."

With regard to the Irish glosses which are found between the lines or in the margin of the Leabhar Breace copy of our hymn, and for the sake of which alone such hymn is here printed, I am of opinion that they are middle-Irish, some of them early middle-Irish, but I can see no evidence that any of them were produced before the eleventh century. Thus we find *m* for Old Irish *b* (nocmaib = O. Ir. nóibaib); *d* for *t* (augdar = O. Ir. augtor); *nd* for O. Ir. *nn* (adbronda, coitchind, colaind, brond, cend). *A* is written for *e* in *sean*, O. Ir. *sen*, for *i* in *an* "in," *at* "in thy," and for *o* in *mara*, O. Ir. mora. *Iu* has become *i* in cind (capiti, W. and Corn. pyn), anciently ciunn. In declension the feminine article has in the nom. pl. masc. usurped the place of the forms proper to the masc., and we find *na* sloig, *na* hescarait, *na* baill, which in Old Irish would be respectively *intslóig*, *indescarait*, *inbaill*. In the dat. pl. the article and adjectives have dropt their labial ending, and we have dona hainglib, cusna hairnib, cumachtaib nemtruailnide, for the Old Ir. donaib ainglib, cusnaib áirnib, cumachtaib nebthrúailnidib. The noun, too, has suffered serious changes: thus all distinction seems lost between the nom., gen., and voc. sing. of *ia*-stems, and we find cride for the O. Ir. cridi (cordis) and a thigerna for a thigerni (domine). In the dat. pl. of macc, a masc. *a*-stem, the old accusative termination seems to have taken the place of the dative-ending, and we find maccu for the O. Ir. maccaib. In a consonantal stem, míl (= milit), we observe in the acc. pl. a passing over to the vocalic declension, and thus ocmiled-u appears for the ancient ocmiled-a. Other such instances will be mentioned in the notes. In the verb the only remarkable form presented by the glosses is *ingerrtha* (gl. lacerandum) for the Old Irish gerrthi. The practice of thus forming the fut.

the hymn leads me to believe in its Cambrian origin. The metre, too, is un-Irish. It seems to be what Welsh writers call *y gyhydedd lues*.

fut. part. pass. by prefixing *in* to the pret. part. pass. has lasted down to the present day. It is noticed in O'Molloy's *Grammatica Latino-Hibernica*, Romæ, 1677, pp. 99, 100, where we find the following:—"Particula autem *in* addita voculæ facit voculam importare participium finiens in *dus* apud latinos, ut *faciendus*, ut *hoc non est faciendum*, hibernicè *ni bhfuil so indeunta*." This, in Old Irish, would be *ni dénti inso*[1].

The text of the hymn is printed as it stands in the MS., save that I have expanded the contractions, severed the prepositions from the words they govern, punctuated, and invariably commenced the lines and the proper names with capitals. The glosses have been placed under the text, their numerous contractions expanded, and such expansions represented by italics.

Gillas hanc loricam fecit ad demones expellendos eos qui adversaverunt illi. Peru[enit] angelus ad illum: et dixit illi angelus. Si quis homo frequentauerit illam addetur ei secul[um] septimm annis: et tertia pars peccatorum delebitur. In quacunque die cantauerit hanc orationem, oratores, homines uel demones et inimici non possunt nocere: et mors in illo die non tangit. Laidcend mac Búith Bannaig uenit ab eo in insolam Hiberniam: transtulit et portauit superaltare sancti Patricii episcopi sauos nos facere, amen. Metrum undecaisillabum quod et bracicatelecticon dicitur quod undecem sillabis constat. sic scanditur,

   [S]uffragare[1] trinitatis unitas, unitatis miserere trinitas,

et sic disponitur:

    Suffragare[2], quaeso[3], mihi possito[4]

                       Ut

GLOSS.—[1] Forgaire ata hic onbrethir choitchind asberar sufragor .i. fortachtaigim . sufragare .i. fortachtaigim, "this is an imperative from the common verb, which is called *suffragor* .i. I assist, *suffragare*, i. e. I assist." [2] INni tra atbert intaugdar [*in marg.*] hic .i. sufragare dobeth forgaire onbrethir choitchind asberar sufragor .i. dotoet uad ifus conidintinit gnima ou brethir gneithig asberar [sufrago] .i. sufragor. fuit sufrago secundum veteres. "Now what the author has said here, i. e. that *suffragare* is an imperative from the common verb which is called suffragor, i. e. it came from it here, [or] it may be an infiuitive active, from the active verb which is called *suffrago*, i. e. *sufragor*. Fuit, &c. [3] .i. deus. [4] .i. iarsuidiugud, "having been placed," lit. "after placing."

---

[1] Ebel (Beitr. 1, 162) has equated the -ti of the O. Ir. part. fut. pass. with Skr. -tavya, Gr. -τέο-ς, Lat. -tivu-s. Z. has compared the Old Breton -*toe*, the Mod. Welsh -*dwy*. Cf. also the Cornish -*dow* in cara-dow, casa-dow, (amandus, abominandus).

The Lorica of Gildas.

4. Magni⁴⁽ᵃ⁾ maris⁵ uelut in periculo⁶.
   Ut non secum trahat⁷ me mortalitas⁸
   Hujus anni⁹ neque mundi uanitas¹⁰,
   Et hoc¹¹ idem peto a sublimibus¹²
8. Celestis¹³ milit[i]e¹⁴ uirtutibus¹⁵;
   Ne me linquant¹⁶ lacerandum¹⁷ hostibus¹⁸,
   Sed defendant¹⁹ me iam²⁰ armis²¹ fortibus²².
   Ut me illi precedant in acie²³
12. Celestis²⁴ exercitus²⁵ m[i]litie²⁶
    Cerubin²⁷ et cerupihin²⁸ cum millibus²⁹,
    Gabrihel³⁰ et Michael³¹ cum similibus³²;
    Opto tronos³³, uirtutes³⁴, archangelos³⁵,
16. Principatus³⁶, potestates³⁷, angelos³⁸.
    Ut m[e] denso³⁹ defendentes⁴⁰ agmine⁴¹
    Inimicos⁴² uale[a]nt⁴³ prosternere⁴⁴.
    Dum deinde ceteros agonetetas⁴⁵,
20. Patriarchas⁴⁶ quatuor quater profetas⁴⁷;
                                                                Apostolos

GLOSS.—⁴⁽ᵃ⁾ .i. mor, "great." ⁵ .i. inmara "of the sea." ⁶ .i. anguasacht, "in danger." ⁷ .i. naromstaine inbas, "that the mortality may not defeat me." ⁸ .i. diabul iarforba mobethad, "the devil after the completion of my life." ⁹ .i. nahamsiresea, "of this time." ¹⁰ nadinnaines intsoegail, "nor the world's vanity." ¹¹ .i. allatum .i. impide, "a supplication." ¹² onabardaib, "from the heights." ¹³ .i. nemdai, "of heavenly." ¹⁴ .i. calmdacht, "soldiery." ¹⁵ .i. nasualaig, "the virtues." ¹⁶ naromfaebat, "that they should not leave me." ¹⁷ .i. ingerrtha, "about to be mangled." ¹⁸ escarait, "enemies." ¹⁹ .i. corumditnet, "that they defend me." ²⁰ .i. cohairithe, "particularly." ²¹ .i. arm. ²² .i. calma, "brave." ²³ .i. corôremtusaigit remumm isnacathaib, "that they may precede me in the battles." ²⁴ nemda, "heavenly." ²⁵ .i. nasloig, "the hosts." ²⁶ .i. nacrodachta .i. comthinol nanaingel, "of the soldiery, i. e. a congregation of the angels." ²⁷ .i. sciencie multitudo. ²⁸ .i. adutes, "burning heat." ²⁹ cusnahilmilib, "with the many thousands." ³⁰ .i. fortitudo dei. ³¹ .i. qui sicut dens. ³² .i. cusnacosmailsib, "with the like persons." ³³ .i. sedes dei interpretatur. ³⁴ .i. iunauirtute. ³⁵ .i. summos nuntios. ³⁶ naprincipate. ³⁷ .i. napotestate. ³⁸ .i. nuntios l. ministros. ³⁹ .i. ontsluag dluith, "with the dense host." ⁴⁰ .i. curaditnet, "that they may defend." ⁴¹ .i. oisluag, "with a host." ⁴² nahescarait, "the enemies." ⁴³ .i. curafedat, "that they may be able." ⁴⁴ aclod, "to overthrow them." ⁴⁵ .i. unde dicitur agonithetas? principes belli .i. nahænachdu. Unde dicitur agon .i. œnach. agon .i. cath l. cuimleng. Unde dicitur liber de agone Christianorum? ex quo fit agonia .i. brug l. athgc. "Unde dicitur *agonithetas?* principes belli, i. e. the presidents of the assembly. Unde dicitur *agon?* i. e. an assembly; *agon*, i. e. a contest or conflict. Unde dicitur liber *de agone Christianorum?* ex quo fit *agonia*, i. e. anguish or struggle." ⁴⁶ patres excelsos. ⁴⁷ .i. neros nuntios.

138   *Appendix.*

          Apostolos[48] navis Ch[risti] proretas[49]
          Et martires[50] omnes peto athletas[51],
          Atque adiuro[52] et uirgines[53] omnes[72].
24. Uiduas[53,a] fideles[54] et profesores[55]
          Uti me per illos[56] salus[57] sepiat[58]
          Atque omne malum a me pereat[59].
          Christus[60] mecum pactum[61] firmum feriat[62],
28. Cuius tremor[63] tetras[64] turbas terreat[65].

Finit primus prologus graduum angelorum et patriarcharum, apostolorum et martirum cum Christo. INcipit prologus secundus de cunctis membris corporis usque ad genua.

          Deus, inpenetrabilis tutela[66],
          Undique[67] me defende[68] potentia[69].
          Mei[a] gibre[70] peruas[71] omnes[72] libera[73],
32. Tuta[74] pelta[75] protegente[76] singula[77],
          Ut non [t]etri[78] demones in latera[79]
          Mea uibrent[80] ut soleant iacula[81].
                                           Gigram

GLOSS.—[48] .i. missos. [49] .i. bruinecha l. nastiurasmaind. A prora .i. onbroine, oucbuirr thussig naluinge, arite nomina ada corr: prora. pupiss, "prow-men, or the steersmen: *a prora* .i. from the prow, i. e. from the foremost end of the ship; for these are the *nomina* of its two ends, *prora, puppis*." [50] .i. credentes. [51] .i. na bocmiledu .i. principes belli. [52] .i. atchimm, "I adjure." [53] oga, "virgins." [53(a)] nafedba, "the widows." [54] .i. indracca, "faithful." [55] nafaismedaig, "the confessors." [56] gnathbugnd trithu, "to use through them." [57] .i. slanti, "safety." [58] .i. coro[m]imme, "that it may surround me." [59] .i. condechat uam foreulu uleu bite foriarair chuirp ┐ anma cechoein, "that back from me may go the ills that are behind the body and soul of every one." [60] unctus. [61] .i. cairdes l. dluthad, "friendship or compact." [62] .i. curabena, "that he strike" [cf. foedus ferire]. [63] .i. in anima et in bono .i. in corpure (sic). [64] .i. grana, "hideous." [65] curauaimnige, "that it may terrify." [66] ininillius nemtbremeta l. nemthroeta, "the security impenetrable or unconquered." [67] .i. di cech leith, "from every side." [68] ditin, "defend thou." [69] .i. dotchunnachtaib nemtruailnide, "with thy incorruptible powers." [70] .i. hominis. gibre. [71] .i. artus .i. compur iochleib, "trunk (?) of the chest." [72] .i. na huile, "all the." [73] .i. sær, "free thou." [74] .i. inill, "safe." [75] .i. sciath, "shield." [76] .i. ditnet, "they protect." [77] .i. membra .i. naball, "the members." [78] .i. granna, "hideous." [79] .i. donatoebaib, "to the sides." [80] .i. narobertnaiget, "that they may not brandish." [81] .i. amal clechtait anurcharu, "as they are used, their darts."

---

                        [a] In the MS. Mee.

The Lorica of Gildas.

Gigram[92], cephale[83] cum iaris[84], et conas[85],
36. Patham[86], lignam[87], senas[88] atque micenas[89]
Cladum[90], carsum[91], mandianum[92], talius[93],
Patma[94], exugiam[95] atque binas idumas[96].
Meo ergo cum capillis[97] uertici[98]
40. Galea[99] salutis[100] esto[101] capiti[102],
Fronti[103], oculis[104] cerebro triformi[105],
Rostro[106], labio[107], faciei[108], timpori[109],
Mento[110], barbæ[111], superciliis[112], auribus[113],
44. Genis[114], bucis[115], internaso[116], naribus[117],
Pupillis[118], rotis[119], palpebris[120], tutonibus[121],
Gingis[122], anclo[123], maxillis[124], faucibus[125].
Dentibus[126], lingue[127], ori[128] et guturi[129],
48. Uue[130], gurgulioni[131], et sublingue[132], ceruici[133],

Capitali,

GLOSS.—[82] .i. incloicend l. inccindetan, "the skull or the top of the forehead." [83] .i. inhaithes, "the crown." [84] .i. capillis. [85] .i. oculos. [86] .i. intetan, "the forehead." [87] .i. dontengaid, "to the tongue." [88] .i. dentes. [89] .i. etiucta fiaccal, "*etiucta* (?) of teeth." [90] .i. collum. [91] .i. pectus. [92] .i. latus. [93] .i. nahinneda, "the bowels." [94] .i. nasliasta .i. infuathroic, "the loins, i. e. the waist." [95] .i. iotarb sliasta l. infothoin, "the bull of the loin, or the buttock." [96] .i. manus. [97] .i. cusnafoiltuih, "with the hairs." [98] .i. mullach, "crown" (of the head). [99] .i. cathbarr, "helmet." [100] .i. slanti, "of safety." [101] .i. Christe. [102] .i. donebind, "to the head." [103] .i. donetan, "to the forehead." [104] .i. donasuilib, "to the eyes." [105] .i. doninchind tredelbdai, "to the triform brain." [106] .i. dongulbain, "to the bill." [107] .i. donbél, "to the lip." [108] .i. donagaid, "to the face." [109] .i. donaraid, "to the temple." [110] .i. donsmeich, "to the chin." [111] .i. donulchain, "to the beard." [112] .i. donamailgib, "to the eyebrows." [113] .i. donacluassaih, "to the ears." [114] i. donagruadib, "to the cheeks." [115] .i. donahóilib, "to the lower cheeks." [116] .i. donetarsroin, "to the *internasus*" (the gristle between the nostrils). [117] .i. dosligtib .i. ua srona, "to (the) passages, i. e. of the nose." [118] .i. dona maceu immlesaib, "to the pupils." [119] .i. donarotlib, "to the irides (?)." [120] .i. donahabrachtaib, "to the eyelashes." [121] .i. donahimmchosnib, "to the eyelids." [122] .i. donamennanib* l. donsmech, "to the double-chin (aux deux mentons), or to the chin." [123] .i. donanáil, "to the breath." [124] .i. donagruadib, "to the cheeks." [125] .i. dongiall, "to the jaw." [126] .i. dona ñaclaib, "to the teeth." [127] .i. dontengaid, "to the tongue." [128] .i. donbeol, "to the mouth." [129] .i. donbragait, "to the throat." [130] .i. dontengaid, "to the tongue." [131] .i. don uball bragat, "to the apple of the throat." [132] .i. dofeith bic bis fontengaid this, "to the little sinew that is under the tongue below" (the frenum). [133] .i. donchuirr bragat, "to the nape of the neck."

* MS. donamennanibus.

Capitali¹³⁴, ccutro¹³⁵, cartilagini¹³⁶
Collo¹³⁷ clemens¹³⁸ adesto¹³⁹ tutamini¹⁴⁰.

Obsecro¹⁴¹ te¹⁴², domine¹⁴³ Jesu Christe, propter novem ordines¹⁴⁴ sanctorum¹⁴⁵ angelorum*¹⁴⁶.

Domine esto lorica tutisima¹⁴⁷
Erga membra, erga mea uiscera¹⁴⁸,
Ut rotundas¹⁴⁹ a me¹⁵⁰ invisibiles¹⁵¹
54. Sudum¹⁵² clauos¹⁵³, quos fingunt¹⁵⁴ odibiles¹⁵⁵.
Tege¹⁵⁶, ergo, deus¹⁵⁷, forti¹⁵⁸ loricca¹⁵⁹
Cum scapulis¹⁶⁰ humeros¹⁶¹ et bracia,
Tege¹⁶² ulnas¹⁶³ cum cubis et manibus¹⁶⁴,
58. Pugnas¹⁶⁵, palmas¹⁶⁶, digitos¹⁶⁷ cum unguibus*.
Tege¹⁶⁸ spinas¹⁶⁹ et costas¹⁷⁰ cum artibus,

Terga,

GLOSS.—¹³⁴ .i. donchendfiacail, "to the foretooth" (?) ¹³⁵ .i. dondibechan, "to the throat." ¹³⁶ .i. donloing brond, "to the cartilage (?) of the belly" (the ensiform cartilage?). ¹³⁷ .i. donmuineol, "to the neck." ¹³⁸ .i. achainuarraig, "O gentle one." ¹³⁹ .i. aratorta, "do thou give." ¹⁴⁰ .i. doninillius, "for the security." ¹⁴¹ .i. aitchimm, "I adjure." ¹⁴² .i. tu, "thee." ¹⁴³ .i. athigerna, "O Lord." ¹⁴⁴ .i. tresna .ix. nordaib, "by the nine orders." ¹⁴⁵ .i. donancemaib, "of the saints." ¹⁴⁶ .i. donahainglib, "of the angels." ¹⁴⁷ .i. athigerna ti atluir[i]g roinill ocumimdegail aramainsib inchentair ⁊ arphein inalltair, "O Lord, be thou a very secure corselet, protecting me from the wiles of this world, and from the punishment of the other." ¹⁴⁸ .i. illcith remballa*ib* ⁊ illeth remindib, "overagainst my limbs and overagainst my entrails." ¹⁴⁹ .i. curathuairge, "that thou mayest hammer." ¹⁵⁰ .i. uaimm, "from me." ¹⁵¹ .i. dofaicsena, "invisible." ¹⁵² .i. inna[m]bir, "of the stakes." ¹⁵³ .i. naclu, "the nails." ¹⁵⁴ .i. delbait, "they form." ¹⁵⁵ .i. diabuli. ¹⁵⁶ .i. ditin, "protect." ¹⁵⁷ .i. dia, "O God." ¹⁵⁸ .i. calma, "brave." ¹⁵⁹ .i. luirech, "corslet." ¹⁶⁰ .i. cusnaclassaib dromma, "with the shoulder-blades," lit. "with the trenches of the back." ¹⁶¹ .i. nafornnai, "the shoulders." ¹⁶² .i. ditin, "protect." ¹⁶³ .i. na rigthe l. nabuille, "the radii, or the elbows." ¹⁶⁴ .i. cusnarigthib l. cusnasliastaib l. [leg. ⁊] cusnadoitib, "with the radii, or with the thighs, or [leg. and] with the hands." ¹⁶⁵ .i. nadurnu, "the fists." ¹⁶⁶ .i. nabassa, "the palms." ¹⁶⁷ .i. namera l. naresi, "the fingers, or the spans." ¹⁶⁸ .i. ditin, "protect." ¹⁶⁹ .i. nalorgdromma, "the backbones" (the spinous processes?). ¹⁷⁰ .i. donasnach, "to the ribs."

---

* In the Leabhar Breacc this unmetrical ejaculation is written as if it comprised two lines. It does not occur in the Darmstadt MS.

ᵇ MS. unginibus.

Terga[171], dorsum[172] neruos[que] cum ossibus.
Tege[173] cutem[174], sanguinem, cum renibus[175],
62. Catas[176] crinas, nates[177], cum femoribus[178].
Tege[179] gambas[180], suras[181], femoralia[182]
Cum genuclis[183] poplites[184] et genua[185].
Tege[186] talos[187] cum tibiis[188] et calcibus[a],
66. Crura[189], pedes[190] plantarum[191] cum bassibus[192].
Tege[193] ramos concrescentes[194] decies[195],
Cum mentagris[196], unges[197] binos quinquies[198].
Tege[199] pectus[200], jugulum[201], pectusculum[202],
70. Mamillas[203], stomacum[204] et umbilicum[205]
Tege[206] uentrem[207], lumbos[208], genitalia[209],
Et aluum[210] et cordis et uitalia[211].
Tege[212] trifidum jacor[213] et ilia[214],
74. Marcem[215], reniculos[216], fitrem[217] cum obligia[218],
Tege[219] doliam[220], toracem[220(a)] cum pulmone[221],

Uenas,

GLOSS.—[171] .i. nadromand, "the backs." [172] .i. indruimseilg, "the back-spleen." [173] .i. ditin "protect." [174] .i. doncholaind, "to the body." [175] .i. cusnahairnib, "with the kidneys." [176] .i. nalessa, "the haunches." [177] .i. natona, "the buttocks." [178] .i. cusnasliastaib, "with the thighs" (from hip to knee). [179] .i. ditin, "protect." [180] .i. cusnahescata, "to the hams." [181] .i. nahoreni, "the calves of the leg." [182] .i. natarbsliasta, "the upper thighs(?)." [183] .i. cusnahairnib toli l. cusnafarclib glun, "with the reins of desire, or with the kneecaps." [184] .i. nahescata, "the hams." [185] .i. donaglunib, "to the knees." [186] .i. ditin, "protect." [187] .i. nabadbronda, "the ankles." [188] .i. cusnacolpthaih, "with the calves." [189] .i. donaluirgnib, "to the shin-bones." [190] .i. donacosaib, "to the feet." [191] .i. nabuind, "the soles." [192] .i. cusnasalaib, "with the heels." [193] .i. ditin, "protect." [194] .i. nagega chomforbrit, "the branches that grow together." [195] .i. dona .x. meraib, "to the ten fingers." [196] .i. cusnaladraib, "with the toes." [197] .i. donahingnib, "to the nails." [198] .i. dona .x. ningnib, "to the ten nails." [199] .i. ditin, "protect." [200] .i. donbruinde, "to the chest." [201] .i. donalt, "to the joint." [202] .i. doucbt nadernainde, "to the breast of the palm." [203] .i. donacichih, "to the paps." [204] .i. dongaile, "to the stomach." [205] .i. animmlind, "the navel." [206] .i. ditin, "protect." [207] .i. donmedon, "to the middle." [208] .i. donahairnib, "to the reins." [209] .i. nahui[r]ge, "the genitals." [210] .i. donbroind, "to the stomach." [211] .i. donspirait beothaig inchride, "to the living spirit of the heart." [212] .i. ditin, "protect." [213] .i. inmace hoe trediuigthe l. inmace hoc trenillech, "the 3-cleft liver, or the 3-cornered liver." [214] .i. nabloingi, "of the lard (?)." [215] .i. selg, "spleen." [216] nalocha ochsal, "the armpits." [217] .i. indriscain, "the ... (?)." [218] .i. inglais, "the ... (?)." [219] .i. ditin, "protect," .i. ingaile, "the stomach." [220(a)] .i. indraip (indrapp?), "the chest (?)." [221] .i. cusinscaman, "with the lungs."

[a] MS. calicibus.

Uenas[222], fibras[223], fel cum bucliamine[224].
Tege[225] carnem, inginem[226] cum medullis[227],
78. Spplenem[228] cum tortuosis intestinis[229].
Tege[230] uesicam[231] adipem et pantes[232]
Compaginum[233] innumeros[234] ordines[235].
Tege[236] pilos[237] atque membra[238] reliqua[239]
82. Quorum forte præterii[240] nomina[241].
Tege[242] totum[243] me cum quinque sensibus[244]ᵃ,
Et cum decem fabrefactisᵃ foribus[245].
Utiᵇ[246] a plantis[247] usque ad uerticem[248]
86. Nullo[249] membro[250] foris[251(a)] intus[251] egrotem[252].
Ne de meo posit[253] nitam[254] trudere[255]
Pestis[256], febris[257], langor[258], dolor corpore[259].
Donec iam deo dante seniam[260]
90. Et peccata mea bonis factis deleam[261].
Et de carne lens[262] labis[263] caream

Et

GLOSS.—[222] .i. nahéte ochta, l. na cuislenna, "the ete (?) of the breast or the veins." [223] .i. nafethi, "the sinews." [224] .i. cusintóin .i. coelan nageraine l. muine. [225] .i. ditin, "protect." [226] .i. inbleoin, "the groin." [227] .i. cusna hindib, "with the entrails." [228] .i. inlu leith, "the spleen." [229] .i. cusna-findchorlanaib cammaib, "with the tortuous intestines" (lit. "white guts"). [230] .i. ditin, "protect." [231] .i. lamannan, "bladder." [232] .i. omnes. [233] .i. nacomdluta, "of the joints." [234] .i. dirim, "innumerable." [235] .i. innahuird, "the orders." [236] .i. ditin, "protect." [237] .i. nafoilt, "the hairs." [238] .i. nahúill, "the limbs." [239] .i. cobulide, "entirely," "altogether." [240] .i. asarsechmaillius, "of which I have passed by." [241] .i. ananmand ("their names") .i. præterii per concisionem causa metri. [242] .i. ditin, "protect." [243] .i. imlan, "the whole." [244] .i. cusna .u. sians[aib], "with the 5 senses." [245] .i. cusna .x. ndoirsib dentæib .i. quinque sensibus anma, "with the 10 doors of . . . i. e. quinque sensibus of the soul." [246] .i. gnath[ugnd], "to use." [247] .i. nabuind, "the soles." [248] .i. inbaithis, "the top of the head." [249] .i. cenni, "without anything." [250] .i. sic. [250(a)] .i. allamuig, "abroad, without." [251] .i. allaastig, "at home," "within." [252] .i. nasroin, "that I may not be sick" (?). [253] .i. nafeda, "that it may not be able." [254] .i. betha, "life." [255] .i. curasroena, "that it may defeat." [256] .i. plag, "plague." [257] .i. fiabrus "fever." [258] .i. indiangalur, "the lethargy." [259] .i. incorp, "the body." [260] .i. curaoentaige dia dam curbamsean friforba mobethad ind etlai ⁊ indendgai, "that God may grant to me that I may be old at the end of my life in purity and in innocence." [261] .i. curadichuirer mopecda domdegguimarthaib, "so that I may displace my sins by my righteous doings." [262] .i. inategim, "in which I go." [263] nel himis .i. onabasaib, "from the deaths (?)."

ᵃ MS. fabrifactis: *in marg*. vel fabricatis f. .i. cusna .x. ndoirsib *cundach*taib.
ᵇ MS. utli.

Et ad alta euolare²⁶⁴ ualeam,
Et miserto deo²⁶⁵ ad etheria²⁶⁶
94. Letus²⁶⁷ uehar²⁶⁸ regni refrigeria²⁶⁹.
Fin. it. amen.,

GLOSS.—²⁶⁴ .i. curaetelaiger cusnabardaib .i. cusnauemdaib, "that I may fly to the heights, i. e. to the heavenly (places)." ²⁶⁵ .i. curaerchisse dia dim, "that God may have mercy on me." ²⁶⁶ .i. cusnanemdaib, "to the heavenly (places)." ²⁶⁷ .i. cofailid, "blithely." ²⁶⁸ .i. coruinimarchoirther, "that I may be borne." ²⁶⁹ .i. ctarfuarad, "coolness"?

NOTES.

PREFACE.—*Superaltare* (sr. altare, MS.) "bifariam sumi videtur, nempe pro Ciborio, quod altari imminet, et Altari portatili."—Du Cange. *Savos*, i. e. salvos. *Undecaisillabum*, i. e. ἑνδεκασύλλαβον. *Bracicateleeticon*, i. e. βραχυκατάληκτον.

TEXT.—V. 4. I take the following quotations from Mone (*Hymni Lat.* i. 370):—An non est mare hoc sæculum, ubi se invicem homines quasi pisces devorant? an parvæ procellæ et fluctus tentationis perturbant hoc mare? an parva pericula sunt navigantium, id est in ligno crucis patriam cœlestem quærentium? S. *Augustini*, sermo 252, 2. *Chrysost.* contra anom. 7, 1. ὁ τῆς δικαιοσύνης ἥλιος τοῦτον ἡμῖν κατευθύνει τὸν πλοῦν. Minæ undæque mundialium nimborum *Sidon. Apoll.* Ep. 9, 4. Salum jactantis sæculi, S. *Cyprian.* Ep. 1. Tibi hoc sæculum mare est; habet diversos fluctus, undas graves, sævas tempestates et tu esto piscis, ut sæculi te unda non mergat.—*Ambros.* de sacram. 3, 1.

V. 19. *Agonetetas*, i. e. ἀγωνοθέτας.

V. 21. Says Mone: A similar putting together of the saints is often found in the Greek songs, e. g. θεηγόροι προφῆται, θεοειδεῖς μάρτυρες, θεῖοι μαθηταὶ τοῦ σωτῆρος, τοῦτον αἰτήσασθε.—*Triodion*, E. 3.

V. 24. *Atque adjuro.* This and the next line are not given by Mone.

V. 25. For *ŭti* (which, as in v. 85, the scholiast mistakes for *ūti*) Mone gives *ut*.

V. 28. For *cujus tremor*, Mone has *timor, tremor.* Note the alliteration in this line.

V. 29. *Inpenetrabilis tutela*, Mone.

V. 31. *Gibræ*, i. e. hominis (*gybræ* in the Darmstadt MS.), gen. sing. of gibra, apparently a corruption of the Chaldee gabrā (Syriac gabrŏ, Hebrew gḗber, Arabic gábrun).

V. 31. *Tetri demones.* Again I quote Mone: "The devil has destroyed the divine order in the creation, and this is expressed in his form, which is an image of the wildest distortion (*verzerrung*), neither human being nor beast, but a self-contradictory mixture of both. To this essentially belongs his black colour, for he is an enemy of the divine light; he shines only as a destroying fire, and has fallen
like

like a lightning-flash from heaven, Luke, x. 18, Matt. xxv. 41. All these representations rest on the Revelation of John, xii. 3, 9, xiii. 2, and other places. Strictly speaking, the devil should only be named serpent, so far as regards the aforetime and the present, for only at the end of the world does he appear as a dragon. *Augustin.* sermon. ined. ed. Denis, p. 39, calls him leo et draco ; quando ut draco serpit non ut leo rugit. *Tertullian.* adv. Marcion, 4, 24, diabolus in serpentis et draconis et eminentissimæ cujusque bestiæ nomine deputatur penes creatorem. *Sever. Sulpit.* epist. 3, calls him cruenta bestia."

V. 34. Mone's MS. reads "mea librent, ut solent, iacula." Here, of course, iacula is a quadrisyllable (i-acula). "The darts of the devil," says Mone, " are called in the Menæa ἰοὶ ψυχόλεθροι. Oct. 11. Thereby is the heart poisoned : ἡ καρδία μου φαρμαχθεῖσα ἰῷ του ὄφεως, Jul. 27. They are a poisonous snake-bite : δρακόντιον δῆγμα, ibid. ἐτραυμάτισεν ὁ ὄφις ὁ παμπόνηρος ὅλην μου τὴν ψυχὴν πονηρῶς. *Triodion*, Il. 3."

Vv. 35-38. These difficult lines stand thus in the Darmstadt MS. :—

> Gigram cepphale cum iaris et conas
> patam liganam sennas atque michi: nas
> chaladum charassum madianum talias
> batma exugiam atque binas idumas.

Gigram, better *gugram* (gugras, i. e. capita, Z. 1097), is possibly taken from Hebr. gulgōleth, or Syriac gōgūltō. *Cephale* (*cepphale*) is of course κεφαλή. For *Iaris* (gl. capillis), leg. *saris*, abl. pl. of sara (-us, -um ?), formed from Heb. sĕ'ār, Arab. sha'run ? This ingenious conjecture is due to Professor Wright. *Cona*, " eye," and *patha* (*pata*) " forehead," have not yet been referred to their sources, whence Eng. *pate !* *Ligna* (*ligana*), "tongue," perhaps for lizna, lizana, a corruption of Syr. lesbōnō (Heb. lāshōn, Arab. lisānun). *Sena* (*senna*), "tooth," obviously, as Dr. Todd remarks, from Syr. shennō, fem. (Hebr. shēn, Arab. sinnun). *Miccnas* (i. e. etiucta faccal). *Miccna* must be some part of a tooth, the enamel, the fangs ? but unfortunately the meaning of *etiucta* is unknown, and *miccna* is equally obscure. *Cladum* (*chaladum*), i. e. collum. If this be not from Gr. κλείς, gen. κλειδός, the collar-bone, we must regard it as for cadlum (cadalum), and compare the Arab. qadhālum (Syr. q'dhōlō), which, as Prof. Wright informs me, is " the back of the head and upper part of the neck." *Carsum* (*charassum*), gl. pectus. I suspect the scholiast has blundered here, for carsum is probably the Chaldee harṣā, " the loins." *Mandianum* (*madianum*), i. e. latus. Perhaps from Hebr. *mothnayim*, which, however, means lumbi. *Talias* (gl. na hinneda, "the entrails, bowels") is obscure to me. *Patma* (*batma*), i. e. na sliasta .i. in fuathroic, "the thighs, i. e. the waist," is also obscure. *Exugiam* (i. e. in tarb sliasta no in fothoin, "the bull of the thigh or the buttock"). Exugia is glossed by *gihsunga* l. *gescincu* (shank ?). Dief. Ælfric has exugium *mecgern*. No one of these A. S. words do I understand. *Idumas* (*edumas*) seems formed from Hebr. yādhayim. The abl. sing. occurs in the Book of Hymns, *Altus*, line 70, "Suffulta dei *iduma* omnipotentis valida," where the scholiast says, " .i. manu, iduma ebraice, cirus [χείρ] græce, manus latine"[a].

V. 39.

---

[a] I am ignorant of the Shemitic languages, and am indebted for the above Shemitic words to Professor Wright and Dr. Todd.

Notes.

V. 39. Mone's MS. has meo ergo cum capillis *et vertici*, which is bad metre and bad grammar. The construction is obviously " Be therefore a helmet of safety to my crown (meo ... vertici), head (capiti) forehead, eyes, and triple brain (right and left lobes, cerebellum), nose, lip, face, temple."

V. 44. *Internaso*. Ælfric has "internasus, *nose-gryslte*."

V. 45. For *Tutonibus*, Mone's MS. has tautonibus, and *tautones* is glossed by A. S. *bruwa*, "eye-brows," in Diefenbach's Med. Lat. Glossary. *Rota* (whence *rotis*) I take to be the circulus pupillæ, ðæs seo bringe of Ælfric.

V. 45. *Gingis*. I have been unable to find this word elsewhere. *Anele*, i. e. anbelæ.

V. 46. Mone's MS. has:—

Dentibus linguæ ori uvæ gutturi
gurgulioni et sublingua cervici.

Ura, "tongue," hence uvula (κίων, columella). *Gurgulio*, "Adam's apple," is glossed by Ælfric *throtbolla* (throat-ball). As to *sublingua*, Ælfric has *sublingium huf*, which Bosworth explains as "a round spongy substance covering the glottis."

V. 49. *Capitali, centro*, with the meanings given in the gloss, are, so far as I know, ἅπαξ λεγόμενα. With *centro*, we may, perhaps, compare chautrum, which Ælfric glosses by *cul throtbolla*. But what is *cal* here? The ejaculation *obsecro te*, &c., is not in Mone's MS.

V. 51. For *domine*, Mone gives *deinde*.

V. 53. For *retundas*, Mone gives *retrudas*, and in illustration of the verse he cites *Triodion*, L. 4, ὁρατῶν καὶ ἀοράτων ἐχθρῶν ῥῦσαι ἡμᾶς, κύριε.

V. 57. *Cubis* (i. e. rigthib). Ælfric glosses the nom. sing. *cuba* by *elboga*.

V. 62. Read *catacrinas* for *catus crinus*; first, because Mone's MS. has the former reading; secondly, because Ælfric has "catacrina *hypeban*," hip-bone, which comes tolerably near the meaning of the Irish gloss.

V. 64. *Genuclis*. The gloss attributes two meanings to this word. The first is "reins of desire;" and here the word probably stands for *genialibus* (though genialia properly means "marriage bed," "marriage"). The second is "knee-caps;" and here it stands for *geniculis* (Ælfric glosses *geniculi* by *cneowwyrste*).

V. 68. *Mentagris* (i. e. ladrnib, "toes"). This meaning suits in the following passage from Cummian's Epistle (*Usher's Works*, iv. 436): " An Britonum Scotorumque particulæ qui sunt *pene extremi*, et, ut ita dicam, *mentagræ* orbis terrarum." Dr. Reeves has kindly referred me to a story in the Acts of S. Baithene (*Acta Sanctorum*, Junii, tom. ii. p. 237, *b*), where the devil says of a possessed man, " per *mentagram* irrepsi in eum."

V. 69. *Pectusculum*. Ælfric glosses this word by *breost-ban*, breast-bone.

V. 74. *Mareem* and *Fitrem* are to me ἅπαξ λεγόμενα. *Obligia* occurs in Ælfric's glossary, explained by *nytte*, and Somner thinks it means ἀκρομφαλον, i. e. the centre of the navel.

V. 75. *Dolium*, apparently for dolium, which properly means a large jar, but may well have got the secondary signification of "stomach" (*gaile*).

V. 76. *Bucliamine*: *bucleamen* is glossed by *heorthama* ("midriff, covering of the heart") in an Anglo-Saxon MS. quoted by Diefenbach.

U V. 81

V. 81. *Pantes*, of course πάντες. This conceit of using Greek words when Latin would have done as well, or better, may be further exemplified by the hymn to Abbot Comgill (Z. 1138):—

<blockquote>
Audite *pantes ta erga* (πάντες τὰ ἔργα)
allati ad angelica, &c.
</blockquote>

V. 91. *Labis* (MS. *iabis*) is for labibus.

GLOSSES.—No. 1. *Forgaire*, "an imperative" (= ver-garia): cf. *forgair* imperat., Z. 440. In co *foringairiu apstil*, "with an apostle's authority," Z. 1060; *foringarthaid*, an imperative, Z. 767, 853, 979; *foringarti jussi*, Z. 473. the preposition seems *forn* (*farnóendeilb*, *forn-óin ńdeilb* "secundum idem exemplar," Z. 583) = Bret. and Corn. *warn*, unless, indeed, this be the Ir. *iarn* = ivarn. The root is GAR. See Commentary, No. 469, and compare γῆρυς, Eng. crow.

Fortachtaigim, I assist, a denominative from *fortacht*, or, as spelt in the Tract, No. 727 (Comm. p. 90), *furtacht*. It may be interesting to put together here the verbal forms found in these glosses:—

Active, Pres. indic. 1st. sing. (î-stems), *fortachtaigi-m*, 1; *atchi-mm*, 52; *aitchi-mm*, 141; *tegim*, 261.
    3rd pl. *ditnet*, 76; *it*, 49.

  Pret. act., 1st sing. *sechmaillius*, 240. 3rd sing. *ather-t*, 2 (an ā-stem); *dotóet*, 2.
  Imper. 2nd sing. act., *ditin* passim; *bi*, 147.
  Conjunctive 1st sing., *sroin*, 252 (leg. *srúinam*?); *dichuirer*, 261; *etelaiger*, 264.
    2nd sing., *torta*, 139; *thairge*, 149.
    3rd sing., *bena*, 62; *feda*, 253; *srocna*, 255.
      ,, *erchisse*, 265; *imme*, 58; *óentaige*, 260; *sraine*, 7; *uaimnige*, 65.
    3rd plur., *bertnaiget*, 80; *remtúsaigit*, 23; *chomforbrit*, 194; *ditnet*, 19; *didnet*, 40; *fedat*, 43; *dechat*, 59.
  Relative present: *bis*, 133.
  Passive, 3rd sing. pres.: *asberar*, 1, 2 (an ā-stem), for asberthar; *imarchoirther*, 268 (conjunctive).
  Pret. participle: *nemtroeta* (troeth-ta), 66; Fut. participle: *ingerrtha*, 19.
  Verbal noun: *elud*, 44; *imdegail*, 147; *gnáthugud*, 56; *suidigud*, 4.

No. 4. *Iar suidingud* (gl. posito). This mode of making the pret. part. pass. is common in Middle Irish; see, for example, Leab. Breacc, 79 *b* (cited Petrie, R. T. 437), where coilech in choimded *iarna* chumtach translates the "calix Domini scriniolo reconditus," of what is said to be the Ven. Bede's abstract of Adamnán's work, *De Situ Terræ Sanctæ*, &c.

No. 6. *Guassacht*, danger; *guassacht*, in Z. 28, 61. Cf. the man's name, Gósact (*Gosactum* filium Milcon Maccubooin, Book of Armagh, 11 *a*, 1).

No. 7. With *sroene* we may perhaps connect W. rhynod, "agitation;" rhynu, "to shiver, to shake:" *sroin*, 252; *srocna*, 255; Mod. Ir. sraoinim, "I defeat;" Gael. *sraon*, "make a false step," "fall sideways," "stumble," "rush forward with violence;" *sróin*, "deviate."

No. 8. *Forba*, cf. *forbe*, Z. 15, dat. sing. iar *forbu* in gnimo, "after the completion of the work," Z. 1068.

No. 10. *Dimaines* would now be *diomhanas*. *Soegail*, gen. sing. of soegal, O. Ir. saigul, Z. 731. I know
not

Notes. 147

not if this be connnected with W. hoedel (vita), Z. 125, Bret. hoal. The resemblance to sé-culnm is, perhaps, deceptive.

No. 11. *Impide* is, perhaps, = *imb-bide*. Cf. Goth. bidjan, bidan, A. S. gebede, Eng. *bid*, *beadsman*, &c.

No. 20. *Co-hairithe* for co-hairighthe, an adverb formed from the adjective airighthe (O. Ir. airegde, Z. 233), by prefixing *co*, now *go*; connected are *airechas* (principatus), Z. 233; *airech* ("primus, anterior," Z. 67, note) = W. arg in arg-lwydd?

No. 28. *Adnlcs*, apparently adan-tes; *adhanaim*, "I kindle" (W. en-*ynn*, root AN?). As to *tes*, v. Commentary, No. 5.

No. 39. *Dluith*, v. supra, Commentary, No. 636. Cf. dluthad, *infra*, No. 61, and W. dyludo, "to adhere," from the W. word it would seem as if dluith stood for du-luith : cf. dlìged = W. dyled.

No. 43. *Fedat* (gl. valeant), *feda*, gl. possit, 89, read *fédat*, *fèda*, and compare nir *fètsat* a hescaine do forchúlu, "they could not avert his malediction." Fled dúin nan ged, 28 ; ni *fedann* for singaile a togluasacht, "a parricide cannot move it," ibid. 82.

No. 44. *Clód* = W. cludd, "an overwhelming." Clód for co-lód. Cf. O. Ir. imchlóud (imm-co-lóud), Z. 768, 847 : *imchloud* ceneiuil na diil, "change of gender or declension," Z. 664: timluad (du-immlód) agitatio, Z. 847 : imluadad (gl. saltabat), ib.; immluadi (gl. exagitat), ib.

No. 45. *Cuimleng*, cf. bid *cuimlengaithi* .i. bid conflechtaigthi (gl. congrediendus), Z. 474 : coimpleanga, O'R., "a race," Skr. root, *langh*? With *brug* cf. the Mod. Ir. *bruighean*, "strife."

No. 49. *Enach*, *enachdu*, in Old Ir. óinach, óinachdu : in oinach l. i taibderce (gl. in theathrum), Book of Armagh, 183 b. Óinach is derived from óin, W. un, Old Lat. oinos, Goth. ain-s, Eng. *one*. M. Pictet (the morning-star of Celtic philology) has compared the Mod. Ir. *aon* with the Skr. demonstrative êna. *Bruincha* (gl. proretas), *bruine*, broine, "prora," are O'R.'s *braine*, "prow," braincach .i. taoiseach, a leader. (Cf. W. blain, *blaenor*, a leader; *blaenu*, to precede, and Corn. brenniat, gl. proreta?). *Stiurasmaind* is a Teutonic word, probably Old Norse, in which language there may have been *stýrismenn*, n. pl. of *stýrismaðr*, though I cannot quote either of these forms. Cf. A. S. steóres man, L. Æselb., *forestéorda* proreta Somn. The Danish styrmand means "a mate." In Breton we have *stur* and *sturia*. *Corr* fem. agrees in gender with Bret. *ker*, a sharp edge. W. *cwr* (for *cwrr*) is masc.

No. 52. With *atchimm* cf. *itge*, a prayer. Book of Armagh, 18 b, 1.

No. 53. *Fedba*, nom. sing. *fedb*, i. e. *fede* = W. gweddw, Corn gueden, Lat. vidua.

No. 54. *Indracca* (gl. fideles) cf. O'R.'s *ionnracain*, and perhaps the O. Ir. *inrice*.

No. 55. *Faismedaig* : the gen. plur. of this word occurs in Patrick's hymn: in ernaigthib huasalathrach, i taircetlaib fatha, hi praiceptaib apstal, in biresnib *fuismedach*, for which we should read fóismedach : cf. fóisite (confessio), Z. 41 ; fóisitnib (professionibus), Z. 589.

No. 58. *Imme*, apparently from a verb, immim, imlim, formed from the prep. imm, imb = ambi.

No. 59. *Dechat* has here, perhaps, a transitive meaning ; but in Z. 1129, arna *decha* means ne veniat. *Uleu*; this is the O. Ir. acc. pl. masc. of *ole* (= Ulko-s, which is found on a Gaulish coin?). *Iarair*, a derivation from the prep. *iar* : cf. rofersam ar*hiarair*, Oingus; ar ar*hiarair*, Corm. Ecc. 60.

No. 62. *Bena*, from *benim*, Z. 933, I strike, now *beanaim*. Cf. Goth. *banja* (πληγή, ἕλκος), Engl. bane, Gr. φόνος. The root is concealed in W. cyminedd, "conflict," cyn-binedd.

No. 64. *Granna*, cf. perhaps W. graen, "rough."

No. 65. *Uaimnige*, a denominative from *ómun*, fear; cf. W. ofni, to frighten; Gaul. Exobnus.

No. 66. *Inillius* (gl. tutela, gl. tutamini, *infra*, No. 140), derived from *inill* (gl. tuta, *infra*, No. 74); *ro-inill* tutissima, No. 147. Z. 731, has *inill* (gl. tutor), but he says the reading is doubtful. *Tremeta* (leg. tremetha?) in nemthremeta (cf. neimhthreabhthe, O'R.), seems a deriv. from the prep. *tremi*, which occurs in composition (tremi-berar "transfertur," tremi-tiagat "transgrediuntur," Z. 850). *Troeta* in nemtroeta appears to be the part. pret. pass. of the verb *troethaim* (O'R.'s traothaim), I subdue.

No. 69. With *truailnide* in *nemthruailnide*, cf. ro-truailled, "was corrupted," Corm. v. *Bráthair*, Eng. *trull*, Bret. trulen, "femme malpropre," are perhaps connected.

No. 71. *Compur*, O'R.'s *compuir*, "body, chest, trunk," is etymologically obscure to me.

No. 75. *Sciath*, Z. 21 = W. ysgŵyd, Old Bret. scoit, Z. 114 (= scêtâ), the relations of which with scûtum, σκῦτος, if existing, I am unable to settle.

No. 80. *Bertnaiget* (gl. vibrent), Z. 436, has ro-*bertaigset*, gl. vibraverunt. Has he left out *n*?

No. 81. With *urchar*, "a dart," cf. W. ergyr-waew, "a flying spear."

No. 82. *Cloi-cend* seems the W. *pen-glog*.

No. 83. *Clechtait* (gl. soleaut), from *clechtaim*, now *cleachdaim*. The same form occurs in the Leab. Breacc : ꝛ *clechtait* doine a thadull ꝛ a póccad, "and men are used to touch it and kiss it" (Petrie, R. T., 437). This seems the W. preithiaw, "to practise."

No. 93. *Inneda*, acc. pl. of inne, O. W. engued, Z. 149; the Corn. encder-en (gl. extum) is from ἔντερον.

No. 94. *Sliasta*, nom. pl. of sliasait (now sliasaid), sliassit, gl. poples, Z. 22 ; sliastaib, gl. femoribus, gl. cubis, *infra*. *Fuathroic*, *fuathrog*, "girdle," O'R., cf. W. gwregys, Corn. grugus.

No. 95. *Fothoin*, I have not met elsewhere, and cannot say whether it is a nom. sing. *fem.* or a nom. pl. *masc.* ; probably the former, as *na* is used in these glosses for the nom. pl. masc. of the article. May we compare the W. *gwadn*, "foundation"? Z. 261, has fotha (gl. crepido), dat. sing. fothu, Z. 999 (roh-fothiged, "ye were founded," ibid; no-fothaiged, "it was founded," Lib. Hymn., ed. Todd, p. 73), which seems cognate.

No. 99. *Cath-barr*, "battle-hat ;" barr (gl. cassis, Z. 51) = O. W. barr (gl. colomaticus). With these, I suspect, are connected Fr. *barrette*, Ital. *berretta*. Diez, however, refers them to the late Latin *berrus*.

No. 106. *Gulbain* (gl. rostro), cf. nom. *gulba* ; cf. O. W. golbinoc (gl. rostratam), Z. 111; W. *gylf*, a bill, or beak, Corn. gelvin.

No. 107. *Bil*, "lip," cf. W. gweft = vo-bel.

No. 109. *Araid* (gl. tempori) for *araig*, dat. sing. of *are*, gen. arach. The acc. dual of this word occurs in the charm against *cengalar* (headache), Z. 926 : im du da *are* ꝛ fort chulatha, "round thy two temples and on the back parts of thy head" (*clais culad*, "hollow of the poll," C.); Corn. *criev*, gl. timpus, W. ar-lais.

No. 112. *Malg*, "eyebrow ;" Bret. *malven*.

No. 113. *Cluassaib* (gl. auribus), from cluas = W. clust.

No. 114. *Gruadib* (gl. genis), from *gruaid*, W. grudd.

No. 115. *Oilib* (gl. bucis), from *oil*, now written *aoil*, with which the W. *ael* may be connected, though this means "a brow."

No. 121.

No. 121. *Imchosnib* (gl. tutonibus) is to me an ἅπαξ λεγομένον: the root seems that of *cosunaim*, I defend. Though *tautones*, according to an A. S. glosser, signifies eyebrows, I think that the Irish scribe understood it as meaning eyelids, especially as eyebrows (*mailgib*) occurs before, No. 112.

No. 123. *Anail* (gl. anele), W. *anadl*, Skr. r. ᴀɴ; an-imus, ἄν-εμος, Skr. anila, wind.

No. 125. *Giall* (gl. faucibus): cf. A. S. ceole, Eng. *jowl?*

No. 135. *Dibechan*, throat : *ncascóid dibeachain* (gl. apostema gutturis), C.

No. 137. *Muincol* (gl. collo), W. *mwnwgl.*

No. 138. For *caimuarraig* read *cainfuarraig*, and cf. fuarrech (gl. clemens), Z. 778 ; fuairrech, Z. 986.

No. 147. *Bí at láirig*, "be thou a corselet," literally "be thou *in thy* corselet," an idiom inexplicable by me. See O'Don. Gram., 165: bhí sé 'n a rígh, "he was a king," lit. "he was in his king." The same idiom is found in the case of the verb subst. *tá:* tú sé 'n a ṡagart, "he is *in his* priest," i. e. "he is a priest," ibid. ; *imdegail*, protection, so in Patrick's hymn : lám dé domm imdegail ; and see Colmán's hymn, cited *supra*, p. 57, *centair, altair*, genitives sing. of formations from *cen*, "cis," and *all* = ἄλλο, by means of the suffix *-tar* = Skr. tara ; with *amainsib* cf. *dimaines, supra*, No. 10.

No. 149. *Tuairge* (gl. retundas), v. *supra*, No. 722.

No. 151. *Dofaiescna* (gl. invisibiles), apparently an adjectival n-stem, nom. sing. dofaiesc, O'R., from the particle *do* and *faiesc*, which I have not met, though *faiesinach*, "visible," occurs. Retla mongach ...do *faicsin*, "a bristly star was seen," Tighernach, cited O'Don. Gr. 443; *faicfi*, 3rd sing. fut. act. of *faicim*, I see, occurs *ibid*, 179. With this verb M. Pictet (Beitr. ii. 87) compares Skr. paç, W. paith, "glance (from pakti), ; Skr. spaça, "spier;" Lat. specio, specto, &c. I have not found this form (with unaspirated *c*) in Old Irish. Z. 933 has a word, *fégad*, which seems connected :—

> Mucholmoc ramcharastar ar *fégad*, ar fis
> Is airái ramcharastar uair is tend mo chris.

> "Mucholmoc ("my little Colum") loved me, for (my) iusight, for (my) knowledge.
> It is for this he loved me, since my girdle is strong."

Oc *fegad* (fégad), "seeing ;" *fégaid*, "see ye ;" *Scirgl. Conc.* Aingil, apstail, ard *fegad*, "angels, apostles, a high vision !" Colm. 44; cf., too, the Mod. Ir. *feuchaim.*

No. 152. *Bir*, gen. *bera* = Lat. veru; birdae, berach (gl. verutus), Z. 46; W., Corn., and Bret. ber. Benfey connects veru with the Skr. r. hvr ; and this would go far to explain the strange phenomenon of initial Celtic *b* = Lat. *v.*

No. 153. *Clu*, clói (gl. clavi), Z. 67.

No. 160. *Classaib*, cf. W. *cluis*, trench.

No. 163. *Uille* (gl. ulnas), W. and Corn. elin. Cf. ul-na, ὠλ-ένη, ellen bogen, Eng. el-bow.

No. 166. *Bassa*, from *bas*, "palm of the hand," probably identical with W. *bas*, shallow, flat.

No. 170. *Asnach* (gl. costas): cf. W. and Corn. asen (there is a W. plur. asen-au). Radically connected with Skr. asthi (by-theme asthan), ὀστέον, os, oss-is.

No. 177. *Tóna*, buttocks: cf. W. *tin*, "a tail, a bottom."

No. 185. *Glúnib* (gl. genua), from glún, W. glin, Corn. (irregularly) elin.

No. 187. *Adbronda* (gl. talos): O. Ir. odbrann, gl. talus, Z. 1102: Leyden Priscian, 37 *b*, Gael. *aobrunn* (where note the non-aspiration of the *b*), W. ufflarn. Probably a compound, the first element of which bas, has, as Dr. Siegfried suggests, perhaps lost an initial p: cf. ποδ-ός, pĕd-is, Skr. pad (Eng. *foot*, Goth. *fôtu* is Skr. pâda).

No. 189. With *luirgnib*, nom. *lorga*, cf., perhaps, W. llorp, shank.

No. 192. *Salaib* (gl. lassibus), from *sal* = W. fäl (or sawdl?).

No. 194. *Géga*, "branches," from gég = W. cang, as dég (10) = W. deng. Perhaps we may compare the Ir. (and British) tribe-name, Gangani (Γάγγανοι).

No. 196. *Ladhar* now means a fork, a prong, the space between two fingers or two toes. O'Reilly, however, has *ladhar*, "a toe," and in Gaelic the word means hoof as well as prong, fork.

No. 198. *Dona s. ningnib, read* dona deich n-ingnib, and note the occurrence of the transported *n* after *deich* (10), that number (Skr. daçan, Lat. decem) having originally ended in a nasal. So we have sccht(n) 7, and ocht (b) 8, *ingnib*, dat. of *inga* = W. ewin, Skr. nakha, ὄνυξ, Germ. nag-el, Eng. *nai*-l.

No. 200. *Bruinde*, "breast, bosom." St. John is called Sean ua bruinne; W. and Corn. bron.

No. 203. *Cich* = W. cyg, flesh.

No. 205. *Imbliud*, navel. Radically connected with ὀμφαλός, umbilicus, navel, Skr. nâbhi.

No. 216. *Ochsal* (which in form is almost identical with Lat. axilla, O. H. G. ahsala) is, I suspect, by metathesis for oschal, aschal: cf. W. asgall, "wing."

No. 220. *Raip* (?) I have never met elsewhere. Can it be connected with A. S. hrife, Eng. mid-*riff*? But the word may, perhaps, be *indraip*, or *draip*.

No. 221. *Seaman* (gl. pulmone), cf. O. W. *scamnhegint* (gl. levant), W. ysgyfaint, "the lights;" Bret. scéveut, Corn. skefans.

No. 224. *Cusin tóin*, "with the anus, i. e. *coelan na geraine no muine*, the gut of fat or lard;" i. e. the large intestine which is covered by the omentum: *coelan*, a deriv. from côil, "slender:" *geraine*, gen. sing. of some word having the same root as *geir*, tallow: *muine*, "the lard which lines the intestines of a pig," C. The Highland Society's Dict. has *muin*, "fat adhering to the entrails of an animal."

No. 228. *Lu leith* "the spleen." Perhaps the mysterious *lewilloit* (gl. splen) of the Cornish vocabulary, may be connected with this.

No. 229. *Find*, "white," W. gwyn, Gaulish, Vindos; root vid, for cvid, Skr. çvid album esse, Goth. hveita, Eng. white. *Cammaib*, nom. sing. *camm*, W. cam = cambo in Cambo-dunum, &c., see Z. 75.

No. 231. *Lamannan*, "bladder," perhaps connected with W. llafanog, "liverwort."

No. 238. *Baill*, nom. pl. of báll, "a member" = φαλλός (Prof. Siegfried).

No. 240. *Asarsechmaillius*, i. e. asa-r'-sechmaillius, *asa*, "whose," (sing. and plur.), I cannot explain. It occurs at least twice in the Félire, and also spelt *isa*, in the *Battle of Magh Rath*. See O'Dou. Gr. 131, 132. *Sechmaillius* is the 1st. sing. pret. act. of a verb which in Z. appears to belong to the â-conjugation (the Latin first): nad *sechmalla* (gl. non omittit), Z. 849; *sechmalfam*-ni (praeteribimus), Z. 437; sechmalfaider, Z. 1067. In Mod. Ir. the verb in question has passed over to the î-conjugation (the Latin fourth), as we see from the form *seachmaill-i-m*; and this change seems to have taken place when our gloss was written, *sechmaill-i-us* being identical in form with rocinn-i-us (gl. definivi), Z. 434; baits-i-us, ibid.; tocuir-i-us (Patrick's Hymn), &c.

No. 245. I do not understand this gloss. Can *dentaib* be for *d'óen-tóib*, "of one side"?

Nos. 250, 251. *Allamuig*, "outside;" *allaastig*, "on the inside." I cannot explain these adverbs. They occur in O'Don. Gr. 263, 269.

No. 258.

Notes.

No. 258. *Diangalur* (gl. languor). This gloss enables me to correct my reading and version of part of one of the S. Gall incantations, Commentary, No. 222. *Diangalar fúail* (languor urinae) is the ailment against which the charm is directed.

No. 260. *Endgai*, innocence, O. Ir *eneae*, fem., Z. 262; inuan ennac (gl. innocentum), Z. 1003. S. Brigit is said to have been *endae*, "innocent," Leb. Breace, cited Todd, Lib. Hymn, 65. The true spelling is *ennaec*, *ennae*, and the words are probably cognate with in-nocens (noceo = Skr. nāçayâmi, "I slay"). *Etlai*, dat. of *ellae*, *etla?* an abstract from the adj. *etal*, the gen. sing. neut. of which occurs in II. 2, 15, fo. 64, *a* (T. C. D.): co fortacht cach *etail* .i. co forithin each glain.

No. 261. *Deg-gnimarthaib*. I have not met the nom. sing. of the *simplex* of this word, which must be *gnimarad*, whence O'R.'s *gniomharthach*, "actual, active."

No. 265. *Erchisse*, better *airchisse*. Cf. airchissi (gl. parcit), Z. 199; airebissa, arcessea, "parcat," Z. 839; bond erchissecht (gl. propitiatione), Z. 839. The root is probably identical with that of *cessacht*, "sparingness," *supra*, p. 64, No. 280.

No. 267. *Cofáilid* (gl. laetus). Cf. fáilte, "gaudium," Z. 94, which Z. connects with Goth. bleiths, O. H. G. blîdi, A. S. blîde, Eng. *blithe*. He also compares Lat. *laetus*, which he supposes to stand for *flaetus*.

No. 268. *Co-ru-m-imarchoirther* exemplifies the system of impersonal flexion which has attained such a development in the Celtic verb, in consequence of the early loss of the first and second persons in the tenses of the passive. Cf. *do-chuiriur*, gl. nscisco, Z. 844; *imm-e-churetar* "qui tractant," Z. 447 (where the *c* is the infixed relative, changed from *a* by progressive *umlaut*); *erchuiretar*, Z. 1016, 467; "ponuntur," *adchuireddur*, "adbibentur," Z. 467; *cuiretar*, "ponunt," Z. 314; *cuire* uait, "pone a te," Z. 457. The third sing. pret. act. of the verb in our gloss occurs in the *Irish Nennius*, p. 110: ro-*imarcor* Artur delb [deilb?] Muire for a gualaind ⁊ ro-teilgistar ua Pagain, "Arthur carried the image of Mary on his shoulder, and cast out the Pagans."

No. 269. *Etarfuarad* (gl. refrigeria), cf. *fuar*, cold. I do not understand the force of *etar-* here.

CORRECTIONS

Appendix.

CORRECTIONS AND ADDITIONS.

Page 2, *for* CARAIG *read* CARRIG (Old Ir. *carric*, Book of Armagh, 10 *b*, 1; Med. W. *carrec*, Z. 814).

Page 4, note 15, *for* amann *read* lamann.

Page 5, No. 55, iolla is for hilla: see Commentary, No. 1005, p. 116.

Page 5, No. 57, *for* ꞃıαċαıꞃe *read* ꞃıαċαıꞃe.

Page 7, No. 132, scama is for squama, and lanꞃ is the O. Ir. *lann*. "Cenni am. blosco am. *lanna*" is the gloss in the Book of Armagh, 176 *b*, 2, on "ceciderunt ab oculis ejus tamquam scamae."

Page 7, No. 147, *for* ταıꞃ *read* ταꞃꞃ.

Page 8, No. 211, *for* fistula *read* festuca.

Page 9, No. 237, *for* monıꞃıcına *read* monificina.

Page 9, No. 254, scupa is certainly for stupa, not scopae.

Page 10, No. 169, *for* cnáımꞃıαċ *read* cnáımꞃıαċ.

Page 10, Nos. 272, 273, *for* chiromantia *read* chiromachia. *For* ꞃτυꞃnα *read* sturna.

Page 11, No. 305, *for* eıꞃınnαċ *read* éıꞃınnαċ.

Page 12, No. 328, *for* ꞃeꞃꞃa *read* ꞃeꞃꞃαċτ.

Page 14, note 4, read merlaime, mer coisi.

Page 17, No. 503, read cnáımꞃıαċ. No. 520, read Locanus, Loċán.

Page 18, No. 575, *for* ꞃaıꞃᵹe *read* ꞃaıꞃᵹe.

Page 19, No. 621, *for* ꞃıαꞃꞃυıleċh *read* ꞃıαꞃꞃυıleċh.

Page 20, No. 643, delete [ventossus].

Page 24, No. 811, the MS. has "ercocledus inleman."

Page 25, No. 826, I should now read this as follows: "hic sibilus est hominis (i. e. is of the masc. gender) sibola [est feminae "is of the fem. gender"]: sermo pri[m]us in ꞃéꞃ ꞃoꞃē.

Page 25, No. 831, delete [pileus.]

Page 27, No. 863, *for* uıꞃcꞃ *read* uıꞃcı. No. 872, read ꞃemċheċταꞃ.

Page 28, No. 890, read ꞃéıꞃc.

Page 31, No. 1019, read ꞃéıꞃeαꞃ.

Page 32, No. 1057, read ꞃoċhınólach.

Page 37,

Page 37, No. 4, *sái, súi*, seems the W. *syw* (Davies). The acc. sing. of the derivative *suithe* occurs (spelt súidi(n)) in the *Cris Finnáin* (Z. 933):—

cris coin muchris
ralég *súidi* nglan

"May my girdle be the girdle of John,
Who read pure science."

Page 37, No. 5, *for* crottārias *read* crottāria-s. As to *cruit*, I am indebted for the following note to Mr. S. H. O'Grady, who has read and annotated the foregoing Commentary with the kindness generally found among men of his wide and accurate attainments:—"Figuratively *cruit* at the present day means 'a hump on the back' (from the shape of the Irish harp), and the word has been introduced into the Anglo-Irish dialect. *He put a critt on himself* (do léig sé cruit air féin) is applied to any one assuming a humpy attitude, as a jockey does when he works himself along in a race," &c.

Page 37, No. 6, the *timpan* (gen. *timpain*), whence *timpanach* was a stringed instrument. See C.'s *Battle of Magh Léna*, p. 50, where occurs the expression an *tiompan* téad-bhinn, "the sweet-stringed *timpan*." Cf. also Girald. Topogr. Hib., "Hibernia quidem tantum duobus utitur et delectatur instrumentis cythara scilicet et *tympano*: Scotia tribus, cythara, *tympano* et choro: Gwallia vero cythara, tibiis et choro."

Page 37, No. 9, cf. the Cornish *renniat*, divisor, which is synonymous with partista.

Page 38, line 10, read 10, *Luchtaire*. I think this word is radically connected with the Latin lucta, "wrestling," luctor, luctator.

Page 38, No. 13, I have now no doubt that *cathir*, &c., are stems in *c*. The stem of cathir (*i* a weakening of *a*) is *catharac*. With *uasal-athair* compare Corn. *huheltat*, A. S. heahfæðer = "high-father." In the second line from the bottom of p. 38 *read* áth *for* ath, and in the last line of the note *for* philosophy *read* poetry.

Page 39, No. 14, read *crosán*. Hence the Mod. Ir. *crosántachd*, which Mr. O'Grady explains as "a kind of composition, part prose, part verse, generally consisting of very far-fetched jokes, and couched in the most difficult and out-of-the-way language at the command of the composer."

Page 39, No. 15, *cestunach*, now *ceisteamhnach*, O'G.

Page 39, No. 16, in O. Ir. the *a* of *ard* is long.

Page 39, No. 17. *cinn* I now regard as the gen. (cf. *gilla nan each, gilla adairce*). The locative sing. of masc. a-stems is in O. Ir., as in Latin, identical with the gen. sing. Thus *puirt*, supra, No. 676, is the loc. of *port*, gen. *puirt*. For examples of locatives sing. of other declensions, see Beitr. i. 335, 336.

Page 40, No. 18, perhaps *birria* stands for *birrus*, "a cloak for rainy weather;" unsmeðe hrægel, "unsmooth raiment," Ælfric.

Page 40, No. 19, W. *gïrydd*, Corn. *gúdh*. See Diefenbach's *Celtica*, i. 134, 135.

Page 40, No. 20, *Ríghan* should be *Ríghain* (W. *rhiain*), as it is in the modern language. In Old Ir. it seems declined like a fem. i-stem. Thus the gen. pl. *rígnae* occurs in an O. Ir. poem to one Áed, for a copy of which I am indebted to Herr Mone, of Carlsruhe :—

"Is bun cruinn mâir miad soerda, fri baig is bunad findae,
is gasne arggait arddbrigg, di chlaind chéit ríg céit rígnae,"

where, though Mone's copy has *phinda* and *ignae*, the corrections are certain.¹

Page 40, No. 24, the *t* in *sagart* may be also explained by reference to the ordinary rise of *rt* from *rd*. See Z. 70.

Page 40, No. 26, cf. the W. *clopen, clopa*, pen-*gloy*.

Page 40, No. 27, read *táiplis*. Cf. A. S. tæfel (gl. alea) Ælf., W. *taflu*, to fling. Perhaps *táiplis* is a Celtic word.

Page 40, No. 30, the Lat. *manus*, O. N. *mund*, should have been compared with *muin*-cille. Cf. also W. *mun, man*.

Page 40, Nos. 33, 35, the genitives sing. of *ciabh* and *dias* are respectively *céibh, déise*.

Page 41, No. 36, cf. the Mod. Ir. *pras*, "hasty, quick, rash;" W. *pres* seems = praestus, *presto, prêt*.

Page 41, line 11, *for* fit *read* faithful.

Page 41, No. 37, I strongly suspect that *fallaing* is cognate with pallium, though Zeuss seems not to believe that a Celtic *f* can ever represent a Latin *p*. Cf., however, con*foi*rem "comparamus," Z. 841, and M. Pietet's paper, Beitr. ii., 84.

Page 41, No. 39, now *gruadh*, pl. gruadhna. Cf. also W. *grudd*.

Page 42, No. 42, hence the Anglo-Irish *losset*, "the long wooden box, with a lid and lock, often standing on trestles in a farmer's bed-room, and in which he keeps his linen and valuables," O'G.

Page 42, No. 44, W. *canwyl*, where *wy* as usual = *ê*.

Page 42, No. 46, I have blundered here. The hard *d* in *fedán* = an O. Ir. *t* (= O. Celtic *tt*), and *fedán* is the W. *chwythu*.

Page 42, No. 47, the root may be VAKS, to grow: cf. the line in Morte d'Arthur, "mixed with the manly GROWTH that fringed his lip."

Page 42, No. 48, cf. *lesmac*, which glosses privignus, in a ninth-century MS. of Priscian,

¹ The MS. from which this poem is taken is preserved in the monastery of S. Paul, Carinthia.

Corrections and Additions.

Priscian, fo. 30, *a*, written by one Dubthach, and preserved in the University Library of Leyden, No. 67. For this and the other glosses in the same MS. I am indebted to Professor Siegfried.

Page 42, No. 49, *sesrach* now means "a yoke of horses," O'G.

Page 42, No. 50. Can this *rón* (gen. *róin*) be = the A. S. *hrón*, "whale"?

Page 42, No. 51, cf. the Gael. *ceann-bhárr*-easpuig, "a bishop's mitre."

Page 42, No. 55, iolla is hilla, see No. 1005, p. 117. *Maróc* = W. *monochen*.

Page 43, No. 59, also *adire-liu* (gl. cornix), Z. 726 (is *liu* = Gaul. λουγος?).

Page 43, No. 61, *riaghail* (*ia* from *è*) is the W. *rheol*.

Page 43, No. 64, perhaps mitreta is for metreta.

Page 43, No. 65, the Mod. Ir. *meadar* means "a vessel," generally a churn. Hence the Anglo-Ir. *mether*.

Page 43, No. 70, *sess* is now "the board thrown out from the gunwale of a boat to the strand, to enable one to walk in dryshod," O'G.

Page 44, No. 71, Gael. *taobhan*, "rafter, beam." "*Taoibhín* means a small patch in the side (*taobh*) of a brogue," O'G.

Page 44, No. 73, *lainnéir* is a living word along the Shannon, and means "lanyard," C. Perhaps both the English and Irish words are taken from the French *lanière*.

Page 44, No. 75, now *coróinn*, gen. *coróinneach*, O'G.

Page 44, No. 77, the reading of the quatrain here given is justified by the fac-simile given by Dr. Ferdinand Keller in his *Bilder und Schriftzüge u. s. w.*, plate xi.: *reimm* should be *réimm*, and *oa*, *ôa*.

Page 45, in the paradigm of the article the hypothetical stem is inaccurate. In the masc. it should be sanda (ex sanna, sa-sma (?)); in the fem. sandâ (ex sa-smâ (?)): in the neut. nom. and acc. sing. sa. In lines 3 and 6, *for* sanad? *read* sa-n?

In the dat. pl. of *dia* read déib = dêvâbo (?), and compare ματρεβο ναμανσικαβο, p. 100, the discovery of which forms overturns Ebel's theory (here followed) as to the origin of the Ir. dat. pl. from an instrumental. O. Ir. *aib* (*-ib*), Ganl. *abo* = *âbus* (fem.), Skr. *âbhyas*.

Page 46, No. 86, *oigheann* now means "a large cauldron," O'G., who quotes from an old song, "do thuit mo bhean a n-*oigheann* na feola."

Page 46, No. 88, *for* panthera *read* pantera. Perhaps this is the French *pantière*, "a draw-net for partridges, &c.," Old Eng. *paunter*:—

> "Pride hath in his *paunter* kanht the heie and tho lowe,
> So that unnethe can eny man God Almihti knowe."
>
> *Political Songs of England*, ed. Wright, p. 344.

Page 46, No. 90, *leth*, W. *lled* = Lat. lătus, Gr. πλάτος (Ebel). Other examples of *leth*, meaning half-, are *leathlobhtha*, "half rotten," *leathmheisge*, "half drunk."

Note 1. If *doiros* in the following Gaulish inscription on the handle of a patera (found in 1853 near Dijon) be = the O. Ir. *dóir*, the opposite of *sóir*, the truth of the conjecture here made is established: DOIROS SEGOMARI IEVRV ALISANV, "a slave of Segomaros made (this) for Alisanos."

Page 47, No. 92, "*craos na haoine*," lit. "gluttony of the Friday," is a phrase now used of eating meat on that day, O'G.

Page 47, No. 93, *mataxa* vel corductum vel stramentum, *stræl* vel *bedding*, Ælfric.

Page 47, Nos. 94, 95, the gen. of *bas* is *baise*. Read basóg.

Page 47, No. 98, dare we connect *cáin* with poena, ποίνη?

Page 47, No. 99, with *féith* cf. Corn. *guiden*, gl. eutulus, i. e. catulus, a kind of fetter; also Skr. vétasa, arundo.

Page 48, No. 104. In the quotation from the Tripartite Life for *atcondaire* we should probably read *atcondarc*, cf. *adcondarc*, "*I perceived*," Z. 930.

Page 48, No. 106, *read* scála, now "a cup;" *caitheamh na scála*, "cup-tossing on Hallow-e'en," O'G.

Page 48, No. 108, "*talamh*, gen. *talmhan*, is now used by correct speakers for the earth = the world, as in *druim na talmhan* = dorsum terræ, the face of the earth. But *talamh*, gen. *taluimh*, is earth in the sense of land, e. g. *dá acra taluimh*, two acres of land," O'G. (O'D. and C. do not recognise this distinction.)

Page 48, No. 110, an earlier instance is in the Book of Armagh, 11, *a*, 2 (top margin), "*is báile inso sis as incertus*," "there is a place here below that is *incertus*."

Page 49, No. 118, as to *grunna*, also gronna, gromna, see Z. 735, note ¹.

Page 50, No. 122, "An old saying is *eró roimh oirc*, 'stye before pigling' = 'counting your chickens before they are hatched,'" O'G. (*eró roimh na horcaibh*, C.).

Page 50, No. 128, *lasair* (= laxarae) is the W. llachar.

Page 50, No. 129, *camradh* is, perhaps, cognate with W. cafn.

Page 50, No. 130, *read* sen (old) = sena-s, W. hen: cf. Zend hana.

Page 50, No. 131, *sech-rán* is obviously a deriv. from the prep. *sech*, W. hep. Lat. secus; Zend, haca.

Page 51, No. 133, delete the statement that in O. Ir. *liacc* is a cc-stem, into which I was led by a misreading of Zeuss's (corrected *supra* p. 80, No. 573); *liacc* was and is a fem. â-stem. As to *lógmar*, v. No. 792, p. 96.

Page 51, No. 137, *ossadh* is cognate with *sossadh* and *fossadh*, the common root being STHÂ.

Page 51,

Corrections and Additions.

Page 51, No. 138, cf. A. S. mele (patera), Ælfr.

Page 51, No. 139. I suspect *cogad* (O. Ir. coccad) is con-cata, the *cata* being cognate with Gaul. *catu*, Ir. cath.

Page 52, No. 141, the dat. sing. *bairgin* is in Z. 738.

Page 52, No. 142, *read* O. W. petguerid in the masculine. And in the third line *read* nómad (Z. 1076) *for* nóim-ed.

Page 52, No. 145, *cogar* is probably con-gar. See p. 76, No. 469.

Page 52, No. 148, at the end *read* san(d)islindeni.

Page 52, note 2, *bliadne*, Book of Armagh (cited *supra*, No. 676), nom. bliadain, is another example of the gen. plur. of a fem. i-stem. So ilar *fochraice*, Patrick's Hymn; nom. fochric: *fochide*, Z. 992, 481; nom. fochaid: *infinite*, Z. 979; nom. infinit.

Page 53, No. 152, cf. the Eng. *butteris*, Fr. boutoir.

Page 53, No. 154, compare with *lúirech*, in its secondary sense, the Vedic charman, lit. a hide.

Page 53, No. 156, cf. W. mèr, a particle, Gr. μέρος, which Benfey connects with Skr. mṛsh. Cf. *tir* with tarsh.

Page 55, No. 170, so biocon, from Viscount.

Page 55, No. 173, *abbdaine* (abbacy) is solely applicable to the office.

Page 55, No. 177, W. *cylwys*, *é* becoming *wy* as usual.

Page 55, No. 179, W. *blisgyn*. *Blaese* is now *plaosg*, "pod," and, jocosely, the "head," O'G.

Page 55, No. 180, *for* sabribarra *read* sarabara: "sarabara sunt fluxa ac sinuosa vestimenta de quibus legitur in Daniele." Isidor.

Page 55, No. 183, see, however, Ebel, Beitr. ii. 82, on the *Vertauschung der spiranten, f, s, h (ch)*, in Celtic.

Page 55, No. 191, *bile* also means lip (of a jug, &c.), O'G.

Page 56, No. 194, *faechoy* is cognate with W. gwichiad, Corn. guihan.

Page 57, No. 207, read *drcolán*, now *dreoilín*, from *deroil*, Corn., now *deireoil*, diminutive.

Page 57, No. 209, *conn* = Lat. canna: W. cawn, conyn.

Page 57, No. 211, *read* festuca *for* fistula.

Page 57, No. 216, *ga* also means "beam:" *ga gréine*, sunbeam; *ga gealaighe*, moonbeam, O'G.

Page 58, No. 217. I think now that the right reading may be *seideth gáithbulya*, the second word being the gen. of a *gáithbuily*.

Page 58, No. 220, for gen. *bláthaiy* read gen. *bláthaighe*.

Page 58,

Page 58, No. 222, *diangalar* is wrongly rendered here: a gloss in Gildas' Lorica shows that its meaning is *languor*. As to the note, I now see that the *t* in perfects like asrubur-t, &c., is nothing but the *d* (of the root dhâ), which, when following *r* or *c*, becomes *t*. This is proved by the occurrence of the form rodam*datar*, "they suffered," in the poem following the Félire (Leab. Breacc):—

iarna techt don rígiu	after their coming to the kingdom
rodamdatar sóethu	they suffered pains.

(The second line is glossed by ".i. rodamsat soethu .i. piana.") And I now believe that the unaspirated *t* in *domeltis*, &c., was preceded by *n*. Cf. dognítis, adsaitis, dofuaircitis.

Page 59, No. 227, cf. in "bello *Roth*," where Adamnán (Vit. Col.) alludes to the battle of Mag-Rath (= Rotomagus).

Page 60, No. 233, the spelling *sirogra* seems to show that chiragra was pronounced *sheeragra*.

Page 60, No. 240, "*cliath fuirsidhe* is a rude kind of harrow, made with a hurdle and stones to weight it, for light work like bush-harrowing. A regular harrow is *bráca*, or *práca*," O'G.

Page 60, No. 245, Schleicher thinks *popina* a loan-word from one of the other Italic dialects (Zeits. vii. 320).

Page 61, No. 246, and lapillula, of course, for lapillulus.

Page 61, No. 248, read *Luch francach*. "A rat is now called simply *franncach*," O'G.

Page 61, No. 251, C. says there is a phrase tug sé *amaise* air, "he made a grab at him."

Page 61, No. 254, *read*, possibly from *es*.

Page 61, No. 256, for *onesta* read *ouesta*, *ovesta*, and cf. *obesta* beost, Ælfr.

Page 62, No. 257, "*baincachlach* occurs in the sense of a female retainer (unconnected with horses) in the tale of Diarmid and Grainne," O'G. (*Toruigheacht D. 7 G.*, p. 98).

Page 62, No. 262, in the fourth line of the quatrain *read* has stuck.

Page 62, No. 264, in the paradigm *read* dib mbethaib.

Page 62, No. 265, is *tiar* = du-iar?

Page 63, No. 266, *ól cormae* would be better rendered "a drinking of ale."

Page 63, No. 272, from dorn comes duirnín, a small handle: *read* nom*durni*.

Page 63, No. 274, *spline*, "a sharp look;" splincín, "a long splinter of bog-pine, used as a candle," O'G.

Page 64,

Corrections and Additions.

Page 64, No. 279, *for* cumail *read* comal, and delete the words *Gaulish ver.*

Page 64, No. 287, I think Ebel (Beitr. i. 163) errs in denying a vowel-changing power to *o, u*, for lenomnaib (gl. lituris), Z. 739, is surely from *l*íuomnaib, Lat. fíno, cercol = circulus, Z. 594; felsub = ph*i*losophus; and I believe that betho, etho (from bith, ith), may also be quoted as examples of the power possessed by *o*. Ebel says that in the latter instances the *o* stands for a prior *a;* and we certainly have *betha, etha*. But these are surely mere instances of *a* for *o.* Cf. the Ogamic genitive *Atilogdo*, which Dr. Graves reads *Apilogdo*, in Mr. Wilde's *Catalogue of the Antiquities in the Museum of the Royal Irish Academy*. Dublin, 1857, p. 136.

Page 65, No. 290. "*Nighean* is heard in Ireland, in names like *Nóra nighean* Aodha, Nora Hays," O'G. (O'D. and C. say this should be written N. *ní n-Aodha*).

Page 66, No. 296. These words seem not Indo-European. "Orientis partibus Adventavit *asinus*" is probably true in more senses than one.

Page 66, No. 300, cf. A. S. feohstrang (pecuniosus), feohhus (aerarium), Ælfr.

Page 66, No. 303, cf. the Corn. diures (gl. exul).

Page 66, No. 305. The theory here set forth is so extremely ingenious that I could not help inserting it. For my part, however, I believe that *Hérinn* is nothing but *Ivernya* ('Ιουερνια), the *v* having passed into spiritus asper, which has then shifted, the *é* standing for *i* (Z. 25), the *nn* for *ny*, as in the Prakrit aṇṇa from Skr. anya, the O. Ir. *moirtchenn*, from morticinium. Thus, Ivernia, hierrna ('Ιερνη), whence by metathesis hirenn, hérenn. As to the irregularity in the acc., *enn* for *inn*, I have found the correct vowel in the Tripartite Life: dorat dia *heirind* duitsiu ("God has given Ireland to thee"), Egerton, 93 (Mus. Brit.), fo. 16 *a*, 2.

Page 68, line 4 from top. The *b* in *marb* (W. marw) is really a *v*, as in O. Ir. *tarb* = Gaulish tarvos, W. tarw, *fedb* = Lat. vidua, W. gweddw, *garb* = Skr. garva, W. garw, *nonbar* = a Skr. navanvara-m.

Page 69, note 2, add: ind réta ad*gúsi* optait, Z. 978, "the things which the optative desires:" assag*uss*im én eechtar mo dá gúaland, "I wish a bird on each of my two shoulders." Scirgl. Conculainn.

Page 70, No. 370, now *macámh*.

Page 70, No. 372. The statement of the regular *lautvertretung* in Old Irish, and the other Indo-European languages, is here given with a brevity which, perhaps, may mislead. The following Table will be useful, and may be relied on so far as it goes, being, with the exception of the Old Irish column, taken from Curtius' *Grundzüge der Griechischen Etymologie* (Leipzig, 1858):—

Appendix.

Indo-European.	Old Irish.	Sanskrit.	Greek.	Latin.	Gothic.	Old High German.	Slavonic.	Lithuanian.
K	c, ch (g)[a]	k, kh, ch, ç	κ	c, q	h (g)	h (g)	k, č, c, s	k, sz
G	g	g, j	γ	g	k	k (ch)	g, ', z	g, ż
GH	g	gh, h	χ	h[b], g[c]	g	g (k)	g, ź, z	g, ż
T	t, th (d)[d]	t, th	τ	t	th (d)	d	t	t
D	d	d	δ	d	t	z, sz	d	d
DH	d	dh	θ	f[b], d, b[c]	d	t	d	d
P	lost[h], c, f[e]	p, ph	π	p	f	f, v (b)	p	p
B	b	b	β	b				
BH	b	bh	φ	f[b], b[c]	b	b (p)	b	b
Ṅ	ṅ, lost?[f]	ṅ	γ before gutturals	n	n	n	n	n
N	n, or lost[g]	n, ṇ	ν	n	n	n	n	n
M	m, n[h]	m	μ, ν[i]	m	m	m	m	m
R	r	r	ρ	r	r	r	r	r
L	l	l	λ	l	l	l	l	l
Y	lost, h?[k]	y	ζ, ´	j	j	j	j	j
S	s, or lost[l]	s, sh	σ, ´	s (r)	s (z)	s (r)	s, ch, š	s
V	f, v[m]	v	F	v	v	w	v	v

[a] When e is, or has been, flanked by vowels, it becomes ch, for which g (i. e. gh) is found.
[b] At the beginning of a word (in anlaut).
[c] In a word (in inlaut).
[d] When t is, or has been, flanked by vowels, it becomes th, for which d (i. e. dh) is found.
[e] O. Ir. f ex p is very rare. See p. 154, addendum to No. 37. I have little doubt that p occurs in inlaut (probably in combination with some other letter), but cannot yet quote a sure example.
[f] In the combination ṅr, so far as I know, the nasal is always lost in O. Ir.
[g] In the combinations nt, ns.
[h] In auslaut, e. g. in the acc. sing., and gen. plur. of a-stems, what I call the transported n represents a primitive m.
[i] In auslaut.
[k] I suspect that initial y is sometimes represented by h, it having (as often in Greek) passed into the spiritus asper.
[l] Lost between vowels, as I believe, invariably; sometimes also in anlaut, e. g. in the nom. and gen. of the article.
[m] Initial v always becomes f. In anlaut and auslaut v (written b, sometimes f in Old Irish, bh in Modern Irish) is preserved in combination with d, l, n, r. It also occurs in varṅ, "your" (cf. Goth. izvara), written barṅ or farṅ in O. Ir., uorṅ in the Tripartite Life, bhar n- in the modern language.

Page 72.

Corrections and Additions.

Page 72, No. 397, a left-handed man is *ciotach*: ciotóg, "the left-hand," O'G. Lhuyd has compared W. *chwith*, "left;" *chwithig*, "left-handed."

Page 72, No. 411, *for* guitter *read* guilter.

Page 72, No. 412, "*breall* is the *glans penis*: also the round knob at the end of the *buailteán*, or striking part, of a flail, by which the thong is kept from flying off," O'G.

Page 73, No. 423, line 8 from top, *read*, 423, Tuata (gl. laicus); cf. Τουτιυς; and in the translation of the Gaulish inscription *read* made this temple for Belesama. Dr. Siegfried now explains ɪ́óʀᴄ, ɪᴄʀᴄ by the Old Ir. root ɪᴄʜ, found in fritamm*iu*rat "me adficiunt," fritamm*ior*sa (gl. me adficiet), Z. 336; *tú*ra*d* (gl. factum est), Book of Armagh, 189 *b*, 1. In the note delete the first sentence. M. Pictet is undoubtedly right in identifying Ουιλλονεοϲ with Villonius (Gruter, 488-5). See his learned and ingenious *Essai sur quelques Inscriptions en langue gauloise*. Genève, 1859.

Page 74, No. 428. I have no doubt now that the MS. is right in its *ruaimnech dubain*. Cf. the Skr. rôman horsehair (from rôhman), and the O. Ir. ruamnac (gl. lodix), Z. 27; W. rhawn, Bret. reûn, Ir. *ruainne* (No. 463) seem connected.

Page 74, No. 429. I think *dilechta* is the pret. part. pass. of a verb *dileicim*: cf. leicim = linquo.

Page 74, No. 430, cf. aon-t-suim, "grand total," O'G.

Page 74, No. 431, delete, gl. tener, *infra*.

Page 74, No. 434, O'G. thinks cúisi (for cúise) the gen. sing.

Page 75, No. 446, read *tige*, gen. of *tig*.

Page 75, No. 462, the acc. plurals here quoted seem (with the exceptions of cairtea, náimtea) to be rather examples of metathesis rather than extension.

Page 75, line 3 from bottom, *for* 469 *read* 463.

Page 76, No. 465, cf. Fr. doigt de pied.

Page 76, No. 479, W. ewpan.

Page 76, No. 482, perhaps W. *od*-n in *eb-odn*, "horse-dung," may be connected.

Page 77, No. 484, *sgagaim*, "I strain, sift, winnow," O'G.; cf. Eng. *shake?*

Page 76, No. 498, delete, compare Eng. *whelp*.

Page 77, No. 508, *preachán* and *préachan* are now "a crow;" préachán na ccearc, "a kite," O'G.

Page 78, No. 545, *c* is *not* aspirated by the influence of *n*. In *sancht* the *cht* has regularly arisen from *ct*. Cf. O. Persian Bakhtris, durukhta: A. S. tæh-te, væh-te, sóh-te, from tæc-an, wræc-an, séc-an. *Conchoinnnenir*, conchechrat, are probably written in the MS. ochoim, ochech, and should have been read cochoim, cochech.

Page 79, No. 561, cf. the N. H. G. *eber*-esche.
Page 79, No. 565, hence *fraochan*, whortleberry, and cf. ἐρείκη, erica.
Page 80, No. 570, *bráthair* now means cousin; *dearbhbhráthair*, "brother," pronounced *dritháir*, derbráthir (gl. germane), Z. 834.
Page 81, line 7, *for* the earth *read* earth.
Page 81, No. 577, *sroll* now always means *satin*; *sioda* is silk, O'G.
Page 81, No. 587, "a bramble-brake is now *driscarnach*, with the termination of which cf. *sgealparnach*, "continued pinching" (*sgealp*, a pinch); *siosarnach*, "continued whispering," O'G.
Page 82, No. 595, the W. *pyrchwyn*, "crest of a helmet;" *pyrgwyn*, "crest of a plume," may be connected.
Page 83, No. 606, *ór* is a neut. a-stem in O. Ir., and occurs in the nom. sing. with the transported *n* in the following verses, for which I am indebted to Herr Mone:—

"Is én immo ñiada sás He is a bird round which the trap is closing,
is nau tholl diant eslinn gúas, He is a leaky ship in perilous danger,
is lestar fás, is crann crín He is an empty vessel, he is a withered tree,
[nach digní toil ind ríg túas.] Whoso doth not the will of the King above.

Is ór áglan, is nem im gréin, He is pure gold, he is heaven round the sun,
is lestar ñarggit cu fín, He is a vessel of silver with wine [in it],
is son, is alaind, is nóeb He is prosperous, is beautiful, is holy,
cach óen digní toil ind ríg."¹ Every one that doth the will of the King.

Page 85, No. 641, read *luathgáirech*.
Page 85, No. 650, *coisínech* would properly be "small-footed."
Page 85, No. 652, add, from *gearb*, a scab.
Page 86, No. 660, *for* sochoise *read* sochoise. I cannot but think the *coscitir* here quoted is cognate with the Lat. consequor. Cf. madu coscedar (gl. ipsa consequatur), Leyden Priscian, 17 b.
Page 86, No. 666, *taithneamh na gréine*, "the shining of the sun," is a common phrase.
Page 87, No. 674, delete line 5 as far as *cruaidh*.
Page 88, No. 700, cf. O. W. cruitr (gl. pala, a winnowing-shovel).

Page 89,

---

¹ This is from the before-mentioned MS. in the monastery of S. Paul. I have ventured to correct Mone's *sar* into sás, his *nan* into nau, his *sin* into fín. Mr. Curry has found a poem in the Book of Ballymote, in which the above verses are incorporated.

Corrections and Additions.

Page 89, No. 709. I have now no doubt that sgeota and sgéotha are different words. *Sgeota* (gl. cartesium, i. e. chartaceum) seems a loan-word from scheda. As to *seéotha*, see Reeves' Vit. Col., 106. Du Cange, sub v. sceta.

Page 89, No. 716, with *bile*, "leaflet, blossom," cf. the Gaulish *Beliocanda*, "Achillæa millefolium." Is not this = folium, φύλλον?

Page 89, No. 717, *cassock*, Fr. casaque, Ital. casaccia, Lat. casa (Diez, E. W., 91), has nothing to do with ceis.

Page 89, No. 720, in Sanskrit svapna sometimes means a dream: cf. Old Eng. *sweren*, somnium, ὕπνος.

Page 90, No. 725. If O'R. be correct in explaining *long* as enclosure, *long-phort* = castrum becomes intelligible.

Page 91, No. 735, *for* áivs-i-s *read* áius-ti-s?

Page 91, No. 740, *for* iii. *read* 111. No. 741, read *Sealladh*.

Page 92, No. 744, Z.'s *muince* is right. Cf. *mjne*, monile, Ælfr., *mene*, Beowulf, 2403.

Page 92, No. 745, druim (notwithstanding the irregularity of *d = t*) is the W. trwm; so días = W. twys.

Page 93, No. 752, *arbe* (not arpe) is the right form. Cf. Goth. arbja, heir, and Skr. arbha, proles.

Page 94. line 5, *for* yávas *read* yavas.

Page 94, No. 769, read *Budhgadh*.

Page 96, No. 782, now *leamhnacht*. Cf. W. *llefrith*.

Page 96, No. 792, *Leasughadh* means, 1, to improve; 2, to manure, O'G.

Page 97, No. 795. Two other forms are *foileastrom*, *oileastrom*, O'G.

Page 97, No. 796, cf. Do *sgairt* sí fá gháiridhe, "she burst out into a roar of laughter," O'G.

Page 97, No. 797, I feel sure that the true reading of Z.'s *rudimm* is rudimin.

Page 98, No. 812, Dia (= divas), "day;" in the acc. sing. *dei* (fri *dei*) is still declined like an s-stem. But in the dat. diu (in*diu*) it has gone over to the vocalic declension.

Page 99. note, *for* Celtic r *read* Gaulish r; see, however, p. 154.

Page 100, line 12 from top, *for* 847 *read* 843.

Page 100, No. 845, for *Coindealbthadh* we should certainly read *Coindealbháthadh*: *coindeal*, from candela; *báthadh*, "destruction, extinguishment." Cf. bathach, leg. báthach (gl. moribundus), Z. 777.

Page 100. No. 846, *Taidbsiu* may be du-ad-*vad*-s-tiân. Cf. W. *gwedd*, "shape," Z. 860; a-gwedd = adgwedd.

Appendix.

Page 100, note, line 11, *read* ad-coth-*ded*-ac; coth = Gaulish cata, W. cyd.

Page 101, No. 851, cf. W. *cor*-lan, "sheep-fold."

Page 101, No. 853, *for* now aifrin *read* now aifrionn : with *aiffrend* cf. W. offeren.

Page 101, No. 854, gradale for graduale; W. *gris*-lyfr, from gressus; W. grisiau, "steps."

Page 102, No. 859, corporale is the napkin which covers the sacred elements.

Page 102, No. 864, now scóraid.

Page 105, No. 884, *read* sólás, happiness, the opposite of dólás.

Page 106, No. 892, read *compántus*.

Page 107, line 11, *for* di[a]áis *read* dia és (dom-héis-se, "after me," Z. 1053). No. 899, *read* denid (facite), Z. 458.

Page 108, No. 903, *read comthromugud*. Comhthrom now means "just, fair."

Page 108, No. 908, now *leoirghníomh*.

Page 109, No. 913, now *comháireamh* (áram = ad-ram ?).

Page 109, No. 916, now *lámhágan* (applied to a child's first attempt at creeping on all-fours), from *lámh*, just as *lapadóireacht*, "groping;" from *lap* and *lapa*, "the hand," O'G.

Page 109, No. 918. *Comma* is, perhaps, a loan-word; κόμμα talcatio (talca, a cutting).

Page 111, No. 937, *for* finlorg *read* fri lorg, "on (the) track."

Page 111, No. 940, cf. in*gerr*tha, gl. lacerandum, Gildas' Lorica.

Page 112, No. 945, now sméaróid: cf. sméar, "a blackberry," O'G.

Page 112, note, frecuirthe céill (gl. recole, i. e. repone sensum), Z. 1130.

Page 113, No. 952, Ir. *gres*, W. *gres*, seem likewise connected with ghrans.

Page 113, No. 955. In the last line of the quotation from Ultán's hymn I should now render *biam* by "may I be!"

Page 114, No. 967. In his A. S. lexicon, p. 690, Ettmüller gives "secóta -an m. tructus, trocta piscis."

Page 114, line 11 from bottom, *for* 995 *read* 975.

Page 114, No. 976, there is no such word as *ainmidheach*, according to O'D. and C.

Page 116, No. 999, delete (from sblurar ?).

Page 117, No. 1006. In the dialect of Vannes, *blonec* means graisse, abdomen. De Courson, *Hist. des origines*, &c. Paris, 1843, p. 409.

Page 118, No. 1017, add W. teneu.

Page 118, No. 1029, *muco mara* is a porpoise.

Page 119, line 8, read 1031.

Page 120,

Corrections and Additions.

Page 120, No. 1040, cf. W. erlyn, "pursuit; dy-*lynu*, "to adhere;" can-*lyn*, "to follow;" *glyn*, "adhesion."

Page 120, No. 1045. The *c* stands, I now believe, for céd, first; and I suspect that *céd grindi foilci* is some kind of warm lotion. The expression occurs in a passage from a medical tract with which C. has furnished me. *Log in baistithi* (nom. *baistedh*) should have been rendered "price of baptism." In the passage from O'Davoren's Glossary *read* intan is i linn ⁊ im biud doberar, "when it is in ale and in food it is given."

Page 121, No. 1052, read *máthair* = mâtar. The *ai* (*i*) is a weakened *a*. So is the *ai* (*i*) of *bráthair, athair*.

Page 125, note. I have erred in regarding and translating *oróit* as from orate. It is explained as a subst. in Cormac, and occurs unmistakeably as such in a piece following Sanctáin's hymn in Lib. Hymn., Rombith *oróit* let a maire, "sit mihi oratio apud te, O Maria!" See also the inscription on the case of the Book of Durrow, *supra*, p. 56.

Page 126, No. 1102. In the quotation from Cormac, *dam* should have been rendered "suffering." See the quotation and gloss from the *Leabhar Breacc, suprá*, p. 158.

Page 128, line 12 from top. I have erred in quoting er-t, var-t, &c., as instances of pronominal agglutination. The *t* here is the regular termination of the 2nd pers. sing. of the Teutonic preterite. The pronoun, however, is agglutinated in the O. H. G., A. S., and Eng. termination of the 2nd pers. sing., *s-t*.

Page 129, line 8 from bottom, *before* méza *insert* Bret.

Page 130, note, *for* Rawlinson *read* Laud.

Page 134, line 20 from top, *read* minimas corporis sui partes.

Page 135, line 19 from top, the Welsh *pyn* occurs in er-*byn*, "against" (Norris).

Page 145, line 8 from top, *for* v. 45 *read* v. 46. *Ginyis* (gl. oslaicib, "openings") occurs in Cormac's Glossary, v. *Gin* (this word is not in the Academy copy).

Page 146, to the verbal forms under the conjunctive 1st sing., add *cu-r-bam*, No. 260. This, indeed, seems the only true form here given of the conjunctive in the 1st pers. sing.

Page 150, No. 220, the gen. plur. *rap* occurs twice in a medical MS. in the library of the Royal Irish Academy (⁴/²), is ann bis an caor ar muine duib n[a] *rap* (p. 2): Loges gaire in gaile ⁊ na *rap* (p. 12). No. 245, *dentæib* is for *déntaib*, "fabrefactis."

Page 151, No. 260, *oentaige*, better *óentuige*, from *óen-tuigim* = O. Ir. óintuccu, "I am of one mind with," "I assent," "I grant." Tuccu (an ia-stem?) seems cognate with the O. Latin tongére, Goth. thagkjan, Eng. think, O. Norse thekkja, O. H. G. denchan.

denchan. Can the Eng. slang-word *twig* (= understand) have been taken from the Mod. Ir. *tuigim?*

Page 151, No. 261, gnimarthaib is for gnímradaib. For *gnímarad* read *gnímrad*. The dat. pl. of *daggnímrad* occurs in the opening of the sermon in the Codex of Cambray (Z. 1003): aire sechethar sclictu ar fédot [nom. féda, fiadu] in *dagnimrathib*, "ut sequatur vestigia dei nostri in bonis operibus," C. *Gníomh* now makes its nom. pl. *gníomha* and *gníomhartha*.

GLOSSES FROM THE BOOK OF ARMAGH.

[The following selection from the Old Irish glosses scattered through the Book of Armagh, may fitly fill a space which would otherwise remain vacant. Of these glosses, as well as of the other contents of that invaluable MS., we may soon expect a complete edition from the Rev. Dr. Reeves.]

Ochen (gl. benignus), 9, *b.* 1; *totmáel* (gl. aurigam totum), 13, *b.* 2; *enga* (gl. aqua supra petram, i. e. fons), ibid.; *duferti martur* (gl. ad sargifagum martyrum), 21, *b.* 2; *gabál oblann* (gl. acceptis autem v. panibus et ii. piscibus), *gabis ailli* (gl. benedixit illis), *combach* (gl. fregit), *fodil* (gl. distribuit), 77, *a.* 1; *áiledu* (gl. stercora), 81, *a.* 1; *indloingtis* (gl. discedabantur), *dúnsit l. congabsat* (gl. continuerunt, aures suas), 175, *b.* 1; *cuimte* (gl. ionuchus), 176, *a.* 2; *tarsende* (gl. Tarsensem), 176, *b.* 2; *etalaeda* (gl. Italica, nom. sing.), 177, *a.* 2; *coibdeliy* (gl. necessariis amicis), 177, *b.* 2; *teeelsid* (gl. acceptor, personarum), 178, *a.* 1; *nudebthi*[*tis*], (gl. disceptabant), 178, *a.* 2; *rechtire forru* (gl. regerent[ur], 179, *a.* 1; *formuichthib .i. moirtchenn* (gl. subfucatis, i. e. suffocatis), 181, *a.* 1; *huasalsichire* (gl. ariopagita), *huasalterchomrietid* (gl. archisinagogus), 182, *b.* 2; *immact* (.i. jecit), 183, *a.* 1; *sachilli* (gl. saudaria), *debai* (gl. simicintia), 183, *a.* 2; *et l. indeb l. tarsichid* (gl. adquæsitio), 183, *b.* 2; *berensdæ* (gl. Beroensis), *derbensde* (gl. Derbius), *arunn*[*f*]*ethitis* (gl. sustinebant nos), 184, *a.* 1; [*ad*]*sluindim* (gl. appello), 187, *b.* 1; *arbir* (gl. co[h]ortis), 188, *b.* 1; *muiride* (gl. civitas Thalasa), *dugaimigud* (gl. ad h[i]emandum), 188, *b.* 2; *dinmuirágu* (gl. cum sustulissent), *crus* (gl. pupi), *innaluæ* (gl. juncturas gubernaculorum), 189, *a.* 2; *fernn siúil l. seól* (gl. artimone), *cimbidi* (gl. custodias), *dlúthsit .i.* infigerunt, navim, 189, *b.* 1; *dindirect .i. rith folo* (gl. disintiria), 189, *b.* 2.

GENERAL INDEX.

(167)

GENERAL INDEX.

[*The numbers refer to the paragraphs of the Commentary, except when the letter " p." is prefixed; then they refer to the pages of this book.*]

Â weakened to *ai*, p. 155; *a* weakened to *ai* (*i*), p. 153, p. 165.
Acta Sanctorum cited, p. 145.
Adamnan's Vision (in the Leabhar Breacc and the Lebar na huidre), cited or referred to, 90, 103; p. 95, note [1]; 1008, 1087.
Adverbs formed by the prefix *co* (*go*), p. 147.
Agglutination, pronominal, 1071; p. 165.
Ælfric's Glossary cited, p. 144, p. 145, &c.
Amra Choluim Chille, cited, p. 37, note.
Archives des Missions Scientifiques et Littéraires, vol. v., referred to, p. 97, note.
Armagh, Book of. See *Manuscripts.*
Article, Old Irish, declined, 78; and see Addenda, p. 155; nom. pl. masc. of article in Mid. Irish, p. 135; article in Old Welsh, Cornish, and Breton, p. 45, note [1].
Assimilation, retrogressive, 458; progressive, 705.
Aspiration, 5, p. 45, note [1]; p. 46, note [1]; 139, 287, 1071.
Aufrecht, Dr. Theodor, referred to, 423, 776.
Autun, Gaulish inscription of, p. 104, note.

B in Old Irish corresponds with Skr. *b*, Gr. β, Lat. *b*; and also with Skr. *bh*, Gr. φ, Lat. *f* (at the beginning of a word), *b* (in a word), 372; p. 160; Indo-European *b*, see p. 160; *b* sometimes for *g*, 784; apparent instance of Ir. *b* = Lat. *v*, p. 149 (No. 152).
Benary's law, 372.
Benfey, Theodor, referred to, 426.
—— his *Griechisches Wurzellexicon* referred to, 700, 1070, 1095.
Beowulf. See *Thorpe.*
Bh, Indo-European, p. 160.
Böhtlingk and Roth, their Skr. Dictionary referred to, 870, 952.

Bopp, Franz, cited or referred to, 158; p. 58, note; 224, 250, 290, 420, 546, 621, 776, 860, 904, 1000, 1068, 1071.
—— his *Vergleichende Grammatik*, quoted, 387, 703.
—— his *Glossarium Sanscriticum* referred to, 1047, 1081, 1133, 1095.
Brogán's hymn (*Liber Hymnorum*), cited 218, 280, 424, 966, 977.
Burn's *Ecclesiastical Law*, cited, 854, 855.

C. Stems in *c*. See *Declension*, and p. 153. Old Irish *c* corresponds with Gr. κ, Lat. *c*, *q*, Skr. *k*, *kh*, *ch*, *ç*, 372, p. 160; *cc* in Welsh becomes *ch*, 439; *ct* in Irish becomes *cht* (*sancht* = *sancta*, 545, see Addenda, pp. 161-162), but *th* in Welsh, 915.
—— *c* (in *inlaut*) lost in combination *cr*, 621, 724; in combination *cn*, 118, and Addenda.
Cianan of Daimliac (Duleek), 35.
Ciaran, St., 1137.
Civilization, material, of Irish ecclesiastics, 740.
Colmán's hymn (*Liber Hymnorum*), cited, 214, 338, 588, 640, 738, 890, 955.
Columcille, p. 37, note.
Comgell, hymn to Abbot, p. 146.
Comparatives, formation of some Old Irish, 1112, 1115, 1133.
Conjugation. See *Verb.*
Cormac's *Glossary* cited or referred to, 38, 42, 70, 90, 112, 115, 120, 136, 146, 155, 159, 184, 216, 218, 255, 256, 266, 555, 578, 588, 651, 814, 843, 873, 889, 897, 933, 966, 1065, 1102; p. 127, note [4]; p. 148, p. 165.
Cormacan écces, cited 39, 56, 226, 866; p. 147.
Ct becomes *cht* in O. Irish, pp. 161-162.
Cummian's Epistle, cited, p. 145.
Curry, Professor Eugene, cited or referred to, *pas-*

sim; his *Cath Maighe Léna* cited, 580; and see *Seirglige Conculainn.*
Curtius, G., referred to, p. 58, note; 245, 860, 871; his *Grundzüge der Griechischen Etymologie* cited or referred to, 792, 948, 999, 1095; p. 159.

D becomes *t* before aspirated *s*, 148, 734; stems in *d*, see *Declension;* Old Irish *d* corresponds with Skr. and Lat. *d*, Gr. δ, and also with Skr. *dh*, Gr. θ, Lat. *f* (at the beginning of a word), *d*, *b* (in a word), 372, p. 160; *d* assimilated to *n*, 914; to *l*, 915; *gh* written for *dh*, 604 (*boghar* for *bodhar*); Indo-European *d*, see p. 160.
Dative plural in Irish, origin of, p. 155.
De Belloguet, Baron, his *Ethnogénie Gauloise* referred to, 423, and note.
De Betouw, his *De aris,* &c., referred to, 1029.
Declension, Old Irish:—
 I. Vocalic: . . . . 1. masc. a-stems, 17, 81; neut. a-stems, 139; masc. ia-stems, 9 (there are neut. ia-stems).
  2. fem. â-stems, 9; fem. iâ-stems, 158.
  3. masc. and fem. i-stems, 2, 42; p. 52, note[2], p. 157; neut. i-stems, 1008.
  4. masc. u-stems, 264 (there are also neut. u-stems, but no fem. u-stems).
 II. Consonantal: 1. Guttural stems: c-stems, 13; g-stem, 1036.
  2. Dental stems: t-stems, 4; ant-stems, 292, 444; ent-stems (*löche,* gen. *löchet*); d-stems, 1; n-stems, 108; mann-stem, 991.
  3. Liquid stems: r-stems, 13.
  4. S-stems, 812; p. 163; ns-stems, 1115.
 III. Monosyllabic stems in *t*, 987.
 IV. Adjectival: a-stems, 803; ia-stems, 803; i-stems, 661 (ili, nom. pl. of il, 565; and see *Beitr.* i., 464).
 V. Pronominal. See *Pronouns, Article.*
Flexion in adjectives preceding the nouns with which they agree, 565; passage over from one declension to another, 87, 726, 1047; p. 135, p. 163; extension of stems, 462, but see p. 161; loss of labial ending in dat. pl., p. 135. See *Article, Pronoun.*
Declension in Welsh and Cornish, trace of, p. 135 (pyn, dat. of pen).
De Courson, his *Hist. des Origines,* &c., cited, p. 164.
Denis, cited or referred to, p. 133, note; 134.

Dh, Indo-European, see p. 160.
Diefenbach, Dr. Lorenz, referred to, 387; his *Celtica* referred to, 121, 266; p. 154; his *Glossarium Med. Lat. Germ.,* cited or referred to, 152, 574, 793, 866; p. 145; his *Gothisches Wörterbuch* quoted, 1073; referred to, 1095.
Diez, his *Etymologisches Wörterbuch* cited or referred to, 107, 708, 852; p. 148.
Dimma macc Nathi, 133, 1080.
Diminutival suffixes, 934; p. 111, note.
Dioscorides, cited, 765.
Dual in Irish, 773.
Dubthach, his MS. of Priscian, p. 155.
Du Cange, his *Glossarium* cited or referred to, 59, 98, 797; p. 143.

Ebel, Dr. Hermann, cited or referred to, 74; p. 61, note[2]; 287, 288, 289, 315, 328, 735; p. 99, note; 1117; p. 136, note; p. 156, p. 157, p. 158.
Eclipsis, phenomena of, 905.
Ettmüller, his *Lexicon Anglosaxonicum* cited, p. 164.

F = *sv*, 777; initial *f* from *v*, 157, 468; from *p*, p. 154.
Féilire Óingusso, cited or referred to, 35, 36, 168, 234; p. 65, note[1]; 391, 812; p. 100, note; 1131, 1133.
Ferguson, Mr. Samuel, quoted, 708.
Festus, referred to, 18.
Fermoy, *Book of.* See *Manuscripts.*
Fiacc's Hymn (*Liber Hymnorum*), cited, 154, 588, 605, 729, 870, 897, 943, 1080; Preface to, cited, p. 112, note.
Förstemann, referred to, 55.

G, loss of, between vowels, 378, 1114; in combination *gn*, 459, 683. Stems in *g*, see *Declension.* Old Irish *g* corresponds with Skr. *g, j*, Gr. γ, Lat. *g;* and also with Skr. *gh, h*, Gr. χ, Lat. *h* (at the beginning of a word), *g* (in a word), 372, and p. 160; *gg* for *ng*, 879; Indo-European *g*, see p. 160.
Gaulish Inscriptions. See *Inscriptions.*
—— derivatives in *anco,* &c., 1006.
Gh, Indo-European, see p. 160.
Gildas, 17.
—— Badonicus, p. 133.
—— *Lorica*, p. 136, *et seq.*
Giraldus Cambrensis, his *Topogr. Hib.* cited, 37; p. 153.
Glück, C. W., his *Keltische Namen* cited or referred to, 46, 133, 139, 258, 328, 430, 533, 558, 656, 666, 667, 957, 999, 1073, 1131.
Gothic *h (g)* = O. Ir. *c;* Goth. *k* = O. Ir. *g;* Goth. *g* = O. Ir. *g;* Goth. *th (d)* = O. Ir. *d;* Goth. *t* = O. Ir. *d;* Goth. *d* = O. Ir. *d.* See Addenda, p. 160.

Greek κ = O. Ir. c; γ, χ = O. Ir. g; δ, θ = O. Ir. d; β, φ = O. Ir. b, 372; and see Addenda, p. 160.
Graves, Rev. Dr., mentioned, p. 159.
Grimm, Jacob, referred to, 387, 423; his *Geschichte der deutschen Sprache* referred to, 250, 784.
—— his *Deutsche Rechtsalterthümer* cited, 1136.
Gunation in Old Irish, 380, 392, 959.

H in Old Irish, p. 68, note.
Haug, his *Die Gâthâ's* referred to, 682.
Highland Society's *Dictionarium Scoto-Celticum* cited or referred to, 66, *et passim*.

Imperative active, Old Irish rare form of 2nd pers. sing., p. 112, note, and Addenda, p. 164.
Indo-European consonants, how represented in Old Irish and other sister languages, p. 160.
Inscriptions, Old Irish, on the case of the *Book of Durrow*, 203; copied by Dr. Petrie, 398; Gaulish, Vaison, 423, p. 161; Nismes, p. 100, note; Dijon, p. 156. See *Ogham*.
Irish Nennius. See *Todd*.

J (= y) lost at beginning of Old Irish words, 758; assimilated to preceding *l*, 765, 884; to *n*, p. 159; to *r*, 1116; passing into spiritus asper, p. 160.

K, Indo-European, how represented in the O. Ir. and sister languages, p. 160.
Keller, Dr. F., his *Bilder und Schriftzüge*, u. s. w., referred to, p. 155.
Kelly, Rev. Dr., his Calendar of Irish Saints cited, 223.
Kirchhoff referred to, 423.
Kuhn, Dr. A., cited or referred to, 108; p. 68, note, 423, 1036, 1038.

L, Indo-European. p. 160; O. Ir. *l*, ibid.
—— assimilating a following *d*, 915.
-lach, 933.
Laidcenn mac Báith Bannaig, p. 133, and note.
Lassen, referred to, 758.
Latin c, q = O. Ir. c; Lat. g = O. Ir. g; Lat. h (at the beginning of a word) = O. Ir. g; Lat. t = O. Ir. t; Lat. d = O. Ir. d; Lat. f (at the beginning of a word) = O. Ir. d, b; Lat. d, b (in a word) = O. Ir. d (and b?), p. 160.
Leabhar Breac, mentioned, p. 132. See *Manuscripts*.
Lebar na huidre cited, see *Manuscripts*.
Lithuanian consonants, correspondence of, with those of the O. Ir., and other sister-languages, p. 160; declension of Lith. stems in -*ter*, 1047.
Locative sing. in O. Irish, p. 153 (and cf. the Mod. Ir. *cois na habhann, láimh re fairge*).
Lottner, Dr. Carl, cited or referred to, 831; p. 100, note; 977, 1124; and see *Verb*.

M, Indo-European, p. 160; *m* in *auslaut* weakened into *n* in O. Ir., p. 160, note; *m* in Welsh represents *mm, mn, mb*, 108.
Macintyre (*Mac int sáir*), 1137.
Manuscripts cited:—
    Book of Armagh (T. C. D.), cited, 75, 114, 203, 264, 342, 366, 383, 387, 390, 398, 424, 425, 427, 439, 580, 583, 588, 607, 616, 676, 693, 729, 745, 746; p. 95, note[2]; 781; p. 100, note; p. 103, note[3]; 871, 879, 909, 948; p. 112, note; 994, 1071, 1085; p. 146, p. 147, p. 152 (bis), p. 156, p. 166.
    Book of Dimma (T. C. D.) cited, 133, 1080.
    Book of Fermoy (Dr. Todd) quoted, 710.
    Book of Leinster (T. C. D.) cited, 555.
    Egerton, 88 (Mus. Brit.), referred to, 301.
    Harl., 1802 (Mus. Brit.), cited, 232; p. 68, note; 1134.
    H. 2, 16 (T. C. D.), p. 37, note. H. 2, 15, (T. C. D.), 1045. H. 3, 18 (T. C. D.), 371, 862.
    Laud, 610 (Bibl. Bodl.) cited, 428; Laud, F. 95 (Bibl. Bodl.), p. 130, note.
    Leabhar Breace (R. I. A.), p. 103, note. See *Félire*.
    Lebar na huidre (R. I. A.) cited, p. 37, note.
    Liber Hymnorum (T. C. D.) cited or referred to, 128, 130, 560, 639, 770, 775; p. 95, note[2]; 867, 894; p. 125, note; 1096, 1134. See *Fiacc's hymn, Broguin's hymn, Colman's hymn, Patrick's hymn, Sanctáin's hymn, Ultán's hymn*.
    Medical MS. ($\frac{32}{7}$), (R. I. A.) p. 165.
    O'Davoren's Glossary (Egerton, 88, Mus. Brit.), p. 44, note.
    Tripartite Life of St. Patrick (Egerton, 93, Mus. Brit.) cited, 104, 110, 189, 320, 518, 784, p. 159; and see *Cormac's Glossary, Félire Oingusso, Mone, Priscian*.
Medials, Irish, 372, and Addenda, p. 160; and see in this Index, *B, D, G*.
Metathesis aspirationis. See *Spiritus asper*: Metathesis vocalium, p. 161.
Middle-Irish, some characteristics of, p. 135.
Middle voice, traces of, in Celtic, 1112.
Mommsen, Theodor, his *Römische Inschriften der Schweiz* cited, 957.
Mone, Franz, his edition of the Lorica of Gildas, p. 134; his commentary thereon cited, ibid., and pp. 143, 144, 145; his copies of poems from a Carinthian MS. cited, p. 154, p. 161.
Müller, Professor Max, quoted or referred to, 584, 1047, 1052.
Muratori, *Thesaurus Veterum Inscriptionum* cited, 1029; his *Antiq. Ital.* cited, 1030.

Myvyrian Archaiology referred to, 21.

N, stems in, see *Declension*. The so-called prosthetic *n*, 85; the combination *nth*, 287; *n* lost before *s*, 285, 807, 880; before *t*, 292 and note [2], 490, 1017; before *f*, 519; *n* from *m*, 305, p. 160, note [b]; the combination *nt* preserved in Welsh and Breton, 772; the transported *n*, 776 and note; p. 103, note [2]; p. 108, notes; 946; p. 150; this *n* becomes *m* before *b*, p. 95, note [1]; *n* assimilates a following *d*, 914, and *y*, p. 159; Indo-European *n*, p. 160.

N Indo-European, p. 160.
Nasalization of initial medials, 776.
Nennius, the Irish translation of his *Historia Britonum*. See *Todd*.
Nismes, Gaulish inscription of, p. 100, note.
Norris, Mr. Edwin, his *Cornish Drama* referred to, p. 109, note, 937, 1039, p. 165.
Numerals, Cardinals, 772 777; Ordinals, 588-593; and see 930, 931.

O possesses umlauting power, p. 159.
O'Davoren's *Glossary*. See *Manuscripts*.
O'Donovan, Dr. John, cited or referred to, *passim*; his *Irish Grammar* quoted or referred to, 90, 139, 155, 161, 168, 208, p. 58, note; p. 70, note; 868; p. 103, note [3]; p. 128, note [3]; pp. 149; his *Fled dúin nan Géd* quoted, 193, 781, p. 100, note; p. 147; his *Battle of Magh Rath*, 303; his *Lebar na Cert*, 747, 837; and see *Cormacán vecs*.
Ogham, 534.
—— inscriptions referred to, 80; p. 159.
O'Grady, Mr. S. H., his assistance acknowledged, p. 153.
Oingus *Céle Dé*. See *Félire*.
Old High German, correspondence of its consonants with those of the O. Ir., and other Indo-European languages, p. 160.
O'Molloy, his *Grammatica Latino-Hibernica* quoted, p. 136.
O'Reilly, his Irish Dictionary cited or referred to, *passim*.
Orelli, 957, 1029.
Oxford Essays. See *Müller*.

P, loss of initial, 13, 493, 746; p. 150; change of initial *p* to *f*, p. 154; change of *p* to *c*, 224; loss of *inlautend p* in the combination *pn*, 720; Indo-European *p*, see p. 160.
Participles in -ων, -οντος, represented by Irish ant-stems, 292; future participle passive, how formed in Old Irish, p. 135, p. 136, note; how in Middle and Modern Irish, p. 136; pret. part. passive, how formed in Middle Irish, p. 146.

Patrick's hymn (Liber Hymnorum) cited, 369, 580, 867, 872, 1071; p. 147, p. 149; Patrick's altar, p. 136; Lassar takes veil from Patrick, 676.
Petrie, Dr. George, referred to, 398; his *Round Towers* referred to, 55, 125; p. 58, note; 847, 933; p. 146; p. 148; his Essay on Tara cited or referred to, 173, 602, 784.
Pictet, M. Adolphe, cited or referred to, 97, 290, 302, 305, 578, 940, 999; p. 147, p. 149, p. 161; his *Essai sur quelques Inscriptions, &c.*, p. 161.
Political Songs of England, ed. Wright, cited, p. 155.
Pott, cited or referred to, 746, 819; his *Etymologische Forschungen* referred to, 426.
Prefixes, *do*, *so*, 85; *mo*, p. 107, note [1].
Priscian, Leyden Codex of, cited, 1102; p. 162.
Pronoun, possessive, of 2nd pers. sing., 570; of 3rd pers. sing., 420; relative, Mid.-Ir. gen., p. 150.
Pronunciation of *c*, *t* before *i*, 884, and note.

R, Indo-European. See p. 160.
Reduplication in Old Irish verb, p. 65, note [1]; p. 100, note; in the Welsh verb, 655.
Reeves, Dr., referred to, p. 133, p. 134, p. 145; his edition of Adamnán's *Vita Columbæ* cited or referred to, 121, 159, 191, 203, 303, 390, 724; p. 163; his list of names in -*gus*, p. 69, note [2]; p. 133, p. 134.
Relative verbal forms in Irish, 1071.
Resolution of *é* into *ia*, 61; of *ó* into *ua*, 955.
Revue Archéologique, referred to, p. 100, note.
Rumann cited, 428.

S between vowels lost, 296; *sn* becomes *nn*, 305; *sr* becomes *r*, p. 160, note [m]; *s* from *x*, Skr. *ksh*, 386, 466; 426; *s* for *f*, 1039; *s* assimilated to following *t*, 556; stems in *s*, p. 163; Indo-European *s*, p. 160.
Sanctáin's hymn (*Liber Hymnorum*), cited, 937.
Sanskrit consonants corresponding with those of the O. Ir., and other Indo-European languages, p. 160.
Schleicher, Professor A., referred to, 1071; p. 158.
—— his *Handbuch der Litauischen Sprache* referred to, 1047.
Scirglige Conculainn, ed. by Mr. Curry (*Atlantis*, Nos. 2, 3), cited, p. 44, note [80]; p. 69, note [2]; 486, 1010; p. 121, note; 1070; p. 159.
Semitic words latinized, p. 144.
Siegfried, Professor R. T., cited or referred to, 89, 99; p. 68, note; 342, 682, 746, 758, 784; p. 100, note; 884, 952, 1071, 1073, 1133; the editor's great obligations to him, p. 132.
Singulative forms, 765.
Slavonic consonants, correspondence of, with those of

the O. Ir., and other Indo-European languages, p. 160.

Spiegel cited or referred to, 55, 96, 130.

Spiritus asper, shifting of in Old Irish, 305; p. 68, note; in Welsh and Cornish, 608.

Suffixes, superlative, 43; -tar, 1014; p. 149; Skr. suffix, -ta, Lat. tu-s, Gr. το-ς, found in Irish, p. 61, note²; O. Ir. -the, -te = -taya, ibid.

Syntax, curious construction with bki and tai, p. 149.

T, use of, in Mod. Ir. declension, p. 58, note; in verbal forms, ibid. (but see *Addenda*, p. 158); stems in *t*, see *Declension*; *t* between vowels, 227; *tt* becomes *th* in Welsh, 230, 957; Old Irish *t* corresponds with Skr. *t*, *th*, Gr. *τ*, Lat. *t*, Goth. *th* (*d*), 372, see Addenda, p. 160; *t* in composition, 430, 1061; loss of *t* before *r*, 466; *t* worn down to *d* in the possess. pron. of 2nd pers. sing., 570; final *t* becomes *s* in Cornish, 772; medialization of *t* by *n*, and subsequent assimilation, 991; Indo-European *t*, p. 160.

Táin Bó Cuailgne cited, 481, 747.

Tenues, Old Irish, 372; and see in this Index, *C, P, T*.

Thorpe, Mr. Benjamin, his edition of *Beowulf* referred to, 752, p. 163.

Todd, Rev. Dr. J. H., his *Irish Nennius* cited or referred to, 14, 229, 557, 817, 975, 1048; p. 151.
—— his edition of the *Liber Hymnorum* cited or referred to, p. 51, note; 218, 267, 320, 481, 691, 695, 727, 745, 770; p. 95, note²; 784, 894, 923, 977, 1078, 1092; p. 148, p. 151.
—— his *Cogad Gaedil re Gallaib* cited, 866.
—— his help acknowledged, p. 2, p. 144.

Tooke, Horne, cited, 595.

U possesses umlauting power, p. 159.

Ultán's hymn (*Liber Hymnorum*) referred to, 943; cited, 955.

Umlaut, 5, 287; p. 159; progressive umlaut, p. 151.

Usury, Old Irish word for, 740.

V between vowels lost, 174, 477; passing into spiritus asper, 305; found in Irish (written *b*) in the combinations *dv, lv, nv*, and *rv*, p. 159, p. 160; also as representing *dv* (aibherscoir, abhcoide, 432); Indo-European *v*, p. 160.

Vaison, Gaulish inscription of, 423; p. 161.

Verb. Old-Irish conjugations: a-stems, p. 150, No. 240; ai-stems, 1080; ā-stems and i-stems, p. 146 (these were first pointed out by Dr. Lottner): ia-stems, p. 165; the *t* in the perf. act. of a-stems, p. 158; pret. part. pass., formation of, p. 146; and see *Imperative, Middle Voice, Participles, Reduplication, Relative Verbal Forms*.

Verbal forms in the Lorica-glosses, p. 146; impersonal flexion in passive, p. 151.

Villemarqué, Vicomte H. de la, referred to, 797.

Vocalism, 5, 287 (but see Addenda, pp. 151, 159).

Vriddhation, 34, 948.

Weakening of *á* and *a* into *ai*, p. 164; p. 153.

Weber, A., cited or referred to, 205, 758.

Welsh, see *C, M, N, Reduplication, Spiritus asper, T*; Welsh Latinity, p. 134; trace of declension in Welsh (*pyn* in *erbyn* is the dat. of pen), p. 135.

Wilde, Mr., his *Catalogue* referred to, p. 159.

Words and forms, historical value of evidence given by, p. 2.

Wright, Professor William, his help acknowledged, p. 144.

Y, Indo-European, p. 160; sometimes passes into *spiritus asper*, ibid., note ᵏ. See *N, T*.

Zeitschrift für vergl. sprachforschung, cited or referred to, *passim*.

Zeuss, his *Grammatica Celtica* cited or referred to, *passim*.

INDICES VERBORUM.

[The numerals refer to the paragraphs of the foregoing Commentary, except when the letter "p." is prefixed; then they refer to the pages of this book.]

I. OLD-CELTIC INDEX.

AD-namatius, 666.
Aedui, 948.
Alisanos, p. 156.
ambi, 670.
Ambitui, 921.
ande, 734.
Andebrocirix, 947.
are, 704.
Argento-ratum, 607.
Argentomagus, 607.
Ar-morica, 704.
asno-s, 296, p. 159.
Atilogdo (gen. sing.), p. 159.
Atrebat-es, 315.

Becco, 664.
Belesama, 423.
belinus, 545.
belio-canda, p. 163.
Bovinda, 21.
brâtu-de, p. 100, note.
Brâtu-spantium, 366.
bretos, 328.
Brettania, 957.
Brettanos, 957.
Brigantes, 292.
Britovius, 957.
Britta, 957.
Britte-burgum, 957.
broci-rix, 947.
Brittus, 957.
Broco-magus, 947.
Brogi-mârus, 663.
bulga, 217.

Cambodunum, p. 150.
casses, 46.
cata-, p. 164.
catu, p. 157.
Catu-slôgi, 1003.
cinco (stem), p. 86, note.
Cintu-genus, 588.
Cluniâcum, 723.
Cocidius, 139.
Cogidumnus, 139.
Com-bretonium, 957.
Cono-maglus, 545.
Con-suanetes, 667.
Con-textos, p. 104, note.
Coslum, 556.
crotta, 5.
Cuno-belinus, 545.
curmen, curmi, 266.

Dânuvius, p. 130.
Darvernon, 554.
dede, p. 100, note.
Dexsiva, Dexivia, 386.
Doiros, p. 156.
Dubis, 381.
Dubra, Dubri-s, dubron, 375.
dula, 765.
dumnos, 994.
dûnon, 21, p. 150.
duron, 608.

eiôru, 423.
Epasnactus, 296.
Epo-mûlus, 295.

ex, 393.
Ex-cinco-mârus, p. 86, note.

Gabro-magus, 372.
Gabro-sentum, 372, 1073.
Gaisati, 216.
Gangani, p. 150.
genos, 588.
Glana, 671.
glastum, p. 91, note.
Gobannitius, 369.
Grannos, 952.

Inntu-mârus, 663.
Iartai : : p. 100, note.
Ierne, p. 159.
ieuru, p. 73, note; pp. 156, 161.
Isarno-durum, 608.
Ivernio-s, Iverni-s, Ivernia, p. 67, note [1]; p. 159.

Labarus, 1133.
Laurentius, 908.
Lauriâcum, 908.
Lauro, 908.
Licca, 133.
Lucterios, 10.
lugos, p. 155.

Magalius, 902.
Magalus, 902.
maglos, 545.
magus (mago-s), 21.
mâros, 423, 621, 663, 902.

matos, 661.
mātrebo, p. 100, note.
Mello-dunum, 258.
Mellosectum, 258.
Moccon (stem), 664.
Moccus, 1029.
Mogit-mārus, 902.
Mogounus, 952.
mori, 860.
mūlos, 295.

namatios, 666.
namausatis, 423.
namausicūbo, p. 100, note.
nemeton, 423.
Nerto-mārus, 663.
novios, 21.

pempe-dula (?), 765.
pompai-dula (?), 765.

raton, 607.
rix, 423.
Rotomagus, p. 158.

sages, 450; sagi, 872.
Salusa, 977.
Santones, 667.
secton, 258.
Sego-māros, 423; p. 156.
senton, 372.
Silius, 1009.
Silo, 1009.
Silus, 1009.
Sirona, 952.
slōgos, 1003.
sole, 558.
sosin, 423.
spantion, 366.
Suanetes, 667.

tarbelodathion (tarvo-tabatio-n),
40; tarvos, p. 159.
Tecto-sages, 450.
Tecto-sagi, 872.
Tento-matus, 661.
textos, p. 104, note.
Togiacus, 994.
Togidia, 994.
Togius, 994.

Togitius, 994.
Togi-rix, 994.
Togo-dumnus, 994.
Toutio-rix, 423.
toutius, 423; p. 161.
tragos, 74.

Ulkos, p. 147.

Velleda, 1.
ver, 74; p. 99, note.
Vergivios, 328.
Vergo-bretus, 328, 366.
Verno-dubrum, 375.
Verno-sole, 558.
ver-tragi, 74.
vidu, 46.
Vidua, 46.
Vidu-casses, 46.
Villoneos, 423.
Villonius, p. 161.
Vindos, p. 150.
Virdomārus, 663.
Volcæ, 1045.
Volcatius, 1045.

II. OLD-IRISH INDEX.

á (prep.), 200, (pron.) 420.
a (interject.), p. 165.
aball, 555.
abbaith, 948.
achéd, 159, 580, 909.
acher, 77.
act, 614, 745.
acus, 203.
adaltras, 882.
adarcdae (-de), 59, 1018.
adbail, 954.
adbar, 161.
adchodadossa, p. 100, note.
adcondarc, p. 156.
adcotedæ, p. 100, note.
adcbuiriur, p. 151.
ade, 676.
adercéne, 1018.
adfiadat, 1080.
adganr, 869.
adgládastar, 128.
adgúsimm, p. 159.
adib, adim, abi (?), p. 127.
adiecht, 1010.
adircliu, 1018; p. 155.

adnacul, 693.
adopart, 948.
ad-ra-nact, p. 61, note; 693.
adruimiter, 738; adrimi, 1080.
adroigegraunatar, p. 100, note.
adsluindimm, p. 166.
A'ed (A'íd), 948.
ágor, 77.
aidlacht, 948.
aidche, 546.
aig, 258.
ail, 91.
aíle, 158.
áiledu, p. 166.
ailigud, 462.
aill, 924.
aille, p. 166.
ainis, 1080.
ainm, 56, 991.
Ainmire, 13.
áir, 873.
airchissim, p. 151.
Airdliacc, 573.
airech, p. 147.
airechas, p. 147.

airgech, 586.
airegde, p. 147.
airi, p. 100, note; 639.
airlam, 884.
airle, 884.
airm, 729.
airthir, 150.
áis, 735, 812.
aith, 155.
aitbech, p. 100, note.
aithle, 155.
ala, 150.
alaile, 872.
álaind, p. 162.
algenaigim, 917.
altóir, 745.
am-, 392.
am, 1112.
amail, 262.
amiressach, 943.
amlabar, 1133.
ammi(n), 85, 1112.
amréid, 890.
an (neut. art.), 78.
ān, 682.

Indices Verborum.

anacul, 570.
anairtúaid, 353.
anais, 897.
analchi, 752.
anamchara, 1082.
and, 676.
anfolmithe, 676.
aníar, 305.
aniartúaid, 353.
antúaid, 353.
apgitir, 21.
ar (prep.), 98, 608, 614.
ara (n), p. 100, note.
araile, 112.
áram, p. 164.
arbar, p. 166.
arbe, p. 163.
arbiathim, 477.
archinm, 35.
Ard-macha, 948.
ardbrig, p. 154.
ard-fégad, p. 149.
are, p. 148.
aren, 752.
ar-unn-fethitis, p. 166.
argat, 607; argget, p. 162.
ar-id-rálastar, 128.
arin, 729.
arbe, p. 163.
ar (n), 884.
arsidi, 722.
artu, 812.
árm, 246, 1011.
as(n), 565, 1112.
asbiur, 639.
asbert, 879.
asbertar, 639.
asigthe, p. 112, note.
asin, 128.
asindisset, p. 100, note.
aslach, 933.
as-m-berar, 578 (asbiur).
ass, 555.
assa, 812.
assagússim, p. 159.
m-aso, m-asu, 1112.
astoidet, 1008.
at, 1112.
atá(n), 565.
athair, athir, 13, 1046.
atlaigthe, 943.
atomsnassar, 817.
atrab, p. 127, note 8.
atrópert, p. 100, note.
m-atu, 1112.
háue, p. 67, note 2.

augtortás, 1107.

bá, 115.
bachal, 262.
bacball, p. 103, note 3.
bad, 729.
bái, 128, 676.
baig, p. 154.
baile, p. 156.
bainne, 966.
bairgen, 141, 722; p. 157.
baithes, p. 100, note.
baitsimm, p. 150.
ball, 638.
bán, 738.
bandach, p. 133, note.
bandea, 289, 1053.
banna, 966.
banterismid, 287.
bar(n), p. 160, note m.
barr, 28.
bas, 881.
bás, 200, 614, 745.
báthach, p. 163.
batar, 36.
bebais, p. 100, note.
bebe, p. 100, note.
becc, 439, 664.
bed, 290, 880.
beith, 745.
bél, 425, 636.
bélre, 176.
ben, 369, 884, 1053.
bendacht, benedacht, 203, 914.
berensde, p. 166.
bertaigimm, p. 148.
bés, 722 (= bías); 745, 1071.
bésgnae, 890.
bethu, 605, 870.
bi, 56.
biad, 477.
biam, 954; p. 164.
bid, 154.
biis, 35.
bind, 115.
bir, 184.
bis, 740.
bithbethu, 640.
bite, 1071.
biu, 154.
bliadain, 676, 745; p. 157.
bláth, 954.
bloscc, p. 152.
bó, 424.
bóchaill, 583.
bocc, 498.

bocht, boctán, 1058.
bói, 948.
Boind, 21, 462.
bolad, 1087.
bolc (bolg), 217.
boltigur, 1087.
bommar, 815.
borg, 555.
bou, 159.
bráge, 292.
brasse, 36.
bráth, 154, 366, 948.
bráthair, 1047; p. 165.
bréc, 958.
brécairecht, 958.
brénaim, 683.
bréntu, 683.
Bretan, 909.
bretha nemid, 578.
bríathar, 812, 897.
bricht (acc. pl.), 369.
Brigit, 954.
brithem, 366.
ron-broena, 1048.
bró, 784.
brónach, 427.
bronnait, 647.
búachaill, 583.
bube, p. 100, note.
buide, adj. 803; subst. 943.
buidech, 884.
buith, 930.
bun, p. 154.
bunad, p. 154.

cách, 154, 729, 815.
cadessin, 948.
cae, 218.
cáer, 267.
cáera, cúira, 13, 851.
Caichán, 676.
caill, 115.
caille, 676.
cúindias, 35.
caindlóir, 44.
caingel, 745.
cúintaidlech, 287.
cúirchuide, 851.
cairtine, 1127.
cairtinigther, 1127.
Callrige, 745.
calad, 280.
canoin, 1080.
car, 280.
cara, 292.
caraim, 280, 815.

Old-Irish Index.

carcar, 262.
carpat, 112, 424.
carric, p. 152.
cathim, 280.
cathir, 13.
cech, 214.
cechaing, p. 100, note.
cechladar, p. 100, note.
cechtar, 1071; p. 159.
cél (celaim), 371.
céle, 882.
celebirsimme, 746.
cell, 203, 948.
cen, 120, 640.
cenél, 676, 745.
cencle, 822.
cenn, 17, 120.
cenngalar, p. 148.
Cennsalach, p. 67, note [2]; 616.
cop, 480.
cerdae, 196.
cercol, p. 159.
cerd, 218.
cerd-chae, 218.
césad, 892, 1131.
céss, 892.
cessacht, p. 151.
cessachtach, 280.
cét, 772; p. 154.
cétamus, 578.
cétlaid, 3.
cétach, 909.
cethir, 775.
cethrar, 398.
ciad-cholomb, 203.
Ciaran, 200.
ciatu, p. 127, note [4].
cid, 1071.
cil, 90.
cimbidi (acc. pl.), p. 166.
cinnim, p. 150.
cis, 954.
cith (cid), 637.
claar, 67.
clam, 424.
cland, 745, 991; p. 154.
cli, 387.
cliab, 1102.
cloce, p. 103, note [3].
clóen, 870.
clú, 812.
clúain, 200, 723.
cluas, 867.
chluichech, 518.
ro-cluinetar, 902.
clum, 262.

cnám, 269.
co, 128.
coccilsine, 882.
cocert, 888.
cofil, 1102.
coibdelach, p. 166.
coibse, 745.
cóic, 776.
cóicur, 398.
coill (caill), 115.
cúimdin, 812; p. 127, note [3]; 1133.
coinnet, p. 103, note [3].
cóimsa (gen. sing.), 757.
coire, 724.
coirnea (acc. pl.), 75.
cúis (acc. sing.), 434.
coisecrad, 880.
coitchenn, 872.
col, 1030.
colann (colinn), 120.
colcaid, 262.
collde, 556.
colinn, 919.
Colmán, 909.
Colomb, 203.
colpa, 146.
comacomol, 1010.
comadnacul, 889.
comain, 897.
comairle, comairlle, 884.
comalnad, 760.
comarpe, p. 127, note [4].
combach, p. 166.
comdlúthad, 636.
coméisséirge, 889.
coméitged, 817.
comirsire, p. 105, note.
comman, 897.
comnactar, 897.
comthúarcon, 722.
con (conj.), 120; (prep.) 580.
conaicertus, 888.
con-a-til, 729.
Conchad, 948.
concheebrat, p. 100, note; p. 161.
conchoinnucuir, p. 161.
Conchuhor, 545.
condaig, 450.
condelg, p. 127, note [4].
conil, 614, 745.
conflechtaiginm, p. 147.
confoircin, p. 154.
congabaimm, 676; p. 166.
contarat, p. 131, note.
contubart, 948.

coniclm, 570.
conmir, 156.
consádu, 1131.
consan, 930.
contuil, 729.
contesbad, 966.
coór, 938.
corcur, 224.
core, 938.
corp, 98, 812; p. 128, note [3].
cos (= coxa), 637.
cosc, 660.
coscelar, p. 162.
coscitir, 660.
coth (?), p. 164.
crag, 203.
cráibdech, 745.
crann, 719; p. 154, p. 162.
creitem, p. 100, note.
Cremthann, 693.
Cremthinne, 909.
cretim, p. 127, note [4].
cretmech, 817.
criathar, 700.
crich, 781, 1073.
cride, 67, 1102.
crin, p. 162.
cris, 1102.
crith, 1102.
croch, 738, 812.
cro-chaingel, 745.
crocann, 56.
crocenn, 56.
croeb, 955.
crottichther, 5.
cruithnecht, 778.
cruithnechtide, 778.
cruth, 380.
cu (co), 168.
cuanene, 986.
cucan, 245, 572.
cucann, 245.
cuibsech, 745, 1071.
cuil (acc. sing.), 262.
cuilech, 1030.
cuilennbocc, 498.
cuiligim, 1030.
ra-chuiliu, 1030.
cuimlengaimm, p. 147.
cuimnigur, 1111.
cuimte, p. 166.
cuinigim, 871.
cuirimm, p. 151.
cuiriur, p. 151.
cuirm, 266.
culatha (acc. pl.), p. 148.

Indices Verborum.

cumal, 909.
cuman, 1111.
cumbre, 678.
Cummen, 909.
cumtach (cumddach), 203, 569, 871, 881, 1098.
curchas, 933.
cúrsagad, 924.
curu (acc. pl.), p. 74, note.
cusecrainm, 879.
cutrumme, 903.
cutruminus, 903.

dá, 112, 773.
dagairle, 884.
dagcomairle, 884.
dagforcitlid, 902.
daggnímrad, p. 166.
daingen, daingnigim, 674.
dairde, 554.
Dallbrónach, 427.
dáltech, 569.
daltæ, 676.
dam (mihi), 1071; (etiam), 752.
dam (bos), 722, 858.
dam (dolor), 1102.
ro-damdatar, p. 158.
damde, 858.
con-dan, 878.
dán, 565; p. 109, note.
dána, dánatu, 1131.
daneu, 738.
darmcbennsa, 635.
daro (gen. sing., nom. *dair?*), 676.
dartinn, 870.
daú (ei), 745; dáu (2), 773.
daur, daurde, 554.
daurauch, 554.
dé-, 773.
dea, 289.
debai, p. 166.
debthimm, p. 166.
décrud, 745.
déed, 815.
deichenbar, 398.
déirce, 626.
delb, 642; p. 146.
denmai (acc. plur.), 214.
dénmid, 899.
dénim, 899.
dénmusach, 899.
dénom, 141, 722, 899.
deóg lái, 120.
derbráthair, p. 162.
derbensde, p. 166.
derc (oculus), 675.

derc (ruber), 565, 738, 939.
dercaide, 939.
dernad, 203.
deruce, 554.
des, 386.
deserce, 626.
dessam, 937.
di (prep.), 676.
di (2), 745, 773.
dia (suo), 450.
dia (deus), 21, 81.
dia (dies), p. 163.
diabul (diabolus), 863.
diabul (duplex), 930.
diade, p. 109, note.
diall, p. 95, note [1].
Dianchride, 1080.
diangalar, 222; p. 151.
dianid, 555.
diant, p. 162.
diar(u), 284, 890.
dias, 35.
dib(n), 773.
dichéin, 878.
didiu, 41.
digéni, 909.
digní, p. 162.
dib, 745.
dil, 1120.
Dimma, 1080.
din, 112.
dind (l. dinn?), p. 37, note.
dindirect, p. 166.
dinn, 292.
dirrógel, 580.
dithrubaeb, 214.
ditiu, 153, 762.
dliged, 87.
dlúith, 636.
dlúth, 636.
dlúthe, 636.
dlúthsit, p. 166.
do- (pref.), 85; (prep.), 112.
do (prep.), 605.
do (pron.), 570.
dó, dóo, 817.
doadbadar, 565.
doadbat, 846.
doairbiur, 660.
doaurchanim, 704, 837.
doblur, 133, 745.
dochuiriur, p. 151.
dochum, 943.
dodcaid, 262.
dofaith, 128.
dofarci, 873.

dofoirnde, 1008.
doförngat, 756.
dofuairce, 722.
dogegat, p. 100, note.
dogniu, 908.
dogrés, 222.
doilbthid, 642.
Doilgus, 342.
dóir, 85; p. 156.
dolbud, 642.
do-m-farcai, 371.
domnn, 812.
domun, 280.
domunde, p. 109, note.
donn, 909.
drochgnim, 752.
dorát, p. 159.
dorchæ, 331.
doroega, 154.
dorcueanas, 837.
dorodba, 954.
doroigu, p. 100, note.
doroiter, 890.
dorónta, 112.
do-s-fiuscad, 605.
dosíathach, 578.
draigen, 559.
driss, 587.
dristenach, 587.
druailuide, 1071.
druid, 369.
druimm, 676, 745.
du (pron.), 570.
du (prep.), 738.
dúaib, p. 100, note.
dub, 381.
dubber, 745.
dubchorcur, 224.
Dubloch, 781.
duécaster, 745.
dúibsi, 1080.
dúil, p. 52, note.
duine, 89, 738.
duit, 943.
dulluid, 879.
du-m-esurcsa, 222 (tesurc).
dún, 674.
dunad (dúnad?), 1131.
dúnn, 98.
dúusit, p. 166.
durind, 880.
durni, 272.
dús in, 745.

e, 637.
hé, 128.

Old-Irish Index.

ech, 17, 909.
Echaid, 13.
écen, 1010.
eclais, 177; eclis, 948.
écosc, 660.
écsamlus, 904.
edocht, 745; edoct, 948.
heirp, 205.
éitach, 757.
éitset, 1101.
héitsid, 1101.
Éladach, 909.
ellach, 933.
emnatar, 1010.
enon, 1010.
én, 371, 746; p. 162.
encae, p. 151.
euga, p. 166.
ennae, p. 151.
éolas, 85.
epistil, 1080.
epscop, 948, 982.
erchissecht, p. 151.
erchoitech, 935.
erchuiriur, p. 151.
hÉrinn, 154, 305, 870; p. 159.
erlabrai, 867.
erlam, 906.
érlam, 955.
ermaisse, 927.
ernaigthe, p. 147.
crnais, 280.
erchuilech, 1030.
erochairchétlaid, 3.
erochuir (-air), 3.
eros, 70, 580; p. 166.
érpimm (airbium), 752.
errach, 1070.
errend, 1006.
erthuaiscertach, 305.
és, dia és, dom héis-se, p. 164.
ésca, 234.
éscae, 234.
escalchaill, 115.
éscide (-caide), 234.
esgre, 738.
eslinn, p. 162.
éstecht, 867.
ét, 635; p. 166.
étach, 501, 757; étacht, 757.
etalaeda, p. 166.
ethar, 70.
Etan, 1102.
étar, 745.
etarscarad, 254.
étmar, 635.

étrad, 166.
étrumm, 639.
étsecht, 176, 1101.
étrumme, 903.
étsid, 902, 1101.

faca, 120.
fácab, 676; fáccab, 948.
fa-des, 128.
fáilte, 161; p. 151.
fairgge, 77.
fáith, 2; p. 147.
fáithsine, 882.
fanacc, 1080.
fannall, 934.
far(ń), p. 127, note ³; p. 160.
fás, p. 127, note ⁴; p. 162.
feblæ, 948.
féda, p. 166.
féisne, p. 100, note.
féith, 99.
fèl, 371.
felsub, 1129; p. 159.
fenechus, p. 127, note ⁴.
fer, 841.
ferb, p. 127, note ³.
ferenn, 390.
ferg, 328.
Fergus, 342.
fergach (fercach), 328.
fernn, p. 166.
ferr, 41, 1116.
ferte, p. 166.
fescor, 224.
fésóc, 47; p. 155.
fess, p. 127, note ¹.
fésur, 392.
féuil, 150.
Fèth, 745.
fiach, 269.
Fiacha, 13, 115.
fiacail, 150.
Fiacc, 880.
fiaclach, 150.
Fiachra, 13.
fiad, 36.
fiaduisse, 959.
fiadu (féda), 292; p. 166.
fiasur, 392.
fichtea (acc. pl.), 676.
fid, 580.
fidbaide, 371.
figim, 1095.
fili, 1.
filus, 738.
fin, p. 162.

Find, 120.
findae, p. 154.
findfolt, 77.
finechas, 745.
Fio, 745.
firián, 681.
firiánigedar, 682.
firiánugud, 682.
firinne, 927.
fir-óg, 954.
fis, 846.
fiss, 1008.
flaith, 338; p. 100, note.
Fland, 203, 948.
fliuchaidatu, 675.
fliuchaide, 675.
fliuchaigim, 675.
fliuchdere, 431, 675.
fó, 1102.
foacanim, 837.
fochaid, p. 100, note; p. 157.
focheirt, 55, 888.
focertar, 222.
fochétóir, 588.
fochlaid, 229.
fochric, p. 157.
fochridigur, 1102.
fochun, 371.
fodil, p. 166.
foedes, 890.
foétsecht, foétsimm, 1101.
fogbaidetu, 740.
foglaim, 890.
fognam, 815.
fogrigur, 611.
fogur, 469.
foigde, 815.
foile, 1129.
foilsignd, 895.
Foirtchern, 871.
folcaimm, 1044.
follus, 895.
fo-m-chain, 371.
for, 387; p. 99, note; 729, 745.
forchanim, 837.
forcetal, 139.
fochell, 98.
forcital, 837.
forcitlaidecht, 837.
forcitlid, 837.
focul, 873.
fóisite, p. 147.
forbe, p. 146.
forculu, 873.
forchun, 837.
fordingair, 578.

2 A

forćir, 660.
forgair, p. 146.
forlóg, 909.
formuichthe, p. 166.
for(n), pron. 635.
forn, prep., p. 146.
forngaire, p. 146.
forngarthaid, p. 146.
for-óenu, 36.
forosna, 168.
forru, p. 166.
fortacht, 727, 890.
fortachtid, 727.
fortiag, 727.
fortrumme, 903.
fot, 677.
fota, 677.
fothn, p. 148.
fothaigim, p. 148.
fotharud, 740, 822.
fri, 112, 369, 635, 815.
frisdúnaim, 287.
friss, 846.
frithiúraim, p. 161.
fróich, 565.
fuacht, p. 103, note 3.
fúal, 222.
fúan, 29.
fuar-both, 120.
fuarrech, fuairrech, p. 149.
fuasnad, 927.
fufuasna, 77.
fuilib (dat. pl.), 608.
fuirsitis, 729.
fulsmelach, p. 147.
fulsam, p. 100, note.
furruimtis, 729.

gabais, 676; gabis, p. 166.
gabál, p. 166.
gabor, 372.
gabsi, 948.
gabul, 135.
gádatar, 870.
gaib, 262.
gúid, 870.
gaide, 216.
gaimigud, p. 166.
gair, 115.
gáith (subst.), 77.
gáith (adj.), 884.
galar, 222.
galla (acc. pl.), , p. 112, note.
gasne, p. 154.
gciuti (acc. pl), p. 100, note.
gelgrian, 168.

genmnai (dat. sing.), 214.
German, 1080.
giall, 216.
gigestesi, p. 100, note.
gilcuch, 933.
gilither, 168.
ginil, 262.
glais, 781.
glan, p. 162.
glanaim, 671.
glas, 738.
glasán, 226.
glicc, gliceu, 1129.
glicce, 1129.
glúne (acc. pl.), 740.
gni (acc. siog.), 902.
guim, 682, 908; p. 128, note 3; p. 146.
gó, 897.
gobann, 369.
góithlach, 933, 1067.
gonas, 940.
gorith, 637.
gorte, 620.
grád, 1040.
grán, 722.
grant, 651.
gres, p. 164.
gréssich, 815.
grian, 952; p. 162.
gruad, 90.
gñala, p. 159.
gúas, p. 162.
guide, 870, 943.
guidimm, 870.
gutae, 1040.

hí, 91.
iach, 216.
iada, p. 162.
iar, 305; p. 100, note.
hiarn, 216, 608, 812.
iarnaid, 676.
iarsichid, p. 166.
iar-suidiu, 879.
iarum, 120.
iasc, 13.
iathmaige, 390.
iarthuaiscerndach, 305.
ibar, 561.
ice, 758.
iccaitl, 605.
icfed, 897.
ichtar, 1014.
idón, 1; page 103, note 3.
idul, 569.

iffern, 519.
il, 13, 565.
ilar, p. 157.
ilurrechtrad, 957.
im, 128.
imb, 578, 784.
imbed, 670, 921.
imber, 465.
imchomarc, 112.
imchlóud, p. 147.
imda, 200.
imdegail, 214, 867; p. 149.
imdergud, 873.
imdu, 299.
imm, 670.
immact, p. 166.
immaircide, p. 128, note 3.
immebuirinr, p. 151.
immib, 757.
immluadi, p. 147.
immo(n), p. 162.
imm-r'ordad, 878.
immunn, 305.
immut, 154.
imorro, 555.
impe, 954.
imthised, 870.
in (prep.), 637.
in (art.), 78.
inad, 516.
inbaid, 954.
ind (art.), 78.
ind (prep.), 734.
indarbe, 752.
indeb, p. 109, note; p. 166.
indiaid, 424.
indlinech, 371.
indlung, p. 166.
indochúil, 450.
indoilbthid, 642.
infinit, p. 157.
ingen, 676.
ingenas, 290.
ingor, 68.
ingruimmim (dat. s.), p. 100, note.
ingrented, p. 100, note.
inill, p. 148.
inis, 462, 1080.
inmain, 955.
inna, inna(n), 78.
innocht, 77.
innunn, 954.
insin, 262.
insnastis, 817.
inso, 222, 745; p. 156.
int, 78.

Old-Irish Index.

intan, 897.
inte, 745.
intech, 872.
intṡerbu, 1132.
intṡliucht, 734.
iráil (cráil, bod. *furáil*), 91.
ire, 13.
hires, 91, 752; p. 147.
iressach, p. 127, note 3.
irladigur, 884.
irlaim, 906.
irlithe, 884.
is, 1112.
isin, 262.
I'su, 758, 954.
it', 154.
it, 1112.
ith, 1038.
íth, 758, 1038.
itge, p. 147.
ithim, 40.
i-timchuairt, 338.
ithland, 132.
indciu (acc. pl.), p. 100, note.
íurad, p. 161.

la, p. 100, note; 605.
labrad, 1133.
labrar, 812; p. 128, note 3.
ro-labrastar, 812.
laechraid (dat. sing.), 77.
Laigen, 954.
laigiu, 923.
laith, 266.
laithe, 154.
laithoirt, 266.
lám, 34, 387, 637, 867.
lámbrat, 740.
lán, 13.
land, 132.
lann (adj.), 77.
lann (subst.), p. 152.
lasan, 203.
lase, 746.
lassais, 128.
Lassar, 676.
lat, 41.
laur, 908.
lebar, 371.
lechdach, 1071.
ledmarb (*recti* lethmarv), 90.
legad, 1071.
légend, 853.
rolég, 1080.
léine, 38.
leis, 879.

lenaimm, 1040.
lendan, 38.
lenomun, p. 159.
leuu, 580.
leosom, 722, 858.
les, 424, 580.
lesc, 382, 815.
lesmac, p. 155.
lestar, p. 162.
let, p. 165.
leth, p. 156.
lethan, 13, 925.
lethchil, 90.
lethgute, 90.
lethit (acc. sing.), 925.
lethmaethail, 90.
lethóm, 90.
lethu (dat. sing.), 640.
lethu (adv. ?), 870.
lia, 13.
lia, 424.
liacc, 133, 573; p. 156.
Liás, 676, 745.
libur, 371.
lige, 812.
lin, 614.
lin, 863.
line, 1080.
linn, p. 100, note.
lobad, 1071.
loc, 879.
loch, 637, 781.
lóche, 292; p. 168.
Lochland, 77.
lóeg (lóig), 424.
lóg, 133, 792, 1085.
lóid, 371.
Lóig-les, 424.
Loiguire, 424.
lon, 371.
lonach, 115.
long, 574.
lór, 860, 908.
lorg (lorc), 937.
losait, 42.
loscud (dat. sing.), 737.
lóthor (-ur), 740.
loure, 908.
lux (acc. pl.), p. 166.
lúath, 371.
lúathchride, 1102.
lub, 114.
lubgartoir, 114.
lubgort, 114.
Lugaid, 13.
lugimem, 923.

luid, 36, 948.
lúrech, 154.
luscu (acc. pl.), 605.

ma, 637, 745.
mac, 115, 200, 757.
maccán, 337.
maccu, 200.
maccu-Nois, 723.
Machae, 943, 948.
mad, 41, 1040.
madu, p. 162.
maethail, 90.
mag, 580.
magister, 365.
maigen, 222.
Máildúin, 200.
Máil Odræ, 909.
Máilsechnaill, 203.
Maire, p. 165.
maisse, 927.
maith, 450, 661, 745.
maldacht, 915.
manach, 745.
manestrech (gen. s.), 726.
mani, 745.
mann, 299.
már, 663; p. 154.
marb, 90, 605; p. 159.
martir, 214.
martre (gen. s.), 738.
martur, p. 166.
máthair, 954.
mátharlach, 933.
mathim, 280.
mcit, 168, 922.
menme, 927.
menn, 77.
menstir, p. 103, note 3.
mér, 465.
mesraigthe, 807.
mess, 154.
messa, 1117.
mí-, 1117.
miad, p. 154.
midus, 1071.
mil, 133.
milte, 133.
mimaselach, 933.
mír, 156.
mirtchaill, 115.
místae, 1050.
mo (pron.), 371; (pref.), 897.
Mochoe, 745.
moirtchenn, p. 159, p. 166.
moithiu (compar.), 394.

molad, 873.
molor, 902.
Monach, 115.
mór, 663.
mórféser, 777.
móru, 1020.
mrecht, 957.
mrechtrad, 927, 957.
mu, p. 107, note.
mucc mora, 1029.
muccfoil, 1029.
mug, 403, 882; p. 127, note 3.
muinæ, 744. p. 163.
muinde, 744.
muine, 128, 583
muinntore, 744.
muinter, 745; p. 127, note 3.
muir, 77, 812, 860.
muirágu (dat. sing.), p. 166.
Muirchad, 200.
muiride, p. 166.
muirmóru, 1020.
Muirsce, 69.
mulenn, 701.
múl, múldae, 295.

na, na(n), 78.
nach, "not," 817.
nád, 371, 639, 745.
námа, 292.
nand, 879.
nascad, 817.
nathir, 13; nathair, 88.
nau (naui?), p. 162.
naucirchinnech, 449.
neb-, 987.
neblesc, 382.
nech, 745.
necht, 224.
neim, 280.
nem, p. 52, note 2; 812, 943;
  p. 127, note 3.
nenaid, 208.
neph-, 987.
nephésicide (-caide), 234.
nescóit, 847.
nessa, nessam, 1117.
ni, 77, 614.
ní (res), 987.
nim, 812.
Nínine, p. 125, note.
nit (gen. sing.), 781.
nóeb, 214, 954; p. 162.
nói, 21.
nóib (nom. pl.), p. 128, note 3.
nóibe, 168.

nóib-bríathar, 812.
nóin, 262.
Nóindruimm, 745.
nónbar, 400.
Nos, 200.
nu, 637.
núæ, 578.
Nuada, 292.
núe, 21, 803.
uns (nús?), 256.

ó, 555.
óa, 77.
óa (minor), 758.
óa (jecur), 1032.
oblann, p. 166.
oc, 299, 815.
óc, 758.
ochen, p. 166.
óclach, 933.
óclachde, 758.
ócmil, 758.
ochter, 580, 909.
odbrann, p. 149.
óg, 954.
óinach, p. 147.
óindæ, 565.
Oingus, 342.
oipred, 889.
óis, 812; p. 127, note 3.
oitherroch, 948.
ól, 266, p. 158.
olambicidsi, 1129.
ole, 578, 662, p. 147.
olachaill, 115.
óm, 90.
omne, 262.
ood, 752.
optait, p. 159.
or, 184.
ór, p. 162.
órd, 943.
órddan, 943.
hóre, p. 100, note.
oróit, 203, 1080; p. 165.
ort, 266.
oslaicib (dat. pl.), p. 165.

Pátric, 676, 745.
pé, 745.
pellec, 136.
peccad, 1040.
pecthad, 1040.
persan, 87.
pólire, p. 103, note 3.
port, 676, 725.

praintech, 729.
precept, 91.
pronn, 815.

ra-, 13.
ráith, 115.
rann, 9, 1071.
ro-ratha, p. 109, note.
rechtaire, 450; p. 166.
réga, 943.
régat, 154.
réid, 890.
réimm, 77; p. 155.
rem, 745.
remthechtas, 872.
remnan, 890.
rét, p. 159.
riagol (-gul), 61.
riat, p. 109, note.
richel, 168.
rici, 264.
rig, 36, 203, 1036; p. 154,
  p. 162.
rigad, 879.
rigain, p. 154.
rige, 1131; p. 158.
rind, p. 67; 1008.
rindaig, p. 133, note.
rith folo, p. 166.
ríthæ, 909.
ro-, 13.
ro-bai, 214.
robbem, 640.
ro-bet, 338.
ro-cét, p. 61, note.
róis, 262.
ro-m-bith, p. 165.
ro-p, 214, 614, 890.
roth, p. 158.
ro-t-chechladar, 656.
ro-t-bia, 161.
ruamnae, p. 161.
ruire, 13.
rúnaid, p. 133, note.
ru-n-dlúth, 636.
sab, p. 37, note.
sachilli, p. 166.
sáchebore, 938.
sáer, 1137.
sácthar, 133.
sáibapstal, 635.
saiget, 214.
saigid (dat. sing.), 1137.
saigul, p. 146.
saile, 651.
sáirdénmidecht, 1137.

sálthar, 1085.
salann, 977.
Salchan, 724.
salm, p. 128, note ³.
-san, -sa, 78.
sancht, p. 161.
santach, 280, 667.
sás, p. 162.
scatan, 967.
scél, 223.
sciath, 214.
scith, 614.
sclictu, p. 166.
scol, 338.
scríbend, 853.
scuchad, 112.
sé, 777.
sech, 112.
sechethar, p. 166.
sechnall, p. 150.
secht(n), 224.
Segéne, 948.
seib, 109.
séim, 636.
séimtana, 1017.
seirge, 924.
selb, 580.
sem, 420.
sen, 735.
sén, 1132.
ron-séna, 1048.
seól, p. 166.
serbe, 1132.
ses, 580.
sesainim, p. 100, note.
sess, 70.
sét, 280.
sét (iter), 490, 729, 1073.
setharoircnid, 320.
sétfethchaib, 826.
siasair, p. 100, note.
sib, 1112.
side, 1088.
sil, 555.
-sind, -sin, 78.
siniu, 130.
-sin(n), 78.
sís, p. 156.
sissi, 1112.
siur, 216.
siurnat, 320.
slabreid, 890.
slébe, 586.
Sléibte, 693, 948.
slemon, 639.
sliassit, p. 148.

slige, 112.
sliss, 32.
slúag, 36, 1003.
slincht, 734.
ron-snádut, 1131.
snáthe, 817.
sned, 649.
sni, 305; snisni, 1112.
so-, 85.
sochoisc, 660.
sóer, 954; ro-n-sóera, 1048.
soerda, p. 154.
sóeth, p. 158.
sóir (sóer), p. 156.
sóirmug, 404.
solam, 740.
som, 420.
son (sonns), 1137.
son, p. 162.
spirut, 565, 1048.
srathar, 262.
suidigud, 1137.
sreihnaide, 794.
srenim, 1039.
srian, 109, 1039.
srón, 1039.
sruth, 999.
suide, 366, 812.
suide (pron.), 1010.
súil, 425.
sunt, 565.
súithe, p. 37, note

t', 570.
tabairt, p. 100, note.
tacáir, 93.
tadbat, 846.
taibderce, p. 147.
taibre, 1040.
taidbsin, 844.
taidlech, 287.
tairchechuin, 837.
tairchet, p. 61, note; 837.
tairchetal, p. 147.
tairmthechtas, 872.
taispenad, 894.
talam, 108, 578.
tamlacht, 781.
tana, 1017.
tanise, p. 58, note.
tar, 740.
tarési(u), 676.
tarfarcennsi, 738.
tarsende, p. 166.
tarslacc, 890.
taschide, 760.

Tassach, 897, p. 104, note.
tech, 569.
tecelsid, p. 166.
tecmallad, 299.
tecnate, 569.
techt, 450, 872; p. 158.
techtaire, 450.
techtat, 639.
teglach, 933.
ten (dat. sing.), 128.
tenge, p. 128, note ³.
teoir, 774.
teora, 774.
terismid, 287.
tét, 1017.
tes, 942.
tiach, 41, 371.
tiarmoracht, 872.
tic, 120.
tigerne, 450, 909.
timluad, p. 147.
timne, 760.
timtherecht, 898.
timthirecht, 368.
timthirthid, 368.
tintarrad, 870.
tintathach, 927.
tír, 703.
Tirechán, p. 95, note ².
tirim, 703.
tirme, 703.
tised, 879.
tissad, 870.
tochuirimm, p. 150.
togu, 878.
Toiguire, 994.
toirthech, 289.
tóisech, 21, 1040.
tol, p. 100, note; p. 162.
toll, p. 162.
torad, 289, 1085, 1106.
tórand, 880.
torc (cor), 1102.
torc, 744.
torec, 373, 729.
torede, 373.
tórmach, 756.
tórmachtae, 756.
tórmachtaid, 756.
tórúther, 1006.
Torrian, 1080.
tosach, p. 100, note.
totmáel, p. 166.
truig, 74.
trastar, 1071.
trefoclæ, 873.

tréide, 578.
tremibiur, p. 148.
tremitiagat, p. 148.
trén, 299, 1117.
tress, 873.
tressa, 1117.
tri, 676.
trí (prep.), 636, 752.
trian, 897.
trimi-ro-thorndiussa, 1008.
trirech, 371.
tróg (truag), 383.
trógún, 383.
tromchride, 903.
tromm, 903.
truag, 262.
truscu (acc. pl.), 605.
tú, 1112.

tnaichle, 1129.
túarcun, 722, 858.
túath, 423, 870.
túathmm, 937.
tucad, 555.
tuccu, p. 165.
tnirind (dat. sing.), 35.
tuislcd, 927.
tús (tnus), 21.
túslestar, 1134.
tuus, 21, 937.

húad, 879.
úadib, 729.
úair, p. 95, note 1.
nan (uainn), 214.
húare, 639.
úas, 371.

húasalathair, 13; p. 147.
búasalsichire, p. 166.
húasalterchomrictid, p. 166.
ucht, 262, 812.
huile, p. 100, note.
huinnius, 557.
uisce, 69.
uisceán, 69.
uisse, 36, 758, 881, 1085.
Ultán, p. 95, note [2].
humae, 611.
úr, 578.
húrde, 578.
urfaisiu, 777.
utmall, 815.

ymmon, 154.

III. MIDDLE-IRISH INDEX.

[*Where there is no commentary on a word, the numerals in this Index refer to the articles in the text, pp. 4-35. Numerals with "gl." prefixed to them refer to the Glosses on the Lorica, supra, pp. 136-143.*]

a (pron.), 420, 421.
a (interj.), p. 112, note.
abb, *see* banab.
abball, 555.
abdaine, 173; p. 157.
abbcoide, 432.
abbracht, gl. 120.
accai, 104.
accadhar, 1096.
aclaidhi, 456.
acra, 869.
adh (agh) allaidh, 387.
adhaig, 866.
adhalltrach, 619.
adhalltras, 883.
adhare, 59, 1018; p. 155.
adhastar, 820.
adbbhar, 161, 849.
adhbhardacht, 835, 848.
adbrond, gl. 187; p. 149.
ad[b]clos, 1030.
adblacadh, 759, p. 23.
adblucadh, 693.
adutes, gl. 28; p. 147.
áe, 975, 1032.
aenach, aenachde, gl. 45; p. 147.

Aengus, 342.
aguidh, gl. 108.
agarh, 385.
aghat, p. 44, note.
aibbirseoir (oibhirscoir), 517.
aicecht, 868.
aidbheadh (gen. pl.), 709.
aidhchidhe, 546.
aier, 105.
aiffrend, 853; p. 164.
áil, 91.
Ailcch, 39.
Ailell, 481.
ailghinecht, 917.
aimfesach, 392.
aimsir, 1048, gl. 9; 847.
ainder, 223.
ainfirénach, 682.
aingil, 460; -gel, gl. 26, gl. 146.
ainim, 288.
ainm, 991; gl. 241.
ainmech, 428.
ainmidhi, 976.
ainmneachadh, 885.
air, 226.
airai, p. 149.

airchindech, 449.
airdi (-de), 926.
airdensbog, 447.
aire, gl. 109; p. 148.
airecht, p. 37, note; p. 95, note [1].
airgi (-ge). 586, 754.
airgeach, 586.
airged, 787.
airgedach, 607.
ait, 191.
aitchimm, gl. 141.
aiteand, 933.
aithléini, 155.
alaind, 226, 234.
Alba, 191.
albanach, 306.
allastigh, gl. 251; p. 150.
allaidh, 297, 417.
allamuigh, gl. 250([2]); p. 150.
Alldghus, p. 69, note.
alltar, gl. 147; p. 149.
almanach, 312.
alt (= artus), gl. 201.
amadán, 302.
amainsibh (dat. pl.), gl. 147.
amaisc, 251; p. 158.

Middle-Irish Index.

ambal, gl. 81.
ambuas, 226.
an (prep.), p. 135; gl. 6.
ro-an, 193.
anál, gl. 123; p. 149.
ancoire, 68.
anmach, 654.
anmain (dat. sing.), 232.
anoir (anoir), 1079.
anum, 406; gl. 59.
Aodh, 948.
aoir, 104.
ar (pron.), 847.
ar (conj.), 847.
ara (d-ara), 589.
ára, 1011; gl. 175, gl. 208.
áirmibh toli (dat. pl.), gl. 183.
arachend, p. 95, note 1.
arain, 163.
arán geal, 286.
arbba, 213, 1038.
archaingel, 461.
ard, 16; gl. 12, gl. 264.
ardeaspoc, 16.
ardrig, 161.
arg, 198.
arm, gl. 21.
arrecaim, 481.
arson anma, 996.
artán (?), 111.
Artglus, p. 69, note.
asa, gl. 240; p. 150.
as-a-aitbli, 193.
asnach, gl. 170; p. 149.
asóer, 937.
assal, 296, 416; p. 159.
assan, 72.
atanach, 596.
at cluic, 26; p. 154.
at pill, 831.
at ("in thy"), p. 149; gl. 147.
athair, 3, 1046.
athair-talmhan, 178.
atbarmarbhthach, 317.
atbél-sa, 104.
atcondaire, 104; p. 156.
athchumiledh, 909.
athfiana, 330.
atchinm, gl. 52, gl. 141; p. 147.
athghabháil, p. 44, note.
atlige, gl. 45.
atuaith, 937.
augdar, gl. 2.

ba, p. 37, note.
baceach, 605.

bachlach, 410.
bachlach breallán, 412.
bachlóg, 696.
bagar, 339.
baile, 110; p. 156.
bainde, 966.
baindea in toraidh, 289.
baindi cich, 326.
baineachlach, 257; p. 158.
baintigherna, 287.
bairin, 28.
bairghen, 141; p. 157.
baistedh, p. 165.
baithes, gl. 83, gl. 248.
ball, gl. 77, gl. 148, gl. 238; p. 150.
ballach, 638.
bam, gl. 260; p. 165.
banab, 22.
bancoig, 247.
banchara, 293.
bannach, p. 133.
banphrioir, 23.
bansagart, 24.
bansaer (-sóir), 292.
bantaisech (-tóisech), 21.
bantracht, 39.
Baothghus, p. 69, note.
bara, 320.
baramhail, 877.
bás, gl. 7, gl. 263.
basóg, 95.
bass, 94; gl. 166; p. 149, p. 156.
báthadh, p. 163.
bathais, 1045.
batar, 36.
bealach, 793.
bean, 1053.
bean do bhráthar, 570.
bean do mhric, 571.
beaunmharbhthach, 321.
bec, gl. 132.
beithi, 560.
ben, 194, 664, 673, 806.
bél, gl. 107; p. 148.
benim, gl. 62; p. 147.
bennacht, 914.
beol, gl. 128; p. 128, note 3.
beóthach, gl. 211.
bérla, p. 37, note.
berradh, 1096.
bertnaighim, gl. 80; p. 148.
betha, 113; gl. 8, gl. 254, gl. 260.
bi, gl. 147.
biadh, 1045; p. 165.
biathadh, 1045.

bicairecht, 171; p. 157.
bidhgadh, 769.
bile (orlus), 191; p. 157.
bile (ventilogium), 716; p. 163.
binn, 223.
bir, gl. 152; p. 149.
biror, 184.
birrach, 18; p. 154.
birur, 823.
bis, gl. 132; bite, gl. 59.
blaesc, 179; p. 157.
bláthach, 220; p. 157.
bláthmhar, 491.
bleoin, gl. 226.
bliadain, 173.
bloingi (acc. pl.? die weichen?), gl. 214.
blonac, 236, 1006; p. 164.
bó, 159, 583.
boc, 1094.
bocasach, 1030.
bocht, 1058.
bocoidech, 653.
bodhar, 604.
bolltanadh, 1088.
bond, 96; gl. 191, gl. 247.
bonn, 190.
bó-sluaigbedh, 300; p. 159.
bothán, 120.
braen aimsire, 1048.
brághe, gl. 129, gl. 131.
braicein, 714.
bráighdech, 444.
braise, 36.
brat, 29.
bráthair, 1047; p. 162.
brátharmarblathach, 319.
breallach, 657; p. 161.
brecc, p. 128, note 3.
brégach, 958.
breitheamh, 366.
brén, 683.
bréntus, 1089.
bretnach, 957.
briathar, 628; gl. 1.
briathrach, 628.
bróce, 1033.
bróg, 445.
broine, gl. 49; p. 147.
brondmar, 647.
brothrachan, 180.
bruach, 947.
brú, gl. 210; b. na hóighe, 576.
brugh, gl. 45; p. 147.
bruinech, gl. 49; p. 147.
bruinde, gl. 200; p. 150.

Indices Verborum.

buachaill bó, 583.
buachaill mucc, 584.
buaile, 174.
buaile dam, 1044.
bunin, 502.
buathbhallán liath, 182.
buidhen, p. 95, note¹.
buidhe, buidhi, 803; p. 128, note³.
buigi, 1119 (see *boc*).
butum, 152; p. 157.

ca, 218.
cabillanacht, 172.
cac gabhar, 1075.
cách, p. 37, note.
caech, 426.
caemh-Dhaire, 191.
caensuaraighi, 1130.
cáer fineamach, 267.
caera, 851; p. 164.
catharach, 1055.
cai, 770.
Caid, 949.
caile, 58.
caile dabhea, 158.
cailleeh, 847; c. ligheoc, 282.
caillué, 336.
caillteamhail, 1061.
cáin, 98, p. 156.
cain (adj.), 234.
cainuarrach, 1130, gl. 138; p. 149.
cairdes, gl. 61.
caire, 36.
caisc, 298.
calma, gl. 22; gl. 158.
calmdacht, gl. 14.
calpach, 164.
calptach, 162.
camm, gl. 229, p. 150.
camra, 123.
camradh, 129; p. 156.
cananach, 437.
cantair, 239.
cantairecht, 63.
caog, 201.
caor. p. 165.
cara, 293, 413.
carain, 191.
ra-m-charastar, p. 149.
carr, 70, 263.
casadh, 1043.
casnoidhi, 253.
casta, 632.
cat, 499.
cath, gl. 23.
cathair airdeasbuig, 176.

cathbharr, gl. 99, p. 148.
catholica, 521.
cealg, 325, 500.
cech, p. 37, note; gl. 59.
céd (primus), 588; (100), 772.
céd grindi foilci, 1045; p. 165.
cedir, 560.
ceilebhradh coin, 746.
ceindetan, gl. 82.
céir, 225.
céirin, 836.
ceis, 717; p. 163.
ceithri, 775.
cenbarau, 181.
cend, gl. 102.
cendaidhi (cennaidhe), 1092.
cend-fíacail, gl. 134.
congal, 149, 911.
i-cenn, 894.
cennaighim, 1092.
cennais, 232.
cennbharr, 51; p. 155.
centar, gl. 147, p. 149.
cep, 480.
cere, 196.
cércaill, 979.
cereall, 475.
cerd, 218, 508.
cerdcha, 218.
cernach, 486.
certachadh, 888.
cessacht, 280.
cestngadh, 891.
cestunach, 15; p. 153.
cethardubhladh, 931.
cét-bhliadhain, 588.
cét-chathach, 772.
cethramhadh, 142.
cethrar, 400, 1092.
cethri, 775.
cethruma, 591.
ciabh, 33; p. 154.
ciarsech, 200.
cich, 100, gl. 203, p. 150.
cichin, 101.
cindchéreaill, 481.
cis, 784.
cisti (ciste), 199.
clais dromma, gl. 160, p. 149.
clár, 67, 560.
clár casta, 1043.
clas guail, 273.
claustra, 818.
cleath, 485.
clechtaim, gl. 81, p. 148.
clóireach, 422, 710.

Clement, 539.
clesamnach, p. 44, note.
co-clethi, p. 37, note.
cliabh, gl. 71.
cliamhuin, 377, 322.
cliavhuinmbharbhthach, 322.
cliath, 126.
cliathach, 712.
cliath fuirsidh, 240, p. 158.
clibhán, 697.
cloc, 26.
cloch, 552; p. 112, note.
clódh, gl. 44, p. 147.
cloirend, gl. 82, p. 148.
cloitheamh, 461.
clu (acc. pl.), gl. 153; p. 149.
cluain gabhida, 723.
cluas, gl. 113, p. 148.
cluithi (-the), 518.
clúmhar, 655.
cnáimh, 193, 296.
cnaimfiach, 269, 503.
cohairithe, gl. 20, p. 147.
cochall, 121, 56.
cocan, 245.
cochtair, 283.
codaltech, 729.
coelán, gl. 224, p. 150.
cofáilidh, gl. 267, p. 151.
cogadh, 139, p. 157.
cogar, 145, p. 157.
coi, 770.
coibhlighe, 847.
coileach, 506.
coilech gaithi (-the), 510.
coill, 115.
coimpert, 847.
coindealbháthadh, 845, p. 163.
coin-mir, 176.
coinnill, 44 p. 154.
coinnlin, 210.
cóir, p. 44, note.
coire (-ri), 724.
cuisinech, 650; p. 162.
coisreagadh, 285.
coissegradh, 880.
coitchend, gl. 1.
colach, 1030.
colaind (dat. sing.), gl. 174.
coll, 556.
colpa, 146, gl. 188.
colum, 203, 504.
Columcille, p. 37, note.
coluud, 919.
combadas, 36.
comhaightech, 314.

Middle-Irish Index.

comhaircachadh, 897.
comhainm, 993.
comhairle, 884.
comhaireuh, 913.
comhaistiu, 518.
comhalta, 486.
comhaltudh, 518.
comhdblúta (gen. pl.), gl 233.
combócul, 873.
chomhforbrit, gl. 194.
combla, 71, 125.
comma, 918.
companach, 378.
companus, 892.
comparaid, 875, 896.
compas, 1137, 1138.
compur, gl. 71, p. 148.
comhradh, 481.
comhruc, 847.
comhsólás, 884.
comhthinól, gl. 26.
combthrom, 960.
comhthromugudh, 903.
conaichi, 1128.
Conall Cernach, 486.
concró, 261.
Conchublar, 545.
conidh, gl. 2.
conn. 209; p. 157.
Conn, 772.
connlach, 209.
connargaibh, 320.
copán, 479.
coraidh, 457.
co-r-bo, 4.
corcach mara, 206, 505.
Corcaigh (dat. sing.), 4.
corcair, 224.
Cormac, 173.
coróin, 75, 76.
corónta, 601.
corp, 812; gl. 259; c. leghas, 1071.
corporas, 859; p. 164.
corr, gl. 49; corr brághat, gl. 133.
corróg, 167.
cos, 466, 560; gl. 190.
coslatra, 36.
cosmhailius, 904.
cosmhailsibh (dat. pl.), gl. 32.
cosolamh, 36.
cotun, 270.
cohulidhe, gl. 239.
craes, 92; p. 156.
cráessach, 644.
crand gius, 563.

crand glésta, 719.
crand laúir, 564.
crand unnear, 566.
crand tochartaigh, 746.
creblhar, 204.
criadh, 1054.
criathar, 700; p. 162.
cridhe, gl. 211.
cris, 720, 1102; p. 149; p. 153.
cris tribhuis, 706.
crisdal, 552.
crismal, 840.
cristaighi (-e), 323.
cristin, 313.
cró, 122, 261; p. 156.
cró carach, 851.
crocan, 56.
crodhacht, gl. 26.
croicinn madra alta, 275.
croidhi (-e), 1102.
croindtille, 651, 844.
croindtilleeh, 651.
crombéol, 708.
crosán, 14.
Cruachan Ráith Chourach, 481.
cruaidh, 674.
cruaidhi, 1118.
crubh eich, 442.
cruit, p. 153.
cruitire, 5, 1015.
cruithnecht, 778, 189.
crapán na lámh, 233.
cú allaidh, 417.
cualli (-e), 495.
Cuangus, p. 69, note.
cugan, 572.
cúig, 776.
cúigedh, 592.
cnigel, 567.
cúigur, 401.
cuilen, 498.
cuimhleng, gl. 45; p. 147.
cuimhneach, 1110.
cuinchidh, 783.
cuindeóg, 165.
cuisle, 99; gl. 222.
cularan, 1049.
cumhacht, gl. 69.
cumair, 678.
cumen, 727.
cumdach, 881.
cumdachta, p. 142, note. ⎱
cumdaightóir, 1098. ⎰ cumh-?
cumtach, 871.
cupris, 560.
curach, 488.

curchuslach, 933.
curracach, 595.
curu (acc. pl.), 428.
cusle, 99.

dá, 773.
dathach, 158, 277.
daingen, p. 37, note.
daingin, 674, 679.
dair, 554.
Daire, 191.
dall, 249, 427, 623.
dallsúlech, 622.
damh, 758, 858, 1044.
dána, 1131.
darahési, p. 112, note; darmési, 937.
dath, 1087.
dea, 289.
dealbh, 642, 936.
dealbhdha, 642.
dealg, 1074.
deallradh, 1031.
dens, 386.
déc, 173.
dechain, 454.
dechnahadh, 43.
Dechtere, 320.
decredech, 12.
deganach, 451.
degh-ghnimhradh, gl 261; p. 151, p. 166.
deirgech, 78.
delbhait, gl. 154.
dénamh, 899.
dénmhusach, 1090.
dénta, gl. 245; p. 165.
deuntar, 1096.
deóir, 550.
deoradh, 303; p. 159
dér, 39, 744.
déreach, 627.
derg, 1048.
dergi (-ge), 939.
dergudh, 481.
dermhár, p. 95, note!; 1008.
des, p. 69, note.
di, gl. 67.
dia, 405, 232; gl. 157, gl. 265.
diablul, 527.
dialhacht, 81, 334.
dianghalur, gl. 258; p. 151.
Diarmaid, 540.
dias, 398.
dias, 35.
dibechan, gl. 135; p. 149.

2 B

dibhlínaibh, 104.
dibh(ń), p. 95, note 1.
dichuirer, gl. 261.
didean, 153.
didin, 762, 995
didnighteóir, 1093.
dighlach, p. 69, note.
dilé, 1121.
dilechta, 429; p. 161.
dilechtach, 83.
dim, gl. 265.
dimaines, gl. 10; p. 146.
din, 193.
dindsenchas, p. 37, note.
diner, 699.
dingbhala, 668.
dírimh, gl. 234.
dithen, 718.
ditoin, 472.
discibul, 438.
dislingudh, 910.
disle, 496.
ditin (acc. sing.), 602.
ditin, gl. 68; ditnet, gl. 19, gl. 76.
dithrebhach, 315.
diumus, 1030.
dlighedh, 87, 879; p. 147.
dlighi, 87.
dlightinech, 433.
dlistinach, 433, 439.
dlúith, 636; gl. 39; p. 147.
dlúthadh, gl. 61.
dó, 193.
dobeth, gl. 2.
dobhrán, 375.
dochinélach, 676, 1057.
dochotar, 894.
doetnir, 1082.
Doedhghus, p. 69, note.
dóenna (= O. Ir. dóinde), 85.
dofaicsena, gl. 151; p. 149.
dogni, 847; doguiat, 1008.
doib, 481.
doilbhtheóir, 1091.
doilbhthiugudh, 900.
dóit, gl. 164.
dolléci, 747.
domblas áe, 975.
Donnchadh, 525.
Donnghus, p. 69, note.
dorátadh, 560, 867.
dorchadhus, 331, 332.
dorine, p. 125, note.
dornadóracht, 272.
dornán bnana, 502.

dorus, 124; gl. 245.
dorus lis, 580.
dot, gl. 69.
dóthengtach, 626.
dothóet. gl. 2.
do-da-trascair, 847.
dreassan, 1012.
dreolán, 207.
dris, 587, 933.
driseain, gl. 217.
droighin, 559.
dromand, gl. 171.
druim, 745; druimseilg, gl. 172.
co-druimne, 4.
dubh, 381, 802.
dubhán, 428.
dubhrudan, 721.
Dubhthach, 1096.
duchu, 1020.
dúil (dúl), 267.
duillen, 765.
duine, 89, 953.
duine beg, 436.
dúl, 1008.
dunmharbhthach, 316.
durnu (acc. pl.), gl. 165.

each, 17, 414, 442.
Eachtghus, 69, note.
eaglas (eaglais), 177.
ealadan, 85.
eallach (?), 71.
earrach, 1070.
eás, 259.
easbog, 448.
easpog, 982.
écas (cccas), p. 125, note.
écna, p. 38, note.
édach, 501, 757.
édail, 694.
édaingen, 680.
édmhur, 635.
edrath, 166.
egcombthrom, 961, 962.
egeusmhai'ius, 905.
eideand, 933.
Eighipt, 581.
eiuech, p. 58, note.
éirindach (éirinnach), 305.
eistidhóir, 1101.
eitelladh, 912.
eithidheamhail, 1068.
ela, 509.
emhnadh, 1010.
endae, p. 151.
endgac, gl. 260.

Eoghan, 543.
éolus, 85, 901.
eorna, 779.
erlabhra, 867.
erchissim, gl. 265; p. 151.
escaine, p. 147.
escara, gl. 18.
escart, 254; p. 158.
escata, gl. 180, gl. 184.
escuing urchoidech, 935.
esga, 234
eslán, 393, 634.
esláiu (-e), 928.
etal, p. 151.
etan, gl. 86, gl. 103.
etarfuaradh, gl. 269.
etarsróin, gl. 116.
éte ochta, gl. 222.
etechail, 1066.
etelaigher, gl. 264.
etincta, gl. 89.
etlae (?), gl. 260; p. 151.
eturru, 481.
examail, 1087.

fabhra (O. Ir. abra, gen. -at), 79.
fáebat, gl. 16.
fada, 677.
faechóg, 188, 194.
Faelghus, p. 69, note.
faicim, p. 149.
faidi (-e), 929.
faidiugudh, 907.
faighin, 157.
failgbeach, 631.
fainleóc, 934.
fairci (fairge), 1103.
fairge, 575, 1103.
fairsing, 640.
faismedhach, gl. 55; p. 147.
faisnéis, 751.
fáistine, p. 38, note.
faith, 2, 350, 351, 352, 958.
fallaing, 37; p. 154.
fallaingech, 599.
farcán, 238.
farcli glún, gl. 183.
farsinge, 640.
feam, 97.
fechug, 185.
fecht, 481.
féd fose[laidh], 826.
fédaim, l. 43, gl. 253; p. 147.
fédán, 46; p. 154.
fedhbh, gl. 53ª; p. 159.
fégadh, p. 149.

Middle-Irish Index. 187

féith, gl. 132, gl. 223; p. 156.
feóil, 193.
feóil na fiacal, 150.
feorus, 582.
fer, 395, 1048.
fer cli, 397.
fer cuisi do condmail, 434.
fér, p. 70, note.
ferand, 390.
ferbóg, 205.
fergacht, 328.
Ferghal, 533.
Ferghus, 486.
fernóg, 558.
ferr, 1116.
fersad (-said), 568.
fersán, 468.
fesach, 392.
fésóg, 47; p. 154.
fésógach, 645.
fétaim, p. 147.
fiabhrus, gl. 257.
Fiac, p. 125, note.
fiacail, 150, gl. 89, gl. 126.
fiadh, 183.
fiadhnaisi (-e), 959.
Fianghus, p. 69, note.
fiar, 621.
fiarśúilech, 621.
fichabhall, 562.
fidh, 46, 267.
fidhbha, 797.
fidubbhuidhe, p. 70, note.
fidhchat, 260.
fidhchilli (gen. sing.), 747.
fighidóir, 1095.
fíl, 104.
filidh, 1.
filidhecht, 833; p. 38, note; 1002.
find-choelán, gl. 229.
find-emhon, 1010.
finemnach, 267.
finemain, 267.
finghaile, p. 147.
fírénach, 681.
firmamint, 749, 1008.
fis, p. 149.
Flathghus, p. 69, note.
fliuch, 675.
fliuchaidhe, p. 111, note.
fliuchidhecht, 1097.
fobith, 486.
fochétóir, 320.
fochluidh (-aidh), 229.
fól, 119.
fofrith, 1048.

foghur, 469.
foighi, 815.
foilci, 1045.
foillsiugudh, 895.
foiltfind, 39.
foiltnibh (dat. pl.), gl. 97.
foiltnin, 464.
foircedal, 837.
foirmtech, 602.
folt, 77, 78; p. 70, note; gl. 237.
fon. gl. 132.
fonamhaideach, 630.
forba, gl. 8, gl. 260; p. 146.
forenlu, gl. 59.
forgaire, gl. 1; p. 146.
foriarair, gl. 59; p. 147.
forithin (dat. sing.), p. 151.
format, 602.
formnai (acc. pl.), gl. 161.
forsgath, 839.
fortachtaighim, gl. 1; p. 146; 727.
fortaighim, 727.
fothoin (acc. sing.), gl. 95; p. 148.
fothragadh, 822.
fraech, 565, 933; p. 162.
francach, 248.
frangcach, 309.
fria, 847; frim, 937.
friss, 125, 847.
fual, 222.
fuathroic, gl. 94; p. 148.
fuil, 1048.
fuiltin, 463.
fuindeóg, 134.
fuindseóg, 557.
fuiseóg, 140.
fundamintech, 612.
furachair, 984.
furtacht (fort-), 727.

ga, 216, p. 157.
gabháiltech, 594.
gabhal, 135.
gabhann, 369.
gabhar, 372.
gaethamhail (góith-), 1067.
gaeth, 428; g. atúaidh, 353.
gaethmhar, 646.
gaibhthi, p. 112, note.
gaile, gl. 219, gl. 220, p. 165.
gaill-mhias, 478.
gaire, p. 165.
gairleóg. 31.
gáith, 1070; gáithbhuilg? p. 157.
galar, 281.

gall, 478.
galldach, 307.
gamain arain, 163.
gammheeh, 428.
garbog, 186.
garrga, 702.
geal, 168, 286, 801, 659, 1124.
gealan na súl, 168.
no-t-gebhtha, p. 112, note.
gég, gl. 194; p. 150.
géidh, 19; p. 154.
geimhel, 226.
gein, 104.
geind, 560.
geinemhain, 887.
genthan, 834.
geocach, 513.
geraine (gen. sing.), gl. 224; p. 150.
gerbach, 652.
gereith (gen. sing.), 125.
gerreach, 494.
gerrchend, 125.
gerrghuin, 940.
in-gerrtha, gl. 17; p. 135.
giall, gl. 125; p. 149.
gileach, 933.
gile, 1124.
gilla adhairce, 1018.
gilla cinn eich, 17; p. 153.
gilla Crist, 523.
gilla Martain, 526.
gilla na naomh, 345.
gilla nan-each, 946.
gilla Patrice, 537.
Gilliam, 532.
Gilliberd, 534.
gius, 563, 560.
glac, 1008; glac-arbha, 213.
glac saighed, 214.
glaine, 191.
glais, gl. 218.
glan, 671, p. 153; glan-mhót, 29.
glas, 29; p. 91, note.
glass(serra), 226.
glocaire, 986.
glic, 1129.
gloinidhe, 1087.
glún, gl. 183, gl. 185; p. 149.
gnáthughudh, gl. 56: gl. 246.
goéthigh (dat. sing. fem.), gl. 2.
gnimh, 908, gl. 2.
gnimhradh, p. 151, p. 166.
goean, 66.
god, 603.
goirt, 637.

2 B 2

Indices Verborum.

gortach, 620.
grádh, 1081.
grainsech, 195.
gramatach, 82.
granna, grana, gl. 78, gl. 64.
gredháil, 854.
greidell, 107.
greim, 144.
grian, 952, 973, 989, 992.
Grighoir, 544; -ghuir, 891.
grinn, 39.
grindi (-e), 1045.
groigh, 742.
gruaidh, 39; gl. 114, gl. 124; p. 148.
gruamdha, 384, 1065.
gruth, 784.
gual, 273.
guala, p. 151.
guasacht, 727; gl. 6.
guidbi (-e), 870, 893.
guirín, 255.
gulban, gl. 106; p. 148.
gus, p. 69, note.

iachtarach, 1013.
iarnaighi (-e), 608.
iarund, 790.
iar-sein, 4.
ibhar, 561; p. 162.
ibrach (?), 832.
ichtar na comhladh, 1034.
idh urchomail, 279.
ifearnadha, 827.
iffern, 519, 520, 825.
ifus, gl. 2.
igha, 244.
ilmhíle, gl. 29; ilrátha, p. 70, note.
ilur, 197.
imad (-adh?), 921.
imarchuirim, imarchor, gl. 268; p. 151.
imdha, 670, 805.
imdhegbail, 154; gl. 147; p. 149.
imell, 69.
imlán, gl. 243.
imm, 784.
immchosnibb (dat. pl.), gl. 121; p. 149.
imme, gl. 58; p. 147.
immles, gl. 118.
imnlind, gl. 205; p. 150.
immun, 891.
impidhe, gl. 11; p. 147.
in (prep.), p. 37, note.
inadh, 516.

inada, 329.
inar, 29.
inarach, 597.
inbher, 428.
inchinn, 747; inchind, gl. 105.
ind (prep.), gl. 260.
ind (subst.), 154.
indilbh (dat. pl.), gl. 148.
indrace, gl. 54; p. 147.
indte, p. 103, note 1.
infinit, gl. 2.
ingar, 839.
inghin, 290; iughen, p. 150; 291.
ingnadh, 229.
inga, gl. 197, gl. 198; p. 150.
inill, gl. 74.
inillius, gl. 66, gl. 142; p. 148.
inmhus, 333.
innarbadh, 752.
innarbthach, 983.
inne, gl. 93, gl. 227.
inne-iachtarach, 1013.
innilt, 25.
innraice (nom. pl.), 36.
inntindeach, 876.
instruimint, 761.
int, 78, 1013.
interiacht, 874.
inti, 867.
inntlecht, 734.
irrlabhra, p. 103, note.
isat, 1008.
ith in arbha, 1038.
iummus, p. 37, note.

la (prep.), 722.
ro-la, 428.
labhar, 376.
labhartaighe, 1133.
lacht, 250.
ladhar, gl. 196; p. 150.
laegh, 424.
láidire, 920.
láidiri, 1113.
láimtech, p. 69, note.
laindér, 73; p. 155.
láir, 294.
laithirt, 266.
lámh, 34, 233, 465; p. 128, note 3.
lámhaccan, 916; p. 164.
lámhann, 34.
lamhannan, gl. 231; p. 150.
lámh-thuagh, 857.
lán, 1008.
land (lann), 132; p. 152.

lá-oirrthi, 1076.
lár, 747.
lasair, 128; p. 156.
lauir (gen. sing.), 564.
Laurini, 538.
leabaidh in daimh allta, 858.
leabhar, 371.
lear, 13.
lebaidh, 481.
lebhar aiffrind, 853.
leca, 89.
léc in árain, 246.
lég, 133, 573.
ra-légh, p. 153.
leghaim, 1071.
leghes, p. 165.
léghtóir, 1080.
léine, 38.
leitheid (acc. sing.), 104.
leithui (-e), 925.
lemhnacht, 782.
lennhunach, 1040.
lepaidh, 481.
Lerghus, p. 69, note.
lesc, 382.
lesmháthair, 48.
less, 580.
lessa (acc. pl.), gl. 176.
leth, 90; gl. 67; p. 156.
leth-ail, 90.
lethchaech, 426, 624.
lethenach, 232.
lethfer, 396.
lethómh, 90.
lethsáthach, 403.
lethtoin, 471.
lexaire, 11.
liath, 182; p. 128, note 3.
ligheóc, 282.
lin uisci, 863.
lind, 221.
line, 232.
linn (lind), p. 165.
liriu, p. 70, note.
liter, 230.
lité, 767.
liubhar, 371.
lubhra, 268.
locha ochsal, gl. 216.
loch, 781.
Lochan, 522.
Lochlann, 541.
Lóegh, p. 112, note.
lóghmhar, 133.
loighed, 923.
long, gl. 49; long luath, 574.

long bronn, gl. 136.
longphort, 725, 813; p. 163.
lór, 908.
lorg, 52.
lorgarecht, 937.
lór-ghnimh, 908.
lorgdromma, gl. 169.
losa feadha, 933.
losad, 42.
loscadh, 737.
lu leith, gl. 228; p. 150.
luach faisnéisi, 751.
luach lesa, 792.
luaidhe, 60, 788, 609.
luaidheamhail, 609.
luath, 574; luathidher, 1070.
luathgháirech, 641.
luch dhall, 249.
luch francach, 248.
luchtaire, 10; p. 153.
lugha, 1115.
luibh (lubh), 114.
luidh, 894.
lúirech, 154; gl. 147, gl. 159.
luirgnibh (dat. pl.), gl. 189; p. 150.
lus, 810, 104, 933.
lus na fiadh, 183.

mac, 407, 408.
mac dilechta, 429; p. 161.
mac inmlesen, 80; gl. 118.
mac imresan, 80.
maccu immlesaib (dat. pl.), gl. 118.
mac na hoidhchi (-e), 546.
mac-lóe, gl. 213.
macámh, 370.
macámh gennti, 473.
machaire, 866, 1060.
madair, 275.
Máel issu, 232.
maeth, 394.
maethsúilech, 431.
magbisder, 365, 392.
maide sgine, 1139.
maighister, 1099.
mailgibh (dat. pl.), gl. 112; p. 148.
maindsér, 861.
mainister, 726.
mainu, 299.
maise, 1083, 1108.
maissi, 927.
maith, 661, 798, 1134.
mallacht, 915.
mallei, 866.
manach, 435.

mani, 104.
Maolsechlainn, 346.
marbhadh, 14.
marbhuudh, p. 70, note.
marcach na comhladh, 127.
marclach, 189.
marce, 55, 1005; p 155.
maróg, 1005.
martra, 738.
marmur, 1104.
Matha, 549.
máthair, 130, 1052.
matal, 490.
mátharmarbhthach, 318.
mathghamhain, 418.
meall, 258.
meata, 1123.
medal, 235.
Medhbh, 481.
medhg, 783.
medhón, gl. 207.
médughuuth, 763.
méid, 922.
méirsi (-e), 780.
mór, 465; gl. 167, gl. 195.
mór-coise, 466.
mór-láimhe, 465.
merdrech, 187.
merlach na comhladh, 944
mésa, 1117.
mesgán, 219.
mesurdha, 807.
mi, 1050, 1051.
mias, 478, 193.
michlúmhar, 656.
michnimhneach, 1111.
midhingbhala, 669.
mil, 974.
mil édaigh, 501.
mil mór, 428, 865.
milan, 138.
milchú, 411.
milech, 648.
mimhaise (-i), 1084, 1109.
min, 430.
mintsúilech, 430.
Miodhghus, p. 69, note.
mir, 156; p. 157; m. pluc, 750.
mirr, 1134.
mirbhail, 695.
mitall, 791.
mithormach, 756.
mó, 1114.
móin, 118.
moladh, 902; -ludh, 894.
Molua, p. 133, note.

monadh, 237, 841.
monadan, 212.
mong in-t-slindéin, 148.
mór, 428, 663, 809; gl. 13.
mórmhargad, 327.
mór-ulchach, 1048.
mucc, 584.
mucc mara, 1029; p. 164.
Mucholmóc, p. 149.
mucor, 566.
mughsaine, 882.
muilleand, 711.
muilind, 701.
muime, 784.
muin, 709.
muinchille, 30; p. 154
muinchillech, 598.
muine, gl. 224; p. 150, p. 165.
muine, 585.
muine draighin, 110.
muinél, 744; muincol, gl. 137.
muir, 144, 860; gl. 5.
múl, 295, 415.
muleán, 243.
mullach, 1007; gl. 98.
mullach tighi (-e), 838.
múr, 476.
Murchadh, 542.
murdhuchu, 1020.

náit, 935.
námha, 1008.
naomh, 345.
nathari (nathair?), 88.
neach (O. Ir. nech), 379.
neimhni, 987, 988.
neimh, 602.
néll, 337.
nélladóracht, 271.
nemh, 812.
nemhdha, gl. 13, gl. 24 g! 264.
nemhdhuine, 954.
nemhfurecháir, 985.
nemhmharbhdha, 1008.
nemhthindisnech, 617
nemhthremeta, gl. 66: p. 148.
nemhthroeta, gl. 66; p. 148.
nentóg, 208.
nertmhar, p. 37, note.
nescóid, 843.
ni, 987, 1112; gl. 249.
Nialghus, p. 69, note.
noemh, gl. 145.
nóin, 1077.
nóine, 335.
nómbadh, 173.

normanach, 308.
nús, 256.

ó, gl. 41.
ochtmhadh, 229.
óen, gl. 59.
oibringudh, 889.
oidhche, 546.
oldi (-e), 1078.
oighen, 86.
oilemhain, 753.
oilithrech, 311.
oinmhid, 512.
oirenin, 493.
obair, 614.
oemhil, gl. 51.
ocum, gl. 147.
óentaighim, gl. 260; p. 165.
ógh, 955; gl. 53.
ógdhamh, 758.
oite, 232.
ol, 847, 1096.
ole, 662, 799; gl. 59.
ómh, 90.
ón, 613.
ór, 606, 786, 1134.
oreni (acc. pl.), gl. 181.
ord, 943; gl. 144, gl. 235.
órdhaighe, 606.
organaidh, 7.
orlár, 704.
ortha, p. 125, note.
ossadh, 137; p. 156.
otrach, 482.

pagán, p. 151.
paiper, 579.
paistí uróg, 445.
parrtus, 553.
partan, 374 (see torpan).
pecadh, gl. 261.
pell, 831.
pellec, 136.
penn, 53.
persnnacht, 170.
pethair (?), 320.
Petar, 528.
pian, 54; gl. 147.
ploir, 1136.
pipur, 1072.
plag, gl. 256.
Plait, 950.
Ploit, 951.
pluc, 750.
póccadh, p. 148.
pólaire (fólaire?), 371.

port, 110.
prebach, 658.
prechán, 507.
prelait, 452.
presen (persen), 524.
primaidecht, 354.
prioir, see banphrioir.
priv, 97.
proindtech, 728.
proisté, 852.
próvinse, 175.
puuc, 474.
punnann, 45.
pupul, 458.

rning ant-sair, 1137.
raip (rapp?), gl. 220(a); p. 165.
raith, 933.
rannaire, 9.
rastail, 814.
rechtaire, 784.
redla, 1008.
réidhi (-e), 890, 191.
reilic, 691.
rem. gl. 148.
remhainm, 992.
remhthechtas, 872.
remhthúsnighit, gl. 23.
remhum, 937; remhomm, gl. 23.
rési (acc. pl.), gl. 167.
retla, 103.
ri, 1035, 1036.
riabhach, 804.
co-riacht, p. 37, note.
riaghail, 61; p. 155.
riccedh, p. 37, note.
righan, 20; p. 154.
rigflaith, 1134; rig-lepaid, 481.
righthe (acc. pl.), gl. 163, gl. 164.
rind, 1008; rinn, 267.
robheg, 808.
Roiberd, 529.
roinill, gl. 147.
rómhánach, 310.
rón, 50.
roth, 227; gl. 119.
rotaidhe, p. 111, note.
Ruaidhri, 535.
ruaimnech dubháin, 428; p. 161.
ruaindi, 463.

sab, p. 37, note.
Sabhull, p. 107, note 1.
aacc, 489.
saebhchoire, 938.
saer, 292, 379, 409.

saer (libera), gl. 73.
saer (artifex), 1138.
Saerghus, p. 69, note.
saethar, 1085.
sugart, 24, 367; p. 154.
sai, 4.
saighed, 215.
sailmchétlaidh, 3.
saithech na tuise, 1134.
sál, gl. 192; p. 150.
salach, 616, 684.
salann, 977.
salm, 467, 3.
saltair, 766.
sanntach, 667.
sanntaighi, 1120.
sáthach, 402.
sbeggach, 629.
sblinach, 274.
sbor, 1041.
sborán, 514.
sbruileach, 1004.
ru-scaith, 894.
scála, 106; p. 156.
scamhan, gl. 221; p. 150.
scáraidh, 864.
sciath, gl. 75; p. 148.
scithech, 613, 614.
scola, 338.
scolb tighe, 446.
sdair, 84.
sdan, 789.
sdocaire, 1016.
sé, 777.
sealladh, 741.
Seán, 151.
sechmaillim, gl. 240; p. 150.
Sechnall, 894.
sechrán, 131; p. 156.
seghdha, 847.
seichi (-e), 732.
séideadh, 1019.
séideth gáithbhulga, 217; p. 157.
séimin, 211.
seirbe, 1132.
séisedh, 593.
séitche, 1073.
selg, gl. 215; sealg, 1012.
sen, 130; senn, gl. 260.
senadh naomh, 551.
senúis, 735.
senathair, 419.
senmháthair, 130.
senóir, 29, 1100.
seomra, 123.
serrach, 494.

Middle-Irish Index.

ses, 70; p. 155.
sesrach, 49.
sét slighedh, 1073.
sgadan, 967.
sgaiguen, 484.
sgartach, 796.
sgél, 223.
sgeota, 709; p. 163.
sgeotha, 710; p. 163.
sgian, 440, 441, 1139.
sgingilóir, 515.
sgiursi (-e), 109.
sgornachán, 707.
si, 847.
siadaire, 57.
sians, gl. 244.
sidhan gaeithe, 997.
sil, 1009.
sillad, 231.
sillaidhi, 231.
sin, 420, 421.
sine ochta, 1059.
sine Seáin, 151.
sitheal, 241.
siur-marbhthach, 320.
slaitin, 117.
slán, 393, 633.
slánti (-e), gl. 57.
slat, 116.
slataidhi (-e), 956.
Sleibte, p. 125, note.
slemain (slemon), 639.
slestán, 32.
sliasit, gl. 94. gl. 164, gl. 178.
slighe, 112, 613; gl. 117.
slind, 1014.
slindén, 148.
slinnebriadh, 376.
slisedg, 1001.
sluagh, 1003; gl. 25, gl. 39, &c.
smech, gl. 110, gl. 122.
smeróid, 945.
smír, 193.
snáithi (-e), 817.
snámhach, 391.
Snedhghus, p. 69, note.
snethach, 649.
so-abb, p. 37, note.
no-sóadh, p. 37, note.
socharthanaighi, 1125.
sochruidhe, 380.
sodain, 747.
soegal, gl. 10; p. 146-7.
sogh allaidh, 297.
soïst (soiphist), 842.
soiler, 740.

súilestar, 795.
soillsi (-e), 998, 1122.
soléghta, 1126.
solus, 665; see follus.
somholta, 1127.
sophistighi (tidhe?), 8.
speilp, 730.
spideóg, 202.
spiu, 933.
spirait, gl. 211.
spuirech, 764.
sraine gl. 7; p. 146.
srathar, 262.
srebhand (-bhan), 794.
srian, 819.
sroenaim, gl. 255.
sroin (?), gl. 252.
sróll, 577.
srón, 1039; gl. 117.
srubhan, 143.
srubán mara, 144.
sruth, 999, 1037, 1042.
stanamhail, 610.
stiurasmand, gl. 49; p. 147.
stoc-ronnadh, 705.
stól, 748.
stuidis, 856.
subhachus, 301.
subdecháin, 455.
sualach, gl. 15.
sui, 4.
sui abb, p. 37, note.
súidhe, p. 153.
suidheovan, 850.
suidhiughudh, gl. 4.
súil, 168, 425; gl. 104; p. 128, note 3.
súilech, 430, 431.
suirgech, 618.
suisti (-te), 278.
súithe (sapientia), p. 37, note.
suithe, 941.
sust, 109.
súthemlacht, p. 37, note.

tabhaill, 62.
tadhbhais, 846; p. 163.
Tadhg, 548.
tadhull, p. 148.
taemhan, 71.
taes, 242.
taibherne, 169, 689.
taili (-e), 739.
tailm (acc. s.), p. 112, note.
táiplis, 27; p. 154.
tairis, 1048.

tairrnge, 443.
tairrsech, 1000.
taisbenadh, 894, 846; p. 163.
taisech, see bantaisech.
taisech eethrair, 400.
taisech cuigir, 401.
taithneamhnach, 800.
taithnemach, 666.
túl, 252.
talumh, 108.
tanic, 110.
tarbh-sliasta, gl. 95, gl. 182.
tardadh, 193, 226.
tarr, 147.
tarrach, 284.
teach, 569.
teachtaire, 450.
teallach, 511.
tech na merdreach, 713.
techat, gl. 59.
tecoisce, 1112.
techtaire, 747.
tédaire, 1017.
tegaisge, 660.
teghim, gl. 262.
teilgim, p. 151.
téine creasa, 720.
teire, 672.
teirci (-e), 924.
tempoll, 688.
tend, p. 149.
tenga, 560; gl. 87, gl. 127, gl. 130; tengadh, 40.
tengthach, 625.
tés, 942, 1086.
tiach, 41, 371.
tiarach, 265.
tidhnachtaidh, 1134.
tigh, 446; p. 161.
tigherna, 287, 404, 453; gl. 143, gl. 147.
tigherna déise, 398.
tigherna trir, 399.
tighernas, 886.
timchell, 691, 1087.
timna, 760.
timpanach, 6; p. 153.
timthirigh, 368.
timthirecht, 898.
tinnisnech (-nach), 615.
tiradh, 703.
tís, gl. 132.
titul, 560.
tochartaigh, 746.
toebh, gl. 79.
togha, 878.

Indices Verborum

toghluasacht, p. 147.
toiu, 470.
tomhliur, 104; toimblid, 193.
tón, gl. 177, gl. 224.
toradh, 289.
torc, 373, 483.
Tordhelbach, 161.
tormach, 755.
torpan, 269 (*see* partan).
torta, gl. 139.
tra, 1030.
tredhelbhdha, gl. 105.
tredhluighthe, gl. 213.
tres, 590.
trenillech, gl. 213.
trethe, 560.
trí, 774.
trial, triallatóir, 1096.
tri-bhith, 229.
tribbus, 324.
tribbusach, 600.
tripulta, 930.
trithu, gl. 56.
triur, 398.
troethaim, p. 148.
troibel, 855.
truagh, 383.
túaidh, 353.
truailnidhe, gl. 69; p 148.
tú, gl. 142.

tuairgin, 722; tuairgim, gl. 149.
tuata, 423.
tucadh, p. 103, note [1].
tuce, 1134.
tuighi (-e), 994.
tuircóg, 64; p. 155.
tunna, 731.
tus, 1134.
tús, 232.
tússigh (dat. s. fem.), gl. 49.

uachtlan, 1064.
uachtlanaidhe, 1063.
uachtar, 192.
uadh, gl. 2.
uaigh, 1069.
uainm, gl. 150.
uaimhnighim, gl. 65.
uainiu, 492.
Uaithne, 547, 768.
uallghubha, 1008.
uam, gl. 59.
uan, 459.
uas, p. 37, note.
uasalathair, 13.
Uater, 530.
ubhall braghat, gl. 131.
ucht, 1059; u. na dernainde, gl. 202.

uchtach, 264.
uchtard, 643.
uchtghel, 223.
ughdur, 1107.
uile, gl. 72.
uille, gl. 163; p. 149.
Uilliam, 531.
uinneambain, 862.
uinniunint, 785.
uir, 578.
uirge (= ἄρχις), gl. 209.
uisci (-e), 160, 863.
uisce iruill, 69.
uisgemhlacht, 932.
uisa (nom. pl. m.), 36.
ulbu, 93.
ulcha, gl. 111.
umhail, 36.
umhamhail, 611.
uraicecht, 868.
urchar, gl. 81.
urchoidech, 935.
urchumail, 279; p. 159.
urlabhradh, 867.
urlamhas, 906.
urraidh, 304.
urralaisti, 1135.
urtan (artán?), 111.
uth, 102, 1056.

IV. WELSH INDEX.

[*The Old-Welsh words in this Index are marked with an asterisk.*]

*aballen, 555.
adau, 746.
ael, p. 148.
*ætinet, p. 59, note; 746.
aflafar, 1133.
afu, 1032.
aguedd, p. 163.
aidd, 948.
amm, 670.
alarch, 509.
amser, 1048.
anadl, p. 149.
angor, 68.

aradu, 1076.
arddangos, 660.
areu, 246, 1011.
arglwydd, p. 147.
ariaut, 607.
arlais, p. 148.
asen, p. 149.
asen, asyn, 296.
atar, 746.
atbrach, 1046.

bach, 439, 664.
bachawg, 605.

ball, 638.
bara, 141.
*barr, p. 148.
bas, p. 149.
bedw, 560.
bendithio, 914.
benyw, 1053.
ber, p. 149.
berw, berwr, bery, 823.
*bicoled, 339.
blas, 975.
blain, blaenor, blaenu, p. 147.
blawd, 491.

Welsh Index.

blisgyn, p. 157.
blodeuog, 491.
bloneg, 236.
bod, 120.
*bou, 158.
*boutig, 158.
braen, braenu, 683.
*brawt, 1047.
*braut, 366.
breuant, 292.
*brith, 957.
bron, p. 150.
*bronubreithet, p. 59, note; 957.
bru, 647.
brycan, 1033.
brysiaw, 36.
Brython, 957.
bugail, 583.
bun, 21.
bwgwlb, 339.
bwrw, 1048.
hwyt, 477.
bycbodawg, 1058.
byddár, 604.
bygyliaeth, 339.
byr, 678.
*bywyt, 113.

cach, 1075.
*cae, 218.
cafael, 594.
cafn, p. 156.
cair, 267.
*caitoir, 1055.
calaned, 919.
calch, 58.
calon, 919.
cam, p. 150.
cang, p. 150.
canlyn, p. 165.
cant, 772.
canwyll, p. 154.
caraut, 292.
cath, 499.
cawn, p. 157.
cedor, cedorawg, 1055.
ceiliawg, 506.
ceiliog gwynt, 510.
cele, 325.
cell, 115.
cengl, 149.
*cenitol, 676.
ceryddu, 888.
cesail, p. 150 (No. 216).
cig, p. 150 (No. 203; correct *cyg*!).
ciglif, 655.

clais, p. 149.
clas, 273.
*claud, 229.
*claur, cloriou, 67.
cledd, 387.
cleddyf, 461.
cloddiaw, 229.
clodfawr, 655.
clopa, p. 154.
clopen, p. 154.
cludd, p. 147.
clust, p. 148.
clyn, 723.
clyw, 655.
*coc, 245.
cogail, 567.
coegfran, 201.
collen, 556.
colomen, 203.
colwyn, 498.
conyn, p. 157.
cor, 457.
corff, 1071.
corlan, p. 164.
craidd, 1102.
cranc, 374.
creyr, 204.
crochan, 56.
croen, 56.
croesan, 14.
croesaw, 92.
*cruitr, p. 162.
crwth, 5.
cunnawg, 165.
cwliawg, 1030.
cwpan, p. 161.
cwr, p. 147.
cwrw, 266.
cwrwgl, 488.
cwyr, 225.
cwyren, 836.
cyd, p. 164.
cyfathrach, 1046.
cyfenw, 993.
cyfrif, 913.
cylor, 1049.
cymanfa, 897.
cymharu, 896.
cyminedd, p. 147.
cymyn, 897.
cynnull yd, 210.
cysegriad, 879.
cystudd, 892.
cystwyad, 891.

chwaer, 320.

chwant, 667.
chwech, chweched, 777.
*chuechet, 588.
chwïawr, 320.
chwegr, 570.
chwerw, 1132.
chwith, chwithig, p. 161.
chwyth, 826.
chwythiad, 217.
chwythu, 57; p. 154.

dafad, dafates, 858.
dalen, deilen, 765.
dall, 249.
dangaws, 660.
delw, 642, 936.
dehen, 386.
deng, p. 150.
derwen, 554.
didryfwr, 315.
delehedion, 87.
*diminid, 237.
dleet, 87.
*doguomisur., 807.
*don, *dui, 773.
*duguohintiliat, 1073.
draen, 559.
drws, 124.
d,ywyn, 207.
dryssien, 587.
du, 381.
duw, 404.
dwrn, 502.
dy, 570.
dyfrgi, 375.
dyled, p. 147.
dyludo, p. 147.
dylynn, p. 165.
dyn, 953; llys dyn, 718.
dysgybl, 438.

eawg, 216.
ebodn, p. 161.
eddestr, eddestl, eddestlawr, 820.
ednyf, 666.
ednyw, 666.
edyn, 746.
efydd, 610.
eglwys, p. 157.
eirif, 913.
eithyr, 1014.
elin, p. 149.
*emed, 610.
emennydd, 747.
*emmeni, 784.
*engued, p. 148.

Indices Verborum.

ennill, 694.
enw, 991.
enynu, p. 147.
erbyn (= O. Ir. archiunn), p. 165.
erfin, 213.
ergyrwaew, p. 148.
erlyn, p. 165.
erw, 1038.
eryr, 197.
*escip, 982.
*eterinn, 746.
*etncoilhaam, 746.
ewin, p. 150.
ewyll, 884.
ewyrdonic, p. 67, note¹.

ffa, 109.
ffal, p. 150.
ffaling, 37; p. 154.
ffroen, 1039.
ffrowyll, 109.
ffrwl, 999.
ffrwyn, 109, 819, 1039.
ffurfafen, 749.
ffust, 109.

gafl, 135.
gafr, 372; gafar, 1075.
galar, 281.
garw, p. 159.
gebel, 135.
gefell, 834.
gel, 940.
Gildas, 17.
glân, 671.
glin, p. 149.
glo, 273.
glwys, 719.
glyn, p. 165.
gof, 369.
goglawdd, 229.
*golbinoc, p. 148.
golchi, 1045.
gorcu, 1116.
gorfynt, 602.
goryn, 255.
graen, p 147.
*gratell, 107.
gre, 742.
gres, p 164.
grisiau, p. 164.
grislyfr, p. 164.
grudd, p. 148, p. 154.
grûg, 565; p. 162.
grwm, 384, 1063.
grwn, 390.

grwysen, 582.
*gudif, *gudhyf, 797.
*guell, 1116.
gwadu, p. 148.
gwaew, 216.
gwain, 157.
gwarchad, 984.
gware, 641.
gwau, 1095.
gwedd, p. 163.
gweddi, 870.
gweddw, p. 147, p. 159.
gwefl, p. 148.
gwel, 1.
gwennol, 934.
*guerg, 328.
gwerneu, 558.
gwerthyd, 568.
gwên, 1095.
gwichell, 140.
gwichiad, p. 157.
gwirion, 681.
gwlybwr, 675.
gwlyp, 675; *rogulipias, 675.
Gwraldeg, 533.
gwregys, p. 148.
Gwrwst, 342.
gwydd, 959.
gwydd, p. 154.
gwyddif, 797.
gwyn, p. 150.
gŵyr, 621, 724.
gwyth, 99.
gylf, p. 148.
gyth, 603.

haearn, 608.
hafal, 609, 904.
halen, 977.
hebawg, 1006.
hen, p. 156.
*henmam, 130.
henwr, 1100.
*hep, p. 156.
hidl, 241.
hil, 1009.
*hinham, 130.
*hint, 490.
hoedel, p. 147.
hosan, 72.
hotan, hotyn, 596.
hun, 720.
hydd, 183.
hynt, 1073.

iâ, 758.

iau, 758.
iawn, 681.
*iechyt, 758.
icuaf, 758.
ieuanc, 758.
*iot, 758.
*iouenc, 758.
*itlaur, 1038.
iwrch, 205.

kentaf, kyntaf, 588.

llachar, p. 156.
llaeth, 250.
llafanog, p. 150.
llafaru, 1133.
llai, 923.
llan, 132.
llath, 116.
llawen, 393.
llawer, 908.
llawn, 13.
llawr, 704.
llech, 573.
lled, p. 156.
llefaru, 1133.
llefrith, p. 163.
lleiad, 923.
lleiaf, 923.
Iliad, Iliaw, 1071.
llin, 38.
llith, 767.
llo, 424.
*logod, 248.
llong, 574.
llongborth, 725.
llorp, p. 150.
llosg, 128, 737.
llu, 1003.
*luit, 182.
lluryg, 154.
llydanedd, 925.
llyfn, 639.
llyfrith, 268.
llyfyr, 371.
llyg, 248.
llygod ffrengig, 248.
llyn, 221.
llynghes, 574.
llyriad, 937.
llys, 580.
llysdad, 48.
llysenw, 48.
llysiau, 810.
llysieuyn, 183.
llythyren, 230.

Welsh Index.

mad, 661.
magwyr, 866.
maidd, 783.
main, 430.
maint, 922.
malu, 701.
man, p. 154.
mantell, 490.
*map, 80.
march, 189.
*marchauc, 127.
marw, p. 159.
marwydos, 945.
mawl, 902.
mawn, 118.
mawr, 663.
maws, 927.
*meichat (-iat), 1029.
meistyr, 365.
mel, 968.
melin, 701.
melldith, 915.
mer, 193.
mèr, p. 157.
*merchet, p. 59, note.
merthyr, 738.
meth, methiant, 1123.
mign, 118.
milgi, 411.
mis, 1050.
moch, 1029.
moel, 258.
moel-ron, 50.
monochen, p. 155.
mor, 860.
morforwyn, 1020.
morhwch, 1029.
*motrwy, 466.
morynyon, 1020.
mul, 295.
munn, p. 154.
mur, 476.
mwnai, 841.
mwng, 744.
mwnwgl, 744; p. 149.
mwyd, 431.
mwy, 1114.
mwyn, 430.
mwyth, 394.
mynydd, 237.
myr, 55.

nadr, 88.
nawf, 391.
nawn, 1077.
nedden, neddog, 649.

nef, 812.
nes, nesaf, 1117.
nifwl, niwl, 337.
nith, 224.
*nottid, 817.

oen, 459.
offeren, p. 164.
ofni, p. 148.
*ois, *oisoun, 735.
orlais, 1135.

pair, 724.
paith, p. 149.
paradwys, 553.
pawl, 495.
pedwardyblyg, 931.
penglog. p. 148, p. 154.
*petguerid, p. 157; *petguared, 142.
*petuar, 775.
*pimphet, 588.
piw, 1056.
plygu, 930.
porch, 493.
porphor, 224.
preithiaw, p. 148.
pren, 719.
pres, p. 154.
priddfaen, 1054.
priddlech, 1054.
pump, 776.
pwn, pyniaw, 45.
pyrchwyn, p. 162.
pyrgwyn, p. 162.
pŷsg, 13.
pystylwyn, 265.

rhagenw, 992.
*rannam, rhan, 9.
*rhascl, rhasgl, 814.
rhawn, p. 161.
rhiain, p. 154.
rhif. 913.
rhod, 227.
rheol. p. 155.
*ro-gulipins, 675.
rhoi, p. 109, note.
rhyn, 1008.

sach. 489.
saer, 1137.
saeth, 214.
sawdl, p. 150.
*scamnhegint, p. 150.
senedd, 551.

serch, 618.
sil, 1009.
sill, 231.
swta, 941.
syw, p. 153.

tad, 1046.
taflu, p. 154.
tafod, 40.
tair, 774.
taith, 450, 872.
tal, 739.
talm, 108.
tant, 1017.
tarw, p. 159.
tes, 942, 1086.
teyrnas, 886.
*tig, 159.
tin, p. 149.
to, 994.
toes, 242.
*traet, 74.
traws, tros, 1000.
*treb, 315.
trech, 1117.
*tri, teir, 774.
triphlygiad, 930.
trothwy, 1000.
truan, 383.
trwm (adj.), 903.
trwm (subst.), p. 163.
trws, 324.
*tût (tud), 423.
twrch, 373.
twysen, 35; p. 163.
tynell, 731.
ty, 569.

uchedydd, 140.
uffarn, p. 149.
uffern, 519.
*unvet, 142.
urdd, 943.
uthr, 1014.
uwd, 1038.

*vndimia (?), 797; p. 163.

wyf, 1112.
wyt, 1112.

ym, 85, 1112.
ymenin, 784.
ynfyd, 512.
ynt, 1112.
ysborion, 764.

ysbwrial, 764, 1004.
ysgadan, 967.
ysgiaw, 440.
ysgien, 440.
ysgin, 515.

ysgŵyd, p. 148.
ysgyfaint, p. 150.
yslath, 116.
ysnoden, 817.
ystlys, 32.

ystrodyr, 262.
yspardun, 1041.
yspar, 1041.
yw, 561.

V. CORNISH INDEX.

aeran, 1011.
ail, 460.
ancar, 68.
arhanz, 607.
asen, p. 149.
avallen, 555.
avi, 1032.

banne, 966.
bara, 141.
barth, 14.
beler, 823.
ber, p. 149.
blez, 491.
bloueg, 236.
bochadoc, 1058.
bothar, 604.
braud, 1047.
brenniat, p. 147.
bron, p. 150.
bugel, 583.
buit, 477.

cans, 772.
cantuil, 44.
kat, 499.
keghin, 245.
chelioc, 506.
kelli, 115.
kigel, 567.
clin, p. 149.
cog, 245.
coir, 225.
coloin, 498.
colviden, 556.
croider, 700.
cugol, 121.
cuic, 426.
curun, 75.

darat (-raz), 124.
dele, 852.
delen, 765.
den, 953.
discibel, 438.
diures, p. 159.
dreis, 587.
duv, 381.
duy, 404.
dyghow, 386.

ehog, 216.
elin, p. 149.
enederen, p. 148.
enef, 288.
ens, 1112.
er, 197.
erieu, p. 148.

fichren, 562.
fruc (friic?), 1039.
firmament, 749.

ghel, 940.
gelvin, p. 148.
glibor, 675.
gof, 369.
grud, 39.
gûdh, p. 154.
guedeu, p. 147.
guein, 157.
guell, 1116.
guennol, 934.
guernen, 558.
guiden, p. 156.
guihan, p. 157.
gurhthit, 568.

haloin, halein, 977.
hivin, 561.

hoern, 608.
huethaf, 217.
hubeltat, p. 153.
huis, 735.

idna, 746.
iffarn, 519.
impinion, 747.
ispak, 982.

lait, 250.
lergh, 937.
leski, 128.
leveriat, 1133.
lewilloit, p. 150.
liver, 371.
loch, 424.
lorch, 52.
lose, 737.
lnu, 1003.
luworch guit, 114.

maister, 365.
manach, 435.
march, 189.
marhaz, 327.
mel, 968.
melin, 701.
mennyw, 1053.
meth, 1123.
mor, 860.
morboch, 1029.
moy, 1114.

nef, 812.
noden, 817.

of, 1112.
oin, 459.
on, 1112.

Breton Index. 197

onnen, 557.
os, 1112.

peis, peus, pows, 717.
pepel, 458.
pér, 724.

reuniat, p. 153.

sair, 1137.

scala, 106.
soued, 551.
skefaus, p. 150.
snoden, 817.
soler, 740.
stoc, 705.

tavot, 40.
tes, 942.
ti, 569.

tonnel, 731.
torch, 373.
truit, 74.
trulerch, 937.

warn, p. 146.

yns, 1112.
yorch, 205.

VI. BRETON INDEX.

amann, 784.
arc'haut, 607.
avu, 1032.

bannec'h, 966.
bara, 141.
beler, 823.
ber, p. 149.
blonec, p. 164.
bouzar, 604.
bragez, 1033.
buez, 113.

cant. 772.
c'houézaf, 217.
chwaut, 667.
compizrien, 1046.

da, 570.
dargreiz, 1102.
delien, 765.
du, 381.

empenn, 747.
éué, 288.
env, 812.
cor, 68.
erer, er, 197.

felc'h, 1012.

gof, 369.
gouin, 157.
guell, 1116.
guénnéli, 934.
gwén, 1095.

gwelaouen, 940.
gwerneu, 558.
gwerzid, 568.

hal, haleu, holen, 977.
hennt, 1073.
hoal, p. 147.

ioul, 884.
iourc'h, 205.
iviuen, 561.

kaz, 499.
kegel (kigel), 567.
kéler, 1049.
kelvézen, 556.
ker, p. 147.
kezour, 1055.
kleiz, 387.
klom, koulm, 203.
koar, 225.
kolen, 498.
kougoul, 121.
krouezer, 700.

lerc'h, 937.
lestad, 48.
lesvab, 48.
lorchen, 52.
losk, 737.
lue, 424.

malven, p. 148.
mel, 968.
meliu, 701.
meulet, 902.

méza, 1123.
moan, 430.
morhouc'h, 1029.
muy, 1114.

nadoz, 817.
neud, neuden, 817.
niz, 649.

oan, 459.
off, 1112.
omp, 1112.
ounnen, 557.

reûn, p. 161.
reiz, 890.

scévent, p. 150.
scuit, p. 148.
skéja, 440.
spern, 1041.
stûr, sturia, p. 147.

tez, 942.
ti, 569.
tonel, 731.
tourc'h, 373.
tréc'h, 1117.
treùzou, 1000.
trulen, p. 148.

warn, p. 146.

yen, 758.
yut, 1112.

VII. LATIN INDEX.

aedes, 948.
aer, 104.
aes, 812, 216.
aestas, 948.
aestus, 948.
agnomen, 991.
agnus (= avignus?), 492.
ago, p. 44, note.
alo, 486.
amb-, 670, 921.
ancora, 68.
animal, 428.
animus, p. 149.
arduus, 16.
argentum, 607.
arvum, 1038.
asinus, 296; p. 159.
atta. 1078.
aurum. 606.
axilla, p. 150.

betula, 560.
bi-. 773.
bos, 159.
brevis, 678.
broccbus, 852.
bubulcus, 583.

caco, 1075.
caecus, 426.
calx, 58.
canis, 411, 1050.
canna, p. 157.
cano, 837.
caper, 372.
carex, 933.
cavea (= O. Ir. cae?), 218.
censeo, 837.
census, 285.
centum, 772.
cera, 225.
certus, 888.
cognomen, 991.
columba, 203.
communis, 897.
comparo, p. 154.
consequor, p. 162.
coquino, 245.
coquo, 245.
corpus, 812.
corylus, 556.
coxa, 466.

crates, 126.
cribrum, 700.
crotta, 5.
cucullus, 121.

dama, 858.
dea, 289.
decem, p. 150.
deus, 81.
dexter, 386.
duo, 773.

edo, 40.
equus, 17.
erica, p. 162.
esox, 216.
est, 1112.
esucius, 216.

faba, 109.
faber, 369.
fero, 835.
fervere, 952.
fircus (Sabine), 205.
flagellum, 109.
flos, 491.
folium, 765; p. 163.
fores, 124.
forma, 642.
frater, 570, 1047.
frenum, 109, 819.
fundus, 96.
furvus. 381.
fuscus, 381.
fustis, 109.

genus, 812.
gilvus, 1124.
grex, 742.
gustus, p. 69, note ².

hirpus, 205.
hircus, 205.

inclytus, 655.
innocens, p. 151.
inter, 490.

jecur, 1032.
justus, 758.
juvencus, 758.
juvenis, 758.

lac, 250.
lacus, 781.
lactus, p. 151.
lătus, p. 156.
lātus ($\pi\lambda\alpha\tau\acute{\upsilon}\varsigma$), 13.
Laverna, 792.
laxus, 382.
lens, lendis, 649.
levior, 923, 1115.
levir, 397.
lien, 1012.
lingua, 40.
lino, p. 159.
linquo, p. 161.
lippus, 675.
liquor, 675.
lorica, 154.
lucrum, 792.
lucta, p. 153.

magnus, 663.
major, 1114.
mantellum, 490.
manus, p. 154.
marceo, 860.
mare, 860.
mater, 130, 1052.
mel, 968.
meme, p. 127, note ⁵.
mensa, 478, 285.
mensis, 285, 1050.
molendinum. 701.
molo, 701.
mors, 315.
mulceo, 243.
mulgeo, 243.
mulus, 295.

natrix, 88.
navis, 21.
uebula, 337.
necto, 817.
neptis, 224.
nex, 693.
noceo, p. 151.
nomen, 991.
nox, 693.

opus, 889.
ordo, 943.
ornus, 557.
os, ossis, p. 149.

Mediæval Latin Index.

pallium, p. 154.
palumba, 203.
pater, 13, 1046.
pectus, 812.
pecus, 389.
penna, 746.
pes, p. 150.
piscis, 13.
plecto, 930.
plenus, 13.
plerus, 13.
plico, 930.
poena, 98; p. 156.
popina, 245; p. 158.
porcus, 493.
pro, 13.
pulsus, 99.
purpura, 224.

quatuor, 775.
quinctus, 588.
quinque, 776.

rastrum, 814.
regina, 20.
ren, 246.
rex, 1036.
rien, 1011.
rivus, 999.
rota, 227; p. 158.

rumis, 999.
ruo, 999.

sacer, 724.
saccus, 489.
sagitta, 214.
sal, 977.
salax, 616.
salicastrum, 795.
salio, 616, 977.
salum, 977.
scutum, p. 148.
seculum, p. 147.
secus, p. 156.
sedeo, 70.
semi, 392.
Seneca, 130.
senex, 130.
septem, 224.
sex, 777.
sextus, 588.
similis, 609, 904.
sisto, p. 100, note.
socrus, 570.
somnium, p. 163.
soror, 216, 320.
specio, specto, p. 149.
stannum, 610.
sum, sunt, 1112.

talea, 252.
taurus (= Gaulish *tarvos*), p. 159.
tellus, 108.
tendo, 1017.
tepere, 942.
theca, 41, 371.
tongeo, p. 165.
torreo, 703.
trans, 1000.
tres, 774.
tribus, 315.

ulna, p. 149.
umbilicus, p. 150.
unguis, p. 150; No. 198.
unio, 862.
unus (oinos), p. 147.

vagina, 157.
varus, 621.
vates, 2.
veru, p. 149.
vespera, 224.
vieo, 99, 1095.
vidua, p. 147, p. 159.
vir, 395.
vita, 477.
vitis, 99; p. 156.
vivus, 113.

VIII. MEDIÆVAL LATIN INDEX.

[*Numerals to which the letter "L." is prefixed refer to the lines of the Lorica, pp. 136-143.*]

abacia, 173.
admidulum, 824.
aglossus, 629.
agoneteta, L. 19; p. 143.
allea, 31.
alministrum, 793.
amusea, 251; p. 158.
aulús, 558.
antela, 264.
anticula, 155.
aptempna, 70.
arcimantrica, 16.
asugia, 236.

babana, 284.
batma, p. 144.

baudaca, 220.
benna, 163.
berrus, p. 148.
binna, 162.
birria, 18; p. 154.
biturrea (-ia), 152.
braxatus, 600.
brecia, 184.
brucus, 565.
brunus, 559.
bucealla, 144.
bucliamen, L. 76; p. 145.

caha, 277.
cadibulta, 274.
callidiba, 278.

camisa, 38.
candalóna, 63.
capitali (dat. s.), L. 49.
caphia, 51.
capula, 266.
carsum, L. 37; p. 144.
cartesium (= chartaceum), 709.
cartilago, L. 49.
catacrina, L. 62; p. 145.
caustoria, 59.
cavicula, 229.
celopidus, 635.
cephale, L. 35; p. 144.
cepus, 480.
centro (dat. s.), L. 49: p. 145.
chautrum, p. 145.

chorus, p. 153.
cipus, 479.
ciratheca, 34.
ciromancia (chiromachia), 272.
cirra, 33.
citola, 241.
cladum, L. 37; p. 144.
clerica. 76.
collacanius, 486.
colomaticus, p. 148.
colosdrigium, 1136.
comprisura, 238.
cona, L. 35; p. 144.
corductum, p. 156.
corporale, 859; p. 164.
corrolus, 556.
creta. 126.
cretella, 107.
cuba, L. 57; p. 145.

dectura, 153.
delipin, 1029.
digma (?), 127.
dolia, L. 75; p. 145.
ducendum, 773.

ea, 186.
edibulta, 275.
emenda, 98.
episcentum, p. 13.
ereocledus, p. 24.
eripica, 240.
erundo, 934.
ethera, 104.

falinga, 37.
fasellus, 488.
ferina, 183.
fessica, 57.
festula (festuca ?), 211.
fethma, 844.
fitrem (acc. s.), L. 74.
fixio, 900.
forcuratio, 899.

gamba, L. 63.
ganea, 187.
garga, 141.
gelima, 45.
genimen, 1010.
genuelis (abl. pl.), L. 64; p. 145.
gernoodum, 708.
gerra, 139.
geta, 19.
gibra, L. 31; p. 143.
gigra, L. 35; p. 144.

gingis (dat. pl.), L. 46; p. 165.
glabella, 78.
glassia, 243.
gletealla, 189.
grangia, 195.
gredale, 854.
grimaga, 257.
grunna, 118; p. 156.
gugra, p. 144.
gurgulio, L. 46; p. 145.
gyrgyrium, 746.

honplata, 148.
honumculus, 436.

iaris (abl. pl.), L. 35; p. 144.
iduma, L. 38; p. 144.
igniferrium, 720.
impedica, 192.
internasus, L. 44; p. 145.
iolla (= billa), 55, 1005.
ionuchus (= eunuchus), p. 166.
irundo, 935.

jacor, L. 73.
juntura, 149.

lapifulta, 246.
lectorie, 856.
licór, 1097.
ligna, L. 36; ligana, p. 144.
limpa, 69.
lucifugia, 204.

malosus, 411.
mancellus, 490.
mandianum, L. 37; p. 144.
manuale, 857.
marcem (acc. s.), L. 74.
mataxa, 93; p. 156.
mentagra, L. 68; p. 145.
mersiamentum, 780.
micena, L 36; p. 144.
milgus, 507.
mitreta, 64; p. 155.
monetola, 201.
monificina, 237.
morelius, 499.
mucledla, 165.
mulcra, 166.

naucula, 71.
nuchum, 794.

oba, 167.
obesta, p. 158.

obligia, L. 74.
obtolmia, 281.
odomen, 1006.
onesta, 256; p. 158.

panca, 235.
pantera, 88; p. 155.
pantes, L. 79; p. 146.
partista, 9.
patha, L. 36; pata, p. 144.
patma, L. 38; p. 144.
pavimentum, 769.
pectusculum, L. 69; p. 145.
pensa, 245.
pestucula, 147.
picuta, 258.
pilomena, 202.
piromanxia, 271.
plumba, 60.
plumpeus, 609.
postella, 265.
presena, 247.
prespiter, 367.
prissura, 244.
profeticum, 796.
proseumeticum, 792.
prostrinum, 711.
punmatus, 473.

quadricentum, 775.
quiucentum, 776.

retor, 1099.
romipeda, 311.
rostigola, 206.
rotis (dat. pl.), L. 45.
rula, 248.
ruter, 1075.

sabribarra, 180; p. 157.
sargifagum (= sarcophagum), p. 166.
saudarium (= sudarium), p. 166.
scama (= squama), 132; p. 152.
scanum, 748.
scilarotica, 168.
sciren, p. 26.
scupa (= stupa), 254.
seua, L. 36; senna, p. 144.
senester, 387.
sepe, 862.
sera, 226.
sexcentum, 777.
simicintium, p. 166.
sindola, 253.
sirogra, 233.

sturua, 273.
sista, 199.
sitarista, 5.
stipifortifartium, 705.
straulium, 717.
subfucatus, p. 166.
sublingua, L. 48; p. 145.
superaltare, p. 136; p. 143.
susurra, 145.

talia, L. 37.
tempe, 806.
tethologia, 81.
tignus, 485.
tipia, 146.
tomus, 587.
treoga, 137.
tribula, 109.
trica, 279.
tricendum, 774.

troclia, 239.
trobiale, 855.
trolla, 42.
tutones, L. 45; p. 145.
tympanum, p. 153.

ugula, 151.
uolua, 181.
urla, 191.
uva, L. 48; p. 145.

IX. GREEK INDEX.

ἄγλυ, 509.
αἰθίοψ, αἶθος, αἴθω, 948.
ἅλλομαι, 616, 977.
ἄλλος, p. 149.
ἅλς, 977.
ἀμέλγω, 243.
ἀμφί, 670.
Ἀμφίμαρος, 860.
ἀμφίπυλος, 898.
ἄνεμος, p. 149.
ἀνεψιός, 224.
ἁπλόος, 930.
ἄργυρος, 607.
ἀρείων, 1116.
ἀρτοκόπος, 245.
ἀρτοπόπος, 245.
ἄττα, 1078.
αὖρον = O. Ir. òr(ń), p. 162.
ἄχεται, p. 44, note.

βάνα, 1053.
βίος, 113.
βίοτος, 477.
βολγός, 217.
βοῦς, 159.
βουκόλος, 584.
βραχύς, 678.

γάλα, 250.
γένος, 812.
γεύω, p. 69, note².
γλακτοφάγος, γλάγος, 250.
γυνή, 1053.

ἀήρ, 397.
ἄκρυ, 724.
ἐξιός, 386.
διπλόος, 930.

ἐόρυ, 554.
ἐρύς, 554.
ἔυς·, 85.

ἐγκέφαλος, 747.
εὖος, 812.
εἰ, εἰμί, εἰσί, 1112.
ἕκτος, 777.
ἑκυρά, 570.
ἑλάσσων, 923, 1115.
ἕλος, 977.
ἐμέω, 97.
ἐμμί, 1112.
ἑξακάτιοι, ἑξήκοντα, 777.
ἐρείκη, p. 162.
ἔργον, 328, 533.
ἐσμίν, ἐστί(ν), 1112.
ἐν-, 85.
εὑρύς, 578.

ζέα, 779.

ἧπαρ, 1032.
ἧσαι, ἧσθε, 1112.
ἤτριον, 1095.

θερμός, 952.
θύρα, 124.

Ἰάων, 758.
ἰθαίνεσθαι, 948.
ἱπποβουκόλος, 584.
ἵππος, 17; p. 68, note; 675.
ἵστημι, p. 100, note.
ἰτία, 99.

κακκάω, κάκκη, 1075.
κανάζω, 837.

κάπρος, 372.
καρδία, 1102.
κίρκος, 507.
κλέος, κλυτός, 656, 812.
κνήμη, 269.
κόνις, κόνιδος, 649.
κόρυλος, 556.
κρησέρα, 700.
κριός, 158.
κύων (= cú, gen. con), 411.

λαμβάνω, 34.
λάτρις, 792.
λείπω, cf. O. Ir. leicim.
λευκός, cf. O. Ir. lóche, 292.
λέχος, 812.
λῇς, 792.
λόχος, 1003.

μακρός, 621, 724.
μᾶνος, 430.
μαραίνω, 860.
μεγάλου, 663, 902.
μέγας, 663.
μέθυ, 968.
μείζων, 1114.
μέλι, 968.
μέρος, p. 157.
μῆνις, 602.
μήτηρ, 130.
μολγός, 217.
μύλη, 701.

ναῦς, 21; p. 162.
νέκυς, 693.
νεφέλη, 337.
νέφος, 812.
νέω, 817.

2 D

νήθω, 817.
νυός, 570.

ὄϊς = O. Ir. ói.
ὁμαλός, 609, 904.
ὀμφαλός, p. 150.
ὄνομα, 991.
ὄνος, 296.
ὄνυξ, p. 150.
ὀργή, 328, 533.
ὀρθός, 16.
ὄρχις (= uirge), gl. 209.
ὀστέον, p. 149.
οὖθαρ, 102.

παρά, 704.
πάτος, 13.
πέμπε, πέντε, 776.
πατήρ, 13.
περαῖος, 13.
πετεηνά, πέτομαι, 746.
πλάτος, p. 156.
πλατύς, 13.
πλείων, 13.
πλέκω, 930.
πλήρης, 13.
ποίνη, 98; p. 156.

πολύ, 13.
πόρκος = orc, 492.
πούς, p. 150.
πτάρνυμαι, 1039.
πυθμήν, 96.

ῥεῦμα, 999.
ῥέω, 999.
ῥύγχος, 1039.
ῥυτός, 909.

σάκκος, 489.
Σελήνη, 952.
σκῦτος, p. 148.
σπλάχνον, 1012.
σπλήν, 1012.
στέργω, 618.
στοργή, 618.
σχίζω, 441.

τάνυμαι, 1017.
τανυ, ταναός, 1017.
ταῦρος = Gaul. tarvos, p. 150.
ταφ, 942.
τέγος, 569.
τείνω, 1017.
τεῖχος, 871.

τέκος, 871.
τελέω, τέλος, 739.
τέρσομαι, 703
τοῖχος, 871.
τόκος, 871.
τρέχω, 74.
τύκος, 871.

ὕδωρ, 69.
ὕπνος, p. 163.
ὑψηλός, p. 68, note.

φαίθω, φάος, 846.
φαγ, 109.
φαλλός, p. 150.
φέρω, 835.
φόνος, p. 147.
φρητήρ, 570.
φύλλον, 765; p. 163.
φώγειν, p. 61, note.

χλωρός, 1124

ὠλίνη, p. 149.
ὠμός, 90.
ὥρα = uair, p. 95, note 1.

X. SANSKRIT INDEX.

aksha, akshi, 426.
anganâ, 290.
anji, 784.
at, 1068.
ati, 155.
attâ, 1078.
adhi, 752.
an, 428; p. 149.
anila, p. 149.
antar, 490.
abhi, 670.
amati, 302.
ayas, 608.
arbha, p. 163.
avara, 305.
açva, 17; p. 68, note.
as, 1112.
asthi, p. 149.
asmad, 305.

âma, 90.
âyu, p. 68, note.
âyus, 812.
âs, 1112.

indh, 948.
ishira, p. 68, note.

utsa, 69.
und, 69.
uru, 578.
urvî, 578.
ush, 606.

ûdhas, 102.
ûrdhva, 16.

edha, edhas, 948.
ena, p. 147.

âidh, âidha, 948.

kanyâ, 158.
karsha, 703.
kâla, 200.
kṛ, 700.
kravya, 919.

gad, 870.
garva, p. 159.
go, 159, 784.
gṛdh, 620.
gṛha, 702.
gnâ, 1053.

gharma, ghṛṇi, 952.
ghraṇs, ghraṇsa, 952; p. 164.

chatur, 775.

Sanskrit Index.

charman, p. 157.

chhid, 441.

jan, 290.
jani, 1053.
janiman, janman, 886.
jalukā, 940.
jīva, 113, 784.
jīvita, 477.

takma, 871.
taksh, 871.
tanch, 872.
tan, 1017.
tantu, 1017.
tap, 942, 1986.
tava, yu-hmad, 570.
tishṭhāmi, p. 100, note.
tu, 423.
tṛ, 898.
tṛksh, 74.
tṛsh, 703.

dakshiṇa, 265, 386.
daçau, p. 150.
dah (dabh), 942.
dā, p. 100, note.
dāru, 554.
dus-, 85.
dṛç (paç), p. 149.
dēva, 21, 81.
dēvara, 397.
dvāra, 124.
dvi-, 773.

dhanvan, 108.
dhā, p. 158.
dhṛ, 642, 819.

nakha, p. 150.
naptrī, 224.
nabhas, 812.
navya, 21.
naç, 693.
nāçayāmi, p. 151.
nah, 817.
nābhi, p. 150.
nēdīyas, 1117.

pach, 245.
panchan, 776.
pad, pāda, p. 150.

parichara, 898.
paç (dṛç), p. 149.
pāthas, pathin = O. Ir. áth, 13.
pitṛ, 13.
puru, ved. pulu, 13.
prch, 930.
pṛthu, 13.
pṛ (par), 13.
pra, 13, 428.
plihan, 1012.

badhira, 604.
budhna, 96.
bṛhat, 292.

bhaksh, 109.
bhiksh, 1058.
bhū, p. 100, note.
bhṛ, 835, 1047.
bhrātṛ, 570, 1047.
hhrū, 79.

maghavan, 952.
mati, 302.
madhu, 968.
man, 302, 1110.
manu, 302.
manthāna, 1139.
mah, 756.
mahat, 663.
mahiyas, 1114.
mā, 1052.
mātṛ, 130, 1052.
mās, 1050.
mithyā, 1117.
mur, p. 76, note.
mṛ, 860.
mṛiṇ, 860.

yam, 635.
yama, 1010.
yava, 779.
yavīyas, 758.
yu, 758.
yuvan, 758.
yushmad, 570.
yos, 758.

rajata, 607.
ratha, 227.
rāj, rājnī, 20.
ruch, 331.
rōman, p. 161.

laghīyas, laghu, 923.
langh, p. 147.
labh, 34.
lōta, 792.

vakra, 621.
vad, 870.
vam, 97.
vara, 397.
varama, 1116.
varīyas, 1116.
vas, 1070.
vasu, p. 126, note.
vār, vāri, 222, 860.
vid, 392.
viṭikā, 99.
vīra, 397.
vṛ, 884.
ve, 1095.
vetasa, p. 156.

çans, 63, 837.
çakṛt, 1075.
çakra, 724.
çatam, 772.
çravas, 655, 812.
çrī, 387.
çvaçrū, 570.
çvid, p. 150.

sad, 70.
sadas, 812.
sama, 904.
saras, 977.
sarit, 977.
salila, 977.
sahas, 663.
sāmi, 392.
sṛ, 977.
sthag, 569.
sthā, p. 100, note.
snā, 391.
snusha, 570.
spaça, p. 149.
sru, 999.
srotas, 999.
svapna, p. 163.
svasṛ, 320.

hari, 1124.
hṛdaya, 1102.
hvṛ, p. 149.

XI. ZEND INDEX.

kainê, 158.
khsvas, 777.
tafnu, 720.
tanch-, 872.
thrishva, 588.
daêna, 89.
nazdista, 1117.
naçu, 693.
panchan, 776.

peretu, 725.
bi-, 773.
maçyêhîm, 1114.
maoirinãm, 55.
mãonh, 1050.
yava, 779.
yaos, 758.
yâna, 681.

rathaêstâ, 227.
verez, 533.
vôhu, p. 126, note.
çatẽm, 772.
hacha, p. 156.
hana, 735; p. 156.
biçtãmi, p. 100, note.
zeredhaya, 1102.

XII. GOTHIC INDEX.

aihus, 17.
aius, p. 147.
aithei, 1078.
andalauui, 792.
ara, 197.
arbja, 752; p. 163.
asilus, 296.
atta, 1078.

balgs, 218.
banja, p. 147.
bidjan, bidan, p. 147.
bleiths, p. 151.
brôthar, 570, 1047; brôthrahaus, 13.

daigs, 242.
daur, 124.
dulg, 433.

eisarn, 608.

faihu, 389.
faihuthraihns, 300.
fidvór, 775.
filu, 13.
fimf, 776.
fisks = iase, 13.
fulls = lán, 13.
fôtu, p. 150.

gamaids, 1122.
gamains, 897.
gasintha, -thja, 1073.
glaggvus, 1129.
gredus, 1081.

hairtô, 1102.
hana, 837.
hardus, p. 64, note [1].
bleiluma, 387.
hunda, 772.
hveita, p. 150.

im, ist, 1112.
izvara, p. 160, nute [m].

jêr = úair, p. 95, note [1].

kiusan, p. 69, note.

laufs, 114.
laun, 133; 792.

magus, 882.
maiza, 1114.
marei, 860.
nikils, 663.
miluks, 243.
missa, 1117.

qvairnus, 784.
qvius, 113.

reiks, 1036.

sakkus, 489.
salt, 977.
sama, 904.
sind, 1112.
sinths, 490, 1073.
skalja, 106.
snur, 570.
svaihro, 570.

triu, 554.
tuggo, 40.

vair, 395.
valdan, cf. flaith, 338.
vast, 1112; p. 165.
viljan, 884.

thagkjan, p. 165.
thaurp, 315.
thaursja, 703.
thiuda, 423.
thragja, 74.

XIII. ANGLO-SAXON INDEX.

âð, 948.
blíðe, p. 151.
braðean, 366.
ceole, p. 149.
dale, 1074.
elch, 205.
feohstrang, p. 159.
garleac (O. N. geirlaukr), 31.
gebede, p. 147.
gerim, 913.
gesið, 1073.

gleav, 1129.
heahfæðer, p. 153.
heado = *cath.*
hlæden, 126.
hrífe, p. 150.
hrón, 50; p. 155.
lagu = *loch*, 781.
mele, p. 157.
mene, myne, p. 163.
naca, 21.

nón, 1077.
rót, 5.
rim, 913.
sceóta, p. 164.
sendan, 1073.
tæfel, p. 154.
treov, 554.
tvi-, 773.
vudu, 46.
yrfe, 752.

XIV. ENGLISH INDEX.

am, 1112.
apple, 555.
art, 1112, p. 165.

bake, p. 61, note 1.
bane, p. 147.
beadsman, p. 147.
bellows, 217.
bid, p. 147.
blithe, p. 151.
booth, 120.
bother, 604.
bottom, 96.
Briton, 957.
brooch, 852.
brogue, 1033.
brother, 570, 1047.
butteris, p. 157.

car, 70.
cat, 499.
choose, p. 69, note.
chough, 201.
clean, 671.
coal, 273.
coracle, 488.
corn = *grán*, 722.
corry, 724.
cow, 159.
cowl, 121.
crowder, 5.
curd, 784.

door, 124.
dough, 242.
dusk, 381.

elk, 205.
ewe = O. Ir. *ói.*

farrow = *orc*, 492.
father, 1046.
feather, 746.
fell, 136.
five, 776.
ford, 725.
four, 775.
fun, 630.

gallon, 106.
garlick, 31.
gavelock, 135.
grail, 854.
greed, 620.
grill, 107.
grum, 1065.

hame, 444.
hard, p. 64, note 1.
hat, 831.
hazle, 556.
hedge, 218.
hound, 261, 411.
hundred, 772.
hurdle, 126.

iron, 216, 608.
is, 1112.

jowl, p. 149.

lanyard, 73; p. 155.
lead, 609.
less, 1115.
linseed, 38.
list, 655.
load, 609.
loan, 133, 792.
loud, 655.
lurcher, 937.

man, 89.
market, 327.
midriff, p. 150.
milk, 243.
mill, 701.
mis-, 1117.
mother, 130.

nail, p. 150.
navel, p. 150.
nit, 649.
noon, 1077.

one, p. 147.
onion, 862.
orc, 608.

paunter, p. 155.
pillory, 1136.
pismire, 55.

quern (Goth. qvairnus), 784.
quick, 113.

rhyme, 913.

salt, 977.
same, 904.
send, 490, 1073.
service-tree, 1132.
shake, p. 161.
shell, 106.
sister, 320.
slaughter, slay, 1003.
six, 777.
smear, 193.

stream, 999.
spur, 1041.
sweven, p. 163.

tailor, 252.
thin, 1017.
think, p. 165.
thirst, 703.
thorp, 315.
three, 774.
tongs, 674.
tongue, 40.
tree, 554.
trowsers, 324.
truce, 137.
trull, p. 148.
tun, 731.
twinge, 674.
two, 773.

udder, 102.
um-, 670.

warm, 952.
wast, 1112; p. 165.
weave, 1095.
white, p. 150.
will, 884.
window, 134.
wit, 392.
withe, 99.
wood, 46.
work, 328, 533.

yellow, 1124.
yew, 561.
young, 758.

XV. OLD HIGH GERMAN INDEX.

blîdi, p. 151.
bodam, 96.
chuo, 159.
cunela, 567.
denchan, p. 166.
diota, 423.
dwingan, 674.
ehu, 17.
eit, 948.
esil, 296.
farah = *orc*, 492.
flehtan, 930.
gelo, 1124.
Iladumûr, p. 86, note.
hafr, 372.

hag, 218.
Hincmar, p. 86, note.
Hlodomâr, 655; p. 86, note.
hlût, 655.
hrêo, 919.
hrotta, 5.
hunta, 772.
îwa, 561.
jâr = *hair*, p. 95.
kisal, 216.
korn = *grán*, 722.
meri, 860.
metu, 968.
milub, 243.
muli, 701.

nacho, 21.
prawa, 79.
salo, 616.
scala, 106.
sind, 1073.
slahan, 1003.
stroum, 999.
sueran, 1132.
umbi = *imm*, 670.
wâr = *fîr*, 954.
weban, 1095.
wida, 99.
wiho, 269.
witu, 46.
zunga, 40.

BENDACHT DÆI FOR HUILI CARATE HÉRINN OCUS A SENBÉLRE.

CORRIGENDA.

[The following have been noticed during the passage of the Indices through the press.]

P. 49, line 4, *for* carpat *read* charpat.
P. 59, line 16, *for* 145 *read* 144.
P. 65, note ª, delete the latter part of this note: *nis gignetar tola* means "desires (lusts) did not wound them," and we have here the 3rd pers. plur. pret. active of the root GON. The 3rd pers. sing. of the same tense—*geguin*—occurs in the Félire, Oct. 23.
P. 107, line 20, *for* tṛ *read* tṛ̇.
P. 108, in the paradigm, nom. and voc. sing., *for* rig *read* ri.
P. 111, line 5, *for* tracing from), lorg *read* tracing), from lorg.
P. 114, line 11 from bottom, *for* 995 *read* 975.
P. 120, line 4 from bottom, *for* bhrátr *read* bhrátṛ.
P. 131, line 11 from bottom, *for* inuirmuith *read* inmir maith.
P. 144, line 16, *for* lens *read* lens.
P. 155, line 11 from bottom, *for* dévabo *read* dévabo.
P. 160, note ᵐ, *for* anlaut *read* inlaut.
P. 166, line 13, *for* aurigam totum *read* totum calvum.
P. 166, line 14, and p. 179, *for* martur *read* martar.
P. 167, col. 2, line 6, *for* Sanscriticum *read* Sanscritum.
P. 168, col. 2, line 3 from bottom, for O. Ir. *d* read O. Ir. *t*.
P. 170, col. 2, at *Prefixes* insert *ro* (*ru*, *ra*), 13, 428, 808.
P. 174, at *barr* insert a reference to p. 148.
P. 181, *insert* tarb, p. 159.

www.ingramcontent.com/pod-product-compliance
Lightning Source LLC
Chambersburg PA
CBHW020833230426
43666CB00007B/1204